The Religious Concordance

Studies in the History of Christian Traditions

General Editor

Robert J. Bast (*Knoxville, Tennessee*)

Editorial Board

Paul C.H. Lim (*Nashville, Tennessee*)
Brad C. Pardue (*Point Lookout, Missouri*)
Eric Saak (*Indianapolis*)
Christine Shepardson (*Knoxville, Tennessee*)
Brian Tierney (*Ithaca, New York*)
John Van Engen (*Notre Dame, Indiana*)

Founding Editor

Heiko A. Oberman†

VOLUME 185

The titles published in this series are listed at *brill.com/shct*

The Religious Concordance

Nicholas of Cusa and Christian-Muslim Dialogue

By

Joshua Hollmann

BRILL

LEIDEN | BOSTON

Cover illustration: Jesus Christ—detail from deësis (δέησις) mosaic, early 14th century, Hagia Sophia, Istanbul. Photographer Edal Anton Lefterov.

Library of Congress Control Number: 2017015575

Typeface for the Latin, Greek, and Cyrillic scripts: "Brill". See and download: brill.com/brill-typeface.

ISSN 1573-5664
ISBN 978-90-04-32677-4 (hardback)
ISBN 978-90-04-33746-6 (e-book)

Copyright 2017 by Koninklijke Brill NV, Leiden, The Netherlands.
Koninklijke Brill NV incorporates the imprints Brill, Brill Hes & De Graaf, Brill Nijhoff, Brill Rodopi and Hotei Publishing.
All rights reserved. No part of this publication may be reproduced, translated, stored in a retrieval system, or transmitted in any form or by any means, electronic, mechanical, photocopying, recording or otherwise, without prior written permission from the publisher.
Authorization to photocopy items for internal or personal use is granted by Koninklijke Brill NV provided that the appropriate fees are paid directly to The Copyright Clearance Center, 222 Rosewood Drive, Suite 910, Danvers, MA 01923, USA. Fees are subject to change.

This book is printed on acid-free paper and produced in a sustainable manner.

Contents

Foreword   VII
Acknowledgments   VIII

Introduction: The Religious Concordance   1
    De Pace fidei in Recent Scholarship   9
    The Word of Concordance   15

1 **The Prayer for Peace**   19
    The Illuminative Word   24
    The Dialectical Word   30
    The Hierarchical Word   34
    The Conversational Word   39

2 **The Search for Peace**   48
    Nicholas of Cusa's Journeys   48
    The Search for Reform   56
    Ascending the Summit of Religious Peace   62
    Late Medieval Christian Approaches to Islam   77

3 **The Mind's Road to Peace**   87
    Hierarchical Dialectics of Peace: Bonaventura's *Itinerarium Mentis in Deum*   90
    Blinded by the Sun: Platonic Influences   100
    From Confusion to Concordance: Reversal of Babylon and the New Pentecost   110

4 **Seeking the Peace of the City**   115
    The New Alexander: Pius II and Mehmed II   115
    War and Peace: Pius II and Nicholas of Cusa   124

5 **Visions of Peace**   143
    Envisioning Peace: *De docta ignorantia* and *De pace fidei*   145
    Envisioning Dialogue: Nicholas of Cusa's *Letter to John of Segovia*   149
    Envisioning Unity: From Council to Pope to Prophet of Religious Peace   154

6 The Word of Peace 177
    The Unfolding Word: *De docta ignorantia* and *De pace fidei* 181
    The Magnetic Word: *De concordantia catholica* and *De pace fidei* 186
    The Inherent Word: *Cribratio Alkorani* and *De pace fidei* 188
    The Enfolding Word: *De visione Dei* and *De pace fidei* 191

7 For the Peace of Jerusalem 198

Conclusion: Nicholas of Cusa's Christocentric Approach to Islam 223

Bibliography 227
Index 242

Foreword

In this monograph Dr Joshua Hollmann charts a highly original, topical, and stimulating thesis on Nicholas Cusanus's (1401–1464) important mature dialogue *De Pace Fidei* (*On the Peace of Faith*). Published in the year of the sack of Constantinople (1453), this seminal work stands at the philosophical interface between Christianity and Islam, and has long been a source of some perplexity among interpreters of Cusanus's thought. Consequently *De Pace Fidei* has been relegated to the side lines of scholarly debate, with the result that relatively scant attention has been paid to consideration of its place and significance in the Cardinal's *oeuvre*. While pursuing his research at the Trier Institute and at the Cusanusstift Bibliothek on the banks of the Moselle River in Germany, Dr Hollmann made profitable use of the opportunity to scrutinise the remarkable collection of Nicholas of Cusa's books and manuscripts in a fashion which contributes very substantially to the advancement of scholarly research presented with such clarity in this volume. Dr Hollmann sets out his original and persuasively revisionist proposal that, far from being a text of peripheral concern, *De pace fidei* in reality embodies a pivotal dialectical synthesis of diverse strands in the thought of this great 15th-century philosopher, theologian, and mystic. Hollmann demonstrates that the arguments of his treatises *De Docta Ignorantia* (1440), *De coniecturis* (1442), *De Visione Dei* (1453), and *De Concordantia Catholica* (1434), among others, coincide in a certain culmination or completion in the discourse of *De Pace Fidei*. His discussion of the latter centres upon Cusanus's audacious claim that Islam, a religious tradition historically antagonistic to Christianity, can be viewed on the level of shared Neoplatonic philosophical theology as being in 'substantial unity' with Christianity by means of their common inheritance of '*logos*' divinity, such that both religions participate in 'the cosmic Word of God'. Cusanus maintains that this shared Word of God stands as 'the Face and Icon of religious peace'. Dr Hollmann's book constitutes a major, ground-breaking and remarkably timely contribution to modern Cusanus scholarship.

Torrance Kirby
McGill University

Acknowledgments

This work would not have been possible without the support of the following: Donald Duclow, Wilhelm Dupré, Thomas Izbicki, Christopher Bellitto, Gerald Christianson and the American Cusanus Society, Gabriele Neusius and the St. Nikolaus Hospital Cusanusstift in Bernkastel-Kues, Walter Euler and the Institut für Cusanus-Forschung in Trier, the International Thomas Merton Society, and the research staff of the Hill Museum and Manuscript Library and the Vatican Library. I wish to thank the Social Sciences and Humanities Research Council of Canada and the Canadian Corporation for Studies in Religion for making possible my memorable research travels abroad. I especially thank Douglas Farrow, Maurice Boutin, Joseph McLelland, Garth Green and Ellen Aitken. I am also grateful to the Order of St. Lazarus of Jerusalem, the Rev Dr Carl Krueger, the Rev Dr Brent Smith, Richard Vernon, Concordia College-New York, and the members of the parishes I served while researching and writing: Ascension Lutheran Church in Montreal and Christ Lutheran Church in New York City. I also extend thanks to Brill, notably, series editor, Robet J. Bast, the expert anonymous reader, Arjan van Dijk, Ivo Romein and Peter Buschman. I thank my family for their unflagging support, my wife Amie and son Elijah. And I am so very grateful for the wisdom, kindness and guidance of Torrance Kirby.

INTRODUCTION

The Religious Concordance

On the Mosel River, near a now rebuilt bridge bombed during the Second World War and across the street from the turn of the century Drei Könige hotel stands the St. Nikolaus-Hospital Cusanusstift. Designed and completed in 1458 under the direction of Nicholas of Cusa himself, it remains the pride of Kues, Germany, and is the largest surviving Gothic structure on the Mosel.[1] Cusanus (1401–1464) used his considerable benefices, which he had accumulated over a successful ecclesiastical career, to establish this hospice as home for thirty-three poor men,[2] thirty-three being the number of years Christ supposedly spent on earth. And, indeed, the hospice still serves its original purpose as it now provides care for elderly men and women. Even now Cusanus, the son of a local boatman who became cardinal of Rome, remains the hometown hero of Kues. The area is especially esteemed for its fine wines, and Cusanus's vineyards still produce much sought after Riesling, which has been poured over the years in support of the work of Christian charity at the Hospital. For Christians like Cusanus the theological virtue of charity flows from the heart of the Christian mystery of Trinity and incarnation.

---

1 On the history of the hospice, see: Jakob Marx, *Geschichte des Armen-Hospitals zum h. Nikolaus zu Cues* (Trier: Druck und Verlag der Paulinus-Druckerei, 1907). See also, Morimichi Watanabe, "St. Nicholas Hospital at Kues as a Spiritual Legacy of Nicholas of Cusa" in *Nicholas of Cusa and His Age: Intellect and Spirituality: Essays Dedicated to the Memory of F. Edward Cranz, Thomas P. McTighe and Charles Trinkaus*, edited by Thomas M. Izbicki and Christopher M. Bellitto (Leiden: Brill, 2002), 217–235.

2 Nicholas of Cusa or Cusanus was formally elevated to cardinal in 1449 and made Bishop of Brixen (Bressanone) in 1450. For a succinct life of Cusanus, see "Life and Works" by Donald F. Duclow in *Introducing Nicholas of Cusa: A Guide to a Renaissance Man*, edited by Christopher M. Bellitto, Thomas M. Izbicki and Gerald Christianson (New York: Paulist Press, 2004), 25–56. The two main biographies of Cusanus are: Erich Meuthen, *Nikolaus von Kues 1401–1464: Skizze einer Biographie* (Münster: Aschendorff, 1985). English translation: *Nicholas of Cusa: A Sketch for a Biography*, translted by David Crowner and Gerald Christianson (Washington, DC: The Catholic University of America Press, 2010). Edmond Vansteenberghe, *Le cardinal Nicolas de Cues (1401–1464): l'action—la penée*, 1920 (Frankfurt: Minverva, 1963). There is also the older English biography of Henry Bett, *Nicholas of Cusa* (London: Methuen & Co., 1932), which is based largely on Vansteenberghe. For primary documents on the life of Cusanus, see the ambitious *Acta Cusana: Quellen zur Lebensgeschichte des Nikolaus von Kues* (Hamburg: Felix Meiner, 1976).

At the heart of the hospice is a small chapel with a well-preserved altarpiece from around 1460, which was probably painted under the direction of Cusanus himself.[3] The central panel of the triptych features Cusanus and his brother Peter kneeling in prayer at the foot of the cross of Christ.[4] At the center of the scene we see Christ on the cross. At the center of the chancel, directly in front of the altarpiece, lies Cusanus's heart, buried beneath a resplendent plaque.[5] Cusanus's now priceless library, which he bequeathed to the hospice, lies adjacent to the chapel.[6] Here, directly over Cusanus's heart, and not far from his books, the mass is still celebrated as it has been for over five centuries. Here at this altar Catholics believe the very Body of Christ is sacrificed anew for the welfare of the world.[7] The Apostle Paul deemed this same crucified Christ to be the very Wisdom of God.[8] Cusanus, a priest, was the first rector of his hospice. Due to the necessity and centrality of the mass in the life of the hospice, Cusanus stipulated in its founding that every rector must be an ordained priest, a rule still enforced today.

It is oddly fitting that the hotel across the street from the chapel bears the name the Three Kings Hotel. Perhaps wise men and women still seek him here.

---

3   For a discussion of the altarpiece, see Helmut Gestrich, *Nikolaus von Kues 1401–1464 Leben und Werk im Bild* (Mainz: Verlag Hermann Schmidt, 2006), 80. I am very grateful for the background information on the alterpiece and Cusanus's family provided through conversation with Frau Gabriele Neusius, the librarian of the Cusanusstift, as well as for the immensely informative and thoroughly enjoyable two summers I spent researching at the Cusanusstift in Kues.
4   Cusanus's brother Peter was a priest and died in 1456. He is buried in St. Michael's cemetery in Bernkastel. Cusanus's sister Klara is also buried in the chapel at the Cusanusstift in Kues. Cusanus appears in the altarpiece with his cardinal's hat. His sister, although married, bore no children. Cusanus's offspring, the continuation of his family line, were the thirty-three men who lived in the hospice he built.
5   Cusanus died in Todi, Italy. His heart is buried in Kues, his body in S. Pietro in vincoli in Rome.
6   For the sometimes inaccurate catalogue to Cusa's library which is still housed at the hospital which he bequeathed in Kues (Latin: Cusa, now Bernkastel-Kues on the Moselle River between Trier and Koblenz), see: J. Marx, *Verzeichnis der Handschriften-Sammlung des Hospitals zu Cues bei Bernkastel a./Mosel* (Trier: Druck der Kunst- und Verlagsanstalt Schaar & Dathe, Komm.-Ges. a. Akt., 1905). Copies of the catalogue are also found at The Hill Manuscript Museum and Manuscript Library, St. John's University, Collegeville, MN. For this study, I have consulted select manuscripts of Cusanus at the Cusanusstift in Kues and at the Hill Museum and Manuscript Library, as well as codices pertaining to Pope Pius II and Cusanus at the Biblioteca Apostolica Vaticana, Rome.
7   Cusanus lived before the Reformation of the sixteenth century, and in this study, unless otherwise noted, the term 'Catholic' refers to the Western (Latin) Church of the Middle Ages.
8   1 Corinthians 1:24.

The three kings of Christian lore heralded from the Orient and sought wisdom. In many ways, Cusanus sought wisdom from afar, especially from the east. His library includes works by Avicenna and Al-Ghazali, the great medieval Muslim thinkers, as well as books from Constantinople and Robert of Ketton's imprecise Latin translation of the Qur'an.[9] Indeed his life and career read as a search for concordance between East and West, Islam and Christianity. Cusanus sought union between the Eastern and Western Churches at the Council of Florence.[10] He further sought out ancient texts of wisdom in his brief visit to Constantinople in 1437.[11] For Cusanus the concordance between Christianity and Islam is founded upon the concept of Divine Wisdom, a concept which lies at the heart of Cusanus's dialogue *De pace fidei* (1453). And, for Christians like Cusanus, this wisdom is the very *Verbum Dei*, both as the *ratio* of the Godhead and of the cosmos, and also as incarnate revelation of religious concordance.[12]

This Wisdom as Word is made known to the wise through words. Cusanus creatively applies Augustinian hermeneutics to his sapiential dialogue *De pace fidei* where he formulates his idea of "one religion in the variety of rites."[13]

---

9   Cod. Cus. 205 includes Al-Ghazali on philosophy, *Lib. De universali philosophia*, with notes by Cusanus, and Avicenna's *Metaphysics* with a note by Cusanus on f. 80v. Cod. Cus. 108 contains Ketton's translation of the Qur'an, with numerous notes by Cusanus. Cusanus brought Cod. Cus. 18 back with him from Constantinople.

10 The Council of Florence, or the continuation of the Council of Basel, was an ecumenical council of the Catholic Church. It is more properly referred to as the Council of Basel-Ferrara-Florence (1431–1445).

11 *Cribratio Alkorani*, prologus; *De docta ignorantia*, epistula auctoris ad Dominum Iulianum Cardinalem. On Cusanus's visit to Constantinople see H. Lawrence Bond, "Nicholas of Cusa from Constantinople to 'Learned Ignorance': The Historical Matrix for the Formation of the *De Docta Ignorantia*" in *Nicholas of Cusa on Christ and the Church: Essays in Memory of Chandler McCuskey Brooks for the American Cusanus Society*, edited by Gerald Christianson and Thomas M. Izbicki (Leiden: E.J. Brill, 1996), 135–164.

12 *De pace fidei* II, 7; V–VI. Cf., *Idiota de sapientia* 21.

13 *De pace fidei* I, 6. English translation by James E. Biechler and H. Lawrence Bond, *Nicholas of Cusa on Interreligious Harmony: Text, Concordance and Translation of De Pace Fidei* (Lewiston, NY: The Edwin Mellen Press, 1990). Unless otherwise noted, English translations of *De pace fidei* in this study are by Biechler and Bond. The Latin text of *De pace fidei* used in this study, unless otherwise noted, is the edition of Biechler and Bond, i.e., the same standard Latin text as found in the Heidelberg *Opera Omnia* edition of *De pace fidei*. *Nicolai de Cusa Opera Omnia*, Vol. VII: *De Pace Fidei*, eds. Raymundus Klibansky et Hilderbandus Bascour, O.S.B. (Hamburg: Felix Meiner Verlag, 1959), xiii–xxvi. This standard critical edition incorporated the Latin text and notes of *De pace fidei* of the earlier Warburg Institute edition: *Nicolai de Cusa De Pace Fidei cum Epistula ad Ioannem de Segobia*, Ediderunt Commentariisque Illustraverunt Raymundus Klibansky et Hilderbandus Bascour,

In *De doctrina Christiana*, the hermeneutical text book of the western middle ages, Augustine famously writes,

> All teaching is teaching of either things or signs, but things are learnt through signs…Words, for example: nobody uses words except in order to signify something. From this it may be understood what I mean by signs: those things which are employed to signify something. So every sign is also a thing, since what is not a thing does not exist. But it is not true that every thing is also a sign.[14]

For Augustine, God as ineffable hidden mystery is nether thing nor sign, but the source of all things and signs.[15] Cusanus posits in *De pace fidei* that God is hidden and known in the Wisdom and Word of God.[16] According to Cusanus, echoing Augustine, religious rites are signs of the truth of one faith which are subject to change. Yet that which is signified, namely the truth of one religion, remains unchanged for Cusanus. At the outset of *De pace fidei*, Cusanus identifies truth as the Word of God in which all things are enfolded (*complicantur*) and through which all things are unfolded (*explicantur*).[17] This Truth, this Word and Wisdom, speaks words of truth and wisdom which in turn reveal, point by point in an unfolding manner, the concordance of one single religion in a variety of rites. Cusanus affirms that between, "contracted wisdom, i.e., human wisdom and wisdom *per se*, which is divine and maximum and infinite, there always remains infinite distance."[18] Thus, in this confusing world of conjectures and similitudes, Cusanus's conception of the incarnate Word in *De pace fidei* utters dialogically the path to the signified one religion by means of a variety of signs.[19] For Cusanus, the human nature of Christ united to the Divine

---

O.S.B., Medieval and Renaissance Studies Supplement III (London: Warburg Institute: 1956), 1–90.

14   Augustine, *De doctrina Christiana*, I, 4–5, translated by R.P.H. Green (New York: OUP, 1999), 8–9.
15   Augustine, *De doctrina Christiana* I, 10: "[The Trinity] is a kind of single, supreme thing, shared by all who enjoy it—if indeed it is a thing and not the cause of all things, and if indeed it is a cause." (translation by Green, p. 10). Cf., *De concordantia catholica* I, 1.
16   *De pace fidei* I, 4; II, 7; V, 13.
17   *De pace fidei* II, 7: "Quae quidem veritas intellectum pascens non est nisi Verbum ipsum, in quo complicantur omnia et per quod omnia explicantur".
18   *De pace fidei* XII, 36.
19   *De pace fidei* II, 7. The Verbum has put on human nature so that humans may attain to the truth of one religion in the variety of rites and eternal felicity: "[Verbum] et quod humanam induit naturam, ut quilibet homo secundum electionem liberi arbitrii in sua

Word leads the imagined, wise readers of *De pace fidei* to the final happiness of religious concord.

According to a more contemporary philosopher of hermeneutics, Hans-Georg Gadamer (1900–2002), Cusanus's starting point is the inexactitude of all human knowledge. Gadamer writes that "Cusa's theory of knowledge is that all human knowledge is mere conjecture and opinion (*coniectura, opinio*)."[20] Furthermore, Gadamer notes, "Just as human knowledge is essentially 'inexact'—i.e., admits of a more or a less—so also is human language."[21] Thus, for Gadamer's reading of Cusanus's use of language, "all actual designations are arbitrary, and yet they have necessary connection with the natural expression (*nomen naturale*) that corresponds to the thing itself (*forma*)."[22] The mind must ascend to the infinite and rise above this inexactness.[23] For Cusanus, Gadamer concludes, "In the infinite there is, then, only one single thing (*forma*) and one single word (*vocabulum*), namely the ineffable Word of God (*verbum Dei*) that is reflected in everything (*relucet*)."[24] As Gadamer concludes, "Essential for him [Cusanus] is the fact that all human speech is related to the thing [the Word of God], and not so much the fact that human knowledge of things is bound to language."[25]

If Gadamer's reading of Cusanus's fundamental concept of the Word is correct, then there appear two aspects, or even opposites, to Cusanus's related conception of Divine Wisdom. This wisdom is hidden or unknowable, as is its corollary of inexact knowledge and language where shadowy signs obscure that which is signified. As another philosopher of language, Michel Foucault, puts it, for Cusanus Wisdom is depth without measure, unutterable in any language, unintelligible to every intellect. Compared to the folly of human wisdom, the Wisdom from God becomes, as Foucault sees it, an abysmal madness, a madness that engulfs all, a nothingness faced with the supreme form of reason alone that alone delineates being.[26] For Cusanus, when this infinite hidden wisdom is understood apart from the incarnate Christ, it may

---

humana natura, in homine illo qui et Verbum, immortale veritatis pabulum se assequi posse non dubitaret." Cf., *De pace fidei* III, 8; *De coniecturis* I, 2.

20 Hans-Georg Gadamer, *Truth and Method*, 2nd Edition, translated by Joel Weinsheimer and Donald G. Marshall (London: Continuum, 2004), 435.
21 Gadamer, *Truth and Method*, 435.
22 Gadamer, *Truth and Method*, 435.
23 Gadamer, *Truth and Method*, 435.
24 Gadamer, *Truth and Method*, 436.
25 Gadamer, *Truth and Method*, 436.
26 Michel Foucault, *History of Madness*, edited by Jean Khalfa, translated by Jonathan Murphy and Jean Khalfa (London: Routledge, 2009), 31–32.

lead to intellectual nihilism or not knowing that which can never be known. According to the argument of *De pace fidei*, Wisdom is unknowable and ultimately unattainable by reason alone. Avoiding nihilism and scepticism, *De pace fidei* connects Wisdom to the Word. Thus, in the dialogue of religious concordance Wisdom cannot be seen apart from the Word, nor sign apart from that which is signified. As Gadamer puts it, for Cusanus "there is a real affinity between word and concept."[27] Furthermore, Wisdom is elaborated in the Word. And the Word, as thing (*forma*) and single word (*vocabulum*) speaks words of religious concordance throughout the dialogue and leads beyond inexact conjectures of diverse religious rites, to the peace of one faith. In fact, in Cusanus's mind it is the Word (*Verbum Dei*) who begins the dialogue proper of *De pace fidei*. The Word dialectically leads from signs to the truth of religious concordance and the lasting peace of faith.

The other aspect or opposite of Divine Wisdom for Cusanus, as unfolded in *De pace fidei*, is that Wisdom is identified as the preincarnate *Logos* through whom all things are unfolded and enfolded, and, thereby, knowable. This Wisdom is rational and seen in the order and symmetry of creation.[28] Furthermore, this Wisdom is incarnate and became flesh in Christ who further and supremely reveals the religious concordance of one religion in this variety of rites. Thus, in the *Logos* and in Christ, this Wisdom is recognizable and attainable by divine illumination, by grace. In *De pace fidei*, after Cusanus proposes that there remains an infinite gap between human and divine wisdom, he goes on to discuss how there is only one Christ, "in whom human nature is united with the divine nature in supposited unity."[29] In Christ the divine intellect is united to the human intellect. In order to reassure Muslims, Cusanus affirms that in this union the unity of God is preserved. For Cusanus, not only are the divine and human intellects united in the Word, but the peace of faith also holds that the human nature is united with the divine nature in the incarnate Christ. He is, as Cusanus writes, "the face of all peoples and the highest Messiah and Christ, as the Arabs and Jews call Christ."[30] Christ is the face of all peoples. And, for Cusanus, Christ's face is especially turned toward the great prophets of the "religio una in rituum varietate".[31] As the preface to Cusanus's exposition on the Qur'an, the *Cribratio Alchorani* shows, this especially includes the

---

27   Gadamer, *Truth and Method*, 436.
28   *De pace fidei* IX, 26.
29   *De pace fidei* XII, 39.
30   *De pace fidei* XIII, 43: "in illo scilicet qui est facies omnium gentium et altissimus Messias est Christus, prout nominant Christum Arabes et Iudaei."
31   *De pace fidei* I, 6.

Prophet Mohammed.[32] *De pace fidei* proposes a global Pentecost—a reversal of the confusion of Babel—the concordance of discordant religious language in the one Word of God. The Wisdom and the Word, words and the Word, signs and that which is signified in everything: for the Word and Wisdom of God, according to Cusanus, flows through all ranks of being and encompasses all things.

The late and noted Cusanus scholar F. Edward Cranz has argued that Cusanus developed an all-embracing Christian philosophy as centered in his ultimately Christological understanding of learned ignorance and the coincidence of opposites.[33] Cranz contends that "Augustine and Nicholas of Cusa are two outstanding representatives of the Platonist phase of the Western Christian tradition." He identifies two main principles in Cusanus as developed from Augustine. The first main principle in Cusanus's thought as transmitted through Augustine is his well-known concept of learned ignorance, and the second is the maxim of the coincidence of opposites. Cusanus was not the first to formulate such ideas. The idea that all opposites are transcended is ancient, and the term *docta ignorantia* appears once in the works of Augustine, who says, "There is in us, therefore, a certain learned ignorance, so to speak, but an ignorance learned from the Spirit of God, who helps our weakness."[34] Cranz shows how Cusanus applies learned ignorance "as a method applicable to all areas."[35] Furthermore, Cranz maintains that Cusanus's understanding of the coincidence of opposites in Christ is similar to Augustine's views of the combination of the temporal and eternal in Christ in book thirteen of *De Trinitate*.[36] "But the approach", Cranz argues, "which Augustine applies to the objects of faith, Nicholas applies systematically to the whole universe. Or one may say that for Augustine the incarnation explains the history of Christianity, while Nicholas finds in it the basis of a complete metaphysic."[37]

---

32   *De pace fidei* I, 6; *Cribratio Alkorani*, alius prologus, 13–15.
33   F. Edward Cranz, "Saint Augustine and Nicholas of Cusa in the Tradition of Western Christian Thought", *Speculum* 28 (1953), 297–315. Reprinted in Cranz, *Nicholas of Cusa and the Renaissance*, edited by Thomas M. Izbicki and Gerald Christianson (Aldershot: Variorum, 2000), 31–40.
34   Augustine, *Epistula 130*, *The Works of Saint Augustine: A Translation for the 21st Century, Letters 100–155*, translated by Roland Teske, S.J. (Hyde Park, NY: New City Press, 2003), 197.
35   Cranz, "Saint Augustine and Nicholas of Cusa in the Tradition of Western Christian Thought", 311.
36   Augustine, *De Trinitate* XIII, Chp. 6, 24–25 on Christ as knowledge and wisdom.
37   Cranz, "Saint Augustine and Nicholas of Cusa in the Tradition of Western Christian Thought", 313.

Cranz's insight marks our methodological point of departure. For Cranz, Augustine and Cusanus are the two great representatives of the Platonist phase of Western Christian tradition. Both Augustine and Cusanus adapted the principles of Platonic thought. Yet, as Cranz observes, while the mature anti-Donatist Augustine ultimately sees the phenomenal world with some suspicion and seeks the solace of the City of God and anti-Pelagian predominance of divine grace, Cusanus sees the entire cosmos through Christian philosophy. Thus, Cranz writes "the more he studies it [the cosmos], the more Christian he becomes."[38] Or, we might conclude, the more he studies the cosmos, the more he sees Christ. Furthermore, while Augustine is sceptical of the Platonic method's ability to rest in the Good, Cusanus accepts the Platonic method as what God has made and through which, as in an enigma, one may know both God and the self.[39] By extension, to know religion is to know Christ as Wisdom and Word and ultimate revealer of one religion in the variety of rites.

As we shall see, Cusanus's Platonically infused Christological approach to Islam as articulated in *De pace fidei* and the circumferential Christology of *Cribratio Alkronai* differs from previous western, medieval, Christian theological engagement with Muslims. The famous scholastic theologian Thomas Aquinas opines in Chapter 2, book one, of *Summa contra gentiles* that since Muslims do not accept the authority of Christian Scripture, theologians of sacred doctrine must have recourse to natural reason, albeit acknowledging the failings of fallen human intellect, in order to compel Muslims to rational assent of the articles of the Christian faith. Thus rightly ordered and carefully argued philosophical propositions advance a sparring path to true faith. For Cusanus, the peace of faith is made manifest through the cosmically cogent and conciliarlly corporeal Wisdom and Word of God as enfolded in hierarchical gradations of being and expounded in Platonic dialogue. His argument and presentation of the faith to Muslims is ubiquitously Christological. Cusanus sifts the Qur'an for Christ who remains hidden and waiting to be heuristically found by ardent seekers of peace. The master of learned ignorance creatively centers his critical and constructive conversation (*De pace fidei*) and polemic (*Cribratio Alkorani*) with Islam on Christ, the revealer of religious concordance through Neoplatonic hierarchy and the diversity of pious rites, who synthesizes universal reason and particular faith both as preincarnate Wisdom and incarnate Word.

---

38   Cranz, "Saint Augustine and Nicholas of Cusa in the Tradition of Western Christian Thought", 298.

39   Cranz, "Saint Augustine and Nicholas of Cusa in the Tradition of Western Christian Thought", 298.

In conversation with Augustine, Auquinas, Gadamer, and Cranz, this work seeks to understand better how the dialogue of *De pace fidei* functions, by placing it within the broader context of Cusanus's all-embracing metaphysic of the Word of God, as articulated in the Christology and corpus of his writings. Our reading of Cusanus's *De pace fidei* focuses on his conception of the all-embracing Word of God. Indeed, the more Cusanus studies Islam, the more he sees Christ. What wisdom, then, can be gleaned from the structure and content of the dialogue *De pace fidei*? More precisely, for Cusanus, what is the course of this unique Christian-Muslim dialogue? How is his conception of "religio una in rituum varietate" realized?[40] And how does this concept shed light in turn on the Christology of his other major writings? What, lessons, if any, may we yet learn from Cusanus and even transmit to Christian-Muslim dialogue today? This study presents Cusanus's unique late medieval Christocentric philosophical and theological contribution to understanding the complex relationship between Islam and Christianity.

De Pace fidei in Recent Scholarship

This study takes its place alongside other works on *De pace fidei*. What follows is a brief survey of select scholarly work on the treatise. We may classify works on *De pace fidei* as mainly hermeneutical or contextual. A prime example of the hermeneutical approach is the director of the Institut für Cusanus Forshung (Trier), Walter Andreas Euler's *Unitas et Pax: Religionsvergleich bei Raimundus Lullus und Nikolaus von Kues*.[41] Euler traces Cusanus's conception of unity and peace, and how these ideas are related to those of Raymond Lull. In English, the main monograph on *De pace fidei* is still James Biechler's *The Religious Language of Nicholas of Cusa*.[42] Biechler adroitly explores the terms and concepts of *De pace fidei*, notably wisdom and unity. He focuses on the text and especially on the symbol-systems of its central themes. Yet Biechler does not explore the underlying metaphysics of how peace between the various religions is realized through the Word and Wisdom of God, nor does he posit how the Christology of *De pace fidei* relates to Cusanus's other main writings. When Biechler wrote his monograph, he stated that "one would be hard pressed to find in

---

40 *De pace fidei* I, 6.
41 Walter Andreas Euler, *Unitas et Pax: Religionsvergleich bei Raimundus Lullus und Nikolaus von Kues* (Würzburg: Echter Verlag, 1995).
42 James E. Biechler, *The Religious Language of Nicholas of Cusa* (Missoula, MT: Scholars Press, 1975).

print today a single book-length study of Cusanus in English."[43] This, of course, has changed in the past forty years. Even with many monographs and published articles on Cusanus having been written, notably the several collections of essays by the American Cusanus Society, there have been no book length studies dedicated primarily to the argument of concordance and dialectical structure of *De pace fidei*.[44] While Biechler and Euler have investigated Cusanus's hermeneutics of religious peace, Cary Nederman has written extensively on the idea of tolerance in Cusanus by placing his views within the context of late-medieval and early-modern discourses on toleration.[45] According to Nederman, the early-modern concept and practice of tolerance has deep roots in the medieval tradition. Nederman places Cusanus's *De pace fidei* within the context of its time and his study contextualizes Cusanus's understanding of religious tolerance as expounded imaginatively in the dialogue *De pace fidei*.

In addition to these hermeneutical and contextual studies of *De pace fidei*, there is a commonly held view that *De pace fidei* is a treatise essentially devoid of metaphysics. How *De pace fidei* has been recently interpreted may be summed up in an influential essay by Thomas P. McTighe, who argues in "Nicholas of Cusa's Unity-Metaphysics" for the absence of metaphysics in *De pace fidei*. McTighe concludes:

> For the stubborn fact remains that if Christianity is the one religion, and it is, then it cannot be a *complicatio* of all other religions. Nor can it be reduced to *explicatio* alongside of other *explicationes* of some *Ur-religion*. In the end, the ambiguities in the *De pace fidei* concerning unity of religion and diversity of rites, or diversity of religions, arise not because of the presence (as some commentators claim) [e.g., Biechler], but precisely because of the absence, of metaphysical categories.[46]

By focusing primarily on the formula "religio una in rituum varietate" and the *complicatio-explicatio* schema of the dialogue, McTighe essentially is left with the contextual position of Cusanus's views as representative of late-medieval

---

43 Biechler, *The Religious Language of Nicholas of Cusa*, v.
44 For example: *Nicholas of Cusa In Search of God and Wisdom*, edited by Gerald Christianson and Thomas M. Izbicki (Leiden: Brill, 1991); *Nicholas of Cusa on Christ and the Church*; *Nicholas of Cusa and his Age: Intellect and Spirituality*.
45 Cary J. Nederman, *Worlds of Difference: European Discourses of Toleration, c. 1100–c. 1550* (University Park, PA: The Pennsylvania State University Press, 2000).
46 Thomas P. McTighe, "Nicholas of Cusa's Unity-Metaphysics and the Formula Religio una in rituum varietate" in *Nicholas of Cusa In Search of God and Wisdom*, 172.

Christendom and thus does not adequately explore the thoroughly Christocentric and sapiential nature of the text, nor how it reveals Cusanus's cosmic understanding of religious concordance.

On the holistic coherence of Cusanus's thought, three recent studies focused on seeing continuity in Cusanus merit special attention. The first, *Becoming God: The Doctrine of Theosis in Nicholas of Cusa* by Nancy Hudson, examines and elucidates the complex doctrine of theosis in the thought of Cusanus. Hudson discovers that in Cusanus's theology, God's immanence, 'woven' into both the person of Christ and the corpus of the church, is counter-balanced by an 'unravelling thread' of negative theology. Hudson shows "that Cusanus is unparalleled in his ability to hold together a variety of tensions, including those between immanence and transcendence, monism and dualism, anticipation of modernity and medieval tradition, and Eastern and Western Christianity."[47] Paralleling Hudson's approach, wherein she first explores the doctrine of divinisation or *theosis* in the Greek Fathers and in Pseudo-Dionysius and then turns to examining *theosis* in Cusanus, this study will begin with philosophical and theological foundations. We shall then proceed to an exploration of Cusanus's thought as a whole, through his doctrine of the Word of God as unfolded in a select reading of his major writings. We will consider, in particular, how Cusanus aims to hold together both Eastern and Western Christianity as well as Christianity and Islam in a creative, dialectical tension. A second monograph by Jovino De Guzman Miroy shows the relationship between Cusanus's early work of *De concordantia catholica* and *De doctra ignorantia* by reading each work philosophically and highlighting the metaphysical and religious foundations of Cusanus's political thought.[48] This study also seeks to focus on Cusanus's metaphysical approach to religious dialogue as centered in his understanding of the Wisdom and Word of God. A final work by Gergely Tibor Bakos focuses on Cusanus's manuductive (Cusanus's neologism) approach to Islam—leading, as it were, by the hand—and places this within the context of faith and rationality in the late middle ages.[49] Bakos compares Cusanus's manuductive approach to

---

47   Nancy J. Hudson, *Becoming God: The Doctrine of Theosis in Nicholas of Cusa* (Washington, D.C.: The Catholic University of America Press, 2007), 9–10. Hudson states that the aim of her study is "to trace Cusanus's intriguing doctrine of theosis in as comprehensive a way as possible" (200).

48   Jovino De Guzman Miroy, *Tracing Nicholas of Cusa's Early Development: The Relationship between De concordantia catholica and De docta ignorantia* (Louvain: Éditions Peeters, 2009).

49   Gergely Tibor Bakos, *On Faith, Rationality, and the Other in the Late Middle Ages: A Study of Nicholas of Cusa's Manuductive Approach to Islam* (Eugene, OR: Princeton Theological Monograph Series, Pickwick Publications, 2011).

Islam with his other main writings. While Bakos's work addresses *De pace fidei*, he does so by relating chiefly to Cusanus's method, and does not focus on the dialogue's content, viz. the dialectics of the Word. Although Cusanus's knowledge of Islam continues to be studied by scholars such as Bakos, and the text of *De pace fidei* has been critically annotated and translated into English, the metaphysics of the dialogue in relation to Cusanus's other major writings have yet to be thoroughly explored. While the collection of essays, *Nicholas of Cusa and Islam* critically, constructively and contextually overviews Cusanus's writings on religious diversity and Christian-Muslim dialogue and polemics,[50] as Jovino Miroy concludes, "The current state of studies on the *De pace fidei* shows that the final word has not yet been written."[51]

While this study by no means claims to offer the final word on *De pace fidei*, it seeks nevertheless to highlight how Cusanus's understanding of Christology remarkably comes to the fore when dealing with Islam. Furthermore, there have hitherto been no major studies devoted to examining the philosophical and theological structure of the dialogue and how it relates to Cusanus's dialectical Christology. Two prominent Cusanus scholars, James E. Biechler and H. Lawrence Bond, classify *De pace fidei* with "the literature of utopia."[52] They also contend that far from being original, or in any sense a synthesis of Nicholas of Cusa's thinking on the philosophy of religion, the work is comprised mainly of "used parts" recycled from his other writings.[53] In response to this somewhat sceptical approach, this research proposes to re-examine the significance of the dialectical structure of the dialogue, to consider how it proceeds to disclose what Nicholas of Cusa calls "religio una in rituum varietate", and to explore how to this end his argument advances metaphysically and dialectically from diversity to unity, from the many to the one, and from discord to concord.[54] Since *De pace fidei* proposes a dialectical synthesis of the world's religions, notably of Christianity and Islam, a critically important question arises, namely how this synthesis relates to the Christology of Cusanus's other dialectical writings, and especially to two of his most famous works, *De concordantia catholica* and *De docta ingnorantia*. Throughout his life Cusanus the philosopher and mathematician sought to square the circle—to reconcile humanity with divinity, reunite the Eastern and Western Churches,

---

50 Ian Christopher Levy, Rita George-Tvrtkovic and Donald F. Duclow, *Nicholas of Cusa and Islam: Polemic and Dialogue in the Late Middle Ages* (Leiden: Brill, 2014).
51 Jovino De Guzman Miroy, *Tracing Nicholas of Cusa's Early Development*, 279.
52 Biechler, Bond, *Nicholas of Cusa on Interreligious Harmony*, xxvi.
53 Biechler, Bond, *Nicholas of Cusa on Interreligious Harmony*, xxxiii.
54 *De pace fidei* I, 6.

bring together council and pope, and seek resolution of the strife between Christianity and Islam. This study seeks to square the circle by exploring some of Cusanus's other major theological writings, to consider how they fit together into a continous argument, namely through Cusanus's governing concept of the Word and Wisdom of God. Hitherto there have been few attempts to examine the underlying metaphysics of *De pace fidei*. While Thomas M. Izbicki, Morimichi Watanabe, Paul E. Sigmund, and Bocken all appreciate the importance and uniqueness of *De pace fidei*, like Biechler they underestimate its far-reaching and synthetic relatedness through the central concept of the 'Word of God' to Cusa's other chief works.[55] Nicholas of Cusa's Wisdom-centered Christology in *De pace fidei* has itself not yet been studied in close detail. Cusanus's Christology has been studied generally by Rudolf Haubst, and cursorily by Bond.[56] While both Haubst and Bond highlight the overall importance of Christology in the thought of Cusanus, neither acknowledges the highly original use of Christology as an instrument of Christian—Muslim dialogue, nor how the Christology of *De pace fidei* relates synthetically to the Christology and Wisdom-Word dialectic of Cusanus's other major treatises *De concordantia catholica, De docta ignorantia, Cribratio Alkorani,* and *De visione Dei*.

Furthermore, Cusanus's career and major writings tend to be categorized largely along political and sharply defined academic-disciplinary lines.[57] Thus, according to the latter criteria, *De concordantia catholica* is seen as a work of

55 Thomas M. Izbicki "The Possibility of Dialogue with Islam in the Fifteenth Century," in *Nicholas of Cusa In Search of God and Wisdom*, 175–183; Morimichi Watanabe, *Concord and Reform: Nicholas of Cusa and Legal and Political Thought in the Fifteenth Century*, edited by Thomas M. Izbicki and Gerald Christianson (Aldershot: Ashgate Variorum, 2001); Paul E. Sigmund, *Nicholas of Cusa and Medieval Political Thought* (Cambridge, MA: Harvard University Press, 1963); *Conflict and Reconciliation: Perspectives on Nicholas of Cusa*, edited by Inigo Bocken (Leiden: Brill, 2004).
56 Rudolf Haubst, *Die Christologie des Nikolaus von Kues* (Freiburg: Verlag Herder: 1956); H. Lawrence Bond, "Nicholas of Cusa and the Reconstruction of Theology: The Centrality of Christology in the Coincidence of Opposites," in *Contemporary Reflections on the Medieval Christian Tradition: Essays in Honor of Ray C. Petry*, edited by George H. Shriver (Durham, NC: Duke University Press, 1974), 81–94.
57 An example of the multi-disciplinary approach to Cusanus's life and thought is found in the chapter structure of *Introducing Nicholas of Cusa: A Guide to a Renaissance Man*. See also, discussion of development in Cusanus in F. Edward Cranz, *Nicholas of Cusa and the Renaissance*, edited by Thomas M. Izbicki and Gerald Christianson (Aldershot: Ashgate Variorum, 2000), 1–18. For a now classic reading on the importance of Cusanus's political thought, as well as changes in his thought and political views, see: Morimichi Watanabe, *The Political Ideas of Nicholas of Cusa with Special Reference to his De concordantia catholica* (Geneva: Librairie Droz, 1963).

political and legal theory, *De docta ignorantia* of philosophical speculation, *Cribratio Alkorani* of apologetics, and *De visione Dei* as mystical and devotional. These writings are further classified politically based upon Cusanus's shift during his career from a conciliarist to a papal monarchist position, to the extent that Cusanus's life and writings are virtually split into two seemingly irreconcilable halves. The interpretation of Cusanus's intellectual development in recent studies has almost led to a Cusanus I and a Cusanus II, demarcated by being either before or after the sea-change of his vision of learned ignorance.[58] Indeed, as Nancy Hudson observes, "Cusanus has been accused of opposite and mutually exclusive tendencies."[59] This study on *De pace fidei* is an attempt to bring together the many Nicholas of Cusas as centered in his engagment with Islam into a single, unified perspective; just as Cusanus's heart lies buried in the chapel at Kues and his body in Rome, the sundering of these parts of his scholarship is an injustice to the whole of Cusanus's work on Christologically understanding Islam. Going to the heart of the matter, we argue that Cusanus's distinctively Christological approach to Islam reveals the centrality of Christology throughout much of his intellectual and pastoral career.

Over against the fragmenting tendency of much recent criticism, this study offers a substantial revision of interpretation in a more unitive direction on *De pace fidei* and Cusanus's Christocentric approach to Islam. Drawing upon the paradigm of Cusanus's own metaphysical claim concerning the coincidence of opposites (*coincidentia oppositorum*) the Christocentric arguments of four of his major treatises—*De concordantia catholica*, *De docta ignorantia*, *Cribratio Alkorani*, and *De visione Dei*—may be seen to fit together in relation to the keystone of Cusanus's Christology and *Logos* theology as articulated and globally expanded in *De pace fidei*. Cusanus's intellectual encounter with Islam illumines his cosmic Christology and the Christocentric structure of his other major works. A keystone in the late-medieval rib-vaulted ceiling in the St. Nikolaus Hospital illustrates Cusanus's Christology and *Logos* theology. Cusanus designed the Hospital himself and the interlocking vaulting shows an architectural example of the *coincidentia oppositorum*. One of the keystones in the vaulting of the Hospital cloisters is embellished with a boss of

---

58   Miroy provides a brief overview of different approaches to Cusanus pre and post his vision of learned ignorance in *Tracing Nicholas of Cusa's Early Development*, 1–2. See also: Joachim W. Stieber, "The 'Hercules of the Eugenians' at the Crossroads: Nicholas of Cusa's Decision for the Pope and Against the Council in 1436/1437—Theological, Political, and Social Aspects" in *Nicholas of Cusa in Search of God and Wisdom*, 221–255; Chapters IX–XI of Sigmund, *Nicholas of Cusa and Medieval Political Thought*, 218–280.

59   Hudson, *Becoming God*, 6.

the face of Christ or Veronica's veil. The arched opposing ribs intersect in the person of Christ.[60] Similarly for Cusanus, Islam and Christianity, and the overarching structure of *De concordantia catholica, De docta ignorantia, Cribratio Alkorani,* and *De visione Dei* intersect in the central concept of the *Logos* and the person of Christ. Moreover, it is our proposal that recognition of the underlying substantial relatedness of these five treatises, the keystone of the Word, provides new insight into the coherence of Cusanus's Christology throughout much of his political career, whether that be on the side of either council or pope. In both instances, as well as in methodology and substance, this study presents a considerable revision of the received criticism on *De pace fidei*, as well as Cusanus's polemic and dialogue with Islam. Former McGill professor Raymond Klibansky explores the medium of Platonic genre and the Platonic-Neoplatonic message as transmitted in the Latin West to the time of Cusanus, in many ways his life-long scholarly project.[61] Our aim is to extend such an approach even further, namely to demonstrate that Cusanus's key concepts of the matrix of learned ignorance and the coincidence of opposites are centred in the synthesis and keystone which is Christ, the Word and Wisdom of God as directly applied to Islam. Following the lead of Klibansky and Cranz, our method aims to emphasize the continuity of Cusanus's sapiential thought on Islam within the Neoplatonic tradition where dialectic and hierarchy in particular are fundamental philosophical presuppositions.

The Word of Concordance

Far from being a mere pastiche of previous writings, Nicholas of Cusa's dialogue of *De pace fidei* presents a profound dialectical and hierarchical account of the cosmos as actively flowing from, centered in, and returning to the Word and Wisdom of God. From within the dialecitical framework of medieval Christian philosophical and theological summations on the Wisdom and Word of God, Cusanus constructively envisions a *concordantia religia* as evidenced in *De pace fidei* and correralry Christocentric writings on Islam. This study on the Cusanian keystone of the Word of concordance comprises seven

---

60 On the face of Christ (Veronica's veil) boss at the Cusanus Hospital in Kues, see Gestrich, *Nikolaus von Kues 1401–1464 Leben und Werk im Bild*, 76.

61 Raymond Klibansky, *The Continuity of the Platonic Tradition During the Middle Ages with a New Preface and Four Supplementary Chapters Together with Plato's Parmenides in the Middle Ages and the Renaissance with a New Introductory Preface*, reprint 1943 (München: Kraus International Publications, 1981).

chapters. We begin by tracking Cusanus's search for religious concordance and exploring the philosophical and theological background of drama of *De pace fidei*, which culminates in Jerusalem, and includes the foremost Platonic and Neoplatonic influences of hierarchy and dialectic as expressed in the thought of Plato, Pseudo-Dionysius, and Bonaventura, as well as the Greek and Christian idea of the polis as nexus of religious concordance. The first chapter, "The Prayer for Peace", discuses Cusanus's unique Christocentric and Platonic approach to Islam through his central conception of one religion in many rites. Chapter 2, "The Search for Peace", traces Cusanus's intellectual journey to the summit of religious concordance, as well as his pursuit of reform. This chapter also places Cusanus's Wisdom and Word dialectical conversation with Islam in the context of other Christian approaches to Islam in the late middle ages. In Chapter 3, "The Mind's Road to Peace", we compare Cusanus's path to religious peace in *De pace fidei* with Bonaventura's famous *Itinerarium mentis in Deum*. In this chapter we will also study the influence of Plato's *Republic* and Christian Scripture upon Cusanus's search for religious peace in *De pace fidei* in connection with his correlative and life-altering theological method of learned ignorance. Along the way, we will briefly and recurrently meet the influential Dionysius. Chapter 4, "Seeking the Peace of the City", offers a discussion of Cusanus and his friend Pope Pius II on their response to Islam and the hope for a potential new Alexander the Great in Mehmed II, as well as confronting the reality of how Cusanus could promote crusade and yet dream of peace.

Chapter 5, "Visions of Peace", looks especially at his two related Divine revelations found in *De docta ignorantia* and *De pace fidei*, and overviews his main theological and philosophical ideas and how they relate to his Christiocentric approach to Islam. This chapter also examines the ordering of the theological loci of *De pace fidei* as indicative of an actual blueprint for dialogue with Muslims, and his plans for a Christian—Muslim council found in his correspondence with John of Segovia, his fellow student of Islam. Here we compare the theological order or talking points of the dialogue of *De pace fidei* with Cusanus's plan for a Christian-Muslim council in his letter to John of Segovia. This chapter also focuses on a discussion of how his metaphysics provide fresh insight on Cusanus's controversial move from the side of the Council of Basel to that of the pope and finally to visionary voice for Christian-Muslim conciliar conversation.

The penultimate chapter, "The Word of Peace", addresses in detail how the structure of the dialogue of *De pace fidei* progresses from the one (the Word and Wisdom of God) to the many religions, and from the many back to the one through exploring various aspects of Cusanus's Christology and how this relates to the Christology of his other major writings. Here we see how

Cusanus's Christology is the keystone connecting the crisscrossing Christological arguments of four of Cusanus's major works. This chapter aims to bring together Cusanus's Christology in *De pace fidei* with the Christology of his other major works: *De docta ignorantia*, *De concordantia catholica*, *Cribratio Alkorani*, and *De visione Dei*. We compare Cusanus's conception of the Unfolding Word (*De pace fidei* and *De docta ignorantia*), the Magnetic Word (*De pace fidei* and *De concordantia catholica*), the Inherent Word (*De pace fidei* and *Cribratio Alkorani*), and the Enfolding Word (*De pace fidei* and *De visione Dei*). The structure of this chapter reflects the metaphysical, arch-like movement of Cusanus's theology which flows from and returns to the keystone of the Word and Wisdom of God. The final and culmative chapter, "For the Peace of Jerusalem", explores and evaluates the exclusivist-inclusivist dynamic in Cusanus's conciliar Christological approach to Islam and ponders what this means for contemporary Christian and Muslim dialogue. This study seeks to further appreciate Nicholas of Cusa's complex and constructive Christology and philosophy of religion as a whole, within the wider context of the metaphysics of Christian-Muslim dialogue. Along the way, we will also discover hints of Cusanus's Wisdom and Word dialectical approach to Islam, as found in the notes he left in the margins of books now kept in Bernkastel-Kues. Throughout these seven chapters, we see the centrality of the Word and Wisdom of God in the life and thought of Cusanus, and especially in his conversation with Islam.

In 2007, amidst the often polarizing tone of contemporary political and religious discourse regarding Islam and the West, various Muslim scholars from around the world jointly published *A Common Word Between Us and You*, an open and pacific letter addressed to Christian religious leaders everywhere.[62] The preface to the letter proposes that since Muslims and Christians comprise more than half of the world's population, "Without peace and justice between these two religious communities, there can be no meaningful peace in the world" and indeed goes on to emphasize that "the future of the world depends on peace between Muslims and Christians."[63] The preface also observes that the source of this peace is found in the revealed sources of both religions. For both the sacred texts of Christianity and Islam believe that God is one and

---

62 *A Common Word: Muslims and Christians on Loving God and Neighbor*, edited by Miroslav Volf, Ghazi bin Muhammad and Melissa Yarrington (Grand Rapids: Eerdmans, 2010), 28–50. *A Common Word Between Us and You* is also discussed in "Inter-Faith Blessing", Chapter 7 of David F. Ford's *The Future of Christian Theology* (Chichester, UK: Wiley-Blackwell, 2011), 137–140.

63 *A Common Word*, 28.

affirm that followers of God should love their neighbours as themselves. In a similar vein, upon hearing the news of the fall of Constantinople to the Ottomans in 1453, the philosopher and prelate Nicholas of Cusa composed *De pace fidei* as a creative prayer for peace and cogent plea for understanding common religious concepts: God, unity in plurality, Wisdom, Word, and peace. For Cusanus the source of peace between Christians and Muslims is found in the source of the cosmos: the Word and Wisdom of God, which the sacred texts of Christianity and Islam affirm. It may be hoped that this study contributes to the ongoing and necessary conversation between Christians and Muslims. In order to further this conversation in pursuit of peace, we first examine the prayer for peace as found in *De pace fidei* and the hierarchical and dialectically unfolding Cusanian religious concordance of "religio una in rituum varietate".

CHAPTER 1

The Prayer for Peace

Blessed are the peacemakers, for they will be called children of God.[1]

∴

After the brutal deeds recently committed by the Turkish ruler at Constantinople were reported to a certain man, who had once seen the sites of those regions, he was inflamed by a zeal for God; with many sighs he implored the Creator of all things that in his mercy he restrain the persecution, raging more than ever because of different religious rites.[2]

∴

One religion in the variety of rites (religio una in rituum varietate)[3]

∴

In the summer of 1453 news about the fall of Constantinople to the Turks shocked Western Europe. While this event is also referred to as the Ottoman conquest of Constantinople, for Nicholas of Cusa and his Western Christian contemporaries this ominous occurrence marked not merely a city's fall, but rather a full-scale catastrophe fraught with foreboding of the impending religious and political conflict now exploding along the eastern front of

---

1 Matthew 5:9 NRSV. Beati pacifici quoniam filii Dei vocabuntur (Vulgate).
2 *De pace fidei* I, 1. Translation by Biechler and Bond. Fuit ex hiis, quae apud Constantinopolim proxime saevissime acta per Turkorum regem divulgabantur, quidam vir zelo Dei accensus, qui loca illarum regionum aliquando viderat, ut pluribus gemitibus oraret omnium creatorem quod persecutionem, quae ob diversum ritum religionum plus solito saevit, sua pietate moderaretur. Unless otherwise noted, Latin quotations of Cusanus are from the Heidelberg critical edition. Cusanus's Latin is condense and rife with neologisms, and as Maurice de Gandillac comments, says exactly what it wants to say (*Neoplatonism and Christian Thought in the Fifteenth Century: Nicholas of Cusa and Marsilio Ficino* (Norfolk, VA: International Society for Neoplatonic Studies, 1981), 144). And note Cusanus's apology for his Germanic Latin in the prologue of *De docta ignorantia*.
3 *De pace fidei* I, 6. Translation by Biechler, Bond.

European Christendom.[4] In tracing the trajectory of the Ottoman-Western European conflict, 1453 punctuates history as a turning point that favoured the eventually Vienna-bound Turks. It is the spark of the subsequent geopolitical stratagems and alliances between Muslim and Christian empires and nations of the early modern era.[5] The Turkish author and Nobel laureate Orhan Pamuk observes that perhaps for some, 1453 was neither a fall nor a conquest, but rather a coercive context in which ordinary men and women found themselves caught between two worlds and had no alternative but to be either Christian or Muslim.[6]

In the pre-enlightenment world-view of the late middle ages, religion and politics, faith and fatherland, prayer and the public square, were fused and easy fodder for sparking conflict. For the late-medieval Neoplatonic and concordant visionary Nicholas of Cusa, theology and philosophy, revelation and reason, St. Paul and Plato, St. Denys and Proclus, divine *Logos* and mortal humanity, Christianity and Islam, even the Abrahamic faiths in all of their sublime complexities, are all intricately interconnected and joined inexorably together on a profound metaphysical and pacific plane. Nonetheless this synthetic metaphysic of unity had for Cusanus real-world implications. Constantinople actually fell and the crash reverberated far beyond the Bosphoros. For in this now strange world of the distant past, even mysticism and the sublime heights of passive contemplation compelled visionaries to launch public careers as manifest, for example, in the frenetic activism of Brigit of Sweden and Catherine of Siena who only a generation before Cusanus's birth urged an end to the pope's 'captivity' in Avignon and restoration of diminished papal prestige. Cusanus's own mystical vision and determined search for religious concordance, *De pace fidei* also addresses both contemplation and action in the concrete realities of religious schism. The now famous dialogue was written in the mystical and conciliar form of a recounted vision of concord and consensus by the representatives of Judaism, Islam, Christianity and Hinduism because of the fall of Constantinople and the news of the suffering caused by religious strife.[7] While

---

4 For a classic overview of the early to mid-fifteenth-century conflict between the Ottoman and Christian powers see Franz Babinger, *Mehmed the Conqueror and his Time*, edited by William C. Hickman, translated by Ralph Manheim (Princeton, NJ: Bollingen Series XCVI, Princeton University Press, 1978).

5 For examples of these complex geopolitical alliances, see Jonathan Riley-Smith, *The Crusades: A Short History* (New Haven: Yale University Press, 1987), 241–254.

6 Orhan Pamuk, *Istanbul: Memories and the City*, translated by Maureen Freely (New York: Vintage, 2004), 172. Cusanus's fifteenth century but forward looking vision of religious harmony in *De pace fidei* reveals peace based on free and fair consensus instead of dictated and oppressive coercion.

7 *De pace fidei* I, 1.

today religion in the post-Enlightenment western world is primarily a private affair, in the late middle ages it was public and all-encompassing.

The thesis of *De pace fidei* is Nicholas's all-encompassing belief that there exists "religio una in rituum varietate".[8] Indeed this is the answer to Cusanus's prayer for peace. This seminal idea of peace comes from the treatise *Lex sive doctrina Mahumeti*, where the text reads: "fides.. una.. ritus diversus." Here in the margin Cusanus emphatically copied along with a pointer, "fides una, ritus diversus."[9] This, *in nuce*, is how Cusanus read Islam. Yet for Cusanus this formula is more than Islamic. In his understanding, at least, this was the case not only from Muslim sources but also more broadly from the prophets of a single religion which also comprises the prophets of Christianity and Islam, as well as the philosophers of ancient Greece and Rome, in so far as they professed one religion in a diversity of rites, mediated by the common agency of the Word and Wisdom of God.[10] His now famous formula "religio una in rituum varietate" arises from his understanding of Islam and Christianity as concordant with his comprehensive understanding of Divine Wisdom and the *Verbum* of God.

Through the Wisdom of God, "religio una in rituum varietate" signifies a synthetic metaphysical element.[11] It stands as formative building block of concord fitted together by the capstone of Divine Wisdom by which the dome of a single religion spans both heaven and earth. The dialogue of *De pace fidei* presents an elaborately structured and multilayered polis-discussion on religion by the philosophers of the world. It is as if with each philosophical and theological proposition discussed, another 'floor' or level of truth is added until the entire unified and completed 'house' of religion towers in perpetuity above the persecutions caused by religion raging below in a dissimilar, unstructured world in turmoil.[12]

---

8   *De pace fidei* I, 6.

9   Cod. Cus. 108, f. 25v.

10 For the term "profferut" in this context see Cod. Cus. 108, f. 25v. In the dialogue of *De pace fidei* the Word (*Verbum*) initiates and leads the discussion and path to truth, which is none other than the Word itself (De pace fidei II, 7).

11 *De pace fidei* I, 6; XIX, 68. The transcendent quality of "religio una in rituum varietate" is seen in these two references, which bookend the dialogue. The dialogue itself builds upon these elements. The first reference contains the speech of the angel before God (eternal court). The second addresses how the ancient philosophers and all the books of the wise affirm this timeless truth and how this peace of faith is realized in Jerusalem (in some sense, the 'eternal' city of God). From Jerusalem, as from the centre, "religio una in rituum varietate" emanates to the end of the world.

12 For Cusanus, philosophy and theology both have the same aim: the attainment of truth and wisdom, and, that truth and wisdom is the Word of God whom nourishes and perfects the intellect (*De pace fidei* II, 7; IV, 16; *De quaerendo Deum* I, 18).

Cusanus's dialogue proper begins with the Wisdom of God, which leads straightaway to the synonymous Word of God. From there the complexities of unity and plurality and Trinity in unity are discussed, followed by a delineation of the tension between finite and infinite in the incarnation of the Word of God. Finally, resurrection, paradise, faith, tradition and rites are serially explored. Together, these propositions or 'storeys' from natural reason to divine revelation further expand one by one the foundational element or building block of "religio una in rituum varietate." What joins these levels of understanding and peace together is the Wisdom or Word of God. For it is the Word (*Verbum*) of God who builds, initiates, furthers, clarifies and finally ratifies the religious discussion. It is, after all, the Word's house of religious peace. According to Cusanus, *sapientia* is unique and through it the cosmos came to be.[13] Furthermore, towards the beginning of *De pace fidei*, *sapientia* is clearly identified as the eternal and generating Word of God.[14] And, the cosmos is, after all—at least according to Cusanus and his western Christian forbears and contemporaries—the created domain of the Word and Wisdom of God.[15]

Ultimately for Cusanus the thesis "religio una in rituum varietate" flows from the wellspring of the Wisdom and Word of God and moves, dialectically and hierarchically, through the cosmos.[16] For Cusanus and his medieval heirs, the world is created in Wisdom, by Wisdom, and for Wisdom. For Christians, this powerful Wisdom of God is further identified with the person and work of

---

13   *De pace fidei* IV, 11: "Non potest esse nisi una sapientia."
14   *De pace fidei* V, 15: "Sapientia igitur est aeternitas"; *De pace fidei* VI, 17: the Arab (as one well acquainted with wisdom in the Arab philosophical tradition) addresses the Word (*Verbum*), "Tue es sapientia, quia Verbum Dei."
15   Cf., Augustine, *Confessions*, XII, xi; XII, xix. Augustine seeks the eternal house of God in the heavens of heavens. This house does not experience the vicissitudes of time. It is the abode of peace and harmony, the goal of the pilgrim. In *De pace fidei*, Cusanus sets his council in the heaven of reason and the court of God (i.e., the house of reason and house or *domos* of God, the place of religious peace and the goal of the pilgrim still struggling in a world torn apart by religious violence). In this heavenly house, the 'Trinity' of memory, understanding and will is one (Cf., Augustine, *De Trinitate* X, iv). For the religious representatives of the world become one in peaceful accord (not only with each other, but also with angels and the Word of God and the saints). They understand "religio una in rituum varietate" and remember what has transpired in the heaven or altitude of reason within (the mind's road to God) in order to will it to reality in the world without (senses) and below (earth). Their actions resemble and participate in the Trinity (by the economy of the Wisdom and Word of God) in memory, understanding, will, and the concord of God's undivided peace.
16   *De pace fidei* I, 6.

Jesus Christ (who, according to orthodox Christian doctrine is, in his twofold nature, both Creator and creature).[17] Thus, the cosmos is rational, and can and should be 'read' by the senses and deciphered in the mind and in the harmonious pursuit of being made wise unto the peace of faith.[18] For Cusanus, Divine Wisdom may be "read" in the mind, although, owing to the ignorance of sin, it is difficult, although not impossible, to decipher.[19] As book one of *De docta ignorantia* shows, the cosmos may be read in geometry and mathematics. It may be read in Holy Scripture, and in the Qur'an.[20] As *De pace fidei* shows, it may also be read in the writings of the ancient Hellenic philosophers.[21] The ultimate way God makes his Wisdom and way to happiness and immortality known is through the incarnation of the Word made flesh, the Word beyond words, the sure via of knowledge, beatitude and peace.[22] Thus, in *De pace fidei*, drastic times (e.g. the fall of Constantinople) call for drastic measures; the Word and Wisdom of God reasons face to face with the religious leaders of the world in order to establish an enduring peace of faith.[23] To realize this peace and avert the maelstrom of religious violence, Wisdom and the Word make opposites known (the many rites and the many adherents of those rites) in relation to the One (both one God and one religion). The highest knowledge Wisdom and the Word impart is the interrelatedness of religions upon which a new polis of world peace is to be established. In this chapter, we will explore four aspects of how, according to Cusanus's prayer for peace in *De pace fidei*, the Word and Wisdom of God reveal one religion in the variety of rites.

---

17 1 Corinthians 1:24.
18 Cf., 2 Timothy 3:15. For Cusanus and St. Paul, Christ, the ultimate Word and Wisdom to whom Scripture testifies, makes seekers of truth and concord wise unto the peace of reconciliation with God and one another, and, hence, harmony between heaven and earth.
19 *De pace fidei* I, 3: "excitatus admiratione eorum quae sensu attingit, posit aliquando ad te omnium creatorem oculos mentis attollere et tibe caritate summa reuniri, et sic demum ad ortum suum cum fructu redire." *De pace fidei* I, 4: "Ex quo factum est, quod pauci ex omnibus tantum otii habent, ut propria utentes arbitrii libertate ad sui notitiam pergere queant." Cf., Aquinas, *Summa Theologiæ*, Ia, 1, 1: "Quia veritas de Deo per rationem investigata a paucis, et per longum tempus, et cum admixtione multorum errorum homini proveniret".
20 *Cribratio Alkorani*, alius prologus, 16.
21 *De pace fidei* XIX, 68.
22 *De pace fidei* II, 7; *De pace fidei* XIV, 49.
23 *De pace fidei* III, 8: "indiget humana natura crebra visitatione, ut fallaciae quae plurimum sunt circa Verbum tuum extirpentur et sic veritas continue elucescat."

The Illuminative Word

'The peace of faith', according to Cusanus, is the all-embracing concordant and eschatological science of God and the blessed, i.e. those blessed to know God, the author of "religio una in rituum varietate", and the imagined everlasting religious and political peace.[24] 'The peace of faith' is a science in the medieval sense in that it proceeds dialectically from higher first principles, which are then exposed, examined, enumerated and elaborated under the aegis of Divine Wisdom which, as one with the Word of God, is first, middle and final principle. This Wisdom not only concerns God (God in God's self), but also God the creator in relation to creatures: the enlightened and blessed (the new eschaton of peace and beatitude), and God in relation to peace (religious and political).[25] Furthermore, this concordance of faith deals with both infinite and finite (God and creation), reason and revelation (philosophy and revealed doctrine), nature and grace. The seemingly opposed religious representatives of the world in the dialogue, especially Muslims and Christians, become blessed through the illuminating and propositional dialectic of Divine Wisdom. To be blessed is to know the religious concordance and live in harmony accordingly forevermore.[26]

This Cusanian Wisdom-Word-dialectic bears striking parallels to the overall structure of Thomas Aquinas' sprawling *Summa Theologiæ* where reason serves to clarify revelation and nature becomes perfected by grace. Cusanus was versed in Aquinas' *Summa Theologiæ*.[27] On a cursory level the all-encompassing structure of the *Summa Theologiæ* and *De pace fidei* share the dialectical format and summational order of *quæstio, ad primum, sed contra, responsio*, and the resulting *ad primum* and *ad secundum*, etc. of the *responsio* as reflective of the unfolding conversation between student and teacher. A brief exploration of this structural similarity serves to further clarify the centrality of "religio una in rituum varietate" and Cusanus's all embracing prayer for peace and search for religious synthesis. This dialectical, *summa*-like conversational outline may be seen, for example, in how Cusanus discusses Wisdom at the beginning of *De pace fidei*.[28]

---

24 Cf. Aquinas, *Summa Theologiæ* Ia, 1, 2.
25 *De pace fidei* I, 1: "sapientum" or the wise men familiar in religion, "religionibus".
26 *De pace fidei* I, 6; XIX, 68.
27 Cods. Cus. 68–74 are works of Aquinas. Cod. Cus. 69 contains the *Summa Theologiæ* Ia–IIæ with a note by Cusanus on f. 124v.
28 It may also be seen in how Cusanus discusses questions on the Trinity and Christology. The Trinity leads to Christology. For each of these, he presents the question and alternative

The 'students' or representative wise of the world commence the dialogue proper. The order of participants is as follows: Greek, Italian, Arab, Indian, Chaldean, Jew, Scythian, Frenchman, St. Peter, Persian, Syrian, Spaniard, Turk, German, Tartar, St. Paul, Armenian, Bohemian, Englishman. The *Verbum* serves as foremost teacher. The Greek who represents Hellenic philosophy, the idea of the *Logos* and the dialectic of ideas, the Socratic method, and the origins of the democratic polis, an idea central to the conciliar character of the dialogue, first praises God for alone being able to bring such a *religionum diversitas* into *uman concordantem pacem*, and straightaway implores the *Verbum* of God to instruct them how this *religionis unitas* could be introduced and implemented.[29] The first subject to be discussed in *De pace fidei* is Wisdom. Thus, the Greek also represents the font of wisdom as transmitted to the Western world through the Romans and Arabs.[30]

This structure is reminiscent of Aquinas' foreword to the *Summa Theologiæ* and the foundational first question of the *prima pars*.[31] In the foreword he commends his, ultimately unfinished, work to the training of beginners in the Christian religion. Aquinas also notes that beginners in the study of the Christian faith are often belaboured with pointless questions. Instead, he devises what he deems to be the appropriate questions in their right order for the sake of clarity and instruction.[32] Understanding the order of the questions is tantamount to understanding the point of the questions. The same dialectical axiom may be applied to *De pace fidei*: understanding the order of the questions is indistinguishable from understanding the point of the questions: the awareness and attainment of unambiguous religious unity and peace. This awareness of the *concordantiam* of religion arises by means of Divine Wisdom (and the *Verbum*) through rightly ordered and necessary conversation between teacher and student (dialectic). The teacher of the peace of faith is the author

---

positions, followed by the definitive response and following points, which then lead to other related questions (*De pace fidei* VII, 21 ff.; XI, 29 ff.).

29 *De pace fidei* IV, 10. The dialogue is imagined by Cusanus as "in concilio" (*De pace fidei* I, 1).

30 The initial hierarchical order of the speakers in *De pace fidei* is important. First, the Greek, followed by the Italian and the Arab, corresponding to the historical transmission of Greek thought through the Romans and Arabs.

31 Cusanus discusses "religio una in rituum varietate" in the prologue to the dialogue itself. This serves as prolegomena to the following questions and responses. This is also similar in style and structure to question one of the *prima pars*, the prolegomena, of Aquinas' *Summa Theologiæ*. In this question, Aquinas presents the overarching subject matter of *sacra doctrina*, which will then be explored in the following parts and questions.

32 *Summa Theologiæ, prologus*, Aquinas writes of the need for an "ordinem disciplinæ". Cf., "unam posse facilem quondam concordantiam" (*De pace fidei* I, 1).

of peace, the *Verbum* of God. He is also Wisdom. For Wisdom concerns God as first cause of creation and giver of religious peace, the end beyond the grasp of reason alone, and, Wisdom governs all knowledge, just as the Word governs all words.[33] The right order of knowledge (ie., the right questions in proper order) point to highest Wisdom which is the harmony of peace.

Throughout *De pace fidei*, the concepts of Word and Wisdom are inseparable. One cannot know Wisdom without words and one cannot know the Word without knowledge. To know Wisdom and the Word is to understand the peace of faith and the concordance of Christianity and Islam and all religion ("religio una in rituum varietate"). While the argument of *De pace fidei* aims to be reasonable, it is also dependent upon a revealed wisdom, as is Aquinas' understanding of *sacra doctrina*. Reason aids in understanding revelation—*fides quaerens intellectum*. For Cusanus, dialectic (reason), is only correctly and surely unfolded by the *Verbum*. Only the Word of God can teach such lasting peace and only the Word of God is reliably knowable. Cusanus writes that after the fall of Constantinople the visitation of the dialogical and conciliar, timeless and hierarchical *Verbum* is needed "since in the sensible world nothing remains stable and because of time opinions and conjectures as well as languages and interpretations vary as things transitory".[34] The *Verbum* of God is truth and one.[35] The only sure truth and unity in a world of conjecture and flux of becoming. For the Word of God is the very religious concordance and Divine Wisdom which reveals the elementary principle of "religio una in rituum varietate".[36] The visitation of the Word in *De pace fidei* is the necessary answer to Cusanus's prayer for religious and political peace.

Returning to Aquinas, we see that divine wisdom is the highest science. In question one, article six of the *prima pars* of the *Summa Theologiæ*, Aquinas argues that *sacra doctrina* is the highest wisdom above all human wisdom. Philosophy, at least in the medieval sense, as transmitted by the Greeks to the Romans and the Arabs, leads to this same higher wisdom. For Aquinas, *sacra docrtina* reveals a surer way (beyond *coniecturis*).[37] Furthermore, in the prologue to question two of the *Summa Theologiæ*, Aqunas sketches the general outline of his magnum opus: "first, of God, secondly, of the journey to God

---

33 Cf., Aquinas, *Summa Theologiæ* Ia, 1, 6.
34 *De pace fidei* III, 8: "et cum nihil stabile in sensibili mundo perseveret varienturque ex tempore opinions et coniecturae fluxibiles, similiter et linguae et interpretations."
35 *De pace fidei* III, 8.
36 *De pace fidei* I, 6.
37 Aquinas, *Summa Theologiæ*, Ia, 1, 1.

of reasoning creatures, thirdly, of Christ, who, as man, is our road to God."[38] The *Summa Theologiæ* advances from God, the first cause, the creator of all things *ex nihilo* (*prima pars*), to humanity (*secunda pars*), then, from humanity to God, and, finally, to the incarnate Word, Christ, the God-man, and perfect return to God (*tertia pars*). In commenting on this fundamental passage, M.D. Chenu observed that the *Summa Theologiæ* follows the Neoplatonic sweep of emanation and return, *exitus et reditus*.[39] This flow from God the first cause is seen in the hierarchy of *De pace fidei,* and is also evident in the grandly conceived treatise that so often overshadows *De pace fidei* in Cusanus scholarship, viz. *De docta ignorantia*.

De *docta ignorantia* unfolds what, according to Cusanus, he received in a celestial vision of knowing which does not know and the coincidence of opposites. The three-part treatise covers first God as unknown first cause; secondly, the universe as unknown first effect; and finally of 'Jesus' as way of unfolding truth, humanity's hierarchical way to God and peace. The synthesis of *De docta ignorantia* is 'Jesus', the *Verbum*. Only the *Verbum* is capable of extending down to the bottom-most grades of being and ascending altogether beyond being to unity with the One. Only the *Verbum* can unite varied languages to the one source in a concordance beyond language. Only the *Verbum* can instruct philosophers on the concordance of religions. According to the structure of *De docta ignorantia*, God is unknown (book one) and the cosmos is also a fluctuating welter of wonder (book three). Hence, the need for 'Jesus,' the via of knowledge and font of wisdom. This is further expanded in *De pace fidei* which presents Cusanus's training for those beginning to seek the peace of the "religio una in rituum varietate".[40] For Cusanus, the religious representatives of the world, and the readers of the dialogue, are noble-minded beginners on the necessary way of conversation to realizing the one concordant peace of faith, religion encompassing of and yet also beyond the discrete religions of Judaism, Christianity, Islam and Hinduism. On their own they are lost in conjectures. By the end of the dialogue, these wise men are to

---

38   Aquinas, *Summa Theologiæ*, 1a, 2: "primo tractabimus de Deo, secundo de motu rationalis creaturæ in Deum, tertio de Christo, qui secumdum quod homo via est nobis tendendi in Deum." English translation from the Blackfriars edition.

39   M.D. Chenu, O.P., *Toward Understanding Saint Thomas*, trans., A.M. Landry, O.P., and D. Hughes, O.P. (Chicago, IL: Henry Regnery Company, 1964), 304–305. See also the description of the Platonic structure of the *Summa* in appendix one of St. Thomas Aquinas, *Summa Theologiæ*, Volume 1 (1a., 1), reprint (Blackfriars edition) (Cambridge: Cambridge University Press, 2006), 43.

40   *De pace fidei* I, 6.

become 'preachers' of "religio una in rituum varietate" through the *Verbum*.[41] In a sense, they are a special order of preachers of religious peace who are now truly wise unto peace and the interconnectivity of religions. While the dialogue gives no indication they are ordained in any way, they are nonetheless eminent philosophers well trained in logic and dialectical argument.[42] The format of the dialogue is conciliar. The interlocutors are both participants and proclaimers of religious peace in and through the *Verbum*. They become enlightened by the idea of religious concordance through the *Verbum* and are ordained to initiate peace. The substantial burden of their message is the religious concordance that embraces Christianity and Islam as one religion in and through the *Verbum* of God.

"Religio una in rituum varietate" is Cusanus's own all-embracing *sacra doctrina* as revealed by the *Verbum of God*. At the beginning of *De pace fidei*, Cusanus prays for religious concordance. This religious harmony is revealed directly by God article by article, question by question, as the divine Word dialectically unfolds the full implications (both philosophically and even politically) of the concordance of religion to those providentially blessed to receive this knowledge. As the preface of *De pace fidei* argues, before this revelation the religious leaders of the world mistook rites for religion. They 'read' and understood religion incorrectly. According to medieval Christian hermeneutics, there are signs and things signified.[43] The religious seekers are lost in rites or in the signs instead of that which is signified. They need the signifier and signified, The Word of God, to reveal himself in the dialectic of peace in order for the religious leaders of the world to recognize religious concordance and read rites correctly as diverse signifiers of higher unified reality. Differing words and differing rites are necessary and yet not to be disassociated from one religion and the one Word. Because of the fog of ignorance and the loquaciousness of interpreters, words no longer express the unity of thought of one religion in the variety of rites.[44] Instead, words confuse rite with religion and divide what is pre-eminently one (viz. Islam and Christianity). Only the ineffable Word can cogently express the unity of God and religion.

While direct citations may be elusive, there is, nonetheless, a structural-dialectical comparison between *De pace fidei* and the *Summa Theologiæ*, that, when applied, sheds brighter light on the brilliance of Cusanus's grand

---

41 *De pace fidei* I, 6.
42 Cf., Cusanus appeal for well trained lay men to participate in a Christian-Muslim dialogue as envisioned in *De pace fidei* and his *Letter to John of Segovia*, see Chapter 5.
43 Augustine, *De doctrina Christiana* I, 4.
44 *De pace fidei* III, 8: "similiter et linguae et interpretationes".

thesis "religio una in rituum varietate" and how the concordance of religious peace becomes realized in heaven and on earth.[45] As the sprawling *Summa Theologiæ* seems to cover all aspects of *sacra doctrina*, so too, in a much more focused and concise way, *De pace fidei* covers all aspects of religion, culture and language (the global scope of the dialogue which spans heaven and earth). And here we see an example of a more focused similarity: *sacra doctrina* as the highest Wisdom, and the revealed way to beatitude. The first and foremost teacher in *De pace fidei* is the Word (*Verbum*) of God who begins the religious council by first positing that the wise men of the world are lovers of wisdom, i.e., philosophers. Thus, the *ad primum*: what is wisdom? The desire for wisdom burns in the minds of the wise, be they Muslim or Christian, as enkindled by wonder. Wonder ignites questions. For Cusanus, these questions address the interrelatedness of religion through the *Verbum* and Wisdom of God. If, therefore, these Christian and Muslim philosophers love wisdom, they assume there is such a thing as Wisdom. The implied *sed contra*: can there be more than one wisdom? It would seem that wisdom is composite given that so many wise seekers from various cultures and contexts desire it. *Respondeo*: since Wisdom exists (and is evidenced by the desire for it), there can only be one Wisdom, for even if it were possible for there to be many wisdoms, they would first have to derive from this one Wisdom. And here Cusanus quotes the authority of Proclus.[46] In the *respondeo*, Aquinas sometimes cites Aristotle or Averroës.[47] It is noteworthy that Cusanus cites a pagan philosopher with whom he was well versed and who provided him with the elements of theology. Thus, the resulting *ad primum et al*: this one Wisdom is invisible and hence images or idols or statues (as discussed in the dialogue by the Indian, or Hindu) are allowed in so far as they point to wisdom which is unseen and initially unknown. From there the discussion moves to the worship of one God who is also ultimately unknown and unknowable. According to Cusanus (reminiscent of Augustine's *De Trinitate* and Denys' *De divinis nominibus* and Aquinas' *Summa Theologiæ* 1a., 13), the names attributed to God are relational and proportional for the sake of creatures.[48] This sacred science of "religio una in rituum varietate" is made known question by question through the agency of the

---

45 *De pace fidei* I, 6.
46 *De pace fidei* IV, 11. "Every manifold is posterior to the One." Proclus, *The Elements of Theology*, trans. E.R. Dodds (Oxford: Clarendon Press, 1963). Prop. 5, p. 5.
47 For citation of Aristotle in the *responsio* see, *Summa Theologiæ, De Deo*, Ia, 4, 1, and Ia. 5, 2. For reference to Averroes, see Ia. 4, 2.
48 Augustine, *De Trinitate* VII, 4; Pseudo-Dionysius, *De divinis nomibus* I, 588AB; *De pace fidei* VII, 21.

Wisdom and Word of God. The dialogue of *De pace fidei* moves from unknown to known, or from what God is not to what God is in the Word. This truth can only be realized by humanity through the subtle art of dialectic, the art of Wisdom as expressed and formulated through words of the Word.

The Dialectical Word

In and through the dialectical, rational and relational *summa* of Divine Wisdom, opposites attract as unity in plurality. This cosmic concordance occurs naturally and enigmatically in creation and providence, and, supernaturally and superlatively in the incarnation, sotieriology and ecclesiology of the Word of God. We have seen how this dialectical concordance echoes Augustine and Aquinas. This elementary and elaborate Cusanian dialectic of the attraction and coincidence of opposites in the Wisdom and Word of God which is given dialogue form and universal reach in *De pace fidei* is also found in a pertinent passage from *De docta ignorantia* (II, 2), which further expands the broad implications of "religio una in rituum varietate" and shows how it relates to the art of dialectic.

We turn to Augustine, Aquinas and now Cusanus himself. Book two of *De docta ignorantia* discusses the universe as created by the absolute maximum (*absoluto maximo*) namely, God (the One who still cannot be named).[49] The second book of *De docta ignorantia* unfolds Cusanus's understanding of natural theology or naturally 'reading' the cosmos. In Chapter 2 of this book, Cusanus observes that creation cannot rightly be called "*una*" as it descends from "*unitate*", nor "*pluralitas*" as contingent on the One (God), nor the copulative of both one and many. Instead, the unity of the universe exists in a kind of enigmatic contingent plurality (*pluralitate contingenter*), which principle, according to Cusanus, ought then to be applied to other opposites (*oppositis*). Furthermore, Chapter 1 of book two of *De docta ignorantia* discusses astronomy, mathematics, music, harmony and proportion, and arithmetic as natural and rational approaches to the investigation of opposites on the continuum of creation from maximum to minimum.[50] These subjects pave the path of attracting opposites and point toward unity. The order matters. For to every thing, God, as maximum in dominical unrivalled power, can provide an opposing thing. Ultimately, the opposite creating and infinite maximum God self-exists as the self-knowing One beyond all opposites: every positive affirmation, and,

---

49 *De docta ignorantia* I, 24, 78.
50 *De docta ignorantia* II, 1, 96.

finally, every negation as well.[51] One can easily get lost in opposing things, and in affirmative and negative thought: for even these are conjectures. Coherence and peace is only found in and through the *Verbum*. Yet, in this context of book two, Cusanus also alludes to 'Jesus', the subject of book three, as the synthesis, who is absolute maximum and absolute minimum, by whom all things were made, in whom opposites coincide, and by whom the lower things are brought to the higher on the continuum of the cosmos, and, according to *De pace fidei*, through whom diverse rites exist conjointly in one religion. The academic subjects of astronomy, mathematics, harmony and proportion, and arithmetic are important paths to exploring the inner workings of nature and they appear in *De docta ignorantia*, in book one through mathematics and in book two, the realm of natural and supernatural Wisdom (natural science and *sacra doctrina*). How they are integrated in the mind and beyond time is the realm of Wisdom (*Verbum*, 'Jesus'), and this is the subject of book three of *De docta ignorantia*, the synthesis, as well as of *De pace fidei* where the religious conversation is joined and integrated by Divine Wisdom, the synthesis of "religio una in rituum varietate".

Diverse religious rites such as ablutions and baptism are naturally contingent on one religion. The order in which rites are discussed in *De pace fidei* matters, as does the order of questions on religion. In *De pace fidei*, religion is discussed before rites, and rites unfold from religion and are enfolded in the *Verbum* they signify. Dialectic is the art of Wisdom by which opposites attract as unity in plurality and religion coincides with rites. God is beyond religion. After the philosophical and theological breakthrough of *De docta ignorantia*, Cusanus often penned dialogues in the genre of Plato.[52] For Plato, the dialogue serves the art of dialectic. Through its very form, its layout and flow on the page, the genre of dialogue embodies the path to transcend conjectures through conversation and unified minds. According to book seven of Plato's *Republic*, dialectic and dialectic alone goes directly to the first principle and thereby forsakes opinions (becoming) for that of truth (being).[53]

In *De docta ignorantia*, Cusanus's shows his predilection for the dialectal method. Returning to Chapter 1 of book two of *De docta ignorantia*, astronomy, mathematics, music, harmony and proportion, and arithmetic fit together through dialectic and lead to the synthesis of book three which is 'Jesus' (hence, the necessary mention of 'Jesus' in this context). Without 'Jesus' these subjects would be cut apart by the jagged edge of knowledge for knowledge's sake,

---

51   *De docta ingorantia* I, 1, 3; I, 26.
52   For example, *Dialogus de Deo abscondito, De ludo globi, De apice theoriae*.
53   Plato, *Republic* VII, 533–534.

instead of being fit together by knowledge for the sake of concordance and peace. With 'Jesus', the Word, they lead to Wisdom (*Verbum*). In *De pace fidei*, dialectic is the art of the *Verbum* ('Jesus'). It is the path of exploring opposites and finally rising above to where ideas originate. As in the mysteries of Diotima and Plato's great sea of beauty, dialectic leads lovers of Wisdom beyond what is transitory to what is eternal. Lovers of Wisdom are led Socratically from transitory rites and violence over the confusion of opinions for the beauty of one religion in the variety of rites and peace without end.

Throughout *De pace fidei* the art of dialectic is the means of the *Verbum* in realizing and implementing religious concordance. Only the *Verbum* bears the Divine-human, signified-sign all embracing complexity to discuss opposites as being opposites and also being beyond opposites and the way beyond opposites. In an axiomatic passage of *De pace fidei* Cusanus speaks of the creating and enlightening Wisdom and the Word of God as reason:

> Therefore, the one infinite reason of all things is God. But reason, which is the *Logos* or Word, emmenates from that which speaks it so that when the Omnipotent speaks the Word, those things which are enfolded in the Word are made in reality, so that if Omnipotence should say 'Let there be light,' then light enfolded in the Word thus actually exists.[54]

Here Cusanus also directly draws attention to the Word as *Verbum* and *Logos* (Latin and Greek) and the complex Stoic philosophical and Johannine antecendents. God is reason, and in reason God speaks through God's *Verbum* and *Logos* all things to be. The fleeting *vox* of God as spoken in the Scriptural account of Genesis conveys the *Verbum* of God as eternal essence and creative force.[55] The scholastic *trivium,* as well as the diverse religious rites, converge on the *Verbum* of God, who is none other than Christ, the source of wisdom and concord. And all things exist in the light of God's Wisdom and according to the divine *ratio* are reasonable.[56] In *De pace fidei* the attainment of wisdom means the rational and consensual comprehension of "religio una in rituum varietate"

---

54 *De pace fidei*, X, 27: "Omnium igitur rerum ratio una infinita Deus est. Ratio autem quae <logos> seu verbum, a proferente emanat ut, cum Omnipotens Verbum profert, facta sint ea in re quae in Verbo complicantur; ut si diceret omnipotentia "Fiat lux", tunc lux in Verbo complicata existit ita actu. " Translation by Biechler, Bond.

55 Eriugena, *Homily on the Prologue to John*. According to Christian theology, the momentary vox of God becomes man in Jesus Christ, the Word made flesh, and permanently changes the relationship between the finite and infinite and gives permanence to the voice of the spoken and recorded Word in Scripture.

56 *De pace fidei* VI, 17; *De pace fidei* XI, 29.

both in the mind of the imagined participants of the dialogue (and Cusanus's fifteenth-century contemporary readers) and, as envisioned at the conclusion of the dialogue, throughout the geo-political world reeling from the fall of Constantinople.[57] Accordingly, as all things are enfolded (*complicare*) in the Word, so also all rites are enfolded in one religion.

As God is one with Wisdom, so religion is one and rational. According to orthodox Christian teaching, as the Word is both God and man (one substance with the Father, two natures), so religion is diverse in rites, yet one in rational substance. As "Father", "Son", and "Holy Spirit" are relational titles that signify God's universal economy of salvation in and for the world, so too the rites in *De pace fidei* are relational in their universal reach and distinct meaning in the varied cultures of the world.[58] That this wise thesis cannot be adequately 'read' except by illumination stems from the 'sin' of ignorance.[59] They might see a vestige of the Trinity, a hint of the *Logos* principle of creation, but enlightenment of the *sacra doctrina* of "religio una in rituum varietate" is still needed and necessary. Cusanus's conception of sin is not exclusively that of ignorance. For as the prologue to the dialogue makes clear, sin also leads to persecution.[60] As antidote to blind ignorance and brutal acts, right thinking leads to right action and unity upheld by the bond of charity. Right understanding of religion leads to right understanding of rites.[61] How one prays is synonymous with what one believes and understands (as in the ancient Christian formulary, *lex orandi, lex credendi*). Above all else, *De pace fidei* is a fervent and reasonable prayer for peace and wisdom. Following Augustine's famous statement in *De Trinitate* "faith seeks, understanding finds" (*fides quaerit, intellectus invenit*) and as transmitted and adapted by Anselm of Canterbury in his *Proslogion*, "I believe so that I may understand" (*credo ut intelligam*),[62] Cusanus seeks and believes one Wisdom and rational Word of God so that he may understand one religion and realize rational peace and comprehend the divinely instituted interrelated diversity of rites. Here again we feel Augustine's weighty influence.

---

57   *De pace fidei* I, 6.
58   *De pace fidei* VIII, 24: "sic res omnis creata geri ymaginem virtutis creativae et habet suo modo fecunditatem". *De docta ignorantia* I, 24, 80: "Et hoc est verum de affirmativis omnibus, quod etiam nomen Trinitatis et personarum, scilicet Patris et Filii et Spiritus sanctim in haditudine creaturarum sibi imponuntur."
59   *De pace fidei* II, 7.
60   *De pace fidei* I, 1.
61   Varied and conjoint rites exist for the greater good of praising God who is one and rational and complex (*De pace fidei* XIX, 66).
62   Augustine, *De Trinitate* XV, prologue; Anselm, *Proslogion* Chp. 1. English translations by Edmund Hill (*De Trinitate*) and Davies and Evans (*Proslogion*).

On the divine origins of unity in and for creation, Augustine argues in book twelve, Chapter twenty-eight of *De civitate Dei* that the goal of humanity is to preserve a single-minded unity.[63] In *De pace fidei* this unity is distorted by sin and threatened by confusing rites for religion. Thus, the *Verbum* will once again visit his creation and in intelligible words reason with philosophers and lead them dialectically to the truth of the religious concordance, the final and greatest single-minded unity of humankind.

Cusanus's other major writing on Islam, *Cribratio Alkorani* (1461), an exploration of the one religion as expressed in the variety of rites in the Qur'an, has more in common with a polemic or apologetic. It primarily covers specific Nestorian-Christological concerns and the multitude of ways of thinking and speaking about Christ, the Wisdom of God. Although *De pace fidei* and *Cribratio Alkorani* are different works written in different genres (dialogue and apologetic), they are hypostatically related through Cusanus's unique understanding of the Word and Wisdom of God, and taken together, present the hierarchical and dialectical complexity of his cosmic and particular Christology as applied to Islam and the global quest for single-minded unity in a harmony of religion.[64]

The Hierarchical Word

In *De pace fidei* the formula "religio una in rituum varietate" as realized through the Word of God is first spoken of by an archangel, which parallels the Prophet Mohammad's reception of the Qur'an from God via his intermediary, the archangel Gabriel.[65] Exploring Cusanus's application of the ministry and hierarchy of angels in relation to Divine Wisdom in *De pace fidei* proves crucial to fully appreciating his cosmological and all-encompassing search for religious synthesis between Christianity and Islam. The dialectical Word and Wisdom of God inaugurates religious peace hierarchically through the sublime order of angels and human beings. Cusanus understands the concordant and Word-revolving ministry and order of angels through Scripture, book eleven of Augustine's *De civitate Dei*, the entire *De coelesti hierarchia* of Pseudo-Dionysius and the discussion of the hierarchy and ministrations of angels

---

63 Augustine, *De civitate Dei* XII, xxviii: "Deus creare voluit unum de quo multitudo propagaretur, ut hac admonitione etiam in multis concors unitas servaretur."
64 *Cribratio Alkorani*, alius prologus, 15.
65 *De pace fidei* I, 6.

THE PRAYER FOR PEACE 35

in the *prima pars* of the *Summa Theologiæ* of Thomas Aquinas.[66] Cusanus structures the dialogue of *De pace fidei* on the hierarchy of God and angels (heaven) and at the conclusion of *De pace fidei* eminent leaders of the regions of the world (earth) are finally centered geographically in the ancient city of Jerusalem as the city of God's peace.[67] For Cusanus, like Denys and Aquinas before him, there exists a sublime order of angels and men in heaven and earth established by and through the Divine Wisdom as affirmed by both reason and revelation. Here we detect the influence of Augustine. In *De civitate Dei* (XI, 1), Augustine begins his theological discussion of the rise, development and ends of the heavenly and earthly cities by first discussing how the origins of these two cities arose from the difference between the good and fallen angels.

The relationship between Divine Wisdom and angels proves to be the initial key for unlocking the fuller mystery of the City of God. Drawing on passages in Scripture, Augustine further says that through the Wisdom of God all things were made and that this Wisdom passes into all souls and makes them friends of God and prophets and informs them soundlessly of the array of God's works.[68] Since the angels of God were created through the Word of God in the first day of Creation ("Let there be light"), they also always behold the illumination of beatitude and reveal the will of God in accordance with the Wisdom of God to those whom it befits to know.[69] In *De pace fidei*, the angels collect the wise of the world's religious sects by divine decree and bear them unto the heaven of reason in order to announce the peace of faith through the Word and Wisdom of God and to become friends of God and of one another whereas before they were enemies on account of the confusion among rites of religion. The angels are illuminative messengers and unifying transporters of God's Wisdom in order that the wise of the world may be enlightened to know (contemplation) and achieve (action) "religio una in rituum varietate" in the city of Jerusalem, the city of wisdom and revelation for Jews, Christians, and Muslims, and from there to the ends of the earth.[70] In *De pace fidei* angels are also set by God over the nations and languages of the world and govern the created order of civilization and culture.[71] Furthermore, in *De civitate Dei*

---

66   *De civitate Dei* bk. XI, Chps. 1, 2, 9, 11, 13, 33–34; Pseudo-Dionysius, *De coelesti hierarchia*; Aquinas, *Summa Theologiæ* Ia. questions 50–64.
67   *De pace fidei* XIX, 68: "cum plena omnium potestate in Iherusalem quasi ad centrum commune confluant et omnium nominibus unam fidem acceptent et super ipsa perpetuam pacem firment".
68   Genesis 1:3; Wisdom 7:27; Proverbs 8:27; *De civitate Dei*, IX, iv.
69   Matthew 18:10; *De civitate Dei* XI, iv.
70   *De pace fidei* I, 6.
71   *De pace fidei* III, 9: "Et advocatis angelis qui omnibus nationibus et linguis praesunt".

(XI, 29) Augustine notes that the angels do not need spoken words to know about God. Instead they know the unchanging Truth of the Word of God and the Trinity by virtue of actual and immediate presence. Through God's Wisdom they also have a better and more complete knowledge of themselves and the cosmos than mortals know themselves and the created world in the art by which it was made. In *De pace fidei*, this knowledge as disclosed by angels in the Wisdom of God also includes the underlying cosmological and concordant principle of "religio una in rituum varietate" that bridges heaven and earth and has existed since the beginning of creation and will abide in an enlightened society of perpetual peace.[72] Thus, in *De pace fidei*, angels, unlike humans, do not require the art of dialectic, since by closer approximation to God on the chain of being they intuitively apprehend the elemental truth of "religio una in rituum varietate."[73]

This concordant society of angelic religious peace serves as the heavenly ideal to be realized by humanity divided by religious confusion. Augustine longs for the holy fellowship and society of the angels in the heavenly city. In *De civitate Dei* (XI, 31) Augustine sighs for the felicity of rest and eternity and permanence of the angels in the commonwealth of heaven. In the prologue of *De pace fidei*, Cusanus sighs after perpetual religious peace in the commonwealth of Jerusalem, the city of God, which through advent of the Word of God spans heaven and earth. The angelic, Wisdom-centred commonwealth regulates and flows by hierarchical gradation through the essence and matrix of the cosmos and underpins the metaphysics of religious concordance. According to the Pseudo-Areopagite, a supreme, divinely emanating sacred order, understanding and activity imitating God by approximation spans and integrates heaven and earth.[74] Angels primarily span the heavenly side of this sacred order. 'Jesus', the Word of God, is the source, revealer and perfection of every hierarchy and he appears prominently at the beginning of both *De coelesti hierarchia* and *De ecclesiastica hierarchia*.[75]

Cusanus transmits the teachings of the Pseudo-Dionysius and Aquinas on angels and hierarchy in the structure and meaning of the dialogue *De pace fidei*. For the *Doctor Angelicus,* angels are more precisely incorporeal and intellectual creatures. Indeed, according to Aquinas the perfection and order of the universe requires incorporeal and intellectual creatures. As incorporeal

---

72   *De pace fidei* I, 6.
73   *De pace fidei* I, 6.
74   *De coelesti hierarchia*, 164D.
75   John 1:1. Note the importance of 'Jesus' in the hierarchies of Denys. *De coelesti hierarchia* 120B–136D; *De ecclesiastica hierarchia* 372A–377B.

and intellectual creatures, angels rank between God and humanity and also more closely imitate the Good in assimilation to God who is Good.[76] In *De pace fidei*, Cusanus (the visioner) ascends by God's grace to an "intellectualem altitudinem" wherein the afore mentioned archangel addresses the King of the Universe.[77] Spatially and metaphysically the angels rank between God and Cusanus. What connects God and angels and Cusanus is the synthetic and enfolding (*complicare*) and unfolding (*explicare*) Word of God.[78] For Cusanus and medieval Christian theologians, the Word of God became man and not an angel in order to reach all aspects of fallen creation. According to Christian doctrine, angels are incorporeal, yet men and women are corporeal as is the world they inhabit. Thus, in order to connect incorporeal with corporeal, the Word of God became flesh and dwelt in temporal matter.[79] In *De pace fidei* angels gather representative eminent and intellectually prone men of the corporeal world to reason face to face in the marked syllables of time with the Word of God and his emissaries in the incorporeal simplicity of the intellectual heights.[80] In Scripture, angels not only deliver messages of peace as in the Annunciation but also implement God's judgment as in bearing souls unto Abraham's bosom.[81] And, as thoroughly noted in Chapter sixteen of *De pace fidei*, Abraham's seed or offspring of Isaac would indeed be a blessing to all peoples forevermore.

There is an angelic eschatological dimension to *De pace fidei*. The dialogue begins with the apocalyptic reality of wars and rumours of war raging over differing religious rites.[82] Cusanus, like the apostles of the New Testament *Book of Acts* before him, dreams in these 'last' days of violence of elusive but perpetual peace and sees the vision of ultimate everlasting religious harmony.[83] Furthermore, the dialogue not only discloses dialectically the *concordantia* between heaven and earth, angels and humanity, but also in time, between the beginning and the end, as centered in Jerusalem. Here, according to Scripture, Jesus Christ, the Word made flesh, rose again and inaugurated a new eschaton of peace between God and humanity and, after ascending to heaven, promised to return once more in order to make all things perpetually

---

76   Aquinas, *Summa Theologiæ* Ia, 50, 1; *De pace fidei* I, 2.
77   *De pace fidei* I, 2.
78   *De pace fidei* II, 7; John 1:51: "et angelos Dei ascendentes et descendentes supra Filium hominis"
79   John 1:14.
80   *De pace fidei* III, 9.
81   Luke 1:26–38; 16:22.
82   Matthew 24:6; *De pace fidei* I, 1.
83   Acts 2:17; Cf., Joel 2:28–32.

new. For those who persecute others over differing rites, the judgment from God himself decrees that this malice arises from misunderstanding wrought by the fall.[84] Beatitude is reserved for those who by free choice and consent find truth in the Word of God (viz. the blessed).[85] Ultimately, the expansive vision of *De pace fidei* accentuates God's illuminating grace as found in the *Verbum* of God, the epicentre of enlightenment, and, hence, offers a strikingly positive and hopeful schema of the interrelatedness not only of religion, but also of the seemingly disjointed cosmos in every member and aspect of its intricate concordant elements. This timeless concordance also touches Cusanus's present moment. As a result of the fall of Constantinople, the angels address prayers to God for peace and an end to confusion over mistaking rites for religion and work to carry out the hierarchical implementation of God's will that there should endure "religio una in rituum varietate."[86] The angels administer the divinely established sacred cosmic order and sacred dialectical understanding of "religio una in rituum varietate" and further Cusanus's own prayer for peace in his time.[87]

For Cusanus angels serve God and penultimately reveal religious concordance. It is God who ultimately reveals the conversation of religious concordance through the Word and Wisdom of God via the agency of angels in the specific mind and memory of Cusanus. It is Cusanus's own vision and retelling of that vision in dialectical and hierarchical form. The dialogical structure reveals the dialectical structure of the peace of faith. The first three chapters of the dialogue not only show the hierarchy of angels, but also the economy of the Trinity: the Father beckons the Son in the nexus of peace (the Spirit). For the polymath Cusanus, numbers clearly matter: three chapters match three persons of the Godhead. And yet, as there are not three Gods but one, there are not three messages in the foundational first three chapters but one: "religio una in rituum varietate."[88] For just as God is not three but one, so also the eminent leaders of the world are to be of one mind concerning one religion. And just as God is one and Wisdom is one and the eminent leaders of the world are one in the one Wisdom, so also there is to be one concordance of lasting peace

---

84   *De pace fidei* II, 7.
85   *De pace fidei* II, 7: "ut quilibet homo secundum electionem liberi arbitrii in sua humana natura, in homine illo qui et Verbum, immortale veritatis pabulum se assequi posse non dubitaret."
86   *De pace fidei* I, 6.
87   *De pace fidei* I, 6.
88   *De pace fidei* I, 6.

as remembered and recounted as dialogue by Cusanus himself.[89] Later in the dialogue Cusanus first names the persons of the Trinity as "unity", "equality" and "nexus", and, then, as Father, Son, and Spirit.[90] Cusanus unfolds his cosmic Christology expressed in the universal concepts of natural wisdom and the potency of unity and the equality of forms in the intellect before he names the Trinity (relational terms for God who is beyond terms). The only sure footing of knowledge is the Word and Wisdom of God (where words are united in the Word, titles to the bearer of titles beyond titles). Christology, in its broadest counters and interspatial sapiential complexities, comes before the Trinity identified in personhood. Yet, the latter does not negate the former, but further elaborates it: from form to name, from idea to person, from God creating the world to God assuming matter and becoming man. Cusanus's Christology is both sacred order and sacred understanding, intellectual and personal as it embraces the transcendent and the immanent.[91] And Cusanus's Christology embraces all people. In *De pace fidei* Cusanus evokes the central image of his mystical masterpiece *De visione Dei*, which was written in the same year and roughly at the same time as *De pace fidei* (1453). Cusanus describes the face of Christ as the face of all people.[92] Christ, then, for Cusanus, is the face of Mehmed II and Pius II, of Muslims and Christians and Jews and Hindus. There are many religious followers embraced by the Word. The Word assumes flesh and creates the way to unity of religion. There are not many Christs, but one Christ, one Word, one Wisdom.

The Conversational Word

Cusanus's understanding of one religion is nuanced. There is one religion, but the concept of one is not simply equated with number or concept. The peace of faith is formulated through cataphatic conversation and apophatic *coincidentia oppositorum*. Religion which is one comprises more than one rite.[93] Religion which is one names the God who is one in many and various ways, yet God exists in unutterable simplicity beyond all names and thoughts.[94]

---

89   *De pace fidei* I, 1: "unam posse facilem quondam concordantiam reperiri ac per eam in religione perpetuam pacem convenienti ac veraci medio constitui."
90   *De pace fidei* VIII, 24.
91   *De pace fidei* X, 27; XIV, 46.
92   *De visione Dei* I, 2: the all-seeing, all-reflecting face of Christ; *De pace fidei* XIII, 43.
93   *De pace fidei* I, 4.
94   *De pace fidei* I, 5.

This religious concordance is realized through faith and revealed dialectically in the intellect through the dialogue of *De pace fidei*. Cataphatic theology (the necessary naming of God) and cataphatic ecclesiology (the necessary rites of worshipping God) coincide with apophatic theology (the un-naming of God) and apophatic ecclesiology (the peace of contemplation). Throughout *De pace fidei* Cusanus deftly weaves cataphatic and apophatic threads into one seamless discussion of "religio una in rituum varietate."[95]

Coincidentally, in the dialogue plurality exists as derived from unity and for the sake of unity, and thus points to unity both in the Godhead and in religion.[96] For the many rites and customs exist for the sake of God whom alone the religious of the world revere. In *De pace fidei* (I, 6) Cusanus alludes to Surah 5:48 of the Qur'an, which says "To every one of you We have appointed a right way and an open road. If God had willed, He would have made you one nation; but that He may try you in what has come to you. So be forward in good works."[97] Diversity in good works heaps praise upon God and instinctively reveals God's oneness both as hidden (through many rites) and revealed (as the One to whom the rites are directed). Cusanus noted this ayah in his copy of the Qur'an, the twelfth-century Latin translation by Robert of Ketton, here writing that this is the cause of diverse sects.[98] Sects lack clarity and obscure God's unity as first source, and sects lack charity and propagate religious persecution.[99] Sects are corrected and unity restored, according to Cusanus, only through being reunited with God the source in greatest love.[100] Since fallen humanity dwells in the umbrage of cavernous shadows, divine illumination blinds as well as makes visible.[101] For God remains "incognitus et ineffabilis" and yet in the dialogue the Word and Wisdom of God makes the peace of faith known.[102] One's eyes need to become accustomed to the light. The eyes or intellects of the representatives of the world's religions in *De pace fidei* adjust gradually and dialectically and hierarchically as the dialogue progresses in the light of God's illuminating Wisdom.

---

95   *De pace fidei* I, 6.
96   *De pace fidei* IV, 11: "ante enim omnem pluralitatem est unitas."
97   *The Koran Interpreted: a Translation by A.J. Arberry* (New York: Touchstone, 1996), 136. Cf., *De pace fidei* XIX, 67.
98   Cod. Cus. 108, f. 45 va "causis diversus sectari" along with pointer by Cusanus.
99   *De pace fidei* I, 1.
100 *De pace fidei* I, 3: "caritate summa reuniri, et sic demum ad ortum suum cum fructu redire".
101 *De pace fidei* I, 3; Cf., Plato, *Republic*, VII, 514–517a.
102 *De pace fidei* I, 5.

Concordance is only achieved at the conclusion of the dialogue and after lengthy, and at times convoluted conversation where wayward eyes become fixed on the light of reason radiating from the Word of God. God is made known through the subtle and taxing art of dialectic. There is no shortcut. Conversation is necessary in order to realize religious peace. Conversation implies voice and voice implies a full-bodied speaker. The main speaker in the dialogue is the Word made flesh, Jesus Christ. His voice speaks peace and concordance in person to representatives of the various religious rites of the world. This conversation through words (cataphasis) leads to thoughts beyond words (apophasis) and finally to *le grand silence* of God in peace being *infinita virtus* and *infinitas*, because, according to Cusanus, "cum finiti ad infinitum nulla sit proportio" and in God all diverse rites and words are ultimately enfolded through the revealed and hidden Divine *Verbum* who is One with God.[103] Owing to human ignorance, the rites are confused with the one religion of the Word. In the dialogue, the Word of God dialectically leads or enfolds the representatives of differing religious rites to realize freely (without coercion), the unity and concordance (*concordantia*) of religion.[104] Since truth is one, for Cusanus it is not possible that it not be understood by every free intellect.[105] And finally this comes together in the intellect of Cusanus himself. For Cusanus, the human mind is a copy of the original. And there exists an inherent connection between word and concept in the medieval discussion of universals. Thus, the Word is from whom and through whom all things exist and find the goal of their existence. And, thus, the one religion of One God, one Word, unfolds into differing devotional practices and systems of ethics and enfolds into the ultimate reality of the inherent relatedness of religion. Religion which is one affirms one God in sublime ineffable simplicity (God's otherness) and revealed through Wisdom (cataphatic) which is one.[106] For Cusanus, the Wisdom or Word of God is one and truth. And this, then, changes how the many rites are understood. The rites are not one, but many. Yet they are from the One. And the One exists with the many and yet is not dependent on the many nor are the many to be confused with the One.

While religion was by no means the only factor in fanning the flame of the ongoing conflict between Christendom and the Ottomans, it was, nonetheless,

---

103 *De pace fidei* I, 5.
104 *De pace fidei* III, 9: "et contentatur omnem religionum diversitatem communi omnium hominum consensu in unicam concorditer reduci amplius inviolabilem."
105 *De pace fidei*, III, 8: "Quae cum sit una, et non posit non capi per omnem liberum intellectum".
106 *De pace fidei* IV, 11.

the major component for conceptualizing humanity's role in a fluctuating cosmos as well as for motivating civic morale and maintaining self-identity and distinction of both sides along the faith divide. This religion was public, but it was also, for Christian and Muslim philosophers and theologians, reasonable. Religion was the highest form of revealed Wisdom, and, therefore, subject to rational discourse. This was true for both Muslims and Christians. Although they may have understood Wisdom differently, they nonetheless assumed Wisdom to be the highest truth. This was especially true for medieval Christian philosophers and theologians. In the final book of the *Consolation of Philosophy*, Boethius's Lady Wisdom enlightens the mind to understand the hidden providence of God.[107] Boethius and his philosophical heirs believed that philosophy and theology were concordant and led to the same Wisdom. The discovery of the interconnectivity of time and space was to be found by means of Lady Wisdom in providence and Proverbs, in both Plato and Paul.[108]

For Cusanus the goal is for the mind to be so stimulated by wonder that it becomes one in peace with the eternal mind through the dialectic of learned ignorance.[109] This is realized through the *Verbum*. In *Truth and Method*, Hans-Georg Gadamer succinctly states Cusanus's understanding of the connection of the finite and infinite mind with the Word of God: "In the infinite there is, then, only one single thing (forma) and one single word (vocabulum), namely the ineffable Word of God (verbum Dei) that is reflected in everything (relucet)."[110] While Gadamer here does not apply this principle of the Word to Islam, nonetheless, the suggestion lingers that it is indeed reflected in all things, and therefore inclusively in Islam. Furthermore, for Cusanus, nothing falls outside the grasp or understanding of the *Verbum*, but not all things may grasp or understand the *Verbum*. As Boethius addresses in book five of the *Consolation*, what at first appears to be incongruent and chaotic in the cosmos (cf., various rites), is revealed by Lady Wisdom to be intrinsically ordered by Divine

---

107   Boethius, *Consolation*, V.
108   *Idiota de sapientia*, I, 3; *De pace fidei* IV, 12: "Omnes igitur vos, etsi diversarum religionum vocemini, unum preaesupponitis in omni diversitate tali, quod sapientiam nominatis."
109   Romans 1:18–25; Plato, *Phaedrus* 250a (Cod. Cus.177, f 102v–111v with numerous notes by Cusanus. This will be discussed in greater detail in Chapter 3); Aristotle, *Metaphysics* I, 2; *De docta ignorantia* I, preface; *Idiota de mente* I, 10; XV, 5; Cf., *De pace fidei* XIII, 40 on the intellectual human nature seeking to adhere to the divine nature. For Cusanus this hypstasis of divine and human intellect is ultimately centered in the Word of God, "aequalitatem" and the form of forms (*De pace fidei* VIII, 24; XI, 29).
110   Gadamer, *Truth and Method*, 436.

Providence.[111] There exits an order or ratio to the cosmos from which the real world originates which consequently may be naturally presupposed by philosophers and theologians.[112] This order becomes clear through the attainment of Wisdom. Wisdom is the all permeating force that establishes and governs the cosmos.[113] Returning to Aquinas, we look again to the foundational first question of the prima pars of the *Summa Theologiæ* where philosophy serves as handmaid to theology and grace does not cast off nature, but crowns it (*gratia non tollat naturam sed perficiat*).[114] The Christian mystery further reveals that the order of the cosmos in Wisdom exists through the Word of God and is perfected by the grace of the Word.[115] For Cusanus, this Word is both thought and expression, divine and human and according to Christian scripture the very wisdom and knowledge of God.[116] Natural knowledge is brought to its fruition through the incarnation of Christ.[117] In Christ, the Wisdom and Word of God full of perfecting and illuminating grace, there exists the ultimate hypostatic coincidence of opposites: finite and infinite, form and matter, words and the Word, God and man and the way of perfection for fallen humanity.[118] In Christ, hierarchy and dialectic, Islam and Christianity converge. Access to this Word may be found wherever the intellect coincides with truth. Truth, for Cusanus,

---

111   Cod. Cus. 191. Boethius, *Consolation*, v, vi, 70; the fundamental difference between *praevidentia* and *providentia*. Through philosophy, which is concordant with theology, Boethius approaches the nature of God's knowledge and simplicity by which all things are measured (*Consolation*, v, vi, 99, the distinctions of the "divini speculator"). Cf., *De docta ignorantia* I, 22: "Et quoniam ex prioribus manifestum est Deum esse omnium complicationem, etiam contradictoriorum, tunc nihil potest eius effugere providentiam; sive enim fecerimus aliquid sive eius oppositum aut nihil, totum in Dei providentia implicitum fuit."

112   *De coniecturis*, I, 1, 5: "Coniecturas a mente nostra, uti realis mundus a divina infinita ratione, prodire oportet." *De pace fidei* XIX, 68.

113   Proverbs 9; Wisdom 11:21; *De docta ignorantia* II, 13, 176.

114   Aquinas, *Summa Theologiæ* Ia, 1. 8.

115   Aquinas, *Summa Theologiæ* Ia, 12, 13: "Dicendum quod per gratiam perfectior cognitio de Deo habetur a nobis quam per rationem naturalem." Cf., *De pace fidei* III, 8.

116   I Corinthians 1:24, 30 Vulgate: "Christo Jesu, qui factus est nobis sapientia à Deo".

117   *De pace fidei* XII, 37.

118   *De docta ignorantia* I, 2: "Et quoniam tale cum absoluto, quod est terminus universalis, unitur, quia finis perfectissimis supra omnem capacitatem monstram, de illo maximo, quod simul est contractum et absolutum, quod Iesum semper benedictum nominamus." This is one of the most intricate descriptions of Cusanus's Christology. Cf. *De pace fidei* XI, 35, contra Eutychianism; Aquinas, *Summa Theologiæ, prima pars*, preface before question three, Christ as via to God. On Cusanus's understanding of the fall in relation to the Word of God and Islam, see *De pace fidei* II, 7.

is ultimately the Word of God through which and to which all things are enfolded and unfolded (*complicantur omnia, omnia explicantur*).[119]

As this study seeks to demonstrate, there exists continuity of this truth through the *Verbum* of God which informs the Christology of Cusanus's major works, and, perhaps, is no where more succinctly stated than in *De pace fidei*. The fall of Constantinople and the rage of religious strife compel Cusanus to clearly unfold his Word (*Logos*) metaphysic and the *complicare-explicare* formula for the sake of revealing and realizing religious concordance. This Word and Wisdom of God may be found in Plato, Proclus or Avicenna and Al-Ghazali, the Bible or even the Qur'an.[120] Yet, this Word is universal and particular: found everywhere and yet fully realized when applied to correcting the destructive force of religious division. Cusanus unfolds a philosophy and theology of the *Verbum* which encompasses both Islam and Christianity as one in essence and many in rites.

Cusanus's understanding of the *Verbum* is also crucial for understanding the full implications of his famous dictum of the *coincidentia oppositorum*. Thus, while Cusanus applies his conception of the coincidence of opposites to various subjects throughout his writings, *De pace fidei* and *De visione Dei* (both written in 1453) show that when applied to Christ it is not only a method or means of knowing, but the very basis of knowing and unknowing the definitive synthesis of God and man.[121] In Christ, the human and divine nature are not dissolved into each other, but are coincident and provide, moreover, an ontological concordance of heaven and earth, divine Mind and human mind in the Truth or *Verbum*-Icon of God. Furthermore, Cusanus's famous dictum,

---

119   *De pace fidei* 11, 7. The *complicare-explicare* concept is oft used by Cusanus. Cf., *De docta ignorantia* 11, 3: "Deus ergo est omnia complicans in hoc, quod omnia in eo; est omnia explicans in hoc, quod ipse in omnibus." According to orthodox Christian theology (contra Arianism), the Word is one with God (prologue to the Gospel of John). Note also *De visione Dei* 111, 8 where Cusanus applies this formula to theology as a complete and complex circle and theological investigation as circular: from the Word-Icon, through the Word-Icon, to the Word-Icon. Thus for Cusanus, as true philosophy is one with true theology, one religion finds its source and summation in the One who is one with the One (Jesus) who was and is and is to come, note the incarnation (*De docta ignorantia* 111, 5. Cf., *De pace fidei*, xiv, 46; *De visione Dei* xix) and ascension-consummation (*De docta ignorantia* 111, 8; cf., *De visione Dei* xxv).

120   Cod. Cus. 205, f. 80v evidences how well Cusanus knew certain writings available to him of Avicenna as well as the Qur'an. Here he wrote in the margin of Avicenna's *Metaphysics* a brief note drawing attention to a section of the text and how it is related to the Qur'an "lege...alchoran." Cod. Cus. 205 also includes texts of Al-Farabi and Al-Ghazali.

121   *Coincidentia oppositorum* indirectly in *De pace fidei* 1, 5, directly in *De visione Dei* ix, 10.

coincidentia oppositorum, is found in the very *concordantia* of religion. Thus the various rites of Islam and Christiaity are not polar opposites, but coincident practices pointing to the higher unified reality of the *religionum concordantiam* in the *Verbum*.[122] There is one religion and peace, but the different rites and regulations coincide in a 'Chalcedonian' communication of attributes (*communicatio idiomatum*) between rites and religion within the hypostasis of the Divine Wisdom.[123] While this idea is mainly noetic, it is not docetic: the participants of the dialogue embody the *corpus Verbi*, the body of the Word of the one religion and the ideal and real community of religious peace. Christ is the Word of God, the ratio of God, the face of all peoples, the magnet, and the structure of the dialogue itself, the way to lasting religious and political peace.[124]

In the medieval mind, natural knowledge of God and revealed knowledge of God are intimately coupled. And what God has joined together, may no one cast asunder. Western and Eastern forms of Christianity were profoundly influenced by Greek thought as transmitted by scribes and scholars through the centuries from Athens to Rome to Damascus to Baghdad to Paris to Cologne and to Constantinople.[125] As Pierre Hadot observes, Neoplatonism, as channelled through and adapted by the great writers of late antiquity such as Augustine and Boethius, together with the Arab translations of ancient philosophical texts and the Byzantine intellectual tradition, provided Medieval Christian thinkers like Cusanus, as well as Muslims and Jews, with a philosophical and theological "dénominateur commun".[126] For the late-medieval Cusanus, religion, which encompassed both Christianity and Islam, was perceived not only as Abrahamic and monotheistic, but also as Hellenic and perennial: processional and plenary, hierarchically dialectical in its ceaseless operations as emanating through the divine *Verbum* and coincident presence in the absence

---

122 *De pace fidei* XVII, 61: "Hanc mundationem in lotione baptismali signatam quisque ostendet fidelis."

123 Wisdom as "verbum seu ratio rerum est" (*Idiota de sapientia* I, 23), and wisdom as synonymous with eternal truth, "quod est veritas absoluta, quae est aeterna sapientia" (Ibid., I, 26). Cf., *De pace fidei* II, 9: "Quae quidem veritas intellectum pascens non est nisi Verbum ipsum".

124 *De visione Dei* XIX, 84: "in ratione, conceptu, causa seu exemplari, et quomodo filius est medium omnium, quia ratio"; *De pace fidei* XIII, 43: "qui est facies omnium gentium"; *De pace fidei* XII, 40: "lapis magnes".

125 On these Hellenistic sources on Islamic mysticism (Sufism), see Massignon, *Essai sur les origins du lexique technique de la mystique Musulmane*, 2n Edition, 50, 73–81. Cf., *De pace fidei* IV.

126 Pierre Hadot, *Éloge de la Philosophie Antique* (Paris: Éditions Allia, 2009), 26.

of intermediate agency.[127] According to Cusanus, the *Verbum* is the ultimate, all-encompassing "dénominateur commun", the minimum and the maximum, and the synthesis of reason and revelation. Cusanus prays for peace and coherence in a world of religious violence and confusion[128] For what at first appears incongruent, even chaotic is revealed to be sublimely ordered and interconnected. The same may be said of the relationship between Islam and Christianity. Cusanus was a man of thought and action, and his thoughts on Islam were provoked by action. This is his prayer for peace, his search for synthesis. *De pace fidei* reveals Cusanus's profound reading of religion and the

127 On descendants of Abraham, see *De pace fidei* XVI, 55–57; *Cribratio Alkorani* III, 13, 15. On hierarchy and God, the Trinity is present to all things, yet not all things are present to the Trinity (Pseudo-Dionysius, *De divinis nominibus* 680B). *De pace fidei* is a hierarchy and a vision: given all at once and approached in gradation. The hierarchy is seen in how the dialogue progresses: the prayer of the visioner to angels to God the Father to the Word to Peter and Paul and then to angels. Yet there is immediacy between God and the viator. He is aassured that his prayers will be answered and in the heaven of reason representatives of the religions of the world are gathered together before the Word of God. He experiences a vision and recounts the vision from the fullness of his memory. Like Augustine, he returns from touching the Divine simplicity to the flux of dissimilarity where every sentence has a beginning and ending (Augustine *Confessions* IX, 10. Cf., *Idiota de mente* 11). Thus, both immediate and by degrees (the creation account and the temple), there is a tension between hierarchy (intellect and angels) and immediacy (creation *ex nihilo*). On Denys the Areopagite (and indirectly on Cusanus), Denys Turner writes, "all creation is hierarchically ranked in degrees of proximity to God and that God is in no conceivable degrees of proximity to creatures" (*The Darkness of God: Negativity in Christian Mysticism* (Cambridge: Cambridge University Press, 1995), 33). At the end of *De pace fidei*, after consulting Marcos Varro (among the Latins) and Eusebius (among the Greeks), Cusanus gives his definition of religion: "Quibus examinatis omnem diversitatem in ritibus potius compertum est fuisse quam in unius Dei cultura, quem ab initio omnes praesupposuisse semper et in omnibus culturis coluisse ex omnibus scripturis in unum collectis reperiebatur." Cod. Cus. 41 contains Eusebius' *De evangelica praeparatione* interpreted by George Trapezuntino with numerous notes by Cusanus. On the *via negativa* in Cuanus: Donald F. Duclow, *Masters of Learned Ignorance: Eriugena, Eckhart, Cusanus* (Aldershot, UK: Ashgate Variorum, 2006). Kurt Flasch "Docta ignorantia und negative Theologie" *Nicolai de Cusa Opera Omnia: Symposium zum Abschluß der Heidelberger Akademie-Ausgabe, Heidelberger, 11. Und 12. Februar 2005*, Edited by Werner Beierwaltes und Hans Gerhard Senger (Heidelberg: Universitätsverlag Winter, 2006), 79–100. Peter J. Casarella, "*His Name is Jesus*: Negative Theology and Christology in Two Writings of Nicholas of Cusa from 1440", *Nicholas of Cusa on Christ and the Church*, 281–307.

128 *De pace fidei* I, 1: Cusanus implores God to answer him and undergoes a prolonged discipline of meditation (*meditatione*). This mediation is tearful-active and follows what is Divinely revealed: *theoria* as passive locution.

interrelatedness of philosophy and theology, heaven and earth, Christianity and Islam in one single concordance. *De pace fidei* is Cusanus's own sincere prayer for peace, so also it hearkens back to salient cries for an end to religious violence following the fall of Constantinople. It is this flux of dissimilarity, this jumble of tears and fears amidst pangs of hope in the elusive search for peace between Christians and Muslims, to which we now turn. In the following chapter, we will place Cusanus's religious concordance in the context of the fifteenth century by exploring its relation to conciliarism and other late-medieval Christian approaches to Islam.

CHAPTER 2

The Search for Peace

Be makam-i Konstantiniyye el Mahmiyye
(Constantiniye—the protected domain)[1]

∴

We exhort, moreover, all Catholics assembled here and others who will come to this sacred synod that they should seek to think on, to follow up and to bring to us, and to this same sacred synod, those matters by which the body of Catholics may be led, if God is willing, to a proper reformation and to the desired peace.[2]

∴

This Teacher had to be the Word Itself, in which are hidden all the treasures of knowledge that can be desired.[3]

∴

---

1 Iliber Ortayli, *Discovering the Ottomans, Osmanli'yi Yeniden Kesfetmek*, 2006, translated by Jonathan Ross (Markfield, UK: Kube Publishing, 2009), 1. Ilber Ortayli is the director of the Topkapi Palace, Istanbul, and one of Turkey's most respected historians on Ottoman history.

2 Council of Constance, Session 1, 16 November 1414. Insuper etiam exhortamur omnes catholicos hic congregatos, et alios ad hanc sacram synodum venturos, ut velint diligenter cogitare, et prosequi, et ad nos et eamdem sacram synodum perducere ea, per quae posit etiam congregatio catholicorum ad debitam refomationem et optatam tranquillitatem Deo iuvante perduci. Latin text and English translation in Norman P. Tanner, editor, *Decrees of the Ecumenical Councils*, Vol. I 'Nicaea I—Lateran V' (London: Sheed & Ward, 1990), 406. This exclamation of ecclesial reform, unity and peace expressed by the fathers of Constance at the beginning of the famous Council would reverberate throughout the fifteenth century and find new voice in Cusanus's *concordantia religionum* as embodied in the imagined global religious synod of *De pace fidei*.

3 Cusanus, *Reformatio generalis, Praefatio*, 1 (1459). Quem oportebat esse Verbum ipsum et magistrum, in quo omnes thesauri desideratae scientiae absconditi essent. Translation by Izbicki.

Nicholas of Cusa's Journeys

For nearly two centuries the Ottomans had steadily overcome the Byzantine Empire. Until 1453 Constantinople stood on the banks of the Bosporus and represented for Western Europe the ancient capital of Greek learning and the Eastern bastion against Islam. Truth be told, by 1453 Constantinople and its environs was essentially a vassal state of the steadily expanding Ottoman Empire, yet for Christians and Muslims alike the city represented more than declining splendour and source of tribute. It was the protected domain, the famous polis, survivor of conquests, wonder of the world. For both East and West Constantinople was still the Roman city of Constantine, Theodosius, and Justinian. Its marvels included Hagia Sophia, the hippodrome, albeit in disrepair, and the basilica cisterns which proudly endured as evocative symbols of the past and the measure of resilience for the present. Even today, though the hippodrome has long since vanished, columns erected by Theodosius, once part of the massive circus, as well as Hagia Sophia and the cisterns remain in the Sultanahmet district of Istanbul. In the late middle ages, Constantinople was the city whose Roman walls would not fall and whose orthodox faith would not yield.

The imperial heritage of Byzantium and the allure of the East were not lost on Western Europe, though they also claimed a holy Roman emperor as their own through Charlemagne and his successors.[4] Eastern and Western Churches had long since parted over linguistic, liturgical, ecclesiological and doctrinal differences.[5] Yet the architecture and mosaics of Hagia Sophia still baffled,

---

4 The western (and Germanic) medieval intoxication and transmission of Eastern art and culture is, perhaps, best seen in the blending of Byzantine and late Gothic architecture of Charlemagne's cathedral of Aix-la-Chapelle. Cusanus's De *concordantia catholica* seeks concordance in the Catholic Church and Holy Roman Empire.

5 This 'Great Schism' (not to be confused with the 'Great Schism' of the Catholic church in the late fourteenth and early fifteenth centuries or the Papal Schism, although it is worth noting that Cusanus career was deeply influenced by the desire to end both these great schisms) is traditionally dated 1054, although the differences between Western and Eastern Churches were apparent long before. In the West, ecclesial negotiations from the pope with the Eastern Church continued for some time after 1054, but ultimately the brutality of the Crusaders in capturing Constantinople in 1204 nullified the attempts of the Second Council if Lyon (1274) and the Council of Basel-Ferrara-Rome (1431–1445; note especially the canons of Florence) to achieve reconciliation between East and West, which ended with the fall of Constantinople in 1453. The Latin text and English translations of the Second Council of Lyon, as well as the Councils of Constance and Basel-Ferrara-Florence-Rome, including critical introductions, are found in: Tanner, *Decrees of the Ecumenical Councils 1*. In this study schism is not

bedazzled and beckoned travellers such as Cusanus himself, who briefly visited Constantinople in 1438. By 1453, the Latin Church and the nascent nations of Western Europe had already long enjoyed more favourable geopolitical positions than their Eastern counterparts. The 'reconquest' of Spain was nearly over. The long 'Babylonian Captivity' of the papacy in Avignon and the great schism that followed had come to an end. The conciliar theory and movement, which once looked so powerful and promising after the watershed Council of Constance (1414–1418), which had been called to end the great schism and the great embarrassment of three feuding claimants to the one sacred chair of St. Peter, as well as ambitiously to seek reform of the catholic church both in head and members, had run its bureaucratic course.[6]

Even by mid-century there endured a still hopeful if slowly fading resolve for ecclesial unity, peace and reform. Appearing throughout the shifting political and religious affairs of the first half of the fifteenth century is the complex life and multifaceted career of the active scholar, preacher, philosopher, and visionary of religious peace, Nicholas of Cusa. In Cusanus's career as canon lawyer,

   neceassarly the same as heresy. Schisms destroy unity (1 Corinthians 1:10 Vulgate). For Cusanus this unity is inherent and emanates from the unity of God (*De pace fidei* IV, 11, "ante enim omnem pluralitatem"). Heresies persist to create competing communities of belief, and intellectually, plural categories of thought. For example in western church history, the Donatists were schismatic. They affirmed doctrine and yet neglected charity. While schism often might lead to the charge of heresy (e.g, the Eastern Church refused to comply with the western church on aforementioned issues, and, according to western perception, further developed their own community of belief), for Cusanus there is ultimately "religio una in rituum varietate" (*De pace fidei* I, 6; Cf., *Idiota de mente*, I, 52). Note that in the dialogue *Idiota de mente*, one faith is synonymous with one ancient philosophy as exposited by the philosopher of the conversation. This unity of faith is unity of philosophy and, therefore, broader than Rome as papacy and curia as it also derives from Athens as Academy and Jerusalem as Temple, Sepulcher and Dome of the Rock. Schisms appear because of ignorance over rites, which, in turn forsakes charity and cause strife. When schismatics persist in schism and what is perceived to be clearly understood false belief (i.e., Nestorius), they are deemed heretics. Learned ignorance (the paradox of passive contemplation and active humility, as well as the coincidence of opposites) enkindled by wonder ("admiratio" *Idiota de mente*, I, 51; *De pace fidei* I, 3; *De docta ingnorantia* prologue) enlightens one to forsake schism and subsequent heresy and embrace concord and unity both philosophically and politically (*De docta ingnorantia* includes both negative theology in book one and ecclesial structures in book three; *De concordantia catholica* covers church and empire). In many ways, Cusanus's whole life and thought may be seen as countering schism and restoring (inherent) unity.
6 The three popes are: Gregory XII (the Roman party), Benedict XIII (Avignon or French camp, antipope according to the Catholic Church), and John XXIII. (also deemed by the Catholic Church to be antipope) The Council of Constance deposed both Benedict XIII and John XXIII, whereas Gregory XII resigned paving the way for Martin V to be elected as sole legitimate pope in 1417.

reforming bishop, and cardinal we find a grand synthesis of conciliar theory and papal power, and even Islam and Christianity, in and through the Word of God. As the noted Cusanus scholar Maurice Gandillac observes, the fifteenth century was "par excellence un temps de transition."[7] The fifteenth-century commenced with the hubris of three bickering popes and concluded with the dawn of the age of discovery and Columbus' voyage to the land beyond maps. Mid-century Johannes Gutenberg developed the movable-type printing press, thereby opening new frontiers of communication which would revolutionize learning and the dissemination of ideas. Given Cusanus's whereabouts and interests, it is not inconceivable that he and Gutenberg met in Mainz around that time. Amidst these far reaching technology-driven changes, we discover transition in the life and work of Cusanus himself. He was a man of transitions in search of religious reform, synthesis and peace. He would find this concordance of religious peace in Greek thought, Christian Scripture and the Qur'an. During an era of transition, he applied ancient and medieval philosophy and theology to the critical issue of his day: namely, the fraught relationship between Islam and Christianity. Is Cusanus to be considered Early-Modern or Late-Medieval? He strides betwixt eras and belies labels. As Sigmund observes, "[Cusanus] stands between two historical ages."[8] He studied medieval canon law and was a humanist in search of ancient sources and new ideas. He moved in the avant-garde of conciliar theology but later became a loyal subject of the pope in the Roman ecclesial establishment. Indeed, he is an elusive case study in the hazy transition from Late-Medieval to Early-Modern Europe. In his enrolment at the University of Heidelberg in 1415/16 his name appears as "Nycolaus Cancer de Coeße clericus Treuerensis dyocesis."[9] The cleric from the ancient diocese of Trier would eventually become cardinal of Rome.

The mystic Cusanus was born in 1401 in Kues, Germany on the Mosel river not far from Trier and Koblenz in what is now Bernkastel-Kues. He studied canon law at Padua and scholastic theology at Cologne. Cusanus became famous for *De concordantia catholica* (1433), a Christocentric work formulating the constitutional unity between council and pope. In 1437 Cusanus left the conciliar camp of the Council of Basel and sided with the pope in his attempt to promote union with the Eastern Church. He eventually became papal legate to reform Germany. Even with the many laurels and accolades, he never forgot his childhood home. Cusanus donated his vast library to the hospice

---

7 Maurice de Gandillac, *La politique de Nicolas de Cues* (Rome: Atti Congresso Internazionale di Studi Umanistici, 1952), 71.
8 Paul E. Sigmund, *Nicholas of Cusa and Medieval Political Thought* (Cambridge, MA: Harvard University Press, 1963), 313.
9 *Acta Cusana*, I, I, p. 3.

he built in his hometown of Kues. The hospice or hospital was intended for the welfare of thirty-three poor and aged men. Today the hospice still stands as the largest Gothic building on the Mosel river. The hospice has weathered the Thirty Years' War, Napoleon's conquest, and the allied bombs during the Second World War. And while today the hospice houses men and women, it sill serves its original purpose: caring for the aged. Cusanus's also left his library to the hospice as a place of research and study which it remains to this day. Many of Cusanus's books still retain his marginalia, making them a treasure trove of discovery for his present day students. It remains unclear how Cusanus collected so many books. Borrowed? Never returned? Cajoled? Bought? Even stole? No one knows for sure. What is known from the size of his vast library is that he was an avid collector and lover of books. Furthermore, he took much of his weighty collection as he travelled around Germany. Upon his death in 1464 his body was entombed at his titular church of St. Peter-in-Chains in Rome. His heart lies buried in the chapel of his hospice, not far from his beloved books.

Much of Cusanus's life was spent on the move: north and south of the Alps in Kues and Brixen, Heidelberg and Padua, across the Mediterranean to Constantinople and Rome, East to West and West to East. While on the move, he embraced and transmitted various ideas, both old and new: the *via negativa*, recent findings in geography and science, rediscovered classics. Like other successful churchmen and wandering scholars of the Middle Ages, Cusanus radiated a restless ambition that would take him from life as a cleric from Trier to being a Cardinal in Rome, and from little known canon lawyer at the Council of Basel to prominent philosopher of learned ignorance. From his first major writing *De concordantia* catholica to his final *De venatione sapientiae* and *De apice theoriae*, he emanated a recurring restlessness in his theological and philosophical concentric search for God and the concordance of all things, whether that be pope and council or Creator and creation.

Cusanus's library and career reveal a simultaneous looking forward and backward, outward and inward: the exploratory interplay of ancient and early modern texts and ideas, writings on Islam and the religions of the East and mystical classics of interior introspection. His wide-ranging medieval and renaissance interests may still be seen in the continued and varied examination of his works by scholars in several fields of study.[10] Just as Albrecht Dürer was

---

10   For example, on Cusanus and mathematics see Jean-Marie Nicolle, *Mathématiques et métaphysique dans l'œvre de Nicolas de Cues* (Paris: Presses Universitaires du Septentrion, 2001). For Cusanus and multiculturalism, see Morimichi Kato "Cusanus and Multiculturalism", which discusses *De pace fidei* and *Cribratio Alkorani* in *Nicholas of Cusa: a Medieval Thinker for the Modern Age*, edited by Kazuhiko Yamaki (Richmond, UK: Curzon, 2002). And for Cusanus imagined in historical fiction see: Wilhelm van Eimeren, *Cusanus:*

the first major northern artist to transmit southern renaissance artistic ideas north of the Alps, Cusanus was the first major transmitter of ancient Neoplatonic and apophatic thought creatively applied to Islam and the new reality of the Ottoman Empire. And as Albrecht Dürer spent the last years of his life searching for the elusive perfect proportion of beauty, so too Cusanus sought the elusive perfect synthesis of Christianity and Islam in "one religion in a diversity of rites".

In mid-July 1453 news about the fall of Constantinople to the Ottomans reached Cusanus in his diocese of Brixen (Bressanone) where he had served as bishop since 1450. Within a matter of weeks Cusanus had written his dialogue on religious peace, *De pace fidei*, shortly after hearing about the fall of Constantinople.[11] The alternative titles of this work are *De pace seu concordantia fidei* and *De concordia Religionum*.[12] Both titles allude to his *De concordantia catholica* where Cusanus seeks concordance of church and empire within Christendom, while hinting at world wide peace. In *De pace fidei*, Cusanus seeks an even more universal concordance of religions. For Cusanus, the title and idea behind the title is nuanced and complex: the concordance of opposites and the harmony of peace. In concordance there is the coincidence of seeming opposites: Christianity and Islam in one concordant faith. There are also striking similarities between *De pace fidei* and the aim of *De concordantia catholica* in which Cusanus sought the coincidence of church and empire, council and pope, heaven and earth. The geographical range is broadened in *De pace fidei* which charts the entire religious world as Cusanus knew it. Since *De pace fidei* was written so quickly after hearing about the fall of the great city, it represents Cusanus's first response to this conflagration of religious violence.

As a highly educated man of his times, Cusanus was well travelled and interested in maps, geography and travel narratives. Here one need only draw attention to the famous "Eichstätt Map" of central Europe of which Cusanus is the acknowledged author. The map is engraved on copper and covers the territory from southern Scandinavia to central Italy to the Black Sea in the East.

Historischer Roman (Münster: Aschendorff, 2008). On Cusanus as transitional and difficult to label thinker, the American Cusanus Society hosts annual sessions on Cusanus at the meetings of the Medieval Congress of North America and Renaissance Society of America.

11 Dated to September 1453. On the dating of the composition of *De pace fidei*, see the introduction by Biechler and Bond, *Nicholas of Cusa on Interreligious Harmony*, ix–xii.

12 Rollin Armour, Sr., *Islam, Christianity, and the West: A Troubled History*, Faith Meets Faith Series (Maryknoll, NY: Orbis Books, 2002), 106. For the complete listing of original titles from the existing manuscripts of *De pace fidei*, see Nicolai de Cusa, *De pace fidei cum epistula ad Ioannem de Segobia*, Edited by R. Klibansky and H. Bascour, O.S.B (London: Wartburg Institute, 1956), 3.

The map focuses on the Rhine and Mosel, Cusanus's home.[13] The engraving claims to date from 1491. Yet it was probably first published later than 1529. The map in the British Library bears a book plate stating that it belonged to the library of Willibald Pirckheimer, a friend of Albrect Dürer, both of whom were early sixteenth-century admirers of Cusanus. It appears now that Cusanus created the lost original map sometime around 1450. The map must have been a collaborative effort and evidences that Cusanus moved in scientific and navigational circles.

Cusanus's search for religious peace in *De pace fidei* is also patterned on his own journeys and the inspiring curiosity of the famous medieval Venetian traveller Marco Polo.[14] Cusanus travelled to Constantinople before its fall, but also throughout northern and central Italy much of Germany and the lowlands, all the while searching for texts, old and new. He also travelled daily within his boundless imagination through reading his books on subjects ranging from alchemy to geography. A copy of Marco's Polo's fabulous travels with annotations by Cusanus now resides in the British library.[15] European travellers in the

---

13   The history and analysis of the map are discussed in: Tony Campbell, *The Earliest Printed Maps 1472–1500* (London: The British Library, 1987), 35–55.

14   On whether Marco Polo went to China, see: Frances Wood, *Did Marco Polo go to China?* (London: Secker & Warburg, 1995), especially on Prester John and the Magi, 23–28. For the classic detailed study of Marco Polo's Travels, see: *The Travels of Marco Polo: The Complete Yule-Cordier Edition*, containing the 1903 unabridged third edition of Henry Yule, as revised by Henri Cordier, together with Cordier's later notes and addenda of 1920, 2 vols. (New York: Dover, 1993). On late-medieval travels, see also: Tamarah Kohanski, *The Book of John Mandeville: An Edition of the Pynson Text with Commentary on the Defective Version*, Medieval and Renaissance Texts and Studies, vol. 231 (Tempe: Arizona Center for Medieval and Renaissance Studies, 2001). *The Mission of Friar William of Rubruck: His Journey to the Court of the Great Khan Möngke 1253–1255*, translated by Peter Jackson, notes by Jackson and David Morgan (London: The Hakluyt Society, 1990).

15   *The Travels of Marco Polo: The Complete Yule-Cordier Edition*, containing the 1903 unabridged third edition of Henry Yule, as revised by Henri Cordier, together with Cordier's later notes and addenda of 1920, 2 vols. (New York: Dover, 1993). On page 531 (vol. 2), brief description of Cusanus's manuscript of Polo's in the British Library, Additional mss. No. 19952 in Latin, Pipino's, small, including on f. 85 et seqq., a note on Mohammad and the Qur'an: "Incipit Noticia de Machometo et de Libro Legis Sarracenorum, etc." This appears, according to the Yule-Cordier edition, to be the work of William of Tripoli. Yule-Cordier also notes that this manuscript was purchased by D. Henry Wolff, 12 August 1854 (Ibid., 531). Cusanus's notes in the marginalia of Marco Polo's *De condicionibus* (Cod. Add. 19952, British Library) are listed in: Herrad Spilling, "Cod. Harl. 3934, 3992 und Cod. Add. 19952", *Mitteilungen und Forschungsbeiträge der Cusanus-Gesellschaft 12* (MFCG) (Mainz: Matthias-Grünewald-Verlag, 1977), 63–64, 67–71.

Middle East were common as the *Travels* or *Rihla* of Ibn Battuta (1325–1354) show.[16] But the daring Venetian's hold on the imagination was stronger. Consider how in book one, Chapter 3 of *De condicionibus et consuetudinibus orientalium regionum* Marco Polo describes how the Turks of Anatolia are Muslims, or in book one, Chapter forty-six he vividly describes how the Tartars believe in a sublime heavenly being.[17] Consider also how Cusanus marks "nestorini" and "machometani ibi vinum bibunt" in the margins of his copy of Marco Polo's tale.[18] Cusanus is attuned to the religious descriptions of the East and the central argument of his *Cribratio Alkorani* is that Muslims are Nestorian. Furthermore, his marginal notes indicate that he is trying to determine if Muslims will drink wine for sacramental reasons, which is traditionally considered by Muslims to be forbidden.[19]

Cusanus's era saw the dawn of the Ottoman golden age and Western exploration culminating in Magellan's circumnavigation of the globe. Fifteenth-century scholars like Cusanus were attracted by the allure of the Orient still too wonderful to believe, too traditional to ignore: the mystique of Prester John and the Magi, the haunts and traces of Alexander the Great.[20] The times exuded an openness to the bipolar world of the fifteenth century where bygone myths met bourgeoning scientific discoveries and launched speculative minds aloft into the mystery of infinity itself.[21] The loquaciousness of Marco Polo's journeys into the unknown gave shape to Cusanus's characterization in *De pace fidei* of the religious sentiments of the Turks, Persians and Tartars. Marco Polo's modern trek from city to city and his fabled descriptions serve as backdrop to *De pace fidei*. The contours of Cusanus's description of the perfect city of peace in *De pace fidei* as heavenly-earthly commonwealth of the wise was influenced by Marco Polo's description of Samarkand, Plato's *Republic* and

---

16 H.A.R. Gibb, *The Travels of Ibn Battuta, A.D. 1325–1354*, translated with revisions and notes from Arabic text edited by C Defrémery and B.R. Sanguinetti, with annotations by C.F. Beckingham, 5 vols. (London: The Hakluyt Society, 2000).
17 *De pace fidei* XVI, 54.
18 Cod. Add. 19952 f. 18r, 15v; *De condicionibus* bk I, Chp. 40, bk I, Chp. 32; MFCG 12, 69.
19 *De pace fidei* XVIII.
20 In his copy of *De condicionibus* Cusanus notes in the margins "presbyter Johannes" and "Allexandriam" (f. 23r, 82r, MFCG, 70–71).
21 On the idea of infinity in Cusanus and Pascal, see "L'uomo e l'infinito nel Cusano e in Pascal" by Sante Pignagnoli. On the principal of inertia in Cusanus and Galileo, see: "Il principio d'inerzia in Cusano e in Galileo" by Vittorio Somenzi in *Cusano e Galileo*, edited by Enrico Castelli (Padova: CEDAM, 1964).

Augustine's *De civitate Dei*.[22] Contrary to the views of Étienne Gilson, *De pace fidei* marks not so much the "passage à la métaphysique" in the renaissance metamorphosis of the Augustinian ideal of the Cité de Dieu[23] as it explicates the metaphysical deepening of transitional earthly reality—i.e. of the *civitas terrena*. *De pace fidei* is Cusanus's passage to peace both inwardly (renewal and reformation) and outwardly (conversation and council). The outward religious persecution and the fall of Constantinople gave rise to the cry to God for deliverance. God answers this real world appeal through his incarnate Word who is hypostatically both divine and human. This hypostatic Word dialogues with Muslims and Christians. Cusanus utilizes Marco Polo's travels to give shape to the characters and talking points of the world-wide religious council. While the twentieth-century writer Italo Calvino inventively conceives of Marco Polo's travels as imaginary and endless "emblems among emblems", for Cusanus the imagined worldwide religious council of *De pace fidei* exists nonetheless as a real attempt at Christian-Muslim dialogue.[24] The argument of *De pace fidei* is grounded in physical reality: e.g. references to Marco Polo's descriptions of far off places and people, realistic descriptions of Muslim beliefs and practices, and the concluding journey to the city of Jerusalem. *De pace fidei* records Cusanus's journey to religious peace through his imagined conversation with Muslims. The dialogue is based on a page-by-page search through the books in his library, his mystical vision of a social imaginary, his genuinely proposed commonwealth of peace in the global urban *ummah* of "religio una in rituum varietate".[25]

The Search for Reform

Cusanus's search for reform and the discovery of religious peace in *De pace fidei* are properly approached after surveying not only late-medieval cartography, but also the history of the conciliar movement of the fifteenth century. Just as a basic grasp of late-medieval monasticism is required in order fully to understand Martin Luther's thought, and especially his dynamic

---

22   Cusanus wrote "samarcha" in the margins, Cod. Add. 19952 f. 17v, *De condicionibus* bk. I, Chp. 39 MFCG 12, 69. For Marco Polo's description of Samarkand, see *Travels*, bk. I, Chp. 30.
23   Étienne Gilson, *Les Métamorphoses de la Cité de Dieu* (Paris: J. Vrin, 1952), 181.
24   Italo Calvino, *Invisible Cities*, translated by William Weaver (Orlando: Harcourt, 1974), 23.
25   *De pace fidei* I, 6. Cf., Charles Taylor, *Modern Social Imaginaries* (Durham, NC: Duke University Press, 2004).

theology of the Word of God, so too, Cusanus's cosmic dialogic theology of the Word of God first needs to be situated in the sundry *sitz im leben* of late-medieval church politics. In 1415 the Council of Constance famously decreed in *Haec sancta* that even popes must obey the assembled general council of the church in matters of faith.[26] In such fashion this proactive Council sought to end schism and promote long lasting unity, counter heresy, and implement far reaching reform.[27] In *Frequens* the Fathers of Constance decreed that in order to guard against future schism more frequent general councils of the church

26 *Haec sancta*, session five of the Council of Constance, 6 April 1415: "Et primo declarat, quod ipsa in Spiritu sancto legitime congregata, generale concilium faciens, et ecclesiam catholicam militantem repraesentans, potestatem a Christo immediate habet, cui quilibet cuiuscumque status vel dignitatis, etiam si papalis exsistat, obedire tenetur in his quae pertinent ad fidem et exstirpationem dicti schismatic, ac generalem reformationem dictae ecclesiae Dei in capite et in membris" (Tanner, *Decrees of the Ecumenical Councils 1*, 409). See also the English translation and discussion in: C.M.D. Crowder, *Unity, Heresy and Reform, 1378–1460: The Conciliar Response to the Great Schism* (New York: St. Martin's Press, 1977), 82–83.

27 The Council of Constance had three main objectives, which also shaped the agenda of the Council of Basel-Ferrara-Rome or what is now referred to as conciliarism or conciliar thought, as well as set the stage for much of Cusanus's own concordance prone career. These three goals were pronounced in session four of the Council of Constance, 30 March 1415: "Haec sancta synodus Constantiensis, generale concilium faciens, pro exstirpatione praesentis schismatic, et unione ac reformatione ecclesiae Dei in capite et in membris fienda" (Tanner, *Decrees of the Ecumenical Councils 1*, 408). First, to restore unity to the church catholic, which meant ending the great schism and ensuring there was only one rightfully elected pope. Second, to combat heresy, which included the condemnation of various articles of John Wyclif (Sessions 8 and 15), and the relinquishing of Jan Hus to the judgment of the secular authorities and his burning at the stake (session 15). This condemnation of Hus and his teachings at Constance was followed by negotiations with the Hussites, which continued at the Council of Basel, of which Cusanus played an instrumental role. Third, promoting a general reform of the church in both head and members. Cusanus spent much of his ministry advocating reform of the church both in its head and members, whether Roman curia or German Benedictine monks. Another emphasis of conciliarism as it developed throughout the Council of Basel was unity beyond Western Europe to include the Eastern Church, which was a long-standing goal of Cusanus and previous councils, notably the Second Council of Lyons (1274). The councils of Constance and Basel called for reform and ending both great schisms (that of three popes in the West, and between Latin and Greek churches). Cusanus own synthetic thought and dialectical method was informed by the actions and thought of conciliarism. In the conciliar formatted dialogue *De pace fidei*, Cusanus applied the conciliar focus on unity to the known religions of the world, notably to Christianity and Islam, and thus, sought to end this greater schism between Christians and Muslims.

be held after five years, then after seven years, and thereafter every ten years in perpetuity.[28] Following *Frequens*, the next council met in Pavia in 1423 and then moved to Siena, but because of the lacklustre attitude of Pope Martin V and national rivalries, the council floundered and fizzled. Constance was followed by the lengthy and contentious Council of Basel, which began in 1431. Basel was a council transferred from Basel by Pope Eugenius IV to three locations: Ferrara, Florence and finally Rome and ended in 1445, hence the elongated name of this shifting Council as that of Basel-Ferrara-Florence-Rome. The multiple changes in location reflect conflicting political and theological agendas.[29]

Although the Council of Basel has been interpreted as meandering or magisterial, protean or precursor to the Reformations of the sixteenth century, nonetheless, by mid-fifteenth century the pope was again the established head of the Western Church.[30] And there appeared then a moment of aspiration,

---

28   *Frequens*, Session 39, 9 October 1417. The Latin text with English translation is found in Tanner, *Decrees of the Ecumenical Councils I*, 438–443; see also: Crowder, *Unity, Heresy, Reform*, 128–129.

29   Sigmund opines that given the rising nationalism of the fifteenth century (as seen at the Council of Constance), if the principle of conciliar supremacy had triumphed, the Catholic Church would have probably separated into national churches (Sigmund, *Nicholas of Cusa and Medieval Political Thought*, 305).

30   On how the council has been interpreted, see: *The Church, the Councils, and Reform: the Legacy of the Fifteenth Century*, edited by Gerald Christianson, Thomas M. Izbicki and Christopher M. Bellitto (Washington, D.C: Catholic University Press, 2008). On Cusanus's efforts at reform of the early 1450s, see Joachim W. Stieber, *Pope Eugenius IV, the Council of Basel and The Secular and Ecclesiastical Authorities in the Empire: The Conflict over Supreme Authority and Power in the Church* (Leiden: E.J. Brill, 1978), 340 ff. On the papacy: "especially in the Empire, the papacy came to be regarded in the later fifteenth century as an opponent of church reform, since the expectations of reform had become inseperably linked with the holding of general councils" (Pope Eugenius IV, Stieber, 346). Stieber also says this of the calls for crusades from Pope Calixtus III and especially Pius II: "After the fall of Constantinople in 1453, such a crusade [called by the pope] would have had two functions from the standpoint of the Roman Curia: (1) to relieve the direct military threat to Italy, and, especially, to the Papal States, and (2) to aid the Greek Christians, some of whom the papacy could no longer regard as schismatics after the papal council at Ferrara and Florence in 1438 and 1439" (Stieber, 342). Stieber concludes that from the standpoint of post-1870 Roman Catholic dogma, "the claims of the Council of Basel may appear untenable or illegitimate." Yet, they did not appear so to the German princes and theologians of the 1440s (Stieber, 335). For more on the papacy and crusade and Cusanus, see Chapter 4. Yet it is also argued that the primary concern of the canonists and theologians was theological, see Antony Black, *Council and Commune: The Conciliar Movement and the Fifteenth Century Heritage* (London: Burnes & Oates, 1979), 4–6. Black downplays the

clarity and clairvoyance, even of synthesis when it seemed that the Eastern and Western Churches, Rome and Constantinople, Rome and Mecca, Christianity and Islam, Jerusalem and the ends of the earth—at least, in the Neoplatonically tuned mind of Cusanus—would find their underlying metaphysical unity and realize their shared philosophical and hierarchical hermeneutical concepts and dialectical categories as shaped by Greek thought and fulfilled through the revelation of sacred texts. Yet that moment was fleeting and ultimately gave way to more religious violence and disunity. In the Balkans, a powder keg of Europe long before the early twentieth century, the Turks continued their advance. In Rome, the renaissance flourished, and the ostentatious trappings and ambitions of the mid- to late-fifteenth and early sixteenth-century pope-princes—as exemplified by the warrior clad Julius II—led to the pivotal posting of ninety-five theses of reform by a persistent German monk and the consequent breakup of Christendom. The late-medieval moment of synthesis had dissipated.

In the East, the situation by early 1453, both ecclesiastically and politically, was bleaker. Representatives of the Eastern Church had agreed to accept Papal primacy and end the centuries old schism between Eastern and Western Churches in exchange for promises of much needed military aid from the encroaching Ottomans. This concord was decreed officially in both Latin and Greek on 6 July 1439, in session six of the Council of Basel, now transferred from Ferrara to Florence. The first session at Florence, or session five of the Council of Basel-Ferrara-Florence, convoked on 10 January 1439, officially transferred the Council to the banks of the Arno. The definition of union between the Western and Eastern Churches begins by honouring in proper hierarchical gradation Pope Eugenius IV and the Byzantine Emperor John Palaeologus (in that order). In florid language the decree describes how both Western and Eastern Fathers had crossed the perilous sea to meet and establish this longed for holy

---

parliamentarian approach for a more nuanced theological, biblical and ecclesiological-political approach. On the complex relationship between conciliar theory, monarchy, and the Turkish advance, Black writes: "The political norm of monarchy, the opposite of tyranny as well as of democracy, was becoming established as a common feature of Christendom, which—as the rulers of Eastern Europe at least saw it—was a political as well as a spiritual entity, with an all too real enemy, the Turk, directed at its very existence as a single community of peoples" Antony Black, *Monarchy and Community: Political Ideas in the Later Conciliar Controversy, 1430–1450* (Cambridge: Cambridge University Press, 1970), 132. For other views on the conciliar movement and its impact see Brian Tierney, *The Foundations of the Conciliar Theory* (Cambridge: Cambridge University Press, 1955); Paul Avis, *Beyond the Reformation? Authority, Primacy and Unity in the Conciliar Tradition* (London: T&T Clark, 2006).

union.[31] The decree affirms the 'filioque' and allows that the Body of Christ is confected in both unleavened and leavened bread. Furthermore, Eastern and Western Fathers side with the great Dominican theologian Thomas Aquinas on his view that the blessed upon death clearly see God as God is while some see Him more perfectly than others on account of their merits.[32] The definition of union also lists the order of patriarchs: first, Rome, and then Constantinople. It was on the perilous ocean that Cusanus crossed to and from Constantinople, and on his return voyage to Venice that he received his apophatic vision of learned ignorance, that is of a paradoxical 'seeing' which does not see God. Citing the New Testament epistle of James, Cusanus records that this method was illumined by God.[33]

In spite of these points of agreement, the Greeks still bitterly remembered the sack of Constantinople by marauding crusaders in 1204 and the subsequent establishment of a short-lived and ill-fated Latin kingdom. And yet Constantinople, the ancient city, remained. The Latins were overcome. The perilous waters of the Sea of Marmara and the golden horn had for centuries—until the devastation wrought by the long range guns employed by the Ottoman Sultan Mehmed II, the Conqueror—naturally formed a stalwart defence for the protected domain of Constantinople. Although the Emperor himself and ecclesial representatives of Byzantium had traversed the perilous sea to overcome centuries of distrust and heterodoxy, hardly surprisingly the Decree of Union of 1439 between Rome and Constantinople was never accepted by the Greek populace or church. Desperate times called for desperate measures and the leaders of what remained of Byzantium were forced to concede the supremacy of Rome. As for the fall of Constantinople, Western Europe was deeply shocked, perhaps unreasonably. In the end, however, Western Europe did very little to help their now reconciled but beleaguered Greek sisters and brothers in the faith. By 1453, the Ottomans controlled Constantinople and firmly established therein the capital of their Islamic empire on European soil.[34]

---

[31] The Latin definition reads (it was also stated in Greek): "Ecce enim occidentales orientalesque patres post longissimum dissensionis atque discordiae tempus se maris ac terrae periculis exponents, omnibusque superatis laboribus, ad hoc sacrum ycumenicum concilium desiderio sacratissime unionis et antique caritatis reintegrande gratia, leti alacresque convenerun" (Session 6, 6 July 1439, Tanner, *Decrees of the Ecumenical Councils I*, 524).

[32] Aquinas, *Summa Theologiæ* Ia, 12.

[33] James 1:17; *De docta ignorantia*, epistola.

[34] For a detailed account of the last days of Byzantium, see: Steven Runciman, *The Fall of Constantinople 1453* (Cambridge: Cambridge University Press, 1969). Runciman sees the

For Cusanus, who as an aspiring canon lawyer had ably reconciled Rome and Bohemia, the Catholic Church and the Hussites, and whose Proclean-Dionysian thought traversed East and West, and embraced both Greek apophatism and Roman canon law, conciliarism and papal monarchism, the decree of union between the Eastern and Western Churches shone as sign of the underlying unity of the *Logos* as emanating from within and without, from imminence to transcendence, transcendence to immanence, from simplicity to hierarchy and hierarchy to simplicity, from West to East and East to West. He broadened the search for a grand synthesis, for a concordance to extend beyond Rome and Constantinople, and to embrace both Jerusalem and Mecca. As Sigmund observes, Cusanus "was looking for harmony, *concordantia*, a unity in diversity—but, first of all, for unity."[35] Sigmund, however, avoids an exploration of how this unity in diversity is heuristically found in Christ and Christocentricity as explicated in *De pace fidei*.

Cusanus's *De pace fidei* presents not only his synthetic search, but also his public call for general reform of the very understanding of religion. In *De pace fidei* Cusanus prays for peace and unity on a global scale. Yet, *De pace fidei* also reads as a call for universal religious reform from a Latin western perspective. Cusanus approaches and adjures "religio una in rituum varietate" from the standpoint of his own western late-medieval ecclesiastical milieu where the idea of reform based upon *Christiformitas* and the person and iconography of Christ were ubiquitous.[36] As the late, eminent American Cusanus scholar H. Lawrence Bond noted, *De pace fidei* was primarily intended for a Western European audience.[37] Cusanus intended *De pace fidei* to be a bold conversation starter for reforming how fellow Western European (Latin reading)

Turkish conquest of Constantinople as inevitable and describes the Western response as pious mourning devoid of any active response.

35   Sigmund, *Nicholas of Cusa and Medieval Political Thought*, 312.
36   The Chalcedonian and ubiquitous Christology of *De pace fidei*, the hypostatic-ontological basis of religious reform, stresses the one person and two natures of Christ, the *Logos*, *Verbum*. See for example *De pace fidei* XII, 39: "solum unum Christum esse posse, in quo natura humana in unitate suppoaiti unita est naturae divinae." Cf., Council of Chalcedon, *Definitio fidei*: "Sequentes igitur sanctos patres umum eundemque confiteri Filium dominum nostrum Iesum Christum consonanter omnes docemus eundem perfectum in deitate, eundem perfectum in humanitate, Deum vere et hominem vere...in duabus naturis inconfuse" (Tanner, *Decrees of the Ecumenical Councils I*, 86). On late-medieval fascination with the human nature and suffering of Christ, see, for example, the cruciform *Shewings* of Julian of Norwich, and the famous Isenheim Altarpiece by Mathias Grünewald.
37   From comments made during the session on Cusanus and Islam sponsored by the American Cusanus Society at the 44th International Congress on Medieval Studies, Western Michigan University, Kalamazoo, Michigan, 7 May 2009.

scholars thought about Islam, as well as serve as a novel proposal for how Christians, like himself and fellow student of Islam, John of Segovia, might actually engage in dialogue with Muslims.[38] The setting of the imagined dialogue is a worldwide council and congregation of philosophers presided over by God almighty through the the Word of God. The council especially focuses on the inner relationship between Christianity and Islam.[39] The traditional medieval Christian response to Islam could be characterized as *reprobatio*. In *De pace fidei*, however, Cusanus provides a unique and conversational *explicatio* of the interconnectivity of Christianity and Islam through the ancient and Scriptural concept of the *Verbum*. His unfolding dialogue, while composed in the context of fifteenth-century western Europe, is also rooted in Greek thought (for example, the centrality of the *Logos* as synonymous with the *Verbum* in *De pace fidei*), which predates both the advent of Jesus Christ and the Prophet Mohammed.[40] His philosophical view is Hellenic in the same way that Islam and Christianity may be considered Hellenic monotheistic religions infused by the categories and concepts of ancient Greek philosophy. His style is Hellenic as well. *De pace fidei* is written in the genre of Platonic dialogue. Cusanus's intended audience of *De pace fidei* is Catholic, but his understanding of catholicity is greater than Christianity or Islam, and this is what makes Cusanus's *explicatio* ancient and Hellenic, while at the same time original, universal and enduring.[41]

Ascending the Summit of Religious Peace

For Cusanus there is one religion in the variety of rites (the interrelationship of the one and the many) and, ultimately, in the cosmic scope and speculative

---

38 Cusanus, *Epistula ad Ioannem de Segobia* II, 1–2.
39 Much of the dialogue is devoted to addressing actual doctrinal questions on Christianity raised by Muslims. For example, the discussion of Christology, which covers Chapters XI–XIII, mainly focuses on realistic questions posed by Persians, Arabs and Turks. See especially, *De pace fidei* XI, 30 where the Persian asks the fundamental Christological question: "Quomodo Deus, qui est immutabilis, fieri posset non Deus sed homo, creator creatura? Negamus enim hoc paene omnes, paucis in Europa demptis."
40 On the *Logos-Verbum*, see *De pace fidei* X, 27, XI, 29. On Plato and Platonic forms, see *De apice theoriae* 14, *De docta ignorantia* II, 9, 141–150.
41 Cusanus's understanding of the interrelationship between Christianity and Islam in *De pace fidei* and even, to a lesser degree, certain synthetic themes in *Cribratio Alkorani*, is similar to contemporary Roman Catholic views on Islam decreed by Vatican II (*Nostra Aetate, Decleration on the Relation of the Church to Non-Christian Religions*, 28 October 1965).

and enigmatic language of *De apice theoriae* (1464), only *Posse* (to be able, possibility-power itself, i.e., God). The summit of contemplation stands also as the summit of catholicity where the one and many, whether it be religion and rites, or the finite and the infinite, or East and West, move in concordant locutions of unity as *Posse* and modes of appearance. In *De apice theoriae*, which was written shortly before Cusanus's death, he notes that those seeking the one and the many looked to *Posse* and the various modes of its appearing.[42] At the pinnacle of Cusanus's own *Itinerarium mentis ad Deum*, all seekers of unity and the One only look to *Posse*, which is prior to and potent progenitor of conjectures and intellectual taxonomic cartography, including the four points of the compass, and the many rites of one religion.[43] As Cusanus states at the zenith of *Idiota de mente*, religion has always been made known to philosophers and especially simple laymen in a diversity of modes.[44]

To put this in terms of the argument of *De pace fidei*, which occurs metaphorically further down the mount of contemplation in the timeframe of Cusanus's life, religious rites, such as sacrifice, ablutions, circumcision and fasting, are devotional approximations and laudable modes of approaching *Posse* in the concordance of one religion. Religious rites from the four corners of the earth are conjectures, and as such, they are matters of faith or belief in things unseen.[45] On religious rites, Cusanus proposes his own religious hermeneutic of concordance: "For they [signs] have been instituted and received as sensible

---

42 *De apice theoriae* 14: "Qui enim unum et multa dixerunt ad posse ipsum et eius multos apparitiones essendi modos respexerunt." Although *De apice theoriae* and *De pace fidei* were written at different times, the ideas expressed in *De apice theoriae*, namely, One as *Posse* and the many as modes of *Posse*'s appearance which finally pass over into concordance, parallel the emanating doctrine of the *Verbum* in *De pace fidei*, from which and through which and to which all things flow in concordance. While *De pace fidei* is not the summit of contemplation per se, it is the summit of religious concordance. Hence, the setting of the dialogue in the "intellectualem altitudinem." For Cusanus, the Triune God is signified as *Posse* Itself (*De apice theoriae* 28). While *Posse* is an ambiguous title for God which embraces and eludes all things, so too, the title *Verbum* is more expansive and encompassing than the name Christ or Jesus. The title *Verbum* or *Logos* conjures up in the intellect the full scope of the Christian teaching of the pre and post incarnate Word of God through whom all things came to be, in whom is life, and by whom exists the way to the summit of contemplation (John 1:1–5; 14:6).

43 *De coniecturis* II, 15, 148–150.

44 *Idiota de mente* XV, 159: "Connata religio, quae hunc innumerabilem populum in hoc anno Romam et te philosophum in vehementem admirationem adduxit, quae semper in mundo in modorum diversitate apparuit". Cf., Aristotle, *Metaphysica* I, 2,982, a recurring axiom for Cusanus.

45 Hebrews 11:1.

signs of the truth of faith. But signs are subject to change, not however that which is signified."[46] (Rites are imprecise and subject to change, yet the Truth signified changest not.) According to Cusanus, the Truth is the *Verbum*, who, according to the Christian New Testament, is the same, yesterday, today and forever.[47] Cusanus states, "The truth which nourishes the intellect is nothing but the Word itself."[48] The metaphysic of the Word is the peace of faith: how it is known and realized. This metaphysic of the Word is also the peace of the cosmos: how Heaven touches Earth, and how God is known. This metaphysic of the Word connects the rites as many modes in one religion, and images of the divine as many depictions in one divine essence. Finally, this metaphysic of the Word is incarnational and relational: consubstantial with God, one distinct person, divine-human names as analogous approximation and bearers of hidden meaning. Since this Truth is one, and knowable in images (by sense perception) or words (symbolics), and which flows hierarchically and dialectically through the ranks of all creation (both within and without the Church), it is not possible that it would not be finally acknowledged by earnest seekers of the True and the Good and the Beautiful.[49]

Cusanus's comprehensive understanding of Truth and dialogue is more than merely intellectual comprehension and imaginary consensus. As his understanding of the extent of catholicity is greater than the limits of either Christianity or Islam, so also his comprehension of hypostatic Truth is greater than any one religion; but not less than the incarnation of the Word of God.

---

46 *De pace fidei* XVI, 55: "Nam ut signa sensibilia veritatis fidei sunt instituta et recepta. Signa autem mutationem capiunt, non signatum." Cf., Augustine, *De doctrina Christiana* I, 1, 4–6; Aquinas, *Summa Theologiæ* Ia. 1, 9–10. In *De pace fidei*, Cusnaus applies Augustine's hermeneutic on signifiers and signified to other religions. Cf., Cusanus ascetics, on images, which are to be connected to the essence they depict, *De pace fidei* VII, 19: "Ymagines quae ad notitiam deducunt ea, quae in vero unius Dei cultu conceduntur, non dampnantur." Cf., Plato, *Republic*, VI, 510b.

47 Hebrews 13:8. The high Christology of the New Testament epistle of Hebrews with its evocative and enigmatic symbolism of Jerusalem informs Cusanus's own Christocentric and Jerusalem based understanding of the peace of faith. As we have seen, the Christology of the Gospel according to John also serves as primary source of Cusanus's Christology. In medieval iconography, St. John the Evangelist was depicted with the eagle of Revelation 4:7 because he soars to the mystical heights of contemplation, and in many churches the lectern upon which Scripture is read (and through which one is transported to sublime mysteries) is shaped in the form of an eagle (as Cusanus soars to intellectual heights of religious concordance through the *Logos*).

48 *De pace fidei* II, 7: "Quae quidem veritas intellectum pascens non est nisi Verbum ipsum."

49 *De pace fidei* III, 8.

In his essay "The Idea of Truth as the Basis for Religious Tolerance According to Nicholas of Cusa with Comparisons to Thomas Aquinas", William Hoye argues that while Cusanus maintains his Christian convictions, he does so in a way that includes the convictions of all noble thinkers.[50] Hoye writes, "He does this, one could say, by climbing to a high degree of abstraction, to a viewpoint, namely, where he can speak of Truth itself as distinct from truths, where truths are seen in the light of Truth."[51] He concludes that Cusanus developed "an intellectual Christology", an "intellectualizing" of the faith as true theology.[52] Hoye correctly notes the importance of Truth for Cusanus not only in *De pace fidei*, but in a number of his writings. He also accurately identifies Cusanus's association of Truth and Christ. Yet by focusing on the intellectualization of Christ and faith, he fails to mention the incarnation of the Word as the divine-human grounding of Truth, as well as the social dimension of religious dialogue and the dialectical-relational and reformational and conciliar path to Truth.[53] Cusanus's inclusive and holistic insight on Truth is centred and revealed in the cosmic and incarnate Christ. The *Verbum* is a word of the same genus as other words, namely a 'sign'. It is also the Word who spoke words, i.e. the thing signified.[54] Thus, it is more than simply the truest word, it is the Word speaking Truth in community (the world-wide dialogue of *De pace fidei* or the general councils of the church).

Cusanus's conception of the *complicare-explicare Verbum* metaphysic of *De pace fidei* is directly unfolded in the hypostasis of the incarnation. Right after the aforementioned Cusanian formulation of the *Verbum*, Cusanus writes

---

50   William Hoye, "The Idea of Truth as the Basis for Religious Tolerance According to Nicholas of Cusa with Comparisons to Thomas Aquinas", *Conflict and Reconciliation: Perspectives on Nicholas of Cusa*, edited by Inigo Bocken (Leiden: Brill, 2004), 161–173.
51   Hoye, 172–173.
52   Hoye, 173. Cf., Kurt Flasch, *Nikolaus von Kues. Geschichte einer Entwicklung: Vorlesungen zur Enführung in seine Philosophie* (Frankfurt am Main: Klostermann, 1998), 373.
53   The religious council of the peace of faith is patterned after the Council of Constance where the nations were represented (as in *De pace fidei*, the regions of the world are represented). At Constance the Truth (Christ as the way to Truth and Truth) was sought to end schism and reform the church. For the council members, this Truth is ultimately Christ. Thus, the council began with a solemn mass and masses were said regularly (the mass as corporate sacral Truth). Council of Constance, Session 4, *Decreta concilii de auctoritate et integritate eius* (30 March 1415), declares that the general council has "potestatem a Christo immediate habeat" Tanner, *Decrees of the Ecumenical Councils I*, 408. Cf., Cusanus, *De concordantia catholica* II, 3, 77.
54   Cf., Augustine, *De doctrina Christiana* I, 4.

that the *Verbum* put on "humanam naturam" wherein dwells immortal truth.[55] Furthermore, for Cusanus the incarnation is the decisive event of God's revelation. Christ, according to Cusanus, is not timeless truth. He is the incarnate, dialogical Truth which inaugurates the end time of the peace of faith.

De pace fidei mainly focuses on Christology. Sounding overtones of the Reproaches from the traditional western liturgy of Good Friday (the commemoration par excellence of the humanity of Christ), Cusanus wonders what more could be done than has already been done?[56] In *De pace fidei*, Cusanus dives to a low point of abstraction to find Christ the Truth. Christ, the Word of God, answers the call to end religious suffering and enlighten the way to the summit of everlasting peace through his own suffering. Every theological proposition, every rite, everything down to the lowest being, must be enlightened and reformed by the Word of God who even gave his life and suffered death on the cross.[57] Due to sin and ignorance in this life of conjectures and approximations, confused and divided human hearts and minds require repeated visitation and council: by prophets, philosophers and gurus, and also the Incarnate Word, in recurring dialogue.[58] Cusanus further writes, "Unde Christus sic natus est nobis, ut sit omnibus hominibus coniunctissimus."[59]

The religious council of *De pace fidei* and Cusanus's real-life desire for a confraternal gathering of high ranking Muslims and Christians as patterned after *De pace fidei* and the Ecumenical Councils of the Catholic Church, both ancient and contemporary (from Nicea to Basel), are one in context and purpose and should not be seen as isolated phenomena.[60] Councils repair division wrought by confusion over authority; Councils derive their legitimacy from the Word of God, and being called by right authority. Thus, after Pope John XXIII (antipope) ingloriously fled the Council of Constance, the assemble general synod decreed that the council still had the authority as gathered by the Holy Spirit for bringing union and reform to the Catholic Church.[61] This, then, set the stage for the famous decree *Haec Sancta* and the claim that the general council was authoritative in matters of unity and reform. The general council

---

55 *De pace fidei* II, 7.
56 *De pace fidei* II, 7: "quid est quod fieri potuit, et non est factum?".
57 Philippians 2:5–11.
58 *De pace fidei* III, 8.
59 *De pace fidei* XIV, 46.
60 *De concordantia catholica* looks primarily to past (*ad fontes*) ancient councils and the teachings of the Church Fathers for contemporary guidance.
61 Council of Constance, Session 3, 26 March 1415, "pro unione et reformatione dictae ecclesiae in capite et in membris".

of *De pace fidei* as imagined by Cusanus is summoned by God. The Word of God (*Verbum*) interacts with the representatives of the world's religions, followed by Peter and Paul who speak on behalf of the Word. The representatives of the world's religions are led dialectically by the Word, Peter and Paul from the many rites to one religion. To put the matter in terms of conciliar theory as developed at the Councils of Constance and Basel, even the highest representatives of the religions of the world must obey the decrees of the general council in ending religious schism.

The council's legitimacy comes from God as exercised through the Word of God. Thus, *De pace fidei* promulgates a global *Heac sancta*. The papal schism of the late middle ages hinged on legitimacy and caused confusion. The schism of *De pace fidei* is caused by confusion over diversity of religion and religious rites. This global religious confusion is corrected by legitimate authority (i.e. by God through the Word as eternal pontiff) and universality (a truly ecumenical world-wide council of religious leaders).[62] Thus, as Cusanus notes in book two, Chapter 4 of *De concordantia catholica*, the greater the *concordantia*, the more infallible the judgment. *De pace fidei* presents Cusanus's greatest, most far reaching formulation of religious *concordantia* in the infallible, divinely bestowed principle of "religio una in rituum varietate". Furthermore, as Cusanus writes in *De concodantia catholica* (II, 3), the universal council is to be public, as in his published vision of *De pace fidei*, and decisions should be arrived at freely in a spirit of consensual tranquillity. In *De pace fidei*, the Word of God is the active agent and chosen authority who brings reconciliation to those who confuse rites for religion.

Throughout *De pace fidei*, Cusanus highlights the necessity of faith as dynamic means of ascent to religious Truth and concordance. There is faith in Truth. Indeed, there is also more than faith. Even for Martin Luther and the magisterial reformers, *sola fide* was never meant to be seen in isolation. Faith orbits *solus Christus* and *sola gratia*. The same may be said of Cusanus's understanding of faith. While Cusanus does not hold to a Lutheran view of passive or forensic justification by faith alone, he does conceive of faith in Christ, the Truth and the Word of God. For Luther, faith is turned outward to its object, namely Christ, whose passive righteousness is alien to fallen men and women.[63] For Cusanus, faith is connected to its object, Christ, yet by way of

---

62 Cusanus affirms in *De concordantia catholica* (bk II, Chp 2) and in his *Epistola ad Rodericum de Trevino* (see especially 12) that the pope is the right authority to call general councils of the church catholic.

63 Luther, *Freedom of a Christian*; *Sermon on Two Kinds of Righteousness*.

dispositive gradation, habitual formation and imitation. The same faith as believed by the prophet Abraham leads to reformative dialectical religious comprehension and concord and in whom every good is enfolded.[64] Faith needs to be connected to its object and goal, namely Christ, who is the *terminus a quo* and *terminus ad quem* of the dialogue and the life of faith.[65] Christ, the Word of God, animates and flows through the ranks of being and leads believers in *De pace fidei* to be *Christiformes*.[66] Without faith and conjectures, mutable rites and signifiers, the moving cosmos and the world in flux, there would be no modes of knowing God, the Prime Mover, who is beyond all knowing, and, no mode of interpreting the natural world.[67] For Cusanus religion is naturally made known by God in a diversity of modes. According to *De pace fidei*, religion, then is naturally made known in a diversity of books. *De pace fidei* ends with the opening of books: ancient books that taught there has always been and always will be "religio una in rituum varietate".[68] The wise of the world are not able to see this owing to the inheritance of sin or being lost in modes of religion. These modes may be numbers, geometry, logic (hence the meandering cataphatic and apophatic modes of books one and two of *De docta ignorantia*), or, in *De pace fidei*, longstanding diversity of religious observances and rites. Modes become subject to the whims of time, the flux of dissimilarity, the calcification of custom. Knowledge puffs up; love builds up.[69] Thus, the layman of *Idiota de mente* must instruct the philosopher in the way of charity. For Cusanus and medieval theologians, charity is the greatest virtue. Love is nexus,[70] the Spirit of God that connects various modes into one and leads to *Posse*. Pride is what caused Augustine to love so late and what causes the wise of the world to persecute and hate one another over a divergence of religious rites. Making sense of conjectures is the métier of reason. Faith, as cardinal virtue, is surer than conjectures. Faith is the métier of theologians. The Word

---

64   *De pace fidei* XVI, 57: "Quapropter oportet credere Deo prout Abraham credidit, ut sic credens iustificetur cum fideli Abraham ad assequendum repromissionem in uno semine Abrahae, Christo Iesu; quae repromissio est divina benedictio, omne bonum in se complicans."

65   *De pace fidei* begins with God the Father entreating his Son in the Spirit of peace to visit the wise of the world and lead them to religious concordance. The dialogue ends in Jerusalem, city of David and Jesus, the mother church unfolding in apostolic and Christocentric hierarchy to the other ancient metropolitan bishoprics: Constantinople and Rome.

66   *De pace fidei*, II, 7; *De concordantia catholica*, I, 2; *Reformatio generalis* 3.

67   *De apice theoriae* 15.

68   *De pace fidei* XIX, 68.

69   1 Corinthians 8:1, a favourite verse of Augustine.

70   Cusanus's title for the Holy Spirit in *De pace fidei*.

and Wisdom of God, Jesus Christ, the Teacher himself, consubstantially unites modes of religion and revelation, philosophy and theology into one grand synthetic search for *Posse*. Throughout his writings, Cusanus consistently refers to himself as theologian.[71]

While true philosophy and true theology have the same aim, namely God, *Posse*, the Good or the One, for Cusanus, true theology is definitively taught by Jesus Christ, who is both Teacher and Subject, both *Posse* and *Posse*'s most sublime and simple appearance. To put it in terms of *De docta ignorantia* (I, 2), Jesus is the Absolute maximum and minimum, unknown and known. This is precisely why so many of Cusanus's speculative and conjectural writings conclude with the invocation of Jesus. *De concordantia catholica* comes to a close with the *corpus Christi* of Christendom. *De docta ignorantia* ends with a detailed discussion of Christology, as does *De visione Dei*.[72] *Apologia doctae ignorantia* ends with the Truth of Jesus in synthetic mystery of learned ignorance.[73] *De dato patris luminum* concludes with the Word of Truth, Jesus, while at the end of *Cribratio Alkorani* we find a detailed discussion of the hypostasis of Christ in whom the intellective is conjoined consubstantially to the sensual.[74] This is more than pious perfunctoriness. Jesus is the one who reforms, transforms and perfects conjectures into Truth (Himself) and makes known the certain way to beatitude, for he is the way and end. Furthermore, faith, according to *De pace fidei*, means trusting in the promises of the Word of God, promises which include the harmonious revelation of "religio una in rituum varietate".[75] Unsurprisingly, *De apice theoriae* concludes with a prayer for faith in and help from Jesus. Only Jesus can definitively lead the conjecture-bound seeker (Cusanus himself) to *Posse* itself and thus to the summit of contemplation.[76] Jesus has promised this ascent to those who earnestly and arduously seek him: the path of reason and revelation. As Cusanus asks at the outset of *De quaerendo Deum* (1445) in reference to the Apostle's Paul famous speech at the Areopagus in the New Testament *Book of Acts*, why would God have created humanity and this world, if men and women were not meant to know

---

71 For example, in the prologue to book one of *De doctra ignorantia*, Cusanus describes his method of learned ingnorance as theological: "in rebus divinis talem qualem ratiocinandi modum suscipe".
72 *De docta ignorantia*, III, which is almost exclusively devoted to matters of Christology, soteriology and ecclesiology; *De visione Dei* XV.
73 *Apologia doctae ignorantia* 35.
74 *De dato patris luminum* 122; *Cribratio Alkorani* III, XXI.
75 *De pace fidei* I, 6.
76 *De apice theoriae* 28.

the One beyond all knowing?[77] Thus, Jesus is the "perfectissima apparitio" of *Posse*, and "veritas intellectum" in "humanam naturam".[78] There are conjectures (e.g. geometry, aesthetics, logic, dialectic), and there are conjecturalists (Plato, Aristotle, Avicenna), and, then, there is faith, and the teacher of the peace of faith—Jesus in *De pace fidei* as well as the followers of Jesus and great doctors of the Latin Church, notably Augustine and Ambrose as prominent influences.[79] Faith as a theological virtue is connected to its object, Jesus, who propels the ascent from approximation to apprehension of *Posse* (*De apice theoriae*) and religious concordance (*De pace fidei*). In *De pace fidei* that promise includes religious harmony.

Throughout *De pace fidei*, faith is required for realizing peace.[80] Yet, according to First Corinthians 13, the classic New Testament mystical text, faith and hope pass away in the fullness of the beatitude of love at the summit of contemplation when the knower is fully known and knows God fully. In faith the seeker ascends to the culmination of seeing and knowing one God fully in Unity and Trinity through seeing and knowing the one true religion fully in the diversity of rites.[81] According to *De pace fidei*, the Word of God unfolds, informs and perfects this via of faith. One begins with religious rites and custom and sense perception: water, food, the elements.[82] One moves, as along Plato's famous epistemological line in *Republic* VI, from opinion (over rites) to imagination (what is possible) to faith and thought and understanding. Sin leads one to dwell in the obscurity of opinions (water for ordinary physical ablutions is different than water for baptism) and the disorientation of religious imagination (baptism and ablutions share nothing in common). Over the years custom gives way to accepted truth and imagination is stifled concerning what could be.[83] Thus, according to *De pace fidei* long-standing rites are observed and confused by religious

---

77   *De quaerendo Deum* I, 17–18; Acts 17:22–34. For Cusanus and his medieval theological predecessors, Dionysius the Areopagite, who is named in Acts 17:34, was St. Denys the Areopagite, the great apophatic theologian and Cusanus's mystical muse.

78   De *apice theoriae* 28; *De pace fidei* II, 7.

79   The revealed art of learned ignorance (*De docta ignorantia* III, 263), guides one to confess and comprehend Christ correctly and fully. In *Apologia doctae ignorantia*, 34, Cusanus states that this teaching on Christ is synonymous with the teachings of John the Evangelist, St. Paul, Dionysius, Pope Leo and Ambrose of Milan, all of whom we will encounter again throughout this study.

80   *De pace fidei* XVI, 55.

81   *De apice theoriae* concludes with Trinity and incarnation.

82   *De pace fidei* I, 3: "excitatus admiratione eorum quae sensu attingit".

83   *De pace fidei* I, 4.

adherents with truth just as the dwellers in Plato's cave confuse opinion (*doxa*) with tethered knowlege (*episteme*). Owing to sin and ignorance, rites are misunderstood. The eternal God made the world, so corporeal things exist in order to lead us to the incorporeal. Yet, as Plato notes, one can become mired in the material: both as physical matter and books of learning.

According to Plato and Cusanus, the seeker of Truth needs to come out of the cave of opinion in order see the light of knowledge: what is temporal (shadows, rituals) diminishes, what is intellectual (forms) endures. This is taught most clearly by Christ. Cusanus writes, "All temporal things diminish, only intellectual things never do."[84] Cusanus marked this sentence in Cod. Cus. 219 which, along with Cod. Cus. 218, contains the collected works of Cusanus in a single binding and style. Both codices were commissioned and reviewed by Cusanus himself. Cod. Cus. 219 includes *De pace fidei* and *De apice theoriae*, which was written in April 1464. On the first page of the codex we read that Cusanus himself edited the volume. Cusanus died in August 1464. Thus, Cod. Cus. 219 was edited by Cusanus sometime between April and August 1464 and, along with Cod. Cus. 218, then, may be considered to be the final authorised edition of his works along with his final notations on his works. Both codices bear Cusanus's markings in the margins.

Nearing the end of his own life, Cusanus pondered the enduring reality of the intellectual realm in what was presumably his last reading of *De pace fidei*. Perhaps, while preparing for Pius II's abortive crusade to recapture Constantinople, Cusanus longed for the peace of faith in the lofty altitude of the heaven of reason. Perhaps, Cusanus, in ill health saw peace only beyond this vale of tears. Perhaps, though, Cusanus again positively affirmed that the way to realizing the peace of faith, and thus peace between Christians and Muslims, was through first properly distinguishing the temporal from the eternal, creation from creator, and rites from religion. This proper distinction is foundational for consenting to the peace of faith here and now in and through Christ. In his final reading of *De pace fidei*, Cusanus also marked Chapter 14, paragraph 49, where he states that in order for humanity to attain the kingdom of heaven, Christ opened it in every possible way. Thus, Christ the divine *Ratio* opens and perfects all paths of reason to *Posse*, in accordance with the Truth, whether that path be found in Plato or the Prophet Mohammad. Christ does so by virtue of his passion. This is the complexity of Cusanus's orthodox understanding of faith: transformation of the here and now through the suffering of Christ, hope of what is to come through the resurrection of Christ. Thus, while Cusanus acknowledges that Muslims, Jews and Hindus should receive

---

84 *De pace fidei* XV, 50: "Omnia temporalia vilescunt, solum intellectualia numquam".

the Eucharist, he understands by the Sacrament a similitude for 'food' of wisdom and eternal felicity signified by it after which all lovers of wisdom seek.[85] Furthermore, how the Eucharist is to be celebrated, as well as frequency of reception are matters of personal belief and may be ordered to preserve the law of the peace of faith in the mode of diverse rites.[86] In *De apice theoriae*, Cusanus would eventually conclude, that all differences finally move into concordance.[87] Concordance, whether it be in the Eucharist or modes of knowing, is sought in all things and realized in and through Jesus, one person in two natures. *De apice theoriae* and Cusanus's speculative musings conclude his confession of the Trinity. Cusanus writes, "By '*Posse* Itself' is signified the three and one God". Thereupon, he implores Christ, the way "to the clear contemplation of *Posse* Itself".[88] This is the summit of a lifetime of contemplation and faith. Cusanus scaled the heights of divine introspection through years of dialectically ascending reflection and belief in and through the Word and Wisdom of God. Along the way, he hunted this same Wisdom in *De pace fidei*'s conciliar dialogue of religious peace. For Cusanus everything except God, the creator of all things, is conjecture. Even God is approached through approximations and faith. Christ leads beyond to the beatitude of *Posse* itself.

Perhaps, then, Cusanus, the speculative philosopher, is an idealist in the classical sense, while *De pace fidei* qualifies as a fine example of esoteric, Renaissance hermeticism rife with utopian delusions. Like Plato's *Republic*, *De pace fidei* may be read as an allegory of the soul in relation to the One and an exploration of how ideas come to be known by the intellect. We have responded to Hoye's characterization of Cusanus's intellectualization of Christ through focusing on the incarnation and faith connected to its center and object. There is also the greater charge that Cusanus sought a "super religion" mounting above and loitering behind every religion. As the twentieth-century Lutheran theologian Herman Sasse said of Augustine, the conception of "*sacramentum* as a universal idea or category that applies to all religions" may also be attributed to the Augustinian Cusanus.[89] Similarly Jos Decorte, the late student of *De pace fidei*, wonders "whether he [Cusanus] is not really striving

---

85 *De pace fidei* XVIII, 65: "similitudo"; *De pace fidei* VI, 16: *sapientia* as "pane suo intellectualis".
86 *De pace fidei* XVIII, 66: "sic quod ob diversitatem rituum per communem legem non minus pax fidei inviolate perseveret."
87 *De apice theoriae* 15: "Talibus igitur resolutionibus vides cuncta facilia et omnem differentiam transire in concordantiam."
88 *De apice theoriae*, 28: "Per posse ipsum Deus trinus et unus" and "claram contemplationem". Translation by Bond.
89 Hermann Sasse, "Word and Sacrament Preaching and the Lord's Supper" (1956), *We Confess Anthology*, translated by Norman Nagel (St. Louis, Concordia, 1999), 13.

for a super religion which, despite his good intentions, cannot deny Roman origins (and will therefore never be feasible, as the history of his attempts at negotiation has shown)."[90] Furthermore, Decorte continues, Cusanus "holds fast to the classical doctrine of the Trinity, exactly because it is the ultimate conjecture."

While the Trinity is the ultimate puzzle for theologians, why does Cusanus spend so much time in *De pace fidei* on Christology? There is, as Hoyle contends, a high level of abstraction of the faith in *De pace fidei*, but what Hoye and Decorte fail to observe is the low level face to face dialogue which pulsates through the council or religious peace. The heart of *De pace fidei* is the incarnate Word of God. For Cusanus the universal Truth is Christ. Christ is the universal, super reality in which all things and all religious rites are explicated. This Truth is dialogical: incarnational, relational and conversational. Cusanus avoids the two extremes of utopia or dystopia: first, by tethering the lofty dialogue to the cities of Constantinople and Jerusalem, and, secondly, by dialectical conversation that cascades from heaven to earth. The cities of Constantinople and Jerusalem have suffered religious violence. Instead of vacating these cities, Cusanus transforms them into cities of refuge where the citizens have been enlightened by the Word of God to know the peace of faith in the variety of rites.

Caution should be taken before dividing action and contemplation, Cusanus the speculative philosopher from Cusanus the reforming cardinal. While both thinking and serving, supernal ideas and concrete reform, require different aptitudes, for the medieval Christian they are undergirded by the same life of faith and pilgrimage. Cusanus, the musing philosopher and reforming cardinal and passionate preacher is grounded in real questions and real hierarchy: What is the relationship between Islam and Christianity? What is the relationship between pope and council? In *De pace fidei* Cusanus explicates "religio una in rituum varietate" through the cosmically *complicare-explicare Verbum* as inclusive of Christianity and Islam, and both true catholicity and true philosophy.

Cusanus's all-embracing late-medieval catholic approach of "religio una in rituum varietate" may also be viewed cosmically and spatially on a macro and micro level or from above (intellectual) and from below (ecclesiological). From above, the peace of faith exists in simplicity and eternity where true religion and true philosophy coincide and beyond which dwells God who cannot

---

90   Jos Decorte, "Tolerance and Trinity", translated by Huub Stegeman, *Conflict and Reconciliation: Perspectives on Nicholas of Cusa*, edited by Inigo Bocken (Leiden: Brill, 2004), 116.

be named. From below, the peace of faith gradates in hierarchy one sentence at a time as expounded by Cusanus in Latin in 1453, and, from where, straining toward what lies above, revelation perfects reason. This side of paradise, unity is fleeting and peace frayed.[91] Synthesis needs to be sewn together one proposition at a time as aided by shared Hellenic and Neoplatonic concepts and modes of reasoning and as finally perfected by God, the Father of lights, who envisions peace in the visionary.[92] From below, what Plato deems to be the shadow lands or what Augustine calls the "flux of dissimilarity", *reformatio* is needed both individually and corporately to restore the peace of faith which comes from above, individually in that faith is personal;[93] collectively in that peace purviews more than the individual.[94] The hypostatic Word is what unites what is above and below, religion and rites, and leads to *Posse* itself. In the realm of conjectures and appearances, reform by the Word is needed. As the discussion of absolution and baptism in *De pace fidei* 17 shows, even words can confuse and must be sorted out and corrected by the right Word of God.

Reform means not only the virtuous desire to return to the original state, which Christians like Cusanus identified as the *imago Dei*, but also to divinely unfold something new: the *imago in Christi* and the renewing of creation in the surpassing peace of God. *De pace fide* begins with paradise in Chapter 2 and concludes with the City of God, the New Jerusalem, paradise restored and surpassed in Chapter 19. In *De pace fidei*, *reformatio* means that the searcher for peace must confront the *coincidencia oppositorum* of "religio una in rituum varietate". The one religion may be obscured, opposed and confused by the various rites. This is a simplistic, non-dialectical, non-hypostatic reading of religion and in need of hermeneutical *reformatio*. It is a level-one reading, or to put it in medieval terms, what Aquinas would famously label a literal interpretation in the *prima pars* of the *Summa Theologiæ*, Q.I. Art. 10. The spiritual does not negate the literal, but perfects it.[95] Cusanus literally prayed (contemplation) and wrote (action) for religious peace. In this praying, supernatural learned ignorance comes to the fore: passive and active. Learned ignorance is contemplation and action. Vision received, vision recounted. Learned ignorance is explicated through the art of dialectic: dialogue to truth, a synod in

---

91   *De pace fidei* II, 7.
92   De pace fidei I, 1; *De docta ignorantia, Epistola auctoris ad Dominum Iulianum Cardinalem; De apice theoriae* 14.
93   *De pace fidei* XVI, 55.
94   *De pace fidei* as symbol (confession) of the faith.
95   Aquinas, *Summa Theologiæ* Ia, 1, 10: "sensus spiritualis; qui super litteralem fundatur et eum supponit."

and by the Word of God. The same may be said of the church. Christian reform is more than ethical, it is the renewing of the mind both individually and collectively through inward renewal and public confessions of faith and synods called and overseen by due authority (the pope as vicar cathedra of Christ on earth).[96] In *De pace fidei* Cusanus aims to reform the mind in the image of God, through the Word of God.

This ancient understanding of reform harks back to the Church Fathers, with whom, as his library attests, Cusanus was well acquainted and of which Gerhart Ladner famously identified in *The Idea of Reform* (*reformatio* or *renovatio ad imaginem Dei*) as return to the original state in the image-likeness of God.[97] The synthesis of action and contemplation in the singular life of renewal and reform is found in the Word of God who became flesh and dialogical synthesis, perhaps most clearly stated by Aquinas in questions one hundred and seventy-nine thorough one hundred and eighty-two of the *Secunda secundæ* part of the *Summa Theologiæ*. For Cusanus, action and contemplation are focused on peace, unity and reform: the peace of faith is the peace of unity. To the Western (Latin) audience, there is the intended reform of thinking about Islam. Islam is not to be seen in isolation from Christianity, but as one religion in the variety of rites only in and through the necessary and salvific reform and centrality of the Word of God. Thus, the aims of *De pace fidei* should not be separated from Cusanus's career as ecclesial reformer. What God has joined together, according to Cusanus, let no one put asunder. In Cusanus's thought and action, in his quest for reform and religious dialogue, both the various rites of Islam and Christianity are wedded by the Word of God, whom Christian Scriptures describe as the bridegroom. In Christian theology, the bride signifies the church. For Cusanus, the bridal church catholic teaches "religio una in rituum varietate".[98]

Cusanus's well-known clarion calls for church reform are exemplified by his legatine tour of Germany and the Lowlands in 1451–1452, and by his *Reformatio generalis* of 1459, which represents, perhaps, the final cogent late-medieval appeal for ecclesial reform in the western Church before Luther.[99] His ideas for reform from this document have been studied in detail by the distinguished

---

96 *De concordantia catholica* bk I, Chps xiv, xvi.
97 Gerhart B. Ladner, *The Idea of Reform: Its Impact on Christian Thought and Action in the Age of the Fathers*, 1959 (Eugene, OR: Wipf & Stock, 2004), 3.
98 *De pace fidei* I, 6.
99 English translations of the *Reformatio generalis* are found in the appendix to "Nicholas of Cusa, A General Reform of the Church" by Morimichi Watanabe and Thomas M. Izbicki, *Nicholas of Cusa on Christ and the Church*, 188–202; Nicholas of Cusa, *Writings on Church and Reform*, translated by Thomas M. Izbicki (Cambridge, MA: Harvard University Press, 2008), 550–591.

Cusanus scholar and founding president of the American Cusanus Society, Morimichi Watanabe, as well as by two other prominent scholars: Brian Pavlac and Thomas Izbicki.[100] Yet the philosophical and theological preface on the Word and Wisdom of God merits more attention, especially in regards to this study. Here we will only touch on a few relevant points. The preface of the *Reformatio generalis* is thoroughly Christocentric: the reformed church is embodied in and patterned on the Word of God. Interestingly, the *Reformatio generalis* begins by citing the Apostle Paul's sermon in Athens to the Greek wise men ("sapientibus Graecis"), analogous to the wise, eminent religious leaders addressed in *De pace fidei*. God, who cannot be named (cf., Cusanus's *Dialogus de Deo abscondito*), makes himself known in order to reform, unify and pacify the church, the cosmic and expansive Body of Christ in the world.[101] The preface focuses on the Word of God as synthesis and source of peace. God has given the books of the wise in order to make Himself known. Yet owing to ignorance and sin (similar to the argument of Chapter 2 of *De pace fidei*), even the wise religious leaders of the world become lost in conjectures.[102] Christ is the enlightener who takes away the ignorance of conjectures and in whom "omnes thesauri desideratae scientiae absconditi essent."[103] Christ is the "Filio et legato, qui et Verbum eius".[104] Christ is "veritas".[105] The Christian life is to be patterned on Christ, the true way and exemplar of the faith.[106] Furthermore, there is another broad parallel in the overall cosmic structure of *De docta ignorantia*: from not knowing God (book one of *De docta ignorantia*, or as *absconditus* in the preface of *Reformatio generalis*) to not knowing the cosmos (book two of *De docta ignorantia libri sapientum* in the preface of *Reformatio generalis*) to finding knowledge which unfolds hierarchically by gradation through the church as centered in Jesus (book three of *De docta ignorantia*, and the remainder of *Reformatio generalis*). This hierarchy of the church needs to be reformed throughout the ranks from pontiff to bishop to deacon and laity, which is the subject matter of

---

100 On Cusanus and liturgical reform, see also: Brian A. Pavlac "Reform" in *Introducing Nicholas of Cusa: a Guide to a Renaissance Man*, edited by Christopher M. Bellitto, Thomas M. Izbicki and Gerald Christianson (New York: Paulist Press, 2004), 59–112; Robert R. Bond, *The Efforts of Nicholas of Cusa as a Liturgical Reformer* (Salzburg: Druckhaus Nonntal, 1962). See also, Watanabe, *Concord and Reform* and Izbicki, *Nicholas of Cusa on Christ and the Church*.
101 *Reformatio generalis*, praefatio.
102 *Reformatio generalis*, praefatio, "coniicere".
103 *Reformatio generalis* 1.
104 *Reformatio generalis* 2.
105 *Reformatio generalis* 2.
106 *Reformatio generalis* 4.

the *Reformatio generalis*. This reform is in the form of Christ who makes known what is hidden and who unites what is divided. Cusanus's originality lies in how he applied these ideas of unity, peace and reform to Islam. As we have seen Cusanus's interaction with conciliarism and reform, we now compare and contrast his creative search for peace with other late-medieval Christian approaches to Islam.

Late Medieval Christian Approaches to Islam

"One thing" wrote the noted medievalist R.W. Southern in his condense and captivating study, *Western Views of Islam in the Middle Ages*, "which became clear in the fifteenth century was that something would have to be done about Islam."[107] As for what to do about Islam, especially since the fall of Constantinople, there had developed by the mid-fifteenth century three main interrelated Western approaches to Muslims: crusade, condemnation and conversion. Ever since Pope Urban II authorized a penitential holy war to retake Jerusalem from Muslim rule in 1095, the crusades continued on and off for the remainder of the middle ages and right through the early-modern period.[108] Cusanus was well acquainted with crusade. His close friend Giuliano (Julian) Cesarini to whom he dedicated his masterpiece *De docta ignorantia*, promoted and led the crusaders against the Ottomans in a disastrous and failed campaign on behalf of Pope Eugenius IV.[109] In fact, Cesarini was killed by the victorious Ottomans probably while fleeing the battle of Varna (Bulgaria) in 1444. Even so, the battle of Varna failed to deter the crusading spirit. Cusanus himself preached crusade and died on route to Ancona to assist Pope Pius II's ill-fated crusade to retake Constantinople.[110] Years later, even the reformer Martin Luther, no friend of the pope or the holy Roman emperor, called on Charles V in his treatise *On War*

---

107 R.W. Southern, *Western Views of Islam in the Middle Ages* (Cambridge, MA: Harvard University Press, 1962), 83–84.

108 On the designation and definition of crusade as a penitential holy war waged by Christendom against its enemies and legitimized by right authority (contra claims of proto western imperialism), see: Jonathan Riley-Smith, *What Were the Crusades?*, third edition (San Francisco: CA: Ignatius Press, 2002).

109 On Cusanus's relationship with Giuliano Cesarini (1398–1444), especially with reference to their formative time together at the Council of Basel, see, "Cusanus, Cesarini and the Crisis of Conciliarism" by Gerald Christianson, in *Conflict and Reconciliation: Perspectives on Nicholas of Cusa*, 91–103.

110 The problem of Cusanus's dreaming of religious peace in *De pace fidei* and preaching crusade will be addressed in Chapter 4.

Against the Turk (1529) to halt the advancing Ottomans who threatened Vienna in 1529, and again, over a century later in 1683.

Besides crusade, there was the polemical option, the path of refutation of the beliefs and practices of Muslims in light of Christian Scriptures and reason. Like the crusades, this condemnatory apologetic approach proved popular throughout the middle ages and beyond and can be seen in the anti-Muslim writings of Cusanus's contemporary Jean Germain who called for a return to the 'glory days' of crusades under St. Louis and Charlemagne. It was around the same time that Bernard of Clairvaux was stridently preaching the second crusade, beckoning the knights of France to take up arms against Muslims, and touting the prowess of the new military monastic orders such as the Knights Templar that the Qur'an was translated into Latin.[111] In order for Christians to engage in polemics with Muslims, they first needed at least a basic knowledge of Islam. It was to better understand Islam in order to refute it as the heresy it was believed by medieval Christians to be (indeed, for Peter the Venerable of Cluny, Islam was the last great heresy to arise) and to promote the extension of Christendom that at the behest of Peter the Venerable, Robert of Ketton translated the Qur'an into Latin.[112] Robert of Ketton's translation of the Qur'an would prove influential throughout the middle ages and well into the Reformation.[113] In the first half of the fifteenth century, Cusanus and later the humanist and reformer Philip Melanchthon, as well as Luther, were familiar with Ketton's Latin translation of the Qur'an.[114] Cusanus used this translation in his systematic and irenic study of the Qur'an *Cribratio Alkorani*.

---

111   Bernard of Clairvaux (1090–1153) stridently preached the second crusade. His support of the Knights Templar is seen in his *In Praise of the New Knighthood*, trans. M. Conrad Greenia, Cistercian Fathers Series: 19B (Kalamazoo, MI: Cistercian Publications, 2000).

112   The Englishman Robert of Ketton completed translating the Qur'an into Latin in 1143. On Peter the Venerable's far-reaching project to comprehensively study Islam from original sources, see: James Kritzeck, *Peter the Venerable and Islam* (Princeton, NJ: Princeton University Press, 1964), which includes a collection of Latin texts from the period.

113   For a study of both the influence and interpretation of the Qur'an in Western Europe from the high middle ages to the Reformation, which includes a discussion of John of Segovia, see: Thomas E. Burman, *Reading the Qurʾān in Latin Christendom, 1140–1560* (Philadelphia, PA: University of Pennsylvania Press, 2007). Burman's work is also a response to Norman Daniel's now classic study in the same field: *Islam and the West: The Making of an Image* (Oxford, England: Oneworld, 1960, second edition, 1993).

114   Cod. Cus. 107–108. Cod. Cus. 107, 1, *Tractatus contra legem Mahometi* (p. 107); 107, 2, *Rinoldus Contra legem Sarrazenorum* (p. 107); 108, 1, *Lex sive doctrina machometi* (p. 107); 108, 2, *Alcoran translatus a Roberto Retin* [Robert of Ketton] (p. 107); 108, 3, *Tractatus contra Sarazenos* (p. 108); 108, 4, *Epistola Petri venerabilis ad Bernardum Clarevallensem de impia secta Muhamet* (p. 108). In 1542 Luther saw Robert of Ketton's Latin translation of the

An example of Christian medieval condemnation and appreciation of Islam is found in two of Cusanus's own books: Codex Cusanus 107 and 108. The two codices were intended as a whole: Codex 108 contains the aforementioned twelfth-century Latin translation of the Qur'an by Robert of Ketton. Owing to their subject matter and Cusanus's unique interest in Muslim thought, these codices are especially well known and display Cusanus's primary source material for understanding Islam.[115] Both are well marked with notes by Cusanus himself in the margins. Codex 107 begins with the *Tractatus contra legem Mahometi* and this is the main work included in this book. This rambling text includes numerous charges against Islam. One need only note the plethora of pejorative 'contras' within the text to see that the work is divided by various articles against Islam. Yet the 'contra' chapters begin with an attempt to comprehend what it is they are contradicting.

The first sections deal more with understanding Islam than with condemning it. These condemnations must be read alongside Cusanus's own commendations in the margins of finding Christ and his prophetic forerunners in the Qur'an. We will explore in particular Cusanus's heuristic reading of the Qur'an (Codex 108) in Chapter 6. Initiailly, we note Cusanus search for *explicatio* of the interrelationship of Islam and Christianity instead of well-worn

---

Qur'an (Martin Brecht, *Martin Luther: The Preservation of the Church, 1532–1546*, translated by James L. Schaaf (Minneapolis, MN: Fortress Press, 1993), 354). Already in 1529 Luther was familiar with the Latin *Refutation of the Koran* by the thirteenth century Dominican, Ricoldo da Monte Croce. In his book, *On War Against the Turk* (1529), the polemical Luther refers to Ricoldo's refutation. He writes, "I have some parts of Mohammed's Koran which in German might be called a book of sermons or doctrines of the kind that we call pope's decretals. When I have time I must translate it into German so that everyone may see what a foul and shameful book it is" (Martin Luther, *Luther's Works, vol. 46, The Christian in Society III*, edited by Robert C. Schultz, and Helmut T. Lehmann (Philadelphia, PA: Fortress Press, 1967), 176). In 1542 Luther published his own revised German translation of Ricoldo's Latin refutation of the Qur'an under the title, *Berlegung des Alcoran Bruder Richardi, Brediger Ordens, Berdenticht und herangegeben von M. Luther, 1542* (*Brother Richard's Refutation of the Koran, Translated into German by Dr. M. Luther*, printed with both German and Latin texts in: *Luther's Werke* (WA), vol. 53 (Weimar: Herman Böhlaus Nachfolger, 1920, reprint 1968), 261–396). For Luther on Islam, see: Adam S. Francisco, *Martin Luther and Islam: A Study in Sixteenth-Century Polemics and Apologetics* (Leiden: Brill, 2007). Melanchthon wrote a short preface to the printed edition of Robert of Ketton's Latin translation of the Qur'an made by the Swiss reformer Theodore Bibliander (Burman, *Reading the Qur'an*, 110–111).

115   For more on the historical background of these codices see, James E. Biechler "Three Manuscripts on Islam from the Library of Nicholas of Cusa", *Manuscripta* XXVII, 2 (July, 1983), 91–100.

Medieval *reprobatio* of Islam. In the third main part of the *Tractatus contra legem Mahometi* on what the Qur'an and the testimony of Mohammad confess about the Virgin Mary and John the Baptist, Cusanus writes in the margins that herein the Islamic tradition rightly praises the Virgin.[116] From his notes, Cusanus is acutely interested in what the Qur'an has to say about the Virgin Mary and Christ, and hence the incarnation of the Word of God. While noting the influence of the polemical aspects of these codices does not excuse some of Cusanus's more blistering attacks in the *Cribratio Alkorani*, it nonetheless behoves the careful reader to place these typical Christian condemnations of Islam in the context of the pugnacious times, as well as within the context of Cusanus's more pacific and creative notes. The majority of Cusanus's notes in the margins of Cod. Cus. 107 and 108 aim at religious understanding and concord according to the Word of God.

By contemporary standards, Cusanus seems schizophrenic in his approach to Islam. One personality cries out in favour of a crusade to recapture Constantinople. The other speaks rationally of one religion and shared wisdom. We shall explore this dichotomy of condemnation and concordance in greater detail in Chapter 4 of this study. Here we only look ahead to comments on the beatitude of the peace of faith. There is an uncharacteristically long note by Cusanus on f. 21r of Codex 107 concerning beatitude and the role of love and seeing, and the plenitude of paradise. This section of the text of *Contra legem machometi* discusses human nature perfected in beatitude. His translation of the Qur'an notes paradise again and again.[117] No doubt in the medieval west there was a tendency to view Islam through the lens of Christianity, which remains a continuing hermeneutical quagmire for religious dialogue today. Cusanus's fascination with paradise perhaps points to a shared insight on what lies above and beyond the text in the heaven of reason.[118] Since Bishop Tempier's condemnations of alleged heretical propositions within the Faculty of Arts of the University of Paris in 1277, differing views on beatitude and paradise had sown divisions between Christians and Muslims. *De pace fidei* proposes a restorative paradise of religious understanding not completely separate from this world. For Cusanus's eschatological world is not abolished, but perfected. Thus, the dialogue ends with a new Jerusalem and a new Constantinople, the commonwealth of heavenly religious peace on earth.

---

116   'laudat virgi[ne]' Cod. Cus. 107, f. 4 (v). The title of Chapter 3 of the *Tractatus contra legem Mahometi* reads; "Scripta Alchorani testimonia Machometi de Maria virgine et Johanne baptista" (f. 4r).
117   Cf., *De pace fidei* XIII, 44–45; *Cribratio Alkorani* II, 18, 19.
118   *De pace fidei* XIX, 68.

Closely related, and, in many ways, overlapping this second path of polemics, with the subset of at least an attempt at intellectual comprehension, however limited that understanding may have been, was a third approach to Islam, namely conversion or mission. In the prologue to *Cribratio Alkorani* Cusanus recounts how during his visit to Constantinople as part of the papally appointed commission on union with the Eastern Church, it was through the Franciscans at the Church of the Holy Cross in Constantinople that he came across a copy of the Qur'an in Arabic, which the brothers attempted to translate for him as best they could.[119] In Constantinople Cusanus not only found a Qur'an in its original language, but also met thirteen Turkish men who had, it seems, converted to Christianity from Islam and for whom he arranged transport and safe transit to Rome.[120] Besides noting Cusanus's own interest in missionary activities, it is also worth noting the Franciscan focus on Christian evangelism to Muslims, as alluded to by the Arabic Qur'an in the possession of the friars minor in Constantinople. Ever since the dynamic founder of the order, Francis of Assisi, had crossed the battle lines in Egypt during the fifth crusade in c. 1221 to boldly discuss religion with the Sultan Malik al-Kamil, the order possessed an often polemical zeal for mission to Muslims.[121] During the thirteenth and early fourteenth century adventurous Franciscan missionaries in the spirit of Francis trekked across Asia through Mongolia, even all the way to Kublai Khan's capital of Beijing.[122] The Franciscan William of Rubroek even carried out a religious council-debate in 1258 in Karakorum with the Nestorians, Muslims

---

119   Cusanus, *Cribratio Alkorani*, prologus, 3.
120   Cusanus, *Cribratio Alkorani*, prologus, 3.
121   For an early account of Francis' meeting with the Sultan of Egypt, see *The Life of Saint Francis* by Thomas of Celano (1228–1229), in: Francis of Assisi, *Early Documents: Volume 1, The Saint*, eds., Regis J. Armstrong, J.A. Hellmann, and William J. Short (New York: New City Press, 1999), 229–231.
122   For a fascinating discussion of the now oft forgotten Franciscan Mongol and Chinese missions which serve as historical background for the religious geography of *De pace fidei*, see: R.W. Southern, *Western Views of Islam*, 47–52 (on the Flemish Franciscan missionary William of Rubroek); John Moorman, *History of the Franciscan Order: From Its Origins to the Year 1517* (Oxford: Oxford University Press, 1968, Chicago, IL: Franciscan Herald Press, 1988, reprint), 226–239; C.H. Lawrence, *The Friars: The Impact of the Early Mendicant Movement on Western Society* (London, England: Longman: 1994), 202–217. In this section C.H. Lawrence also discusses the Franciscan mission to the Mongol empire until the ascendency of the anti-foreigner Ming dynasty. And for letters, journeys and texts from the Franciscan missionaries, as well as other related primary documents, see: Christopher Dawson, ed., *The Mongol Mission: Narratives and Letters of the Franciscan Missionaries in Mongolia and China in the Thirteenth and Fourteenth Centuries*, translated by a nun of Stanbrook Abbey (London, England: Sheed and Ward, 1955).

and Buddhists before the Great Khan himself. Cusanus was also familiar with the eclectic theologian, student of Islam, and lay missionary to Muslims, who was closely associated with the Franciscans, Raymond Llull (or Lull).[123] Llull was born in Majorca, and proved to be a keen student of Islam. He learned Arabic, a rare feat for a Christian of his day, and spent his career travelling around Western Europe in order to secure support for his passion in life: the conversion of Muslims. Nicholas of Cusa's personal library in Kues not only includes a copy of Ketton's translation of the Qur'an, but also a number of manuscripts by Ramon Llull.[124] As seen in his own collection, Cusanus was well acquainted and intrigued not only by the Qur'an itself, but also by the writings of Llull, his predecessor in mission to Muslims. The structure and aim of Nicholas of Cusa's own dialogue toward achieving religious concord, *De pace fidei* bears similarities to the conclusion of Llull's dialogue *Liber de gentile et tribus sapientibus* (*The Book of the Gentiles and the Three Wise Men*) between a philosophically adept Gentile and three wise religious men: a Christian, Jew and Muslim.[125] Both works end with an agreement among those who have conversed about religion to seek unity of faith not though force, but through unforced consent.[126]

While western medieval approaches to Islam—crusade, condemnation and conversion—continued to find new expression and vigour during the fifteenth century, there also, at the same time arose a new expression of Christian

---

[123] For a study of Ramon Llull's (1232–1316) theology and mission, see: Mark D. Johnston, *The Evangelical Rhetoric of Ramon Llull: Lay Learning and Piety in the Christian West around 1300* (Oxford: Oxford University Press, 1996).

[124] For works of Llull in Cusa's personal library: Cods. Cus. 37, 2, Raymundi Lulli *Liber de homine* (Marx, p. 31); 37, 3, *Grammatischer Traktat* (attributed to Lull, Marx, p. 31); 81–88, *Raymundi Lulli Opera* (Marx, 81–90); 118, 1, Raymundi Lulli *Liber de predicacione* (Marx, p. 115). On Cusanus and Llull'a approach to Islam see Walter Andreas Euler, *Unitas et Pax: Religionsvergleich bei Raimundus Lullus und Nikolaus von Kues* (Würzburg: Echter, 1995).

[125] English translation of *Liber de gentile et tribus sapientibus* is found in: Anthony Bonner, ed., trans., *Selected Works of Ramon Llull*, vol. 1 (Princeton: Princeton University Press, 1985), 110–304.

[126] *De pace fidei* ends with the representatives of the world's religions now intellectually united adherents of one religion returning to their nations to lead others to religious harmony. They are commanded by God to assemble together in Jerusalem as common center of one common faith and the perpetual reality of one common peace (*De pace fidei* XIX, 68). Llull concludes his *The Book of the Gentile and Three Wise Men*, with these optimistic words, "They [the three wise men] decided on a time and place for their discussions, as well as how they should honor and serve one another, and how they should dispute; and that when they had agreed on and chosen one faith, they would go forth into the world giving glory and praise to the name of our Lord God" (Bonner, *Selected Works of Ramon Llull*, 303).

engagement with Muslims, what may be called a dialogical approach as seen in Nicholas of Cusa's own harmonious *De pace fidei*, and hinted at over a century earlier in Ramon Llull's *Book of the Gentile and the Three Wise Men*. This new, more pacific approach is also partly seen in the writings of the Dominican missionary Riccoldo da Monte Croce (c.1243–1320) who had lived in Baghdad. His most famous work was *Contra legem sarracenorum*. Although this work has a polemical bent, it also included Riccoldo's own personal experiences of living in a Muslim context, as well as showing serious study of Islam. Cusanus's library includes this work by Riccoldo (Cod. Cus. 107), and as his notes in the margins show, Cusanus studied it carefully.

Cusanus was also in contact with John of Segovia, an acquaintance from their time together at the Council of Basel. Rather late in life while in seclusion at a monastery in Savoy because of following an antipope, John of Segovia gave himself completely over to studying Islam. Not only did he make a new translation of the Qur'an from Arabic into Latin (now lost), he also called for a world-wide conference or *contraferentia* of Muslims and Christians of which he wrote to the now famous cardinal Nicholas of Cusa, and to which Cusanus responded and concurred.[127] Rather than the centuries-old option of crusade, John of Segovia and Cusanus provided a dialogical or conferential approach to Islam. They sought the mind's road to peace (*itinerarium mentis in Deum*): conciliar dialogue advancing by consensus to religious truth. Cusanus suggested in his letter to John of Segovia of December 29, 1454 (after the completion of *De pace fidei*), an accommodating addition for the plan of conference (*contraferentia*), that the Christian side be run by laymen rather than clergy because the Turks would prefer this arrangement.[128] Here Cusanus not only shows cultural sensitivities towards the Muslims he hopes will attend the

---

[127] An overview of John of Segovia's interest in Islam and plans for dialogue are found in R.W. Southern, *Western Views of Islam*, 86–92 and Anne Marie Wolf, *Juan de Segovia and the Fight for Peace: Christians and Muslims in the Fifteenth Century* (Leiden, Brill: 2014).

[128] James E. Biechler, "A New Face Toward Islam: Nicholas of Cusa and John of Segovia" in: *Nicholas of Cusa in Search of God and Wisdom*, 200. See also, *Epistula ad Ioannem de Segobia*, Appendix, in: *Nicolai de Cusa De Pace Fidei cum Epistula ad Ioannem de Segobia*, Ediderunt Commentariisque Illustraverunt Raymundus Klibansky et Hilderbrandus Bascour, O.S.B., Medieval and Renaissance Studies Supplement III (London: Warburg Institute: 1956), 91–102, where Cusa writes: "Non est dubium medio principum temporalium, quos Teucri sacerdotibus praeferunt, ad colloquia posse perveniri, et ex illis furor mitigabitur et veritas se ipsam ostendet cum profectu fidei nostrae. Verum quia in terries Sarracenorum reperiuntur multi zelosi fideles, qui et mores atque fundamenta eorum optime sciuntet simper student ipsis obviare, illos colligere ex Kayro, Alexandria, et Caffa expediret, et mercatores modum haberent eos adducendi. Sunt etiam quidam religiosi

proposed council, but also an awareness of keeping necessary practicalities in mind. All of which points to the conclusion that Cusanus thought the possibility of such a high level multi-religious dialogue was far from fantasy. Cusanus and John of Segovia's experience years before at the Council of Basel, especially with Cusanus's successful negotiation of peace with the Bohemians, as well as his *De concordantia catholica* in which he described the "profunda divina ecclesiae harmonia" (I, 1), which extended from church to empire, reveal that both men were motivated by the universal principle of concordance, and thought that well-learned Muslims and Christians could indeed sit together and seek the underlying unity of all religious rites.[129] Read in this context, *De pace fidei* is a highly imaginative rendition of what such a real dialogue between Christians and Muslims might have sounded and looked like. Furthermore Cusanus's *Letter to John* of 1454 proposes specific talking points for the planned Christian-Muslim dialogue. We will explore this letter in more detail in Chapter 5. It will suffice for now to take a cursory look at the letter's broad theological outline. In his *Letter to John*, Cusanus moves first from that which is most agreeable (unity or the One), to that which is less agreeable (the many). He begins the discussion by affirming the points of agreement among Christians and Muslims, namely the Oneness of God, and how in unity there is plurality. Cusanus then moves to the Word of God, which aggrees with the Qur'an, Surah 3:45, where Christ is identified as the Word. Cusanus had marked this ayah in his copy of Robert of Ketton's translation of the Qur'an.[130] From Christology Cusanus then proceeds to discuss how the Scripture and the Qur'an compare on the topics of paradise, the cross, and the sacraments. It is interesting to note that the order or discussion here is almost the same as that found in *De pace fidei*. In this letter, as in *De pace fidei*, Cusanus devotes the bulk of his attention to Christology.

As the more detailed discussion in *Cribratio* shows, Cusanus was concerned with understanding Islam in order to understand Christ better. In his prefatory address to his friend Pope Pius II, who wrote his own letter to Mehmed II seeking religious unity, Cusanus states that he composed *Cribratio Alkorani* in order that the pope, like his fifth-century predecessor Pope Leo the Great who defended orthodoxy against the Nestorians through his famous Tome accepted by the council of Chalcedon (the fourth oecumenical council), might defend Christendom against the revival of the Nestorian sect now believed to be found in Islam. Cusanus writes to him about specific rudimentary

---

nostril, qui habitant inter eos tam in Armenia quam Graecia; hii similiter audiendi essent ut mature consilio haec res initiaretur" (97).
129 Cusanus, *De concordantia catholica* I, 1.
130 Cod. Cus. 108 f. 37v.

"principles"[131] These principles cover what the Qur'an has to say concerning the Good, God or the One, and how, as Cusanus contends, even the Qur'an discloses that the Gospel is true.[132] For Cusanus, the Qur'an shows that Christ was the Word and that because of corruption of and misunderstanding of the text and tradition, Muslims or adherents of the Qur'an have become Nestorians by not seeing the one person of Christ in two natures. This means, according to Cusanus, that Muslims separate the two natures of Christ. While the *Cribratio* offers original criticism of the Qur'an, it is, given the times, a fairly positive Christian approach to Islam. In it Cusanus affirms that the prophet Muhammad received divine revelation and inspiration. And, overall, the *Cribratio* avoids outright polemics and instead seeks Christ who makes known the one religion in the variety of rites.

The *Cribratio* discloses, along with *De pace fidei*, Cusanus's unique Christocentric and conciliar approach to Islam. As noted, the *Cribratio* presupposes the Gospel of Christ and sifts the Qur'an for Christ, the transcendently-imminent Word of God. In this sifting, faith is aided by reason. This echoes Thomas Aquinas, a theologian with whom, as we have seen, Cusanus was well acquainted. In book one, Chapter 2, of his *Summa contra gentiles* (1, 2), Aquinas posits that since Muslims do not accept the uncorrupted authority of the Christian Scriptures, Christian preachers and theologians (the intended audience of the *Summa*), must have recourse to reason. The *Doctor angelicus* died while on his way to the Second Council of Lyons in hope of finally ending the great schism between Eastern and Western churches. Like Cusanus, Aquinas also sought religious unity and theological synthesis. While condemnations and crusades persisted well beyond the late middle ages, there emerged a new, if nonetheless nearly forgotten, reformational, rational and Word-*Logos* approach to Islam in the first half of the fifteenth century, one that creatively sought concord through conciliar consent and understanding through dialectical discourse. What R.W. Southern refers to in his *Western Views of Islam in the Middle Ages* as the "The moment of vision."[133] This new approach was formulated by Cusanus, and also, to a lesser extant, John of Segovia, as evidenced in their correspondence and exchange of their writings on Christian-Muslim dialogue, which we will explore in greater detail in Chapter 5. This approach is thoroughly Christocentric. For in Christ is *Posse* itself, and

---

131 *Cribratio Alkorani*, prefatory dedication to Pius II.
132 *Cribratio Alkorani*, prologus.
133 The title of Chapter 3 of R.W. Southern's now classic lectures *Western Views of Islam in the Middle Ages* (Cambridge: Harvard University Press, 1962), 67–109.

wherever it does not shine forth lacks hypostasis.[134] Christ is the hypostatic and lasting principle of religious reform and the paradigm for reforming misunderstanding of the *Verbum* through unfolding "religio una in rituum varietate".[135] As we have explored the context of Cusanus's search for peace, unity and reform, we now turn to prominent philosophical and theological sources for his *concordantia religionum*, and, especially, the great Franciscan mystic Bonaventura.

---

134 Cusanus, *De apice theoria* 27: "Et ubi non relucet illa carent hypostasi".
135 *De pace fidei* I, 6.

CHAPTER 3

The Mind's Road to Peace

In the beginning I call upon that First Begnning from whom all illumination flows as from the *God of lights,* and from whom comes *every good and perfect gift.* I call upon the eteneral Father through the divine Son, our Lord Jesus Christ, that through the intercession of the most holy Virgin Maary, the mother of that same Lord and God, Jesus Christ, and through the intercession of blessed Francis, our leader and father, God might grant enlightenment to the eyes of our mind and guidance to our feet on the path of peace—that *peace which surpasses all understanding.* This is the peace which our Lord Jesus Christ proclaimed and granted to us. It was this message of peace which our father Francis anncounced over and over, proclaiming it at the beginning and the end of his sermons. Every greeting of his became a wish for peace; and in every experience of contemplation he sighed for an ecstatic peace. He was like a citizen of that Jerusalem about which the man of peace—he *who was peacable even with those who despised peace*—says: *Pray for those things that are for the peace of Jerusalem.*[1]

∴

The mystical theologian Bonaventura (c.1217–1274) begins his famous *Itinerarium mentis in Deum* with an invocation of Jesus Christ and St Francis of Assisi and a plea for the peace of Jerusalem. The echo of this plea for peace reverberates throughout Cusanus's *De pace fidei.* As the seventh Minister General of

---

1 Bonaventura, *Itinerarium mentis in Deum, Prologus,* English translation and Latin text from: *Works of St. Bonaventure, Vol. II,* edited by Philotheus Boehner and Zachary Hayes (St. Bonaventure, NY: Franciscan Institute, 2002), 34. In principio primum principium, a quo cunctae illuminationes descendunt tanquam *a Patre luminum,* a quo est *omne datum optimum et omne donum perfectum,* Patrem scilicet aeternum, invoco per Filium eius, Dominum nostrum Iesum Christum, ut intercessione sanctissimae Virginis Mariae, genitricis eiusdem Dei et Domini nostri Iesu Christi, et beati Francisci, ducis et patris nostri, *det illuminatos oculos* mentis nostrae *ad dirigendos pedes nostros in viam pacis* illius, quae *exsuperat omnem sensum;* quam pacem evangelizavit et dedit Dominus noster Iesus Christus…*Rogate quae ad pacem sunt Ierusalem.* Italics indicate passages from Scripture. English translations of the *Itinerarium* in this study are from this edition.

the Franciscan Order and the esteemed second founder of the Brothers Minor, Bonaventura was influenced by divisions developing within the budding mendicant movement. These were concerned with the organizational practicalities of realizing the apostolic and Christ-patterned ideal of poverty and renunciation of potential ecclesiastical entanglements.[2] Yet the *Itinerarium* is celebrated not for its troubled context, but for its sweeping and Christoform mystical theology: how Bonaventura masterfully and methodically ascends from the porous book of nature through the crucified Christ to the sheer silence, simplicity and serenity of God, whose abode is the peace of Jerusalem.

Bonaventura wrote his treatise at a time of increasing religious tension for the Franciscan community. Cusanus wrote *De pace fidei* in the context of outright religious division following the fall of Constantinople in 1453. The dialogue of the latter concludes in Jerusalem, the dwelling place of peace. What makes *De pace fidei* endure, and even sound modern, is his concordant thesis of "religio una in rituum varitate" as channeled through the Word of God as example *par excellence* of his innovative dialogical Christology. Both *De pace fidei* and the *Itinerarium* share a distinctive theological emphasis on Christ as the way and means of peace, which is to be realized dialectically and hierarchically. Both share an emphasis on symbolic characters and place: St. Francis at the start of *Itinerarium*, Cusanus in the preface to *De pace fidei*, and Jerusalem.[3] In both mystical treatises there is a concerted search for peace and unity in the midst of division, and the discovery of that peace and concordance in the person and work of Christ. Peace is realized dialectically in *De pace fidei* through the Word's dialogue with Muslims, Jews and Hindus, and hierarchically through the gradated relationship between Word, angels, saints, philosophers and the representatives of the world's religions. Cusanus offers not a religious debate, but rather a combination of a Platonic dialogue and a Christocentric hierarchy in the paradigm of Bonaventura's *Itinerarium*.

The first three chapters of this work see Cusanus as a sojourner in search of the peace of faith and concordance between Christians and Muslims and looks at the sources and context of this journey towards concord. In the first chapter, we explored Cusanus's creative synthesis of religious peace: "religio una in rituum varietate" and the intricate dialectical hierarchy of the *Verbum* as explicated in *De pace fidei*. In the subsequent chapter we contextualized Cusanus's *De pace fidei* within the religious and political currents of late-medieval

---

2 For the classic account of the troubles within the Franciscan order following the death of St. Francis, see John Moorman, *A History of the Franciscan Order: From its Origins to the Year 1517*, 1968 (Chicago: Franciscan Herald Press, 1988).

3 *De pace fidei*, I, 1; XIX, 68.

Christendom. We looked at the complex interplay of the conciliar movement, the ideal of church reform and late-medieval Christian approaches to Islam in comparison and contrast with Cusanus's own Christological and conciliar understanding of the concordance of religion. In the following chapter we will explore the controversial matrix of the papacy and crusade, the Ottomans and the Christian powers of Latin Europe. In Chapter 4 we will also discover more definitively what it means to call Cusanus a sojourner, and how during his lifetime he sought an elusive peace between Christians and Muslims. For Cusanus, this peace is fully realized only in the heavenly Jerusalem. Cusanus's sojourn in search of religious peace lasted his whole life and he, like Bonaventura and St. Francis before him, considered himself to be a citizen of Jerusalem.[4]

In this chapter we will explore pertinent philosophical and theological sources on Cusanus's search for religious peace in *De pace fidei*. The purpose of this chapter is to shed further light upon the philosophical and theological background of Cusanus's unique Christological approach to Islam and his method for the attaining of religious peace in *De pace fidei*. This light, like the sun in Plato's allegory of the cave, may at times confuse, disorient and even blind. Students can, no doubt, spend hours trying to see the theological and philosophical sources behind Cusanus's religious concordance and method of learned ignorance only to be lost in a cloud of unknowing and miasma of footnotes. Furthermore, the bright light of sources may cause one to grope after distinctions and separate what should be seen as whole, thus severing Cusanus the mystic from Cusanus the dialogist. One must become accustomed to the distinctive light in which Cusanus himself reasons and proposes concordance between Christians and Muslims. Here we observe how Cusanus's dialectical hierarchy of *Verbum* in *De pace fidei* relates to the logic of Bonaventura's *Itinerarium*. We have already seen in Chapter 1 how the other great theologian of the thirteenth century, the Dominican Thomas Aquinas, influenced Cusanus's *concidentia religionum* of "religio una in rituum varietate". Here we meet Aquinas's Franciscan rival, the *Doctor seraphicus*, and measure his effect on Cusanus's search for religious peace. In this chapter we will also study the influence of Plato's *Republic* upon Cusanus's search for religious peace in *De pace fidei* in connection with his correlative and life-altering theological method of learned ignorance. We will also consider *De pace fidei* as a new global Pentecost and reversal of the confusion of Babel to the concordant language of religious peace. Along the way, we will briefly and recurrently meet the elusive Dionysius. We begin with Bonaventura.

---

4 Ephesians 2:19; Revelation 3:12; Bonaventura, *Itinerarium, prologus*, 1.

Hierarchical Dialectics of Peace: Bonaventura's *Itinerarium Mentis in Deum*

Bonaventura begins the *Itinerarium mentis in Deum* by citing the Epistle of James (1:17): "every perfect gift is from above, coming down from the Father of lights"[5] As the epigraph to this chapter shows, Bonaventura proceeds to the overarching theme of the *Itinerarium*: namely, the search for peace. For Bonaventura the annunciation of peace is found in Jesus Christ and St. Francis, both of whom, by varying degree, point the way to concordance. This passage from James is the very same verse cited by Cusanus in the epilogue of *De docta ignorantia* as central to what he believed to be his divinely received vision of learned ignorance and the peace which comes from knowing that one does not know.[6] This mysterious vision and enlightenment is further deciphered in Cusanus's *Apologia doctae ignorantiae*, which lauds Dionysius and the *via negativa*, and *De coniecturis*, where, according to Cusanus's method of learned ignorance, all knowledge this side of heaven may be considered to be conjectural.[7] Peace, however, lies beyond conjecture and human knowledge, because, according to the epistle of James, it comes from heaven. According to the *Itinerarium* and *De pace fidei*, heavenly peace encounters earth most fully and personally in the Word incarnate, Jesus Christ.[8] In *De pace fidei*, peace is one with the Word, Wisdom and Truth of God, all of which transcend the finite and span the hierarchy of divine permanence and fluctuating human knowing in and through the person of Christ.[9] This peace is realized by human minds hierarchically. Bonaventura writes that in and through Christ, "when our spirit has been brought into conformity with the heavenly Jerusalem, it is ordered hierarchically so that it can ascend upward."[10] The same idea of hierarchical ascent to the one peace of Jerusalem is evident in the structure of Cusanus's *De pace fidei*. Due to the limitations of the finite realm and the flux of the earthly life, this eternal peace may be grasped in the temporal sphere by means of dialectic and by degree.

---

5   Vulgate: "omne datum optimum et omne donum perfectum desursum est descendens a Patre luminum."
6   *De docta ignorantia*, epistula auctoris ad Dominum Iulianum Cadinalem.
7   *Apologia doctae ignorantiae* 6–7, 17, 32; *De coniecturis*, I, 2.
8   Bonaventura, *Itinerarium, prologus* 1, IV, 3; VII, 1: Christ appears most prominently at the beginning, middle and end of the *Itinerarium*; *De pace fidei* II, 7; IV–V: the *Verbum* of peace as *sapientia* of peace.
9   *De pace fidei* I, 1; I, 6; II, 7; III, 8; VI, 17; XII, 40; *De concordantia catholica* I, 2, 10.
10 *Itinerarium* IV, 4: "spiritus noster hierarchicus ad conscendendum sursum secundum conformitatam ad illam Ierusalem supernam." Cf., *De pace fidei* XIX, 68.

While the aforementioned verse from the epistle of James was a favourite of medieval mystical writers, its prominent placement at the beginning of the *Itinerarium* and at the end of *De docta ignorantia* further reveals that for both Bonaventura and Cusanus the divinely given annunciation of peace descends as illumination to be realized here and now one sentence at a time. Cuanus unfolds this peace from heaven in regards to Islam in *De pace fidei*. This also explains why the *Itinerarium* concludes by trailing off into silence through a concordant string of Scriptural quotations as the mind comes to rest in God.[11] The sojourner passes over from symbols to simplicity and therewith only stammers the wonders of God's revelation. Furthermore, at the end of *De pace fidei*, religious peace is realized in Jerusalem, the heavenly and earthly city, which for medieval Christians, was "*mater nostra.*"[12] According to the *Itinerarium* and *De pace fidei*, this peace comes from God and descends most perfectly in the person and work of Jesus Christ and to a lesser degree in the person and work of St. Francis (in the *Itinerarium*) and St. Peter and St. Paul (in *De pace fidei*).[13] Furthermore, just as the fullness of deity dwells in Christ through his incarnation, so also Cusanus receives the vision of learned ignorance all at once. According to Christian teaching, this fullness of deity in the incarnate *Logos* then entirely embraces the fullness of human experience through the life and death of Christ. Analogously, Cusanus unpacks the fullness of his vision of learned ignorance through the remainder of his life.

In *De pace fidei*, Cusanus applies this subtle art of knowing that one does not know (*docta ignorantia*) to Wisdom's relationship with Islam. He envisions Peter and Paul carrying on the dialogue on Christology (Peter), the sacraments and ethical practices of "religio una in rituum varietate" (Paul) under the authority and by the commission of the *Verbum*.[14] Peace is given at once by way of a vision to Cusanus at the start of *De pace fidei*. It is recalled on vellum in the genre of a conciliar dialogue and in the *Itinerarium* as a sevenfold mystical path.[15] Both *De pace fidei* and the *Itinerarium* begin with strenuous and devoted meditation. Cusanus weeps and prays for the peace of Constantinople and receives the vision of religious concordance. He calls to mind his journey to the Bosporus as well as the ancient import of Constantinople. Bonaventura ascends to Mount Alverna, figuratively in the footprints of Moses (Mount

---

11   Bonaventura, *Itinerarium*, VII, 6. Cf, Dante, *Paradiso* XXXIII, 120–123.
12   Galatians 4:26.
13   Bonaventura, *Itinerarium* prologus; *De pace fidei* X 28; XVI, 55.
14   Peter: *De pace fidei* XI–XV; Paul: *De pace fidei* XVI–XIX; *De pace fidei* XVI, 55: "Tunc Paulus, doctor gentium, ex commissione Verbi exorsus est dicens."
15   *De pace fidei* I, 1: "eam quantum memoria praesentabat, plane subter conscripsit."

Sinai), Elijah (Mount Horeb or Sinai) and Jesus (the Mount of Transfiguration), literally in those of Francis, who made the same climb.[16] Bonaventura writes that while he was on Mount Alverno, he reflected "on certain ways in which the mind might ascend to God" and he recalls "that miracle which the blessed Francis himself had experienced in this very place, namely the vision of the winged Seraph in the form of the Crucified."[17] Here we see the immediacy of the vision: God present to all things. We also see that all things are not present to God.[18] Here too we see the typology and the *exitus-reditus* arc of ecclesiastical hierarchy: from Moses to Elijah to Jesus (the pinnacle) curved down to Francis and Bonaventura.

Hierarchy's hold on Cusanus is evident in his service as reforming bishop and later cardinal under the pope and is depicted iconically in the altarpiece from the chapel of his hospice in Kues. In the center of the triptych, which was completed before Cusanus's death, we see Cusanus with his red cardinal's hat kneeling in adoration with his brother under the cross of Christ. They are in the scene, but not of the scene. They appear smaller in size than the crucified Christ and the other Biblical characters. Thus, they are both there and not there. There is simultaneously absence and presence. Close to Christ, but by degree. Christ is present to them, and in Christ the Trinity; yet not all things are present to Christ. They are present through the invitation of Christ or his state of humiliation. For both medieval Christians and Christians today, divine peace is centered in Christ who gives his body and blood for the concordance of humanity and divinity. The central painting of the altarpiece depicts what is happening on the altar below as the crucified Christ descends again into the sacrament of the mass as a sacrifice for sins. Mass is still celebrated at this altar under the triptych with the crucified Christ at the center. *De pace fidei*, like the *Itinerarium*, is a search for and discovery of peace in a broken world. The search for peace is the overarching theme of the *Itinerarium*. The central question of *De pace fidei* is how the divinely given annunciation of "religio una in rituum varietate" is unfolded and realized. And, perhaps unsurprisingly, this religious concordance unfolds hierarchically and dialectically in and through the incarnate and crucified Christ.

---

16 Exodus 19; I Kings 19; Mark 9 where Moses and Elijah appear on the mountain with the transfigured Jesus.

17 Bonaventura, *Itinerarium, prologus*, 2: "dum mente tractarem aliquas mentales ascensiones in Deum, inter alia occurrit illud miraculum, quod in praedicto loco contigit ipsi beato Francisco, de visione scilicet Seraph alati ad instar Crucifixi."

18 Dionysius, *de Div. Nov* III, 680B; Cf., on rest in relation to presence, *Bhagavad Gita* 9, 4: "All beings have their rest in me [Krishna], but I have not my rest in them" (translated by Juan Mascaró (London: Penguin Books, 2003), 43).

A contemporary interpreter of Bonaventura's *Itinerarium*, Denys Turner, notes that the mystical treatise exhibits an "interiorized hierarchy": a creative dynamic of Augustinian interiority and Dionysian hierarchy as centered in Christ.[19] Building upon Turner's analysis, we would add that Cusanus applies this interiorized hierarchy to his interpretation of Islam in the context of his conciliar and Christocentric dialogue *De pace fidei*. The *Itinerarium* is Christocentric and the mystical ascent is realized in and through Christ. Bonaventura finds his theological inspiration in the most famous theologian of the Latin Church, St. Augustine. The Augustinian St. Francis of Assisi, beloved saint of the thirteenth-century western Church, appears as mystical muse at the beginning and end of the *Itinerarium*. His hierarchical path from the world (*ab exteriora*) into the mind (*ad interiora*) and upward to God (*ad superiora*) inspired by Augustine is also deeply influenced by Denys the Areopagite, as Turner demonstrates and as is clearly seen in the final chapter of the *Itininerarium* where Bonaventura directly quotes the *De theologia mystica*.[20] While Dionysian dialectic shapes the path to God, Francis in the spirit of Christ inspires the journey. As the first modern and influential biographer of St. Francis, the French Protestant scholar Paul Sabatier declared, "François d'Assise a été par excellence le saint du moyen âge."[21] The incarnate and crucified Christ appears in the pivotal middle of the *Itinerarium* as the ladder to God and doorway of peace. Chapter 4 is the central chapter of the treatise. In this chapter Bonaventura explicates how Christ is the ladder to God and the Truth in human form illuminating the way to Jerusalem, the concordant dwelling place of God.[22] The *Itinerarium* comprises seven books and Christ appears squarely in the middle of *both* the Augustinian arc "from without to within to above" *and* the Dionysian path from cataphatic emenation to apophatic mystery.[23] Interestingly Christ also appears at the center of *De pace fidei* as questions on Christology

---

19 Denys Turner, *The Darkness of God: Negativity in Christian Mysticism* (Cambridge: Cambridge University Press, 1995), 103, 117–127.

20 Bonaventura, *Itinerarium* v, 2: "Dionysius sequens Christum dicit, quod *bonum* est promum nomen Dei." Cf., Dionysius, *de Div. Nov.* 3:1.

21 Paul Sabatier, *Vie de S. François d'Assise*, (Paris: Librairie Fischbacher, 1894), viii.

22 Bonaventura, *Itinerarium* IV, 2: "Et quoniam, ubi quis ceciderit, necesse habet ibidem recumbere, nisi apponat quis *et adiiciat, ut resurgat*; non potuit anima nostra perfecte ab his sensibilibus relevari ad contuitum sui et aeternae Veritatis in se ipsa, nisi Veritas, assumpta forma humana in Christo, fieret sibi scala reparans priorem scalam, quae fracta fuerat in Adam." Cf., Cusanus, *De pace fidei* XI, 29, 35.

23 For medieval Christians, seven is the number of completion and goodness. According to the narrative of creation in the book of Genesis, God created the heavens and the earth in six days and rested on the seventh, declaring everything to be "valde bona."

dominate the middle of the dialogue and form the corpus of the discussion on religious concordance.[24]

The Christ of Bonaventura's *Itinerarium* and Cusanus's *De pace fidei* is more than mystical. Yet it is not the mystical Christ that propels the mind's road to God or indeed the mind's road to religious concordance. Neither is this the mythical Christ of Rudolf Bultmann, nor the historical, apocalyptic Jesus of Albert Schweitzer. We have seen in the first two chapters that Cusanus's Christology of *De pace fidei* is neither mystical nor docetic, but rather cosmic and incarnate, or in terms of the argument of book one, Chapter 2 of *De docta ignorantia*, absolute maximum and absolute minimum. For Christ as cosmic and incarnate spans the whole spectrum of the chain of being, from the ethereal heaven above to the lowest being below. The believer is met by the human nature of Christ in order to be drawn to his divine nature and the fullness of Deity. The flow is from above to below (divine invitation and accommodation in the human nature of Christ) and back to above (theosis and assumption of the human nature of Christ in the Godhead). This Christocentric heavenly-earthly-heavenly movement explains why Cusanus devotes much of the third book of *De docta ignorantia* to the ministry of Jesus from incarnation to ascension, and finally unfolded in the hierarchy of the church.[25] For through this synthesis of divine and human natures, the seeker becomes wise in the art of learned ignorance where God is both known in Christ and yet not known in Christ. In the epilogue of *De docta ignorantia* Cusanus states that it was through the one who is Truth, namely, Christ, who set loose the theological method of learned ignorance in three books. Cusanus writes, "This learned ignorance I have, in the one who is the truth [Jesus], now set loose in these books, which on the basis of this same principle can be compressed or expanded."[26] The same Christ binds together "incomprehensibilia incomprehensibiliter" (*De docta ignorantia*) and various religious rites into one (*De pace fidei*).[27] Cusanus's theological method of learned ignorance and religious concordance unfold through Christ. Jean Gerson (1363–1429), a contemporary of Cusanus and participant in the Council of Constance, puts it this way: "Mystical theology is experiential knowledge

---

24   *De pace fidei* XI–XIV, roughly the middle section of the dialogue.
25   On the life and ministry of Christ from birth to second coming: *De docta ignorantia* III, 5–10. On hierarchy and the church: *De docta ignorantia* III, 12.
26   *De docta ignorantia*, epistola: "Quam nunc in eo, qui veritas est, absolvi hiis libellis, qui ex eodem principio artari possunt vel extendi." Cf., *De pace fidei* II, 7.
27   *De docta ignorantia*, epistola.

of God attained though the union of spiritual affection with Him."[28] Different ways developed in the Middle Ages to find this union. Many roads led to one destination. There were, of course, various opinions on the nature of this union. Even so, by and large, medieval Christian mystical paths led to union of some kind between God and believer as centered in Christ who is both God and man. Indeed, a defining mark of especially late-medieval and western mystical theology is Christ as the way and the guide to union with God.

That Cusanus favoured the *via negativa* as path to union with God is well known. That his favoured path to union was thoroughly Christ-centered may be less well known today. Even for Cusanus, Christ-centered union with God may also be approached through aesthetics, as in the spirit of Plato's *Symposium* one moves from beautiful objects to the sea of beauty itself.[29] *De visione Dei* beckons the sojourner to God with an omniscient icon of Christ. Cusanus's hospice and chapel in Kues with their intricate late-medieval vaulting and changing traceries of the windows of the cloisters, which were designed under his direct supervision, illustrate his understanding of the *coincendentia oppositorum* and *concordantia catholica*, unity and plurality as centered in the Christ focused sanctuary. Furthermore, the vivid original murals in the chapel and the glittering liturgical vessels and crucifixes direct the mind to contemplation of the creator and of Beauty itself. There is as much Abbot Suger of St. Denis in Cusanus as there is the author of the *Cloud of Unknowing*.[30] There is a mystical, Christ-centered quality to *De pace fidei*. It is also a mystical path to union of one religion: one faith and one Lord, yet with a variety of members and religious practices as realized dialectically and hierarchically in the Word and Wisdom of God. According to Cusanus, various ethical practices and rites of Muslims and others beckon the seeker of religious peace to God and the concordance of "religio una in rituum varitate".[31]

De pace fidei is both dialogical and mystical. Turner notes that in modern conceptions of mysticism we have retained ancient and medieval words and metaphors while casting them adrift of their dialectical and hierarchical moorings.[32] The same summation may be applied to Cusanus's *De pace fidei*.

---

28   Dennis Tamburello, *Ordinary Mysticism* (New York: Paulist Press, 1996), 25.
29   Plato, *Symposium* 210b–212c.
30   *The Cloud of Unknowing*. trans. A.C. Spearing (London: Penguin, 2001). Abbot Suger, *De administratione*. Latin text and English translation in: *Abbot Suger On The Abbey Church of St.-Denis and its Art Treasures*, 2nd edition, edited and translated by Erwin Panofsky (Princeton: Princeton University Press, 1979), 40–81.
31   *De pace fidei* i, 6.
32   Turner, *The Darkness of God*, 267.

One cannot correctly and contextually understand "religio una in rituum varietate" without understanding the ancient and medieval Christ-centered dialectics and hierarchy of his religious concordance. Without the benefit of such strange-sounding structural and ontological categories, the contemporary interpreter of *De pace fidei* is left to flounder in the epistemology of taxonomy and the hermeneutics of language. For example, James Biechler's *The Religious Language of Nicholas of Cusa* provides an excellent study of the language and themes of *De pace fidei*. Yet the insightful monograph does not connect the prominent religious concepts of *unitas* and *sapientia* to the central ontological hierarchical dialectics of Christ, the *Verbum* who is the very path to religious concordance. It follows that when one neglects the *Verbum* dialectic in *De pace fidei*, one also fails to see the inherent relationship between mysticism and dialogue assumed by Cusanus.

The Christ of Bonaventura's *Itinerarium* and Cusanus's *De pace fidei* is more than cosmic. He is incarnate, crucified and the way to binding what was loosed. In the *Itinerarium* Christ and St. Francis appear at the beginning of the path to God. St. Francis cheerfully called his admirers back to the ideal of apostolic times and embodied the life and suffering of Christ. He was said to have received the stigmata and upon his death bore in his flesh the marks of the crucified One.[33] To put it in terms of Augustinian hermeneutics, Francis serves as a thirteenth-century signifier pointing to Christ who was signified in his own body and in Bonaventura's own time. The hierarchical path moves from Francis, the literal, to God, the spiritual, through the incarnate Christ, who is both finite and infinite. St. Francis was a simple but sublime mystic, and his creative spirituality effused the peace of the crucified Christ in his own body.

Francis also sought peace between Christians and Muslims through his (failed) attempt to end the fifth crusade by physically crossing the battle lines and entreating peace. Like Bonaventura, whose life and career were so formed by the vision of Francis, Cusanus was formed by the vision of learned ignorance and the vision of *De pace fidei*. At the beginning of *De pace fidei* Cusanus feels the pain inflicted by religious violence and fervently prays for the revelation of peace. This revelation is realized through the Word of God, the incarnate and crucified Christ. As with Francis, there is a desire to return to apostolic times. Francis initially sought to awaken and rebuild a dormant and

---

33   The stigmata is attested by Brother Leo and included in the earliest and most reliable account of Francis's ministry, *The Life of St. Francis* by Thomas of Celano written in 1228–1229. For English translation of Thomas's early *Life of St. Francis* on the stigmata, book two, Chapter 3 see: Francis of Assisi, *Early Documents: Volume 1, The Saint*, 263–265.

dilapidated church; not to establish a new religious order. The same may be said, at least indirectly, of Cusanus's *De pace fidei*: he sought not to make a new religion, but to awaken the wise of the world, and reform the divided church of his time according to the timeless truth of one religion in the variety of rites.

This awakening called for a new angelic annunciation of the Word made flesh. The desire to return to apostolic times is seen in the dialogue's proleptic eschatology and divine annunciation of peace: the angelic revelation 'now' at the beginning of the dialogue of "religio una in rituum varietate" and the 'not yet' realization of this religious concordance in Jerusalem at the conclusion of the work. It is also seen in the emphasis on those ancient rivals, the metropolitan bishoprics of Constantinople to Jerusalem, and in the ministerial ethos of Peter to Paul.

Returning to Francis, he is, above all, the preeminent, popular, medieval proponent of the effusive and holistic peace of Christ's humanity as exemplified in the crèche of Greccio and the stigmata at Mount Alverna.[34] For Sabatier, Francis had been brought into direct, personal, even intimate contact with Jesus Christ. Sabatier praises Francis as layman, prophet, poet, proto-modern freethinker and artist. Indeed, Sabatier writes, "À son tour il voulut faire comme Jésus, et l'on peut dire que sa vie est une Imitation du Christ singulièrement plus vraie que celle de Thomas à Kempis."[35]

While Sabatier is the great modern proponent of Francis's enduring image and appeal, Bonaventura is the great medieval conveyer of the affective and approachable spirituality of Francis and the *Itinerarium* is his mystical masterpiece centered on the crucified Christ as the method and destination of the mind's road to peace. It is the crucified Christ who is able to bind what is broken, whether that be communion between humanity and God (*Itinerarium*) or Islam and Christianity (*De pace fidei*). God became man and not angel because human beings dwell in the middle of the angelic and ecclesiastical hierarchies and, therefore, given their unique position in the chain of being, may ascend to the highest or descend to the lowest grade of existence. Unlike angels, which were understood as intellectual creatures, human beings are comprised of soul and body. Furthermore, human language dwells halfway between signified and signifiers: image and icon, the Word and words. Christology appears in the middle of the way to God in the *Itinerarium* and the way to the concordance of religion in *De pace fidei*. Christ the broken (the crucified) puts together broken

---

34 The miraculous manger of Greccio is recorded in book one, Chapter thirty of Thomas of Celano's *Life of St. Francis, Francis of Assisi: Early Documents: Volume 1, The Saint*, 254–257.

35 Sabatier, xii.

syllables and reaches below where angels could go, and that is why the angel in *De pace fidei* is only able to announce peace while the Word incarnate can enact this peace through religious dialogue. And in *De pace fidei* only Christ can finally put religious signs together with that which is symbolized, whether that be ablutions or baptism, food of wisdom or holy Eucharist. According to *De pace fidei*, the cosmic, crucified Christ flows through the various ethical practices of Muslims, Jews and Hindus and channels these various rites within the hierarchical dialectic of one religion.

As the late H. Lawrence Bond, a noted American Cusanus scholar, has shown, Cusanus was well aware of Bonaventura's *Itinerarium*.[36] As cardinal and reforming papal legate to Germany, Cusanus would have been no stranger to the *Ordo Fratrum Minorum*, and he even heard the famous Franciscan Bernardino of Siena preach in Padua in 1423.[37] By Cusanus's day the once austere Franciscans were firmly established and richly endowed in the universities and cities and towns of Western Europe and beyond. As evident by the imposing basilica built in Francis's honor following the newly canonized saint's death, Francis's courtly devotion to Lady Poverty was compromised in the affairs of the affluent Franciscans. Sabatier's comment "La Réforme n'a su que substituer l'autorité du livre à celle du prêtre" is hyperbolic.[38] Yet Sabatier's maudlin descriptions often contain a modicum of truth.

The Franciscans were from the start part of the high medieval papal establishment. Francis was a faithful son of the church and of pope of Innocent III, and yet he was prophetic in his message and popular in his appeal. He was also international as his journey to Egypt shows. The new mendicant orders of the thirteenth century, much like the heresies they found themselves combating, were borderless. The Franciscans and the Dominicans were international. And as with the Jesuits later, the Franciscans and Dominicans were mobile missionary forces under the authority of the papacy. By the fifteenth

---

[36] Bond demonstrates that Cusanus was very familiar with Bonaventura's *Intinerarium*. Cusanus had a copy of the work in his possession from his time as a student at Heidelberg or Cologne. H. Lawrence Bond, "The Journey of the Soul to God in Nicholas of Cusa's *De Ludo Globi*" in: Christianson, Izbicki, *In Search of God and Wisdom*, 73, no. 4. Bond compares Cusanus's work, completed late in his career, *De Ludo Globi*, written in 1463, to Bonaventura's *Itinerarium*. I am not aware of any work which compares the path toward religious peace of Cusanus's *De pace fidei* with Bonaventura's path toward God in the *Itinerarium*.

[37] Morimichi Watanabe, "Cusanus's Contemporaries: St. Bernardino of Siena," *American Cusanus Society Newsletter* XXVI: 1 (August, 2009), 22–30.

[38] Sabatier, v.

century, the Franciscans were also the Latin caretakers of the holy sites in the Levant and beyond.

Cusanus was well aware of the Franciscans and their orthopraxis. The first prologue of the *Cribratio Alkorani* states that Cusanus found a copy of the Qur'an in Arabic among the Franciscans watching over the Church of the Holy Cross in Constantinople. Like Bonaventura's *Itinerarium*, Cusanus's *De pace fidei* is a Christocentric mystical treatise of peace. It is international. It moves from the realm of nature and the dissimilitude of discord, to the heavenly council of concord and the supernatural grace of Jerusalem. The *Itinerarium* and *De pace fidei* are Christ-centered theological method and mystical treatise: a dialogue or dialectic to concord and ascent to peace. They are both interiorized hierarchies in the sense that move from without to within by gradation. Both the method and mystical elements of these treatises are centered on Christ as incarnate Word of God. There is an overarching goal of union in Cusanus and a predilection for religious concordance: be it the soul with God, pope and council, Eastern and Western Churches, or Islam and Christianity.

In our search, thus far, we have looked at Bonaventura's influential *Itinerarium* and how it relates to *De pace fidei*. We now explore how Plato and Platonic sources as well as Scripture (reason and revelation), guided Cusanus's Christ-centered dialectical and hierarchical path to the peace of faith. In general, this study does not purport to see Christ everywhere in the writings and life of Cusanus. This study looks at Cusanus's Christological concordant approach to Islam in *De pace fidei* and how this then relates to Christology of his other works. Cusanus's religious ideas were not without controversy in his time. Argument fosters clarification as iron sharpens iron, so Cusanus's response to attacks on his *docta ignorantia* reveal ever more about his Christology and concordance of religion. What comes first heresy or orthodoxy? We also see how debate unveils his sources. His philosophical and theological sources are many, here we focus on three: Bonaventura, Denys the Areopagite and Plato. Lest we neglect Aristotle, we add in passing that Cusnus's search for religious concordance begins with wonder as Aristotle states in the opening chapter of Book A of his *Metaphysics*. In the margins of Cardinal Bessarion's translation of this text,[39] Cusanus wrote that "admirando" is indeed the beginning of philosophy. The text reads: "philosophai a principio quidem admirando". The codex is dated 1453 on the last page (f. 102v), as a better and more reliable translation of Aristotle made by the Cardinal of Nicaea from the original sources. We may safely presume that this note in Cusanus's hand is from the same year as he wrote *De pace fidei*. Cusanus's path to union

---

39   Aristotle, *Metaphysics*, Cod. Cus. 184, f. 2v.

with God, the revelation of *docta ingnorantia* and "religio una in rituum varitate" begin in rapt wonder. And yet wonder, as we shall soon see, can both beckon and bewilder. Both *De pace fidei* and the *Itinerarium* are Christocentric writings on peace. Ultimately, for Bonaventura and Cusanus, the wonder stirring annunciation of peace is found in Jesus Christ who points the way to concordance, be it of mind and God or one religion in the variety of rites.

Blinded by the Sun: Platonic Influences

In 1449 Cusanus wrote *Apologia doctae ignorantiae*. The *Apologia* directly responded in an indirect style to the forthright refutation launched against Cusanus's most famous treatise *De docta ignorantia* (1440) by the Heidelberg doctor of theology Johann Wenck. In 1442–43, Wenck wrote his response to *De docta ignorantia*, *De ignota litteratura* or *On Unknown Learning*.[40] As this polemical work shows, Wenck is concerned with finitude and *sedes doctrinae*, as well as clearly distinguishing Creator and creation, sight and modes of seeing, illumination and blindness, and hence the cogent need for divine accommodation for fallen humanity to realize the Gospel. Wenck pens propositions. He begins with a diatribe against the vice of curiosity, which he sees to be unleashed in *De docta ignorantia* and even labels Cusanus with the errors of the Waldensians, Eckhartians and Wycliffians. Of the laundry list of late-medieval heresies or alleged heresies only Huss seems to be missing.[41] Aside from all the theological bluster and orthodox bombast, which abounds throughout the treatise, Wenck is acutely alarmed by what he deems as Cusanus's wily stratagem of the coincidence of opposites in the divine simplicity. For Wenck this doctrine destroys the fundamental principle of non-contradiction or that it is impossible both to be and not be the same thing, and indeed that a thing is one thing and not another. Throughout the attack the scholastic Wenck strikes nominalist overtones.

---

40 The Cusanus-Wenck controversy is briefly covered in: Erich Meuthen, *Nicholas of Cusa: A Sketch for a Biography*, 58, 85. The philosophical underpinnings of the Cusanus-Wenck nominalist-realist debate are explored in: Edmond Vansteenberghe, *Le Cardinal Nicolas de Cues, L'action—La pensée*, Part 2, Chapter 2 'Le philosophe,' especially pages 262–267.

41 *De ignota litteratura*, 21, from the Latin text collated by Jasper Hopkins. For English translation, see Jasper Hopkins, *Nicholas of Cusa's Debate with John Wenck: A Translation and an Appraisal of De Ignota Litteratura and Apologia Doctae Ignorantiae*, 3rd Edition (Minneapolis: The Arthur J. Banning Press, 1988), http://jasper-hopkins.info/Wenck12-2000.pdf.

As Jasper Hopkins points out in his essay "Nicholas of Cusa and John Wenck's Twentieth-Century Counterparts" what is at stake here is a matter of method and methodology. Effectively, Wenck truncated Cusanus's elaborate and theologically intricate method of *De docta ignorantia* and focused on obscure parts instead of the coherent whole. Wenck heard dissonance while Cusanus played the polyphonic harmony of the coincidence of opposites. In the prologue to *De docta ignorantia*, Cusanus refers to the treatise as a theological 'method' of reasoning.[42] Yet even this whole is both coherent and incoherent, a method and a critique of method—the paradox of learned ignorance or knowing and unknowing, reasoning and unreasoning. There is a demure dialogical quality to Cusanus's *Apologia*. While the method of *De docta ignorantia* is as inclusive as conclusive, the *Apologia* is as coy as it is combative in style: a defense in the guise of Platonic dialogue. For Cusanus, echoing Plato's allegory of the Cave at the beginning of book seven of the *Republic*, Wenck is chained to platitudes in the cave of his own didactic method, lost in the manyness of mere images instead of seeing the unity of the whole or the sun.[43] Cusanus, like Socrates, sees the sun, but that means also being directly blinded by the sun and knowing that one does not know. Wenck only hears second-hand reports about the sun's brightness and supposes, according to Cusanus, that from understanding these reports he knows something about the sun. Yet he remains ignorant because he does not follow the Delphic oracle. Wenck fails to know himself and thus fails to know the Good, the One, the sun of righteousness.[44] Knowing this directly means also unknowing this directly.

By the time Cusanus wrote the *Apologia* he had read Petrus Candidus Decembrius' Latin translation of Plato's *Republic*, completed in 1439.[45] This date is clearly marked on the last page of this manuscript which is a finely made edition and no doubt one of Cusanus's prized books. There are some notations or marks (not many) by Cusanus in the margins.[46] Most of his markings are found in the pivotal book seven. Cod. Cus. 177 includes various writings of Plato (*Meno, Phaedo*, etc.) with prefaces by Leonardi Arestinia and his brief synopsis of Socrates' *Apology* (to which Cusanus refers at the beginning of his own *Apologia*, thus his Apology is patterned after Socrates' fatal quest to know one's self), along with the Latin translation of Plato's *Phaedrus* by Antonius

---

42 *De docta ignorantia*, prologus: "in rebus divinis talem qualem ratiocinandi modum suscipe, quem mihi labor ingens admodum gratissimum fecit."
43 *Apologia doctae ignorantiae* 2.
44 *Apologia doctae ignorantiae* 2, 12, Malachi 4:2.
45 Cod. Cus. 178.
46 Cod. Cus. 178 fs. 49, 133, 134, 139, 144.

Luscus.[47] We know from Cod. Cus. 177 that Cusanus read and studied *Phaedrus* carefully. There are numerous notes by Cusanus in Cod. Cus. 177, especially on the famous sections towards the end of the dialogue that deal with the immortality of the soul, the loss of memory and the need for remembering what was lost.[48]

Cusanus's style of writing in the *Apologia*, as is the genre of *De pace fidei*, the shape of his search for understanding and concordance, is adroitly Platonic. He brilliantly employs Platonic rhetoric and dialectic to both uncover *and* cover his method of the coincidence of opposites further. For example, in the *Apologia* Cusanus frames the entire debate with Wenck through a conversation with one of his students, a dialogue within a dialogue. Wenck is so blinded by reports of the sun that he does not deserve to be addressed directly. Indeed, Wenck, like Plato's philosopher-king is chained in the cave in the shadows of the sun. If Cusanus, whose eyes have been actually blinded by understanding God, were to speak face to face with Wenck, Wenck would no doubt label Cusanus a madman and his fate may be the same as what befell Socrates. Wenck must then be approached by degrees, by accommodation, in order that he too may perceive this hidden wisdom. The goal, then, of the *Apologia* is not merely a defense of learned ignorance, but to lead Wenck to the truth of the method of learned ignorance, as Socrates guided his disciples to know themselves and therein know the Good, or even, as Flannery O'Conner put it, "the life you save may be your own."[49]

Concerning method or seeing the one and not just the many, on Wenck, Cusanus says much the same as Hopkins. Yet he speaks in analogies, the groping language of half sight.[50] In the *Apologia* he uses the analogy of a poisonous animal; thus, if a snake (Cusanus does not say snake, the addition is mine) possesses venom and is viewed only by way of the venom, then the snake is seen as altogether dangerous. Yet when the snake is viewed as a complex whole, while dangerous, it is also approached as a creature of fearful wonder. Cusanus then cites Aquinas in the *Contra Gentiles* on St. Dionysius who writes in the *Coelestis hierarchia* that God is the Being of all things upon which certain minds were

---

47   Cod. Cus. 177 f. 102v–111v.
48   For notes or marking by Cusanus in Cod. Cus. 177 see: fs. 30–41, 101r, 101v, 102v–111v, 90v, 108v, 109v, 110r, 110v, 111r.
49   Flannery O'Connor, 'The Life You Save May be Your Own' in *A Good Man is Hard to Find and Other Stories*, first published in 1948.
50   *Apologia doctae ignorantiae* 4, 11.

led to say that God is all things.⁵¹ They failed, though, to understand the Areopagite's entire corpus. In *De divinis nominibus* Denys says that God is the Being of all things in such a way that he is not any of these things.⁵² And God is present to all things, as cause is to effect, as the unnamed is to names, and yet all things are not present to God as God is beyond causality, name and number. Wenck begins with the many apart from participating in unity, he takes the part for the whole, propositions while disregarding the chain of being, perspicuity instead of hidden wisdom, and ends up in a cul-de-sac of disparate reasoning.⁵³ Cusanus was well versed with thinking in terms of unity and contraction. Contraction, for Cusanus, connotes the art of bringing things together and is, therefore, directly related to unity.⁵⁴ He was also well acquainted with the entire known corpus of Dionysius. Even in his first major work, *De concordantia catholica*, especially the first three chapters of book one, which serve as foundation for the entire treatise, we discover Cusanus's principles for his method of concordance, which reveals syntheses of seeming polarities: church and empire, pope and council, church and world, all of which would be further elaborated and modified as the coincidence of opposites. These first three seminal chapters of book one of *De concordantia catholica* also focus on Trinitarian theology and Christology, plurality, unity and nexus (incarnation).⁵⁵ At this early point in this career, Cusanus had indirectly imbibed the Dionysian hierarchical gradations through writings on the angelic ranks by Bonaventura and Hugh of St. Victor, and directly through his regular involvement in the western rite of the medieval mass, perhaps, the most potent demonstration of the fusing and application of Dionysius's celestial and ecclesial hierarchies.⁵⁶ By the time Cusanus wrote his *Apologia* and *De pace fidei* he had read Denys' works in Latin translation.⁵⁷

The influence of Neoplatonic thought on Cusanus in general is evident in his library in Kues which contains works of Proclus, especially his *Elements of*

---

51   *Apologia doctae ignorantiae* 17; *Contra Gentiles* I, 26; *Coelestis hierarchia* IV, 1, 177D; *De divinis nominibus* I, 7, 597A.
52   *De divinis nominibus* I, 2, 589B.
53   *Apologia doctae ignorantiae* 18.
54   *De docta ignorantia* I, 2. See "Contractio" in "A Brief Glossary of Cusan Terms" in *Nicholas of Cusa, Selected Spiritual Writings*, Bond, 337.
55   See especially *De cocordantia catholica* I, 2.
56   See the note by Sigmund on Cusanus's early imbibing of Dionysius, *Catholic Concordance*, 9.
57   *Apologia doctae ignorantia* 10. Cf., Ludwig Baur, *Cusanus-Texte III. Marginalien 1. Nicolaus Cusanus und Ps. Dionysius im Lichte der Zitate und Randbemerkungen des Cusanus* (Heidelberg: Carl Winter, 1941). Cusanus's notes in the margins of the works of Dionysius in Cod. Cus. 96, pages 94–113.

Theology with numerous notes by Cusanus.⁵⁸ Hans Werner Hoffmann's dissertation, *Nikolaus von Kues und Proklos*, contains an analysis of Cusanus's marginalia of his copies of Proclus's writings.⁵⁹ Hoffmann notes that for Cusanus, citing Proclus, the "*perfecta unitas*' ist Gott". According to Cusanus, this *pefecta unitas* is both personal and intellectual and found in the person of Christ. As perfect unity of human and divine, Christ is approached only by the way of learned ignorance as seen in *De docta ignorantia* and as compared with *De pace fidei*.⁶⁰ For Cusanus, the Word is Reason and Form of forms coinciding with Being ultimately beyond knowing, yet being the Word who makes modes of knowing possible. We find a similar point in *Cribratio Alkorani*.⁶¹ This way of learned ignorance is also dialectical (question and response) as seen in the dialogical structure of *De pace fidei* (from ignorance to coherence) and in Cusanus's own untitled Christological questions and responses in Cod Cus. 40 which move from faith to understanding on the matter of the person of Christ.⁶² Cod. Cus. 195 includes the *Liber de Causis*, a favourite text of Aquinas. Cusanus's library also has the collected works of Pseudo-Dionysius, which contain numerous notes and markings by Cusanus.⁶³ By the late 1440s he knew the writings of Dionysius so well that in Cod. Cus. 45, where half of the Areopagite's Eighth Letter is missing, Cusanus wrote "The text here is greatly incomplete."⁶⁴

On philosophical sources from Cusanus's library, we turn to Cusanus's notes in Cod. Cus. 41, a well marked copy of Eusebius's *De evangelica praeparatione*. Cusanus marks names in the margins as a mnemonic device. The names he lists are of philosophers. These philosophers prepare the way for Christ. Here philosophy and theology have the same goal. Both lead to Wisdom, the Word, Jesus Christ. According to Eusebius and Cusanus, these Greek philosophers are shared partakers of Divine Wisdom and the *Logos*. At first glance, there appears nothing new here. Plato is the Greek Moses. Upon closer inspection, Cusanus's

---

58   Cod. Cus. 195. Hans Gerhard Senger, *Cusanus-Texte III. Marginalien 2. Proclus Latinus: Die Exzerpte und Randnoten des Nikolaus von Kues zu den lateinischen Übersetzungen der Proclus-Schriften 2.1 Theologia Platonis, Elementatio theological* (Heidelberg: Carl Winter, 1986). Karl Bormann, *Cusanus-Texte III. Marginalien 2. Proclus Latinus: Die Exzerpte und Randnoten des Nikolaus von Kues zu den lateinischen Übersetzungen der Proclus-Schriften 2.2 Expositio in Parmenidem Platonis* (Heidelberg: Carl Winter, 1986).

59   Hans Werner Hoffmann, *Nikolaus von Kues und Proklos. Eine Interpretatio Christiana* (Düsseldorf: Philosophischen Fakultät de Universität Dissertation, 1998).

60   *De docta ignorantia* I, 2, 7–8; *De pace fidei* 11, 29.

61   *Cribratio Alkorani* I, 13.

62   Cod. Cus. 40 fs. 144–146v.

63   Cod. Cus. 43–45, 96.

64   Cod. Cus. 45 f. 89r: "Hic deficit multum."

THE MIND'S ROAD TO PEACE   105

notes in the margins of Cod. Cus. 41 reveal the philosophical sources behind his method of learned ignorance and religious concordance as centered in Christ the Wisdom of God. On Cusanus's predilection for Plato and his preparation for the prophets and coming of Christ, he writes in the margins 'Plato et Moises[ß]'.[65] The full note reads: "Plato et Moises[ß] attire loquens[ß]". Cusanus notes Plato in his notes in the margins on numerous folios, with reference to "Timeaous" and the beginning, in "principius", and with Pythagoras, "Plato Pytagorirus".[66] Pythagoras is mentioned again, along with Xenophon, "Heraclitus" and even Plotinus ("Plotino") in the key section on *De verbo*.[67] Plotinus is also mentioned in the text of this chapter on *De verbo* which reads "Plotinus".[68] Porphyry is mentioned in a note by Cuanus. Philo is noted as well.[69] Plato is by far the most frequently noted philosopher named by Cusanus. Eusebius covers the natural theology of the ancient Greeks in some detail before dealing with particulars of the preparation: *De verbo*, etc.[70] *De pace fidei* shares this same chronology as Eusebius's *De evangelica praeparatione*: the dialogue begins with Greek philosophy as represented by the first dialogist to be engaged by the *Verbum*, and then Latin thought as represented by the second speaker, viz. the Italian. In *De pace fidei*, we find the dynamic pairing of Hebrew Scriptures and Greek thought: the ideas of Moses and Plato on reason and commandments, the same pairing that appears in Eusebius's *De verbo*.[71] In *De pace fidei* and for Eusebius, the fulfillment of the nations is in the person and work of Christ, the Word made flesh. Furthermore, there are numerous notes in Cod. Cus. 41 by Cusanus on the *imago Dei*. Intellectual vision appears in *De verbo*.[72] The chapter on *De verbo* immediately follows chapters on "Deus ineffabilis" and "Deus bonus est". *De verbo* addresses the Son of God as Word, Lord, and God from God as prefigured in the Hebrew Scriptures and elsewhere.[73] The text goes on to show how the testimony of Plato and the Platonists and Plotinus affirms what is in Hebrew Scripture concerning the Word of God.[74] In the chapter,

---

65   Cod. Cus. 41 f. 152r.
66   Cod. Cus. 41 fs. 26v, 28v, 149v, 151r, 153v, 155r, 157r 166v, 167r, 169r, 170r, 171r, 175r, 184r, 185v, 188v, 189r, 190r, 194r, 'Plato and Pytagorirus' 194v.
67   Cod. Cus. 41 f. 62 Pythagoras, f. 186r Xenophon, f. 186v Heraclitus, f. 155v Plotinus.
68   Cod. Cus. 41 f. 156r.
69   Cod. Cus. 41 fs. 95v, 105v, 114r, 115r, 154v, 159r.
70   Cod. Cus. 41 f. 16v, 27–21.
71   *De pace fidei* XVI, 58–59.
72   Cf., earlier chapter on *De verbo*, Cod. Cus. 41 f. 95–96v; Cod. Cus. 41 fs. 154r–157v.
73   Cod. Cus. 41 f. 154. Cf., *De pace fidei* III, 8.
74   Cod. Cus. 41, f. 155–156.

"De Bono", Cusanus writes "via intellige de bono".[75] This intellectual way is the way of hidden wisdom as revealed in Christ. This hidden way was prepared by Plato and the other aforementioned philosophers. According to Cusanus, the Qur'an also affirms the Gospel, as does Plato and Plotinus. In the prologue of *Cribratio Alkorani*, Cusanus writes, "Ego vero ingenium applicui, ut etiam ex Alkorano evangelium verum ostenderem".[76] Thus even the Qur'an, like the writings of Plato and the other philosophers that Cusanus so diligently and methodically marked in the margins of his copy of Eusebius's *De evangelica praeparatione*, affirm the Gospel.[77] Only, for now, we encounter again Wenck and his attack on Cusanus's theological method. Wenck fails to see how Cusanus's transmits his Gospel preparative philosophical sources to his theological art of learned ignorance as coalesced in Christ.

Where Wenck is pointed, Cusanus is circumspect. Where Wenck is clear, Cusanus is enigmatic. In his *Apologia* Cusanus himself argues that his works should be seen as a whole and that his foray into hidden wisdom is beyond dissection, even beyond contradiction, as God ultimately transcends the coincidence of opposites, the law of non-contradiction, even language and logic. There is the 'Wenckian dilemma' of isolating Cusanus by work, doctrine, or philosophy, rather than by theology. Cusanus defends seeing philosophy and theology as interwoven and aiming at the same goal, namely union with God and beatitude in all of its complexities, which is perhaps most fully explored in his *De visione Dei*. There is something intentionally slippery, even serpentine (back to the analogy of the snake), about Cusanus's method, or way, of learned ignorance and the coincidence of opposites. It is presented in *De docta ignorantia* as negation and cataphatic science. The *Apologia* is indirect in style and yet ends with Jesus, the concrete way to synthesis. Cusanus's *Apologia* presents not only a defense of one work, but of his entire method of knowing God and the cosmos, his way as elucidated in *De docta ignorantia*. Indeed, for Cusanus, the related method of the coincidence of opposites is the starting point of the mystical way of knowing God and the self.[78]

As we have seen, Jasper Hopkins is correct in noting the importance of methodology in the debate between Wenck and Cusanus, between attending to parts or the whole, and yet this debate is also ultimately Christological.[79]

---

75   Cod. Cus., f. 158.
76   *Cribratio Alkorani*, prologus 4.
77   Cod. Cus. 41.
78   *Apologia doctae ignorantiae* 6.
79   Jasper Hopkins, "Nicholas of Cusa and John Wenck's Twentieth-Century Counterparts" in *A Miscellany on Nicholas of Cusa* (Minneapolis, MN: Arthur Banning Press, 1994), 3–38.

At stake is how one understands Christ's cosmic role and his human self-emptying, hypostasis and kenosis, theosis and incarnation; how Christ is both the coincidence of opposites and beyond the coincidence of opposites.[80] Heracleitus said, "The way up and down is one and the same."[81] For Cusanus, as for Denys in the *Coelesti* and *Ecclesiastica hierarchia*, the way up and down is Jesus who is the way (*via*).[82] As noted in the last chapter, *De docta ignorantia*, *Apologia* and *De visione Dei* all conclude with a section on Jesus. It is certainly no coincidence that many of Cusanus's works conclude with Jesus: *De concordantia catholica* also finishes with the Christocentric metaphor of the body for church and empire or church and world. The same may be said of Wenck's attack, much of which deals with Christology. Wenck is so strident in his assault, because, for him, what is ultimately at stake is Christological in import, the very epicenter of the Christian faith. Just as the iconoclastic controversy of the early Byzantine Empire was essentially Christological, so too is Wenck's debate with Cusanus.[83] For Cusanus 'Jesus' is more than the center of his speculative method, 'Jesus' is the method from whom all being emanates and through whom creation returns to the Creator. Professor Douglas Farrow has echoed the Wenckian view that Cusanus held pantheistic tendencies. In *Ascension and Ecclesia*, Farrow observes that the hidden Christ is not much different than the hermetic philosopher's stone.[84] In response to this charge, Cusanus writes in *De docta ignorantia* that Christ is "contractum et absolutum".[85] This contraction, or the assumption of the human nature in Christ in the incarnation, is hereafter permanent. Christ is contracted and absolute, human and divine as ascended to the Godhead. Thus, in *De docta ignorantia*, on the Ascension of Christ, Cusanus notes that while there is one humanity, this humanity is contracted by various and diverse principles as applied to various and diverse persons.[86] In Christ these principles unite to Divinity: "in Jesus Christ these principles were only the most perfect and most powerful and the nearest to

---

80   *Apologia doctae ignorantiae* 15.
81   *The Essential Plotinus: Representative Treatises from the Enneads*, translated by Elmer O'Brien, S.J. (Indianapolis, IN: Hackett Publishing: 1964), 176.
82   *De coelesti hierarchia* I, 1, 120B, IV, 4, 181C; *De ecclesiastica hierarchia* I, 1, 372A, VII, 11, 568A; *De pace fidei* II, 7.
83   Bilal Baş, *Ecclesiastical Politics during the Iconoclastic Controversy (726–843): The Impact of Eusebian 'Imperial Theology' on the Justification of Imperial Policies* (Montreal: McGill University PhD Thesis, 2008), chaps 6 and 7.
84   Douglas Farrow, *Ascension and Ecclesia: On the Significance of the Doctrine of the Ascension for Ecclesiology and Christian Cosmology* (Grand Rapids, MI: Eerdmans, 1999), 162–163.
85   *De docta ignorantia* I, 2, 7.
86   *De docta ignorantia* III, 8, 227.

the essence of the humanity that was united with the divinity."[87] On what this contracted union and ascension means for the *telos* of humanity, Cusanus concludes that the ascended (human and divine) Christ is the way for rational creatures to find concordance between the Creater (God) and creatures.[88] Furthermore, the Christ of *De pace fidei* is the Word made flesh in full bodied, serious and timely dialogue for the *telos* of ascending to religious concordance. This Word converses with Jews, Muslims and Hindus in the mind of Cusanus and in the context of the fifteenth century. For Cusanus, *De pace fidei* represents what he thinks a real conversation between Christians and Muslims could potentially be. One reading of Cusanus (i.e., Wenck's) focuses on his blurring of the line between the finite and infinite. The other reading of Cusanus (i.e., our reading) sees Christ's transcendence in his immanence and immanence in transcendence in a contracted way or in a manner seeking unity. While Cusanus's contracted, Christ-centered way of seeking unity through the subtle art of learned ignorance is both method and critique of method, his Christology (Christ being the synthesis of the absolute maximum and absolute minimum, where God is all things and not anything) is both the way and not the way, both revealed in the Word and hidden beyond words.

There is not one Platonic or Neoplatonic influence on learned ignorance and the coincidence of opposites, but many: Plato, Aristotle, Proclus, Denys, Avicenna, Aquinas, and Eckhart. Throughout all of these sources, Cusanus somehow uncovered the ubiquitous Word of God and plurality in unity and unity in plurality. Thus the Word of God, ultimately Christ, is both unique and not unique. As the first chapter of John's Gospel states, a pericope that was read at the end of the every celebration of the mass, Christ is identified as the Word of God through whom all being comes into existence.[89] The Word also became flesh. Thus the Word is common and uncommon, universal and particular.

Cusanus transmits and fuses concepts on the One, God, the Good, into his own unique method of learned ignorance and the coincidence of opposites as centered in Christ. While God is beyond the coincidence of opposites, God also, in Christ, is the coincidence of opposites. This follows the Plotinian

---

[87] *De docta ignorantia* III, 8, 228: "in Iesu Christo errant solum perfectissima et potentissima et essentiae humanitatis propinquissima, quae divinitati unita fuit." Translation by Bond.

[88] *De docta ignorantia* III, 8, 228: "Qui cum Deus et homo esset, propria virtute resurrexit, et nullus hominum praeter ipsum nisi in Christi virtute, qui Deus est, poterit ut Christus resurgere." Cf., *De docta ignorantia* III, 8, 232.

[89] This practice continued after Trent and is even used by some Anglicans to this day.

maxim: the essence of something is not that something.[90] And yet according to the Athanasian maxim: in order for man to become God, God became man. This is also why in the *Apologia* Cusanus begins his defense with pointing to Christ his teacher and the wisdom hidden therein. This is also ultimately why he employs his indirect dialectical style. For Christ's human nature distances one from God as much as it unites one with God. And this is finally why Cusanus ends his *Apologia* by invoking Jesus, the synthesis and hope for entering the cloud of unknowing and the rest and silence beyond in the divine simplicity where all coincidences and contractions cease.[91] Furthermore, Cusanus concludes the *Apologia* with the related theme of peace, a theme at the centre of *De pace fidei*.[92] For Cusanus, writing about Jesus is problematic. Seeing him as he really is is as complicated as Cusanus's *De visione Dei* shows. Jesus may be approached directly by accommodation in the sacraments and hierarchy of the church, and indirectly through contemplation of the hypostasis. The Gospels present what is hidden, the kingdom of God is within (the realm of the knowing self), and the church and Christ are one as bride to bridegroom. True theology, then, cannot be committed to writing.[93] It is hidden in Scripture and above and beyond human conjecture. The words of Scripture, following Augustine's *De doctrina* are sacred signs of things signified, yet not all things can be signified.[94] For the Trinity is not a thing.[95] Yet Trinitarian language is relational. Only for Cusanus the method or way is also a critique of method, a way and not a way. This is similar to Meister Eckhart's German Sermon Eighty-Three, where he exhorts his hearers to love God as non-God and to love as detached from all else, even the way of love, indeed, from love itself.[96] For Cusanus, the way and not the way, the way of cataphatic wordiness and apophatic silence, must be initiated by divine illumination.

Cusanus attests that the method of learned ignorance was revealed to him by divine illumination—a vision of some kind, much like that of Plato's philosopher-king being blinded by the sun. Writing about Jesus is difficult and full of potential pit-falls, the hazy no-man's land between orthodoxy and heresy. And yet as Plato's philosopher-king in the *Republic* is compelled to return to the realm of shadows in order to show others the way to truth, so too Cusanus

---

90 Plotinus, *Ennead* VI.9.3.45-50, VI.9.11.
91 *Apologia doctae ignorantiae* 35.
92 *Apologia doctae ignorantiae* 35.
93 *Apologia doctae ignorantiae* 4.
94 *De doctrina Christiana* I, 4–5.
95 *De doctrina Christiana* I, 10.
96 Meister Eckhart, *The Essential Sermons, Commentaries, Treatises and Defense*, edited and translated by Edmund Colledge (New York: Paulist Press, 2002), 207.

is compelled to write about Jesus in order that Wenck and others would see the transfiguration of the sun.[97] This also explains why Cusanus was compelled like Augustine (following in the footsteps of the barefoot Socrates and Jesus), to dedicate so much of his labour to the active arena of ecclesial life or what might be labeled late-medieval blood sport.

Plato's *Republic* concludes with the Myth of Er.[98] The warrior Er recounts how he saw what lies beyond and the inter-connectivity of time and space. Plato tells us about Er and what he saw. Reality twice removed. Cusanus wrote down the method of what he saw in a vision, or as much of the vision as he could remember for the benefit of others. The act of writing in order to remember and realize anew what has gone before is a subject Plato explores in the dialogue *Phaedrus*.[99] In it, Socrates shares the story of Thamus, the wise king of the Egyptians. One day Theuth, the Egyptian God of writing, urged Thamus to disseminate the art of writing throughout Egypt. Yet, Thamus warned that writing would produce forgetfulness. Those who write will not practice the art of memory. Instead, they will put their trust in writing, which gives only the appearance of wisdom, not really wisdom of one's own. Cusanus's Latin translation of *Phaedrus* is extensively marked here.[100]

Cusanus's *Apologia* is written for Wenck and for his students. Yet Cusanus, a gifted rhetorician, also knew the fate of another great synthesizer. At the end of his life Thomas Aquinas was reported to have received a vision of some intensity while at mass. Following this vision he wrote no more, concluding that all of his works, his entire theological enterprise of studying God and the blessed, the many and the one, was but straw.[101] Ultimately, as far as Cusanus was concerned, when it came down to defending his way of learned ignorance to the Johann Wencks of the world, some things are better left unsaid.

From Confusion to Concordance: Reversal of Babylon and the New Pentecost

More may be said, about the path to peace and religious concordance in *De pace fidei*. Another important and easily overlooked interpretative source

---

97 Plato, *Republic* VII, 517; *Apologia doctae ignorantia* 2.
98 Plato, *Republic* X, 614–621.
99 Plato, *Phaedrus* 274c–275b.
100 Cod. Cus. 177 fs. 108–111.
101 On this transformative event, see Josef Pieper, *The Silence of St Thomas: Three Essays*, 1953, translated by John Murray, S.J. and Daniel O'Connor (South Bend, IN: St. Augustine's Press, 1999).

which sheds light on how to make sense of the dialectical and hierarchical structure and argumentation of *De pace fidei*, or why Cusanus puts things in this particular way, is the *Acts of the Apostles*, an ancient book of apologetical and missionary journeys. In Acts, Chapter 1, verse eight, the risen Jesus of Nazareth, who, according to the narrative, is about to ascend into heaven, declares to his gathered apostles that they will be his witnesses in Jerusalem, Judea and Samaria, and to the ends of the earth.

This calling charts the itinerary of *Acts of the Apostles*. Initially, the Christian movement is centered in Jerusalem, the locale for much of Acts Chapters 1–7. Samaria is the setting for part of Chapter 8, while Judea plays a prominent role in chapters ten through twelve. From Chapter 13, until the end of the book, Paul travels through the Eastern Roman Empire. The *Acts of the Apostles* ends in Rome with Paul under house arrest awaiting trial.

Paul is on the way to his long anticipated imperial trial; he has not yet achieved what he desires. Likewise *De pace fidei* ends while looking forward to and striving for a general council of religious harmony in Jerusalem and worldwide peace without end. As the *Acts of the Apostles* progresses, more and more geographical areas and nationalities are included both in the work itself and in the Christian community. The same is true in *De pace fidei*: as the dialogue advances, more and more representatives of differing religions and regions take their turn discussing Christianity in the work itself and in accepting it as completely reasonable, thereby confessing to be Christians or part of the *concordantia religionum*.

The itinerary of the *Acts of the Apostles* also progresses by way of two key characters. Peter plays a prominent role until Acts Chapter 15. From there, Paul is the focus of attention. In *De pace fidei*, first the Word dialogues with various representatives of the world's religions, followed by Peter and then Paul. Paul is the last to speak on behalf of Christianity, just as he is in the *Acts of the Apostles*. In *De pace fidei*, Paul is also identified as the teacher of the gentiles, the calling given to him by the risen Lord as recorded in Acts, Chapter 9.[102] In *The Gospel of Luke*, which is traditionally seen to be the precursor to *Acts*, the Word is revealed. The Word, Jesus Christ, traveling Judea and Galilee proclaiming the good news of the kingdom of God.[103] *Acts*, then, continues the proclamation of the Word, Jesus Christ, through the Holy Spirit and through the preaching and teaching of the apostles, notably Peter and Paul. As in the *Acts of the Apostles*, there is a apologetic objective, albeit one marked by rationality and intellectual and consensual decision making, driving the dialogue forward

---

102   *De pace fidei*, XVI, 55: "doctor gentium"; Acts 9:15.
103   Luke 4:43.

in *De pace fidei*, the shape of which bears the imprint of the structure of the early Christian community as recorded in the *Acts of the Apostles*. In *De pace fidei*, the diverse representatives of the world's religions as gathered from the ends of the earth are on the way to Jerusalem. An early name for Christianity as founded in Jerusalem and recorded in the *Acts of the Apostles* was the "via."[104]

In Christian tradition and interpretation, the event of Pentecost as recorded in *The Book of Acts* reverses the confusion of Babel.[105] Jerusalem is the epicenter of the event of Pentecost: the polis of the outpouring of the Holy Spirit upon the enlightened and polyglot apostles. *The Book of Acts* constitutes an inspiration for *De pace fidei*. The argument of the latter is like the narrative of the great commission in reverse, and a second Pentecost of religious understanding and harmony. In *De pace fidei*, the representatives of the world's religions are led to consent to one religion in the diversity of rites through hearing. *De pace fidei* presents a global Pentecost—a reversal of the confusion of Babel—the concordance of discordant religious language in the one Word of God. In the Babel of religious misunderstanding, humanity, according to Cusanus, confuses religious language by taking long standing religious customs as truth.[106] As in the biblical narrative of Pentecost, Cusanus is enlightened by the Holy Spirit in order to bring religious unity and peace.[107] Furthermore, for Cusanus, the Holy Spirit is identified as 'nexus': nexus of Father and Son, and nexus of God and soul in the *imago Dei*.[108] Thus, the Spirit unites humanity with God, and, in the structure and flow of the dialogue, unites the many rites and one religion. In *The Book of Acts* we also read of the first general council held in Jerusalem, one that seeks to bring gentiles into the early Jewish-Christian community.[109] This council, much like the Pentecost-Babel event, seeks concord over discord. Jerusalem, symbolizing revelation and peace, is central in both *Acts* and *De pace fidei*. Yet Athens, as paragon of reason and ancient philosophy, also appears in the itinerary of *Acts* and on Cusanus's way of religious concordance in *De pace fidei*.[110]

We find one final overarching example of source material for the structure of *De pace fidei* in the overall dialectics of Platonic dialogue, the search for

---

104   Acts 9:2; Cf., John 14:6.
105   Genesis 11:1–9; Acts 2.
106   *De pace fidei* I, 4, 6; III, 8, 9; XIX, 68. Cf., Acts 1:8.
107   *De pace fidei* I, 1: "forte ex diuturna continuata meditatione, visio quaedam eidem zeloso manifestaretur"; *De pace fidei* I, 2: "raptus".
108   *De pace fidei* VIII, 24.
109   Acts 15.
110   Jerusalem: Luke 24:47–49; Acts 1:8, 2:5, 14, 15:4. Athens: Acts 17:16–34. Jerusalem: *De pace fidei* III, 9; XIX, 68. Athens: the Greek dialogist, *De pace fidei* IV, 10.

Wisdom in the realm of reason. As the classicist Christopher Gill observes, the point of the Platonic dialogue form is "the Socratic idea of philosophy as a continuing search for objective truth."[111] For example, Plato's *Symposium* begins with two men on their way to Athens. While on the way, one of the men retells the famous drinking party years prior when Socrates and others discussed the meaning and nature of love. The story of the drinking party is told while on the way to Athens. We have charted Jerusalem, now we look for Athens. Plato's *Symposium* climaxes with Socrates' dialogue with Diotima. In this dialogue within a dialogue, Diotima tells Socrates to turn his mind towards the beautiful, which always is and always will be. Socrates has not yet reached this perfect beauty. At the end of the *Symposium*, after an entire evening of drinking and discussion, Socrates goes off and spends the day as he usually did, continually searching for truth, and, we may assume, continuing on the path to Athens. Thus, the *Symposium* reveals, both in its shape and content, the still incomplete quest for wisdom, beauty, truth, and perpetual peace. The influence of *The book of Acts* with its emphasis on journeys to and from Jerusalem, and the *Symposium* with its symbolism of Athens, show the hypostatically united cities of Athens and Jerusalem, reason and revelation, in the search for religious peace in *De pace fidei*.

On the Christocentric and dialogical purpose of *De pace fidei*, we return to the Franciscan Bonaventura's classic mystical guide, *Itinerarium mentis in Deum*. As we have seen, Cusanus was familiar with Bonaventura's *Itinerarium*. Although written in differing contexts for dissimilar reasons, the structure and flow of the *Itinerarium* inform the purpose of *De pace fidei*. Like the *Itinerarium*, which was written in the setting of mysticism as a real map for the mind to progress into God, *De pace fidei* is an interiorized hierarchical progression within the context of meditative prayer and vision toward actually realizing peace among the eminent and wise scholars of the world's religions by consent in their minds to the reality of the Word and Wisdom of God. Indeed, the *Itinerarium* begins with the desire for the peace of Christ. The *Itinerarium* proceeds as a kind of Augustinian dialogue from the world into the soul and the soul upward to God.[112] The path concludes with tranquil words of Scripture. Bonaventura's own words trail off. The hurried human voice is stilled. Only the very words of God reverberate from the mystical union of the

---

111 Plato, *The Symposium*, trans. Christopher John Gill (London: Penguin Books, 1999), xvii.
112 Augustine, *Confessions* I, 1: "quia fecisti nos ad te et inquietum est cor nostrum, donec requiescat in te." Cusanus read Augustine's Confessions. See his reference to the *Confessions* in *Apologia doctae ignorantia* 15.

knower with the known where peace beyond comprehension endures.[113] *De pace fidei* begins with the Word who speaks of the underlining harmony of all religions. The dialogue concludes with free consent to one religion in the variety of rites, and the peace of Jerusalem, which has no end. Christology, in all of its cosmic dimensions forms the beginning and end, the substance, movement and goal of religious peace as expressed in Nicholas of Cusa's *De pace fidei*.

In this chapter we have explored the Christ-focused dialectical path to the peace of Jerusalem and the concordance of religion. Bonaventura's *Itinerarium* served as our hierarchical and Christ-centered guide. We also looked at the Cusanus-Wenck controversy and Platonic influences on Cusanus's art of learned ignorance. And we saw how *De pace fidei* proposes a reversal of Babel: a new Pentecost where the world comprehends religious concord. We now move onto another central idea: the polis as nexus of peace. And we will directly face a question that has been lurking behind this dialogical study: how could Cusanus dream of peace in *De pace fidei* between Christians and Muslims and still preach crusade against the Ottomans?

We began this chapter with St. Francis and we conclude by once again returning to this paradoxical barefoot innovator and beloved saint, originator of the urban Franciscan movement and faithful son of Pope Innocent III. It was this same complicated and nuanced St. Francis who yearned for mystical peace atop Mt. Alverna and conversed on religious concord with a Sultan. It is another Sultan, Mehmed II, and the fraught relationship between religion and violence in the sojourning and complex career of Cusanus, to which we now turn.

---

113   Peace is mentioned in the prologue of the *Itinerarium*, while the final chapter (Chapter 7) ends with Scripture. This chapter does not contend that Bonaventura's *Itinerarium* and Cusanus's *De pace fidei* share the same context, content or intent. We here compare the overarching structure, Christocentricity, and Christ propelled nature of both mystical and dialectical writings.

CHAPTER 4

Seeking the Peace of the City

> Arma virumque cano, Troiae qui primus ab oris Italiam fato profugus Lavinaque venit litora … (Arms and the man I sing, who first from the coasts of Troy, exiled by fate, came to Italy and Lavine shores …)[1]

⋮

> Seek the welfare of the city where I have sent you into exile, and pray to the Lord on its behalf, for in its welfare you will find your welfare.[2]

⋮

The New Alexander: Pius II and Mehmed II

In late 1460 or early 1461 Pope Pius II composed a letter to the conqueror of Constantinople, Mehmed II, "Fatih" (the Conqueror), praised in his Empire and feared in the West.[3] Mehmed II was the son of Sultan Murad II. His mother

---

1 Virgil, *Aeneid* 1, 1–2. Translation by H.R. Fairclough.
2 Jeremiah 29:7 NRSV. Et quaerite pacem civitatis ad quam transmigrare vos feci et orate pro ea ad Dominum quia in pace illius erit pax vobis (Vulgate).
3 Pius II was pope from 1458 to 1464. Mehmed II reigned from 1444 to 1446, 1451–1481. On the dating of this letter, R.W. Southern opts for 1460 (*Western Views of Islam in the Middle Ages* (Cambridge, MA: Harvard University Press, 1962), 99). J.N.D. Kelly marks the date as roughly 1460–61 (*The Oxford Dictionary of Popes* (Oxford: Oxford University Press, 1986), 248). Based on a note from a copy of the letter in the Bodleian, R.J. Mitchell notes that the letter was probably written in Siena in 1460 (*The Laurels and the Tiara: the Life and Times of Pius II, Scholar, Poet, Statesman, Renaissance Pope* (Garden City, NY: Doubleday, 1962) 155). An example of the praise afforded to Mehmed II by his people is seen in his ornate tomb at the grand imperial mosque (Fatih Camii) he built in Istanbul, which is still a shrine to this day. The original mosque was destroyed in an earthquake in the late eighteenth century. It has since been rebuilt. An example of how the nations of Europe feared Mehemd II is from an anonymous Greek chronicle of the Seventeenth Century (*Codex Barberinus Graecus* 111). The author claims that the Ottomans wrote an inscription on Mehmed's tomb, saying: "Rhodes and Italy: You have been liberated" (*Byzantine Europe and The Early Ottoman Sultans 1373–1513, Late Byzantine and Ottoman Studies, 4,* translated and annotated by Marios Philippides (New Rochelle, NY: Aristide D. Caratzas, 1990), 93). On Pius II and Islam and Mehmed II, see also:

was a slave, probably of Byzantine ancestry.[4] Murad II had tried unsuccessfully to capture Constantinople in 1422. Before assuming the papacy Pius II was Aeneas Silvius Piccolomini, a prominent Italian humanist, poet and novelist, who was a friend of the cardinal and philosopher Nicholas of Cusa.[5] Like Cusanus, he was an avid collector of ancient manuscripts and his passion for the classics and predilection for Greek philosophy appear throughout the long letter replete with florid rhetoric and dialectical arguments on the nature of wisdom and the universal human quest for happiness and concord.[6] Indeed, many of the themes in the letter are the same as those found in Cusanus's *De pace fidei* and which we have already mentioned in previous chapters, especially the religious concordance. Mehmed II was more than just the conqueror of Constantinople, he was also a scholar of ancient Greek thought. He was

---

Franz Babinger, "Pio II e l'oriente maomettano" in *Enea Silvio Piccolomini Papa Pio II: Atti del Convegno per il Quinto Centenario Della Morte e altri Scritti Raccolti da Domenico Maffei* (Siena: Società Tipografica «Multa Paucis» Varese, 1968), 1–13.

4   Mehmed's maternal ancestry is shrouded in mystery. Franz Babinger notes that his mother was a 'slave', which ensures that she was not of Turkish origin, and that she probably was of Greek descent (Franz Babinger, *Mehmed the Conqueror and his Time*, edited by William C. Hickman and translated by Ralph Manheim, Bollingen Series XCVI (Princeton: Princeton University Press, 1978), 12). In Chapter 33 of his *Byzantine History*, (composed some years after the Ottoman conquest of Constantinople), the fifteenth century historian Michael Ducas writes that Mehmed's mother was a slave. English translation of Chapters 33 through 42 are found in: *The Siege of Constantinople 1453: Seven Contemporary Accounts*, translated by J.R. Melville Jones (Amsterdam: Adolf M, Hakkert, 1972), 56–116. For a more recent and accessible biography of Mehmed II see John Freely, *The Grand Turk: Sultan Mehmet II—Conqueror of Constantinople and Master of an Empire* (New York: The Overlook Press, 2009).

5   Aeneas Silvius Piccolomini was crowned poet laureate by German king (later Holy Roman Emperor) Frederick III. His works include his widely read novel *Lucretia and Euryalus* and the erotic comedy *Chrysis*. For Latin text of *Chrysis*, see Anton F.W. Sommer, editor, *Enea Silvio Piccolomini (Pius II) Euryalus und Lucretia (De Duobus Amantibus), Epistolae Selectae, Chrysis Comedia* (Vienna: Editiones Neolatinae Tom. 43, 2004), 191–250. His fascination with 'Asia', geography and views on the Ottomans are explored in Chapter 2, 'Barbarians at the Gates', of Margaret Meserve's *Empires of Islam in Renaissance Historical Thought* (Cambridge, MA: Harvard University Press, 2008), 65–116. On the transformation of Aeneas to Pius see the biographical introduction and select translated letters in *Reject Aeneas, Accept Pius: Selected Letters of Aeneas Sylvius Piccolomini (Pope Pius II)*, translated by Thomas M. Izbicki, Gerald Christianson and Philip Krey (Washington DC: Catholic University of America Press, 2006).

6   Early on in his career, Cusanus testifies to his life-long collecting of books in the preface of his first major work *De concordantia catholica*: "Originalia enim multa longo abusu perdita per veterum coenobiorum armaria non sine magna diligentia collegi. Credant igitur, qui legerint, quia omnia ex antiquis originalibus, non ex cuiusquam abbreviata collectione, huc attracta sunt." And, one of his final works, *De venatione sapientiae*, presents Cusanus's philosophical reading list.

interested in the works of the Neoplatonist Byzantine scholar Plethon, as well as Ptolemy.[7]

In his letter to Mehmed II, as one philosophically inclined scholar to another, Pius II boldly attempts to woo the sultan to become Christian and thereby secure eternal salvation and earthly glory. Pius was a humanist and a scholar of ancient texts, but also pope and head of the Catholic Church. Mehmed was a scholar and philosopher, but also a brilliant military strategist and powerful sultan. Pius writes in the most direct and famous passage of the letter,

> If you [Mehmed II] want to extend your power over Christians and render your name as glorious as possible, you do not need gold, weapons, armies, or fleets. A little thing can make you the greatest, most powerful and illustrious man of all who live today. You ask what it is? It is not difficult to guess, not far to seek, and is everywhere to be found: it is a little bit of water by which you may be baptized and brought to Christian rites and to belief in the Gospel. If you receive this, there will not be any leader in the world who can surpass you in glory or equal you in power. We will call you ruler over the Greeks and the East; what you now hold by force and injustice, you will rightfully possess.[8]

While today this request seems brazenly apologetic, at the time it represented a pragmatic and novel Western approach to the expanding political and religious reality of Islam. Pragmatic in the sense that far from belittling Mehmed, as was the norm in western caricatures of the great Ottoman ruler, Pius goes to

---

7   Freely, *The Grand Turk*, 101–102.
8   Latin text and English translation are found in: *Aeneas Silvius Piccolomini, Epistola Ad Mahomatem II*, edited and translated by Albert R. Baca (New York: Peter Lang, 1990), II, 13. pp. 17–18. Si vis [Mehmed II] inter Christianos tuum imperium propagare et nomen tuum quam gloriosum efficere, non auro, non armis, non exercitibus, non classibus opus est. Parva res omnium qui hodie vivunt maximum et potentissimum et clarissimum te reddere potest. Quaeris quae sit? Non est inventu difficilis, neque procul quaerenda, ubique gentium reperitur: id est aquae pauxillum, quo baptizeris et ad Christianorum sacra te conferas et credas Evangelio. Haec si feceris, non erit in orbe princeps qui te gloria superet aut aequare potentia valeat. Nos te Graecorum et Orientis imperatorem appellabimus et quod modo vi occupas et cum iniuria tenes possidebis iure. Cf., Aeneae Sylvii Piccolminei, *Opem quae exstant omnia*, Basiliae, Henrici Petri, circa mid sixteenth century (reprint, folio, Frankfurt: Minerva G.M.B.H., 1967), 874. In this sixteenth century print edition (1571), the letter appears under the heading: '*Epistola* CCCXCVI', '*Pius Episcopus Servus Servorum Dei, Illstri Mahometi principi*'. Cf. Pius II. Papa, *Epistola ad Mahumetem, Einleitung, kritische Edition, Übersetzung*, edited by Reinhold F. Glei and Markus Köhler (Trier: WVT Wissenschaftlicher Verlag Trier, 2001). See also Nancy Bisaha, *Creating East and West: Renaissance Humanists and the Ottoman Turks* (Philadelphia: University of Pennsylvania Press, 2004).

great lengths to praise him, and not merely flatter him, as the would-be new Alexander and Constantine, the chosen one to renew the Augustan golden age of poetry.[9] Pius had penned a brief treatise on the capture of Constantinople, which shows that he had researched the life of Mehmed II and the rise of the House of Osman or the Ottomans. He sought out first-hand accounts about the Ottoman conquest of the city, especially that of the Genoese archbishop of Lesbos, Leonardo Giustiniani of Chios.[10] Throughout the letter Pius shows a profound respect for Mehmed and his military manoeuvres and jurisdictional acuteness. Indeed, for Pius, Mehmed is seemingly the only world leader who would be able to bring peace not only between Christians and Muslims, but also between perpetually warring Christian states.[11] In the epistle, Pius II speaks pragmatically as the pope and principally reasons in the manner of a Socratic philosopher, and he writes for far greater aims than that of historical record or détente. He observes that both Muslims and Christians believe in the same God and that both faiths affirm this same God as creator and preserver of all things, and the ultimate goal of all existence.[12] As with Cusanus's *De pace fidei*, Pius II seeks concordance, a coincidence of seeming opposites: Rome and Constantinople, West and East, Christianity and Islam.

In this chapter we will continue our look at Cusanus the sojourner on the path to religious peace by exploring the *coincidentia oppositurm* of Islam and Christianity, Rome and Constantinople, Sultan and Pope, crusade and peace through first examining Pius's famous letter to Mehmed II and how it relates to Cusanus's *De pace fidei*. We will then briefly consider Pius's ecclesial relationship with Cusanus and with a view to addressing directly the elusive question of how Cusanus could dream of peace in *De pace fidei* and yet support Pius's ill-fated crusade of 1464. In order to answer this question we will contextualize the interrelated ideas of crusade and reform in the life and thought of Pius II

---

9   *Epistula ad Mahomatem* II, 1, 4; II, 17, 20; III, 30–34; XIX, 211.
10   *De Captione Urbis Constantinopolis Tractatulus.* An annotated Latin text with English translation are found in: *Mehmed II The Conqueror And the Fall of the Franco-Byzantine Levant to the Ottoman Turks: Some Western Views and Testimonies*, edited, translated and annotated by Marios Philippides (Tempe, AZ: Arizona Center for Medieval and Renaissance Studies, 2007, 93–120). On Pius and Giustiniani, see: Ibid., 17–18. Cf., *De constantinopolitana clade & bello contra turcos congregando, Oratio XIII* (1454), Pii II P.M., *Aeneae Sylvii Piccolominei Senensis Orationes Politicae, et Ecclesiasticae*, Edited by Joannes Dominicus Mansi, Pars I (3 parts bound in two volumes) (MDCCLV), 263–286.
11   *Epistula ad Mahomatem* I, 1. Pius begins his letter by proposing to set out a few matters as pertaining to the peace of many nations: "Scripturi ad te aliqua pro tua salute et gloria proque communi multarum gentium consolatione et pace."
12   *Epistula ad Mahomatem* III, 22; IV, 39–40; V, 55; IX, 88–89; XI, 112–115.

and Cusanus. In this search, we detect a curious dialectical analogy between Cusanus's promotion of crusade and reform with simultaneously being in favour of papal monarchy and the conciliar principle in his first major work *De concordantia catholica*. We embark upon a journey to cities of fame and yore, literal reality and symbolic inspiration: Troy, Athens, Jerusalem, Rome, Constantinople. In so doing, we attempt to pinpoint how Mehmed, Pius II and Cusanus, all sojourners on the elusive way of religious concordance, intersect on the map of Christian-Muslim relations at the close of the middle ages and the dawn of the renaissance.

Pius's letter to Mehmed mentions ancient cities and ancient leaders, notably Alexander, whose aura emanates through history as the noble and ideal conqueror.[13] Alexander is praised in both West and East, Greece and Persia; each of these ancient civilizations would have a profound effect upon the culture and politics of the Ottoman Empire.[14] Alexander the Great also represents the penetrating and lasting influence of Hellenic thought on Anatolia, the Levant and beyond. Pius's *Letter* further praises Mehmed II as potential new Caesar Augustus.[15] Augustus expressly patterned his own carefully cultivated youthful and commanding image on that of Alexander the Great.[16] And it was Augustus, of course, who was the first Roman emperor and one of the most famous leaders in world history. For Pius, Mehmed the Conqueror is the new would-be Alexander and Augustus.

Mehmed II saw himself as heir of both Constantine even Justinian, and the Byzantine-Roman Empire, and the ancient axiom stating that he who holds Constantinople holds the Empire was as true for Mehmed as the Byzantine emperors who ruled before him.[17] The Byzantine scholar Marios Philippides observes that the term 'Byzantine' was coined by French historians of the seventeenth century and that the population of Constantinople and its domain

---

13 *Epistula ad Mahomatem* IV, 42, 44–47; V, 49. Cf., III, 29, 34; XV, 167.
14 On Alexander or Sekandar in Persian mythology, see Abolqasem Ferdowsi, *Shahnameh: the Persian Book of Kings*, translated by Dick Davis (New York: Penguin Books, 2006), 456–528.
15 *Epistula ad Mahomatem* II, 17.
16 For example, see the eternally young image or ancient busts of Augustus as patterned on the young Alexander. This was the standard portrayal of Augustus throughout his long reign and how he wanted his subjects to see him.
17 Babinger, *Mehmed the Conqueror and his Time*, 416. Ilber Ortayli describes how Constantinople was 'the protected domain,' '*Be makam-i Konstantiniyye el Mahmiyye*' (Ilber Ortayli, *Discovering the Ottomans*, translated by Jonathan Ross (Markfield, UK: Kube Publishing, 2009), 1).

knew their empire as *the* Roman Empire.[18] For Mehmed, the capture of Constantinople cemented his expanding Empire, an Empire both ancient (Roman) and new (Ottoman), and, which, to Pius, would potentially usher in a new *Pax Romana*. Even while Pius finds injustice in what he understood as Mehmed's taking of Constantinople, he nonetheless envisions that by virtue of his abilities and firm hold on the ancient city of Constantinople he will be the potential chosen one to bring about the final union and peace of faith between Christians and Muslims.

We also detect a millennial glow to Pius's *Letter*. The *Letter* flickers between past and present in the hope of a brighter future of world peace. Pius's *Letter* points to the possible fruition of Christendom through the advent of Mehmed II as potential leader destined rightly to unite and restore the divided and sullied grandeur of the Holy Roman Empire.[19] For example, in Chapter 3 of the *Letter*, Pius promises that no age will cease to utter Mehmed's name if he would but procure world peace by embracing the Roman faith.[20] Pius is not alone in his optimism for world peace, however improbable it would prove. Cusanus's *De pace fidei* also hopes, ideally and imaginatively, for religious concord to emanate from Jerusalem to the ends of the earth. Thus, as Jesus of Nazareth proclaimed in the New Testament *Book of Acts* that beginning in Jerusalem his message would be preached to the ends of the earth, so too, at the conclusion of *De pace fidei*, the heavenly message of one religion in the variety of rites as imparted by the Word of God is to be propagated from Jerusalem.[21] There is also Cusanus's intriguing short tract of 1446, *Coniectura de ultimis diebus*, which shows his interest in eschatology and that he was aware of the Augustinian and Joachite traditions of medieval prophetic speculation, speculation that would run rampant just a generation later in the fiery apocalyptic milieu of Savonarola and the Reformation.[22] Even so, these lofty speculations of millennial triumphalism and enlightenment were

---

18   *The Fall of the Byzantine Empire: A Chronicle by George Sphrantzes 1401–1477*, translated by Marios Philippides (Amherst, MA: The University of Massachusetts Press, 1980), 1.

19   Cf., Cusanus, *De concordantia catholica* III, 41, the conclusion of the treatise which compares the ideal Christian emperor to that of a fully functioning, all-embracing body.

20   *Epistula ad Mahomatem* III, 34: "in orbe et nomen tuum nulla silebit aetas." Cf., *Epistula ad Mahomatem* XIX, 211.

21   Acts 1:8; *De pace fidei* XIX, 68.

22   For the late fourteenth, early fifteenth century apocalyptic fascination, see Abrecht Dürer's famous Apocalypse woodcuts and Andrew Cunningham and Ole Peter Grell, *The Four Horsemen of the Apocalypse: Religion, War, Famine and Death in Reformation Europe* (Cambridge, UK: Cambridge University Press, 2000).

grounded in real Western European concern over the seemingly unstoppable surge of Ottoman military might. Indeed, as far as the Western European powers were concerned the Ottomans had staying power. Margaret Meserve writes that when the Ottomans were seen as an expanding, yet stable empire, it would not be difficult "to address their needs rationally, by searching for opportunities for cooperation and collaboration with them, even diplomatic *rapprochement*".[23] Pius's *Letter* reflects not only millennial optimism, but also pragmatic détente.

We have seen how Pius's *Letter* to Mehmed II pragmatically understands the sultan's power and the potential for him to be a new Alexander the Great. What is novel about Pius's approach to Islam in this letter is the way in which he presents Christianity to Mehmed. He does not seek to disparage and condemn Mehmed's faith, which was common for the times, especially when seen in comparison with the numerous and ineffectual calls for crusade bellowing out of pulpits throughout Western Europe after 1453. Indeed Pius says he is only hostile to Mehmed's actions and not to his great intellect or person.[24] Instead the *Letter* explains the Christian faith to Mehmed and to his Muslim subjects primarily through the shared concepts and categories of Hellenic philosophy. The *Letter* proceeds from a discussion of the immortal soul's quest for the good to the unity of wisdom, to unity and plurality, plurality and unity. Pius knew of Cusanus's *De pace fidei* and the structure of the letter matches Cusanus's dialogue, as well as the outline for Christian-Muslim dialogue that Cusnaus proposed in a letter to John of Segovia, a fellow student of Islam and former colleague from the Council of Basel.[25] Cusanus's *Letter to John* of 1454 outlines in proper order the theological topics for how a potential dialogue between Christians and Muslims would proceed. The order begins with a discussion of Christ as the Word of God.[26] Similarly, in his letter to Mehmed II Pius explicates the understanding of God as the Good as fully known through the

---

23   Margaret Meserve, "Italian Humanists and the Problem of Crusade" in *Crusading in the Fifteenth Century: Message and Impact*, edited by Norman Housley (New York: Palgrave Macmillan), 38. On the crusade in Hungry in the mid-fifteenth century and John Hunyadi, see: Norman Housley, "Frontier Societies and Crusading in the Late Middle Ages" in *Intercultural Contacts in the Medieval Mediterranean*, edited by Benjamin Arbel (London: Frank Cass, 1996), 104, 119.
24   *Epistula ad Mahomatem* I, 2: "Operibus tuis, non tibi sumus infensi".
25   This letter is found in *Nicolai de Cusa, De Pace Fidei cum Epistula ad Ioannem de Segobia. Ediderunt Commentariisque Illustraverunt Raymundus Klibansky et Hilderbrandus Bascour, O.S.B., Medieval and Renaissance Studies Supplement III* (London: Warburg Institute: 1956), 93–102. This letter will be discussed in more detail in Chapter 5.
26   For more on Cusanus's *Letter to John of Segovia*, see Chapter 5.

Wisdom and *Logos* as Christ and the Trinity in unity, and unity in Trinity. Yet, he does so in a distinctively Platonic fashion. One example of this is found in his discussion of the Word of God. As with Cusanus's *De pace fidei*, Pius focuses on the Word of God, the *Logos*. Indeed, as Cary Nederman observes, "It is this belief in the relevance of *Logos* (in its classical sense) to religion that clearly stands behind the Christian-Muslim dialogue literature of the Middle Ages."[27] This insight proves to be especially true in both Pius's letter (itself an invitation to dialogue) and Cusanus's *De pace fidei*. Echoing book seven of Augustine's *Confessions*, Pius writes that the Platonists had agreed with much of the prologue to John's Gospel. That the Word was with God and that it was God, and that everything came into being through the Word are all to be found in the writings of the Platonists. Everything, that is, until John, Chapter 1, verse fourteen, which describes the incarnation of the Word. This doctrine, as Augustine well knew, was not found in the books of the Platonists.[28]

There is something old here, very old, and something new. Old in the return to Augustine and Plato, and new in how this is applied directly to Islam (at least to a Muslim ruler) as a way of explaining the nature of God and Christian Scripture. There is the assumption that Mehmed will naturally understand this way of thinking and that this is a natural theology as informed by Greek thought. Pius II and Cusanus were both humanists. They loved ancient texts, visited ancient places, and were visionaries: they traveled and discovered, translated and transmitted ancient texts, and applied them to Islam. Their approach to Islam was initiated by history, place and circumstance: Athens and Jerusalem, Rome and Byzantium, Rome and Istanbul, the city, both old and new. The name Istanbul is from the medieval Greek for 'eis tan polin,' 'into the city' or 'Stambul.'[29] Upon conquering Constantinople, Mehmed passed through At Meydani (Hippodrome) and went to pray in the heart of the city: Hagia Sophia, which became the mosque, Aya Sofya.

The continuity of the name is important. The use of the same name for both mosque and basilica, Holy Wisdom, reveals the continuity of thought shared by the two religions: the same Divine Wisdom. There is one Wisdom, the same divine and holy Wisdom praised and sought by Mehmed, Cusanus and Pius II. The Turkish scholar M.C. Sehabeddin Tekindag relates how the Sultan behaved respectfully toward this church now turned mosque, which

---

27   Cary J. Nederman, *Worlds of Difference: European Discourses of Toleration, c. 1100–c. 1550* (University Park: The Pennsylvania University Press, 2000), 119.

28   *Epistula ad Mahomatem* VII, 70; Augustine, *Confessions*, book VII, Chapter IX.

29   On the Greek origins of the name 'Istanbul' see: Babinger, *Mehmed the Conqueror*, 102; and Philippides, *The Fall of the Byzantine Empire*, 2.

bore terrible memories from the Latin looting and sack of 1204. When Mehmed first entered Hagia Sophia, he is reported to have covered his head for prayer and announced to those hiding there that they need not fear for their lives. Throughout his reign he afforded great care to the maintenance both of the magnificent structure and to its historical records.[30] Mehmed probably never received Pius's letter. In any event, Tekindag also observes, Sultan Mehmed tried to attract Christians to live in his newly conquered Roman capital and sought peace in the city for both Christians and Muslims[31] He read Latin and knew Greek, and, like Aeneas Piccolomini, was a famous poet. He even is reported to have kept and revered Byzantine icons in the inner chambers of his court and was known to be spiritually eclectic. In 1479 he welcomed the famous Venetian artist Giovanni Bellini to Istanbul who painted there his famous portrait of Mehmed now in the National Portrait Gallery in London.[32]

There is continuity and discontinuity, concord and strife, a new empire in place as the old, ancient wisdom as well as new misunderstandings. The symbolic importance of Constantinople for Mehmed II is well known as is his predilection for ancient Greek thought. He also famously visited Troy and saw himself as the avenger of its inhabitants so long ago vanquished but now restored in Ottoman likeness.[33] Troy was also important to Pius II and the other Italian humanists in connection with the foundation myth of Rome.[34] Yet the

---

30 M.C. Sehabeddin Tekindag, "The Conqueror and the Hagia Sophia" in *Lectures Delivered on the 511th Anniversary of the Conquest of Istanbul* (Istanbul: Fen Fakültesi Döner Sermaye Basimevi, 1967), 53–58.

31 "Thoughts on the Letter Sent by Pope Pius II to Sultan Mehmed the Conqueror" by M.C. Sehabeddin Tekindag in *Lectures Delivered on the 511th Anniversary of the Conquest of Istanbul* (Istanbul: Fen Fakültesi Döner Sermaye Basimevi, 1967), 43–44. He also notes that no copy of Pius's *Letter* is found in the library of Mehmed II at Topkapi Palace or in the collections containing non-Islamic handwriting (43).

32 Freely, *The Grand Turk*, 151–152.

33 Freely, *The Grand Turk*, 73.

34 Vat. lat. 1786 f 148v, 18 shows Pius's fascination with Troy. Vat. lat. 1786 is a collection of Pius's Letters and various epigrams. The text or ode to Troy reads: Tradunt Eneam Hectore bello inferiorem Prudentia autem superare Troianos. Inceteris vero his dignum laudibus quibus Hectorem asseuerant earum vero rerum quae addeos pertinent. Et que deleta Troia fato sibi [e]u[e]n[e]runt cognitionem habuisse perhibent eum quidem nullus aratione timor rectoqus consilio ei[c]i[e]bat. In horrendis enim rebus maxime utebatur ratione. et intellectu. unde Greci Hectorem Troianorum manum. Eneam autem intellectum appellabant. At qui eum moderatione utentem plures Grecis molestias afferre. qui surentem Hectorem traditum est. Erant autem et etate et statura pares. forma autem Enee minus iocunditatis habere videbatur compositi et grauis viri speciem magis habebat. Ad comeuero cultum ne diligens quidem erat nequs eam tollerabat-nequs seipm [?] come

fall of the "Asiatics" of Troy represented the supremacy of Greece and Europe. Greece would give way to Rome and the rise of the Western world. We turn to Tertullian's famous conundrum: What has Athens to do with Jerusalem?[35] But what does Troy have to do with Athens? Pius II and Cusanus both believe in a common source of Wisdom as conceptualized in ancient Greek thought and shared by Mehmed II and the humanists of Europe.[36] Even so, shared wisdom was not enough to avert collective mistrust and Europe and Asia seemed to be on a collision course much like that of ancient Athens and Troy. The European Renaissance humanists and the Ottoman Trojans interpreted their actions in light of both ancient philosophy and history.

War and Peace: Pius II and Nicholas of Cusa

Pius II and Cusanus were well acquainted and they exchanged numerous letters in the course of their ecclesial careers. Both were humanists, lovers of wisdom, churchmen and students of Islam. This relationship was well established before Pius became Pius, and, thanks to the work of the prominent Cusanus scholar Thomas M. Izbicki, is well known in renaissance scholarship today.[37] For the purposes of this study on the dialectics of peace in *De pace fidei*, the Pius-Cusanus-crusade connection may be illustrated by briefly examining four manuscripts in the Vatican Library as well as Pius's final crusade oration of 1464.[38] No doubt, Pius and Cusanus would approve of going back to the primary sources—*ad fontes*. It is the opening of ancient books at the end of *De pace fidei* that confirms what is agreed upon in the heaven of reason.[39] Here we have an opening of late-medieval, hand-written manuscripts that affirm agreement between Cusanus and Pius II on the interrelationship between the papacy, ecclesial power and the medieval idea of crusade.

These finely crafted codices date from the mid-fifteenth century and contain letters of Aeneas Piccolomini before he became pope, from the period

---

subiciebat solam virtutem suum ornamentum esse existimans. Quandoquidem oberrantes in tuc[e]retur non ea vehementia eoqus vultu inspiciebat ut ipsos deterreret.

35 Tertullian, *De praescriptione*, vii.
36 *Epistula ad Mahomatem* XVII, 183; *De pace fidei* IV.
37 See the introduction of Izbicki, et al. *Reject Aeneas, Accept Pius: Selected Letters of Aeneas Sylvius Piccolomini (Pope Pius II)*, 3–57.
38 Ott. lat. 347; Urb. lat. 401; Vat. lat. 1787; Vat. lat. 5994.
39 *De pace fidei* XIX, 68.

1449 to 1456.[40] Yet given papal insignia inscribed in two of them, as well as the similar content, they had to have been completed after 1458 when Aeneas became pope.[41] They are books of letters, and letters were the penchant of humanists like Pius and Cusanus. These codices of letters of Pius II are a beautifully written pair, no doubt held in esteem as official record, and individually written as a whole. Each has the same style and were no doubt a set of some kind. Both contain a number of the same letters of Pius and both will serve to establish the Pius-Cusanus connection in a time of struggle and crusade. In this section we will contextualize the central question of this chapter: how could Cusanus and Pius II propose peace and preach crusade?

Aeneas Piccolomini's relationship with Cusanus is illustrated in a number of letters and writings from the three aforementioned manuscripts in the Vatican Library. Letter 26, dated 18 January 1455, where Aeneas refers to "difficile mihi hoc negocium de Duce Sigismundo."[42] The letter refers to the ongoing struggle between Cusanus and Archduke Sigismund, ruler of the Tyrol, that would engulf much of Cusanus's career and energy. We also see the fog of war in Letter 171, dated 8 July 1454, titled, "Difficultat Expeditionem Contra Turcos". In the Letter Pius reviews the state of affairs concerning the proposed expedition with the "Venetos [Veneti]…Alemani…Franci…Polonos…Borgundie…

---

40   Letter 176 ("CLXXVI"), dates from December 1449 (f 241v–242r). Cf., Ott. lat. 347 f 242v. In Urb. lat. 401, the majority of letters date from 1454 to 1455. Cf., Vat. lat. 1787 (many of the same letters, similar codex). For the year 1456, see Vat. lat. 1787 f 373r. Cf., Vat. lat. 1787, f 373r same date: 1456 on final page. Vat. lat. 1787, Urb. lat. 401 and Ott. lat. 347 are similar in content and form and all three are hand written on vellum.

41   In Ott. lat. 347, the papal insignia of the threefold tiara over the crossed keys of St. Peter are luminously inscribed in brilliant gold, crimson, purple, blue and green on f 13r, f 262v, with a decorative muli-colour banner aruond the edge of the text and on the bottom, reads: Pius Eneas Papa Secundus". Cf., Urb. lat. 401 f 9r with referene to "Pius Secum[n]dus". Cf., Urb. lat. 1787 f 2, title on top of page: "Epistolarum Pontificalium Æneæ Silvii Piccolominei Epi Senensis qui tandem Romano Pontificio præfectus Pius ii". Urb. lat. 1787 also includes Pius' *Oratio pro auctoritate Romani Pontificis adversus Austriales* (fs 214v–260v, with many markings in the margins).

42   Ott. lat. 347, f 36r (the date is found at the end of the letter on the top of f 37r "decima octaua Ianuarii MCCCCLV"). Cf., Urb. lat. 401, Epistola XXVI: "difficile mihi hoc negocium de duce Sigismundo" (f 45v), the same date, 18 January 1455 is found in the text at the end of the letter (f 46v; "xviii Januarii"). Cf., Vat. lat. 1787, "Epistola XXVI", f 39r–f 40r; roughly the same text: "Difficile mihi hoc negociuz de duce Sigismundo," and same date, here marked, "decima octaua ianuarii MCCCCLV". Urb. lat. 1787 f 29v with markings, pointers in the margins of this page, i.e., meaning it was noted.

Bohemis…Hungaria."[43] This highlights his awareness of the geopolitical situation, an awareness shared by Cusanus, which would be played out again after Aeneas became pope.

One of these finely crafted books of letters in the Vatican Library also includes Pius's *Oratio pro auctoritate Romani Pontificis adversus Austriales* along with numerous markings and annotations in the margins.[44] It is one of the longer works in this codex and highlights the authority of the Roman church in antiquity and later. Both Pius II and Cusanus were staunch supporters of the primacy of the Roman see. This *Oratio* was composed while Nicholas V was pope (1447–1455). Aeneas mentions him at the beginning of the treatise.[45] It was the bibliophile and humanist Tommaso Parentucelli who, as Pope Nicolas V, is considered to be the real founder of the Vatican library owing to the twelve hundred Greek and Latin manuscripts he left to the now famous collection. In 1453 following the fall of Constantinople to the Ottomans, Nicholas also tried unsuccessfully to rally the Christian powers of Europe for crusade. While no date is given in the codex of Pius's works in the Vatican library, it follows the letter from 1454 and refers to events in Hungary and Bohemia from this time in regard to the primacy of Rome.[46] The *Oratio* also mentions three great defenders of ecclesiology in the Latin church—Cyprian of Carthage, Pope Leo the Great, and Gregory the Great.[47] In the preface to the *Cribratio Alkorani* of 1461 Cusanus would even brave Pius II to become a new Pope Leo the Great and write a new tome of Christological concordance that would unite Christians and Muslims in one faith. The *Oratio* includes a history lesson of sorts of the Hellenic world from paganism to Christianity to the demise of the Western Roman Empire and the rise of the Holy Roman Empire: from Solon, Alexander the Great, and Augustus to Leo the Great, Gregory the Great, and further on to Charlemagne.[48] These names, many of which are the same as those found in his letter to Mehmed II, and the movements and thought they represent, find their fulfillment, according to Pius II, in the church of Rome and cathedra of

---

43 Ott. lat. 347, Epistula CLXXI, fs 172v to 173r; date on f 173r "viii Iulii MccccLiiii". Cf., 7r "contra turchos expeditio", (CLXXI), and 218v "viii Iulii 1454". Vat. lat. 1787 f 212v–213r "viii Iulii MCCCCLiiii".

44 Urb. lat. 1787, hand written, same style throughout, indicating one codex, same first letter of each letter in box in gold, red, blue or green, one complete whole or put together this way, also includes Pius' *Oratio pro auctoritate Romani Pontificis adversus Austriales* fs 214v–260v.

45 Urb. lat. 1787 f 215r: "rex Ladislaus" of "hungarie ac bohemie".

46 Urb. lat. 1787 f 18r.

47 Urb. lat. 1787 f 222v, f 222r.

48 Urb. lat. 1787 f 240r, f 241r, f 242r, f 242v, f 244r.

St. Peter. Aeneas, even before he was Pope Pius II, shows his interest in Rome as the eternal city and the ancient idea of a world-wide religious and political empire, themes which are remarkably similar to his open *Letter* and unsuccessful wooing of Mehmed II. The *Oratio* concludes with a section on how Lucifer has obscured Roman authority and unity in Christendom, which caused the fall of Egypt and Libya to Islam, furthered the demise of Greece, and led to the eventual rise of the Ottoman Turks.[49] In this *Oratio* we again encounter the concentric themes of papal authority and the spiritual realm, Rome as both place and portent, geography both West and East, and Islam as represented by the Ottomans. As is so often the case in Pius's humanist and ecclesial career, as well as, to a limited degree, in Cusanus's own life and works, we find a fascination with Islam and desire to engage the new Ottoman reality both philosophically and militarily.

Pius II and Cusanus, like Pope Nicholas V before them, were active supporters of plans between 1459 and 1464 for a crusade to Constantinople.[50] They were humanists but also realists, reformers and crusaders. These plans for crusade to Constantinople began with the Congress of Mantua in 1459, which, according to Pius's own autobiographical *Commentaries*, was considered by him

---

49 Urb. lat. 1787 f 259r, lines 19–28: "In oriente sicut hieronymus aut Lucifer ille qui ceciderat super sidera posuit tronum suum ubi obruta sulcis frumenta in lolium auenasqus degenerant. ægyptus & libya dum christum qui rome predicatur audire contemnit pseudo prophetam Maumethen admittit & sequitur ad infernum. Grecia duus superbit ac romane maiestatis primatum negare presumit; sexuire turchis cogitur; & hostibus christiani nominis tributa pendere." Cf., Cusanus, *De pace fidei* II, 7.

50 William Boulting, *Æneas Silvius (Enea Silvio De' Piccolomini—Pius II): Orator, Man of Letters, Statesman, and Pope* (London: Archibald Constable and Company: 1908). Boulting writes that the Letter to Mehmed was written at the end of 1461. And he notes the argument thus of his age, "men believed in the sovereignty of reasonable propositions; they gilded the pill with persuasive language" (340). Boulting also notes that Pius was not without precedent. For the Franks, like the Ottomans, had conquered part of the Roman Empire and had been converted. Pope Leo I was presumed to have halted Attila and the Huns by eloquent and reasonable appeal, and the conqueros of Italy in the fifth century accepted the Roman faith and pope (Ibid.). Cf., Pastor, *History of the Popes*, English translation, vol. III, p. 256, n. On the speech of Pius II of September 26, 1459 at the Congress of Mantua of which copies were circulated throughout Europe, he directly cites Urban II and the call from the crowd at the ready: "Deus lo vult, Deus lo vult!" As quoted in *A History of the Papacy from the Great Schism to the Sack of Rome*, vol. III, M. Creighton (London: Longmans, Green, and Co., 1897), 225. Pius's own account of his speech at the Congress of Mantua is found in his *Commentaries*, book III, Chapter 1. For Latin and English text of his speech, see: Pius II, *Commentaries*, vol. 2, edited by Margaret Meserve and Marcello Simonetta (Cambridge, MA: Harvard University Press, 2003), 3–6.

at least to be the pivotal moment of his papacy. Pius describes how at Mass in the cathedral of Mantua on 26 September 1459, he called for crusade much like Urban II had done at Clermont in 1095.[51] Clermont was a reforming council which inaugurated the great era of church reform of the twelfth century. Pope Urban II announced the crusade as surprise. By the fifteenth century the novelty of crusading had worn away, and it came as no surprise that few heeded the call, no matter how grand and bellicose it sounded. Yet this lack of interest did not deter Pius II. Indeed, so much of his time went into this preparation for crusade that he left few other monuments of his papacy. He attempted diplomacy, as his evident in his *Letter* to Mehmed II. Nancy Bisaha concludes that Pius "tried diplomacy, eloquence, coercion, his own good example, even martyrdom."[52] There has been much made of the connection between the call to crusade in the fifteenth century and the need for church reform.[53] Pius II never gave up hope in the power of reform and crusade. He is heir to the conciliar movement and the papal crusading enterprise as established by his predecessor Pope Urban II. For Pius, as for Urban II, the institution of the papacy was central to the idea and reality of the crusade. On 14 January 1460, following the prerequisite of right authority, Pius II declared war against the Ottoman Turks at the Congress of Mantua.[54] Feuds closer to home, though, kept him from realizing this confrontation as did lack of enthusiasm and real support for a crusade. War in the Germanies between various princes and cities gave Pius considerable concern throughout his pontificate.

Even with a busy schedule amidst wars and rumours of war, Pius II found solace and strength in the past, notably, in Bernard of Clairvaux's *De consideratione*. Here again we see the medieval connection between the papacy, church reform and crusade. Pius references *De consideratione* in his Bull *In minoribus* or the Retraction Bull of 26 April 1463 and based on Augustine's *Retractations*.[55] *De consideratione* is a book of advice to his former Cistercian monk, now the busy administrator Pope Eugene III. It is also a treatise on papal authority, the papal-led crusade and the politics of theocracy. Bernard had vehemently, even rashly, championed the disastrous second crusade and he

---

51 Boulting, *Æneas Silvius*, 269.
52 Nancy Bisaha, "Pope Pius II and the Crusade" in *Crusading in the Fifteenth Century: Message and Impact*, edited by Norman Housley (New York: Palgrave Macmillan), 52.
53 Margaret Meserve, "Italian Humanists and the Problem of Crusade" in *Crusading in the Fifteenth Century: Message and Impact*, edited by Norman Housley (New York: Palgrave Macmillan), 13–38.
54 Boulting, *Æneas Silvius*, 278.
55 Izbicki, et al. *Reject Aeneas, Accept Pius: Selected Letters of Aeneas Sylvius Piccolomini (Pope Pius II)*, 52.

responded to its failure in an apologia on the plight of Jerusalem at the beginning of book two of *De consideratione*. Bernard also memorably wrote that the pope wielded two swords, the spiritual and temporal, pointedly restated by Pope Boniface VIII in his Bull *Unam Sanctam*.[56] The Battle of Varna of 1444, in which the papal army was routed by the Ottomans and Cusanus's mentor Julian Cesarini was killed, failed to diminish the crusading spirit of Cusanus and Pius. Indeed, like Bernard of Clairvaux after the second crusade, Pius and Cusanus remain undeterred after the fall of Constantinople. The crusade went on. Reform went on, albeit haltingly. Bernard of Clairvaux, Pius and Cusanus all sought reform of the church. Reform and crusade were inextricably linked from the twelfth century onward.

Following the Congress of Mantua, and now nearing the end of his pontificate, on 23 September 1463, Pius II convened the cardinals in secret conclave and urged them once and for all to join him on crusade as recorded in the *Oratio ad sacrum senatum de profectione contra Turcos*.[57] In the *Oratio*, Pius summons the power and primacy of the Roman see and right authority in order

---

56   *De consideratione* IV, III, 7. For English translation, see Bernard of Clairvaux, *Five Books on Consideration: Advice to a Pope*, translated by John D. Anderson and Elizabeth T. Kennan (Kalamazoo, MI: Cistercian Publications, 1976). Bernard writes, "Both swords, that is, the spiritual and the material, belong to the Church; however, the latter is to be drawn for the Church and the former by the Church" (*Advice to a Pope*, 118). The two swords are temporal and spiritual and based on an interpretation of Christ's words in Luke 22:38. English translation of *Unam Sanctam* is found in Brian Tierney, *The Crisis of Church and State 1050–1300* (Toronto: University of Toronto Press, 1988), 188–189. Interestingly, in stating papal supremacy over every human creature, Boniface cites Dionysius directly after he indirectly cites Bernard of Clairvaux's *De consideratione*. Boniface writes, "For, according to the blessed Dionysius, it is the law of divinity for the lowest to be led to the highest through intermediaries" (Tierney, 189). The fifth and final book of *De consideratione* also covers hierarchy as Bernard focuses on the heavenly hierarchy of the church. An influence, perhaps, on Dante's *Paradiso* where Bernard is the last of the intermediaries to guide Dante to the beatific vision in the hierarchy of heaven. Both Pius and Cusanus were inheritors of the Dionysian tradition of cosmological and ecclesiological hierarchy.

57   Boulting, 343. His oration is also found in: Mansi, *Pii II, Orationes II* (bound in volume II), 168–181. Pius begins, "Vos, qui tantopere nos adhortati estis in Turcos moveti bellum, domi in otio remanere non decet. Oportet membra suo coaptari capiti, & illud sequi quocumque jerit. Quod agimus necessitatis est" (Mansi, *Oratio*, 168). See also, Pii II. Pont. Max., *Oratio, De bello turcis inferendo, eruta ex schedis autographis*, Stephano Borgia, Sacrae Congreg. De Propaganda Fide, a secretis (Rome: Apud Benedictum Francesium, 1774), 53. Oratio: pages 53–66. In the Borgia edition, the beginning of the oration reads: "Moneta aurea cusa Fulginei, quum Pius II. P.M. bellum sacrum adversus Turcas parans Anconam proficisceretur An[no] MCCCCLXIIII Oratio Pii Papae II".

to call on crusade against the Ottomans in aid of besieged Christian powers.[58] What is interesting to note about this final and impassioned appeal for crusade to Constantinople is the accentuated authority of Rome. The crusade was a papal-led movement as seen in the first crusade to the Levant up to the naval Battle of Lepanto in 1571. Appealing to crusade meant appealing back to Urban II, to the Gregorian age of papal reform begun around 1050 that remade the papacy. Pius even cites Troy and again we see the renaissance fascination with the past.[59] Pius attempts to rouse his cardinals to action in the name and power of the chair of Peter.[60] Pius then lists the needed virtues and qualities of the cardinals and again appeals to the power of the Roman pontiff, a list Cusanus took seriously as is evident in his decision to follow Pius to Ancona.[61] Pius calls the cardinals to join the white-robed army of martyrs.[62] He decries the cardinals, who counselled war against the Turk but who remain at home in ease. The members of the body must follow the head.[63] His speech also noted

[58] Borgia, *Oratio*, 56: "Iuvenes bellatores, expertos duces, numerosos exercitus Turconica bella requirunt. Utilius domi manebit Pius, emisso legato cum copiis, qui prose pugnet. Qui hoc pacto ratiocinantur, nec vires Apostolicae Sedis, nec mores hominum satis metiti sunt. Perparum est, quod aerarium Ecclesiae Romanae conferre potest: nec principes, aut populi sunt, qui tam legatum Pontificis, quam ipsum Pontificem sequi velint. In auctoritate, & reverentia vires nostrae, non in opibus consistunt. Matthias Rex Ungariae magnanimus, & clarae memoriae Iohanni genitori suo persimilis, dubius erat, an hoc anno in Turcos arma proferret: At audita profectione nostra: en, inquit, Summus Sacerdos cano capite, debilibusque membris in castris erit; & ego iuvenis robusto corpore domi manebo? Non faciam, iussitque mox cuncta parari ad bellum necessaria."

[59] Mansi, *Oratio*, 171: "Quid Trojana victoria gloriosius, in qua omnes hostium vires in unum conjunctae infelix proelium commisere?".

[60] Mansi, *Oratio*, 168: "Petri cathedram."

[61] Mansi, *Oratio*, 175–176: "Abstinentia, castitas, innocentia, zelus fidei, religionis fervor, contemptus mortis, martyrii cupido Romanam Ecclesiam toto orbi praefecerunt. Primi Petrus & Paulus inclyto martyrio dicaverunt; sequuti deinde pontifices, alter post alterum longa serie ad gentilium tribunalia rapti, dum falsos Deos accusant, Christumque verum & singularem Deum manifesta voce fatentur, exquisitis suppliciis mortem obiere, eoque pacto novellae plantationi consuluerunt. Credidere discipuli magistros vera loquutos, qui suam doctrinam morte firmassent, nec ullis potuerunt ab ea tormentis avelli."

[62] Mansi, *Oratio*, 176.

[63] Boulting, *Æneas Silvius*, 345. Cf, Pii II. P.M. olim Aeneae Sylvii Piccolomini Senensis, *Orationes Politicae, et Ecclesiasticae, Quarum multas ex MSS. Codd. nunc primum eruit; reliquas hinc indè dispersas collegit, & ad MSS. CODD. recensuit*, Argumentis, adnotationibus, et praefatione exornavit, atque appendice aliarum lucubrationum ineditarum auxit Joannes Dominicus Mansi (Rome: 1755–57), three parts bound in two volumes (volume I date: 1755; volume II: 1757). *Pii II, Orationes II* (pars II and bound in volume II), p. 177: "Vos, qui tantopere nos adhortati estis in Turcos moveti bellum, domi in otio remanere non decet.

how others saw the cardinals as rich and out of touch with the plight of ordinary Christians and the nitty-gritty realities of religious persecution.

The vast majority of cardinals paid little heed to Pius's summons, save Cusanus and Cardinal Carvajal. Pius's emphatic charge for the cardinals to join the crusade was tied to the reality of reforming the cardinals and church in both head and members, and to refute charges that the cardinals and members of the curia lived in opulence, instead of being would-be martyrs. How were they to react to this injunction? The opulent cardinals chose to ignore it. Cusanus, the idealist prone to concordance in action as well as contemplation, like his mentor Cesarini before him, answered the call to crusade and reform. Most of the cardinals, however, were opposed to Pius's crusade from the start. And it failed right from its hasty conception. Even so, much of Pius's time and effort were invested in this failure.

Pius himself departed for Ancona in intense pain and in rapidly deteriorating health. The crusade from Ancona was ill conceived and poorly organized: little was ready even when Pius II finally arrived after suffering from the arduous journey across Italy in the intense summer heat. Boulting writes how only six Papal ships were in harbour, none of them from Venice.[64] Eventually a small fleet arrived from Venice immediately before Pius's death. He apparently never heard of the death of his friend Cusanus at Todi.[65] Pius died with Cardinal Bessarion present and his final words urged his brothers of the cross not to shrink from God's work but to go on crusade.[66] His final plea was to no avail. The Venetians hurriedly returned to Venice and the cardinals to Rome. Constantinople remained safe from any papal attack.

This narrative of Pius II's failed crusade leads us to the question lurking behind this study of religious concordance: how could Cusanus and Pius II both aspire to peace and concord, yet preach crusade? It is a difficult, troubling question that will probably never be adequately answered. This is only an attempt to contextualize the question in the thought and ecclesiology of the fifteenth century or to simply let the conflicting narratives and data remain what they are. For Pius and Cusanus, the crusade was part of the necessary reform of the church. The papal crusade must be seen in the context of reforming the cardinals first and the church at large second, or, in terms of Constance, in head and members. Pius and Cusanus both saw this as necessary:

> Oportet membra suo coaptari capiti, & illud sequi quocumque jerit. Quod agimus necessitatis est."

64 Boulting, *Æneas Silvius*, 354.
65 Boulting, *Æneas Silvius*, 355.
66 Boulting, *Æneas Silvius*, 356–357.

(1) to keep Christians from fighting each other; (2) to show that the cardinals were not elitist or out of touch with ordinary Christians called to defend their homeland;[67] and (3) to lay claim to legitimate authority. We have seen the influence of Bernard of Clairvaux and now we turn to another medieval saint. Perhaps additional clarity might be sought in the form of an unlikely heroine: Saint Catherine of Siena.

Pius himself had canonized Saint Catherine. Aeneas Piccolomini was Sienese, or at least, had had a childhood in Siena and later in life considered the city his home.[68] He was very fond of his hometown heroine. He wrote the papal Bull elevating Catherine to sainthood with his own hand in June 1461.[69] Her elevation had been delayed mainly on account of the manoeuvring of the Franciscans who had hoped Pius would canonize the Franciscan crusader Capistrano, whom Pius had known and yet still deemed unfit because of his lack of displaying miraculous graces.

In a long letter dated 12 January 1455, Pius II had corresponded with Capistrano and addressed the crusading Franciscan to "fratri iohanni de capistrano ordinis minorum".[70] True to form, Pius the humanist makes reference to Julius Caesar, Pompey and Virgil.[71] Among other matters, which included the ongoing reform in Frankfurt, as well as difficult relations with Duke Sigismund, something Cusanus knew all too well, the letter unsurprisingly addresses the ongoing and pressing conflict with the Turks.[72] Although the letter responds to the needs of the moment, as letters often do, we also see three main themes of Pius joined together: classical philosophy, ecclesial reform, and crusade against the Ottomans.

These three themes of classical thought, church reform and crusade intersect and leads us back to Catherine of Siena and Pius's final attempt at

---

67 Thomas Izbicki reminds us that after the battle of Varna (1444) in which Cusanus's close friend and mentor Julian Cesarini was killed, the crusade was no longer primarily understood to be about the recovery of the holy land, but rather the defence of Europe and turning back the Ottoman advance (Comments made at The Gettysburg Conference, The Thirteenth Biennial Conference of the International Seminar on Pre-Reformation Theology and the American Cusanus Society: Christian-Muslim Dialogue in the Late Middle Ages, 12–14 October, 2012, Gettysburg Lutheran Seminary).

68 Pius II was born in the small town of Corsignano. He later became bishop of Siena in 1450.

69 Boulting, *Æneas Silvius*, 336.

70 Vat. lat. 1787, f 140v–145v. Letter 110. The quote is from 140r. The date from 145v.

71 Vat. lat. 1787, f 142v.

72 Vat. lat. 1787, f 141r "frankfordie", "congregato concilio", f 143v "Sigismundus", f 45r "turchorum...conflixit".

crusade. Pius wrote a *Carmina* to Catherine of Siena.[73] It is included in a small, hand-written manuscript of various pithy writings, epithets, orations, etc. of Pius II.[74] This manuscript also includes a nine-line epithet to another contemporary famous Sienese, Bernardino of Siena, honouring the Franciscan for his great preaching.[75] Pius extols Catherine as celebrated by the whole world.[76] She is enraptured.[77] The song lauds her dignity as pilgrim and praises her "stigmata."[78] According to Pius, Catherine is a prophetess filled with the fullness of the divine flame that burns in both war and peace.[79] She is beatified for her devotion to Rome and to the concordant unity of the Catholic Church.[80] This prophetess was a prophet of Rome for Rome. As the last line makes clear, she was regarded by Pius as more than just a Sienese saint, but a Roman heroine in peace and in war and especially in the struggle for concordant unity.

For Pius, this struggle for unity would include reforming the church to her apostolic ideals and also restoring the unity of the now lost Christian environ of Constantinople. In this same manuscript in the Vatican library in which Pius's *Carmina* is found we also discover a note penned by Pius's secretary Jacob of Lucca describing how Pius took the cross and departed Rome for Ancona in preparation for a grand expedition against the Ottomans.[81] Jacob notes at the end of this codex how he saw the great lord leave the gate of Rome.[82] The renaissance prince on his way to battle. Followed by the death of Pius in Ancona while preparing for crusade to Constantinople.[83] The manuscript bears a final handwritten date of 1472.[84] In this small manuscript we meet

---

[73] Vat. lat. 5994, f 85 v, f 85r. There are two versions of the *Carmina*: one on f 85r, the other on f 85v. The version on the front appears in the earlier version. Each version is written in a different hand and script. Both songs are twenty-five lines long, though slightly different. The last four lines of each song are the same.

[74] Vat. lat. 5994, f 1r, heading at top: "Pius Papa Secundus" with a note by his secretary "Jacobus de Luca Secretarius", the date "1460" appears here.

[75] Vat. lat. 5994, f 2v is a nine line epithet to Bernardino of Siena where Pius honours the Franciscan for his great preaching "sermone decoro" (line 4).

[76] Vat. lat. 5994 f 85v line 3 "totum celebrata per orbem."

[77] Vat. lat. 5994 f 85r line 1 "ad sidera rapta est."

[78] Vat. lat. 5994 f 85v line 6 "viator", f 85r line 5 "stigmata."

[79] Vat. lat. 5994 f 85r lines 10–11 "Illa propheta quidem divino flamine plena / Et pacem et bellum."

[80] Vat. lat. 5994 f 85r and f 85v lines 24–25: "Millequs tercentis simul octaginta sub armis / Inclita rome obiit [recto reads: obyt] Caterina beata (verso reads: beatai) senensis."

[81] Vat. lat. 5994 f 87r "Jacobus de Luca", "Pius papa Secundus" on "xviii Iunii 1464", "Turchos."

[82] Vat. lat. 5994 f 87r "Ma nota...dela porta de Roma disse in pontia de molii grandi Signori."

[83] Vat. lat. 5994 f 87r "In theucros [Turks] bellum dum parat obiit."

[84] Vat. lat. 5994 f 86r.

Bernardino of Siena, Catherine of Siena, the theme of crusade and the death of Pius II.[85] (There are ninety folios in this codex and it ends on 90 recto). Each of the manuscripts of Pius II in the Vatican Library surveyed in this chapter focus again and again on the interrelated themes of reform and crusade, even the one which so creatively lauds Catherine of Siena.

It was Catherine who courageously urged the Avignon captive popes to return to Rome. The Roman pope had a duty to unify the church: first by reason, then, if needed, by sheer will and force of arms. It was poor Catherine who brought about so much: reform of the papacy, a restoration. What if the same could be said of the curia in Pius's day and for the moment of retaking Constantinople. Like Pius and Cusanus, Catherine was devoted to contemplation and possessed a strongly mystical side. Like Bernard of Clairvaux, though, she coupled contemplation to action and sought ecclesial unity and the authority of Rome. Pius sought to end schism and combat the heresy of the Nestorians much like Leo the Great before him.

In a Letter dated 15 February 1380 to Pope Urban VI Catherine writes, "Dearest and sweetest father in Christ gentle Jesus"[86] And, "Oh dearest Father! I won't be silent about God's mysteries."[87] She refers to the pope as her daddy. She then writes a call to action to Pope Gregory XI in Avignon in June or July of 1376, a bold summons worth quoting in full,

> Sweetest and most Holy Father, Catherine, your unworthy daughter in sweet Jesus, recommends herself to you in his precious blood. I desire to see you a real man, fearless and making no concessions to self-love, whether for yourself or for any of your blood relations, for I believe and see in the sight of God that this more than anything else is keeping you back from your good and holy desire and thwarting the honour of God and the exaltation and reform of holy church. For this reason, my soul's one desire is for God, in his infinite mercy, to take all disordered affection and lukewarmness out of your heart and make a new man of you, that is, remake you with glowing and ardent desire, for in no other way can you hope to implement what God wills and his servants long for.[88]

---

85 Vat. lat. 5994 has ninety folios.
86 Letter T373/G102 in Catherine of Siena, *The Letters of Catherine of Siena, Vol. IV*, translated by Suzanne Noffke, O.P. (Tempe, AZ: Arizona Center for Medieval and Renaissance Studies, 2008), 364.
87 Catherine of Siena, *Letters*, Noffke, 365.
88 Catherine of Siena, *I, Catherine: Selected Writings of St Catherine of Siena*, edited and translated by Kenelm Foster, OP and Mary John Ronayne, OP (London: Collins, 1980), 123.

Stirring stuff. A young woman from Siena inspiring action and reform at the highest level of Christendom. Catherine challenged the pope to be a real man of reform, or in Biblical and prophetic parlance, to gird up his loins and get down to action. Pius knew this fiery spirit well. Through canonizing Catherine he effectively canonized her call to reform and action.

The crusade is a troubling feature of Pius and Cusanus's careers as reformists and adherents to Roman authority. On the one hand you have *De pace fidei*, and Cusanus's unique vision of religious peace. And given Cusanus's correspondence with fellow student of Islam and friend from his Council of Basel days, John of Segovia, that both John and Cusanus unsuccessfully planned for an actual dialogue or council between Christians and Muslims in order to realize religious peace. In his *Letter to John* of 1454, Cusanus even called for the conversation to be led by Christian laymen, as he thought this would be more agreeable to Muslims.[89] And yet, on the other hand, we find Cusanus promoting crusade in 1454 and again with Pius II in 1464. On the eleventh of August 1464, Cusanus died at Todi while on his way to Ancona to assist his long time friend in preparations for a proposed crusade to Constantinople that never made it past the planning stages. Pius died within days of Cusanus on the fifteenth of August 1464. It would seem that the circumstance of religious violence is the cause of Cusanus's quest for peace and, paradoxically, that religion is also ultimately the answer to this quest. Yet for Cusanus, violence erupted owing to the confusion and conflation of religion with various religious rites, the many for the one while the promise of peace rested in discernment of a concordant higher wisdom beyond the diversity of these rites.[90]

For Cusanus, the one Wisdom and Word of God extends by gradual disposition throughout all beings, and through employing an image from his earlier work *De concordantia catholica* (I, 2), he seeks to unite the diversity of religions of the world in *De pace fidei*, notably Islam and Christianity, within the power of a single magnetic stone. As there is one God, one Word and Wisdom of God, plurality in unity and unity in plurality, Christianity and Islam are ultimately in their common adherence to this common Word one and the same religion. They differ in their rites, piety and practices. When seen on the vertical Neoplatonic chain of being, the practices or rites of

---

89 *Epistula ad Ioannem de Segobia* II.
90 Cusanus, *De pace fidei* I, 1: "Fuit ex hiis, quae apud Constantinopolim proxime saevissime acta per Turkorum regem divulgabantur, quidam vir zelo Dei accensus, qui loca illarum regionum aliquando viderat, ut pluribus gemitibus oraret omnium creatorem quod persecutionem, quae ob diversum ritum religionum plus solito saevit, sua pietate moderaretur."

Christianity are nearer the One or God, the source of the hierarchy, than the rites of Islam. One sees this vertical ontological view in the unfolding dialogue of *De pace fidei* as Cusanus moves from the one religion to the many rites. While according to the dialogue there is one religion in the variety of rites, nevertheless, certain Christian sacramental practices, such as baptism and communion, are understood by Cusanus as higher signs of sacred realities than ablutions, circumcisions or other sacred meals.[91] Indeed, for Cusanus, these two main rites (baptism, Eucharist) are confessed by faith and understood as sacramental sign.[92] This fits with Augustine's definition of sacrament as visible word as well as his distinction between sign (*signum*) and reality (*res*).[93] In *De pace fidei* Cusanus combines this Augustinian theory of signification with the Dionysian hierarchy of the unfolding and enfolding Word of God.[94] When the one religions is seen as a whole or seen in the entirety of rites, there is but one faith in many concordant practices.[95]

A poetic and imprecise, but interesting, parallel to Cusanus's concordant hierarchy of the Word of God and one religion in the variety of rites as both signifier and signified is found in Canto Four of Dante's *Paradiso*. Dante wonders how the blessed in the lower spheres of heaven remain happy knowing that there are many other souls above them. To this one the blessed, Piccarda dei Donati, says, "These showed themselves here, not because this sphere is allotted to them but to afford sign of the celestial grade that is least exalted. It is needful to speak thus to your faculty, since only through sense perception does it apprehend that which it afterwards makes fit for the intellect."[96] For Dante, heaven is one sweet eternal life diversified. From the perspective of human frailty, one sees diversification. From the perspective of perfection, one sees the whole in its entirety. For Cusanus, the magnetic Word of God, represented on earth as the hierarch and active in the hierarchy (as in Dante as well), moves through the chain from higher to lower, and through the incarnation of Christ, from lower (human nature of Christ) to higher (divine nature of Christ),

---

91   *De pace fidei* I, 6; XVII; XVIII, 64–66; XIX, 67.

92   *De pace fidei* XVII, 61: "Nam non est aliud baptismus quam fidei illius confessio in signo sacramentali."

93   Augustine, *Ev, Joh.* 80, 3; *De doctrina Christiana* I, 2, 2.

94   *De pace fidei* II, 7.

95   See *De pace fidei* I, 6 as spoken by the archangel in the dialogue from the perspective of heaven. Cf., *De pace fidei* I, 2: "Raptus est enim ad quondam intellectualem altitudinem, ubi quasi inter eos qui vita excesserunt examen huiusce rei in concilio excelsorum, praesidente Cunctipotenti, ita habitum est."

96   Dante, *Paradiso*, Canto IV, 37–42. *The Divine Comedy, Paradiso 1: Text*, translated by Charles S. Singleton (Princeton, Princeton University Press, 1975), 39.

and, finally, to the abode of Deity, the unified perfection of heaven. Because of ignorance due to sin, human sense perception divides and catalogues while subsequent fallen human intellect reasons discursively.[97] Thus, the imagined dialogue and discussion, set in the heaven of reason, makes religious unity fit for the intellect to put it in Dante's words. Thus, to put in Cusanus's words, "a single easy harmony [of religion] could be found and through it a lasting peace established by appropriate and true means."[98] This religious unity is made fit for the intellect through connecting the many rites to the one religion through the single easy harmony of the Word of God which extends to all things, enfolding and unfolding all things.[99] From the perspective of human ignorance, one sees rites in diversity of religions. From the perspective of enlightened perfection, one sees religion in the diversity of rites.[100] Cusanus begins *De pace fidei* with the Neoplatonic and Dionysian movement from God to the Word of God, God from God (Christ) to the angels to the representatives of the world's religions. As Proclus, the great systematizer of Neoplatonism, begins his *Elements of Theology* with the One and not the many and moves from the simple to the complex, the whole to the parts, from the One to the henads, so also Cusanus starts his dialogue with the One God and then discusses the Trinity, Christology, Sacrament, and rites and ethics of the church.[101] For Cusanus the many rites emanate from one God and one religion. At each point in his ecclesial and philosophical career Cusanus sought the underlying concordance of all things, whether that be of the council of Basel and the pope, Eastern and Western Churches, or, ultimately, Christianity and Islam through the magnetic and dialectical Word and Wisdom of God. In this search for concordance, perspective matters. From which religious vantage point does one see? This side of heaven, one's sight obscured by ignorance confuses rites for religion. In the heaven of reason, the enlightened sees one religion in the diversity of rites and freely consents to the concordance of Islam and Christianity.

Even so, how could Cusanus and Pius II reconcile the promotion of crusade with that of Christian-Muslim dialogue? More specifically, how is it possible for Cusanus to engage in Christian-Muslim dialogue based on the ancient Greek principle of *sapientia* while also promoting crusade and religious

---

97   *De pace fidei* II, 7.
98   *De pace fidei* I, 1; English translation by Biechler and Bond; "unam posse facilem quondam concordantiam reperiri".
99   *De concordantia catholica* I, 2; *De pace fidei* II, 7.
100 *De pace fidei* I, 1.
101 Proclus, *The Elements of Theology*, props. 1 and 5, translated by E.R. Dodds (Oxford: Clarendon Press, 1963), 3, 5.

violence? There is an interesting analogy here to the structure of Cusanus's first major work *De concordantia catholica*, which, in turn, leads to a conjectural answer. We have already seen how according to the foundational book one of *De concordantia catholica*, the Word of God extends by gradation to all ranks of being. This Word of God flows down the chain of being from the one heaven or dwelling of God (beyond gradation). Furthermore, in *De concordantia catholica*, Cusanus envisions the ultimate harmony of church and empire and church and world through the hierarchical and conciliar Word of God. The Word of God expands to all creation, even all being. The truth of the Word of God is present to all things.[102] All things are not present to the truth of the Word of God.[103] Furthermore, we have seen how perspective matters and how the dialogue of *De pace fidei* imaginatively occurs in the heaven of reason in order to enlighten those lost in the flux of temporal confusion over religion and religious rites. Thus, Cusanus's dialogical construct of religious participants in the heaven of reason are nearer to the Word of God and the truth of the peace of faith, while those below are stuck in the tangled web of religious misunderstanding and persecution, and, thereby, further away from both the Word of God and corollary religious concordance.[104] *De pace fidei* covers religious harmony, but also captures Cusanus's grand conception of the Word of God (*Verbum Dei*) in relation to the cosmos. *De concordantia catholica* covers the relationship between church and empire, council and pope, but also begins with Cusanus's sweeping conception of the Word of God in relation to all ranks of being. The specific arguments of both *De pace fidei* (religious concordance) and *De concordantia catholica* (concordance of church and pope, church and empire) are grounded on Cusanus's understanding of the inherent interrelatedness of Word and world, Word and gradations of being.

In both *De concordantia catholica* and *De pace fidei*, Cusanus's goal is to find and realize religious harmony. This harmony is centered in the Wisdom and Word of God which flows through everything. *De concordantia catholica* and *De pace fidei* begin with the centrality of the dialectical and hierarchical Wisdom and Word of God.[105] Both also begin in the realm of enlightened perfection, the heavenly context of unity. Thus, *De pace fidei* commences in the

---

102 *De pace fidei* II, 7.
103 Thus, according to *De pace fidei*, the need for enlightenment through the Word of God in the form of dialogue. Cf., *De concordantia catholica* I, 1 focuses on Scripture, God's revelation. Cusanus begins *De concordantia catholica* with enlightenment through the Word of God.
104 *De pace fidei* XIX, 68.
105 *De pace fidei* II, 7; *De pace fidei* IV; *De concordantia catholica* I, 2.

heaven of reason with the intellectual beings prior to the heavenly council of religious representatives, while *De concordantia catholica* begins with the celestial marriage of Christ and the church and the mysterious Trinity in unity of the divine Essence.[106] In *De concordantia catholica* Cusanus first considers the concordance of the church as a whole, before discussing the intricate interplay between pope and council, church and empire.[107] Furthermore, both *De concordantia catholica* and *De pace fidei* conclude with the theme of unity flowing forth into the cosmos in concentric and circulatory movements. *De pace fidei* ends with the wise religious representatives of the world returning to the ends of the earth in order to lead all nations to the unity of faith in a sweeping emanation of concord radiating from the center of the heaven of reason.[108] *De concordantia catholica* ends with the analogy of the human body as illustration of the interrelatedness of church and empire with the priests as the soul and the faithful as the body.[109] The animating life-force of the body, according to Cusanus, flows from the Holy Spirit, whose creative breath inspires the church to charity, unity and reform.[110] In *De pace fidei*, Cusanus identifies the Holy Spirit as nexus of unity (the Father) and equality (the Son), and, as nexus of charity whose power is diffused throughout the universe. The Holy Spirit-nexus-charity unites the many into one and connects to unity and equality and the peace of faith.[111] Both at the beginning and end of *De concordantia catholica* and *De pace fidei*, Cusanus returns to the whole, the nexus of unity: as the peace of one religion and as the body of Christendom.

While *De pace fidei* and *De concordantia catholica* begin and end with unity, in the middle of each work we find the coincidence of opposites: in *De pace fidei*, one religion in the variety of rites, the Word and words, and in *De concordantia catholica*, the pope and council, church and empire. The overarching goal is harmony. This side of paradise dialectical hierarchy flows from and returns to cosmic concordance. Finding and realizing that essential harmony in temporal flux, assumes, for Cusanus, the need for revelation and the nexus of divine aid.

---

106 *De pace fidei* I, 2 angels as "intellectuales virtutes", Cf., Dionysius, *De coelesti hierarchia*, Chp. 9; *De pace fidei* XIX, 68; *De concordantia catholica* I, 1, 6, see also the preface to *De concordantia catholica* in which Cusanus describes the whole of the work: the one harmony of the church in body (laity) and soul (priesthood).
107 *De concordantia catholica*, preface, 3.
108 *De pace fidei* XIX, 68.
109 *De concordantia catholica* III, 41.
110 *De concordantia catholica* III, 41, 580. Cf., *De concordantia catholica*, preface, 3.
111 *De pace fidei* VIII, 24; *De pace fidei* X, 27: "Hinc amor, qui Deus est seu caritas. Dici potest hic spiritus cuius vis est diffusa per universum; ita quod nexus quo partes ad unum seu totum connectuntur, sine quo perfectio nulla subsisteret, habeat Deum suum principium."

In Cusanus's mind, the peace of faith and the concordance of Christendom are eternally realized in heaven and revealed point by point in the cascade of temporal dialectics. From beginning with the church as a whole in the preface of *De concordantia catholica*, Cusanus moves onto his delicate balancing act of holding together the seemingly opposite views of papal authority and conciliar power and consent.[112] Yet, ultimately, for Cusanus, the council and pope, the priesthood and laity form one body with many parts as appears in his final analogy of the work.[113] In *De pace fidei*, Cusanus begins with the divine revelation in the heaven of reason of one religion in the variety of rites. From there the religious representatives of the world are imaginatively gathered and begin to dialectically realize, point by point, this fundamental concordance in a kind of enlightened speculative state of learned ignorance. And, for Cusanus, the hidden, infinite Godhead from whom flows all perfection and peace, eludes human conjecture and discursive reasoning.[114]

Cusanus was a mystical, Neoplatonic theologian, but also a committed cardinal of the Catholic Church, a coincidence of opposites of sorts where action coincides with contemplation. Indeed his life was often stuck in discursive and volitional dilemmas, whether it be contenting with Duke Sigismund or dutifully preaching crusade. Violence, while not the first option for Cusanus, may be deemed necessary by him and his contemporaries in order to restore fractured unity and realize peace this side of paradise.

Ultimately, though Cusnus never actually went on crusade, he died while preparing to venture forth to Constantinople. He did indeed promote crusade. According to Cusanus, this fallen world is the realm of action and conjectures, where sinful ignorance leads to confusing religious rites for religion.[115] Cusanus sought actual religious dialogue in his *Letter to John of Segovia* of 1454. What occurs in *De pace fidei* figuratively represents Cusanus's literal plans for dialogue. It is imaginatively set in the celestial altitude of reason, and intended for a Western European Christian audience in order that heaven and earth may one day agree on religious peace between Christians and Muslims. This vision of peace remained, finally, only a vision as seen by Cusanus from afar, blurred by the fog of war.

There seems to exist in Cusanus's mind an uncanny ability to hold together various speculative formations of the coincidence of opposites and

---

112   On the authority of the pope (hierarchy) and council (consent), see, for example, *De concordantia catholica* I, 15, 61; II, 7, 95–96a; II, 13, 115–118; II, 15, 135–136; II, 18, 156–164.
113   *De concordantia catholica* III, 41.
114   *De pace fidei* I, 4; *De coniecturis* I, 2.
115   *De pace fidei* II, 7; III, 8.

infinite unity beyond the coincidence of opposites. He is prone to exploring theological paradox and enticed by the enigma of Deity. God is *non aliud* and the Word made flesh, infinitely unknown and finitely knowable. Cusanus also seems willing to adhere to religious dialogue and crusade. It would seem that for Cusanus, violence may be needed to restore unity in church and empire, but only after dialogue and dialectic fail. Furthermore, violence is neither the primary nor preferred option. *De pace fidei*, written shortly after the fall of Constantinople, represents his primary response to what he perceived to be the Ottoman threat. As history regrettably shows, it was not his only response. For Cusanus, in line with medieval-western church teaching, this violence, should it finally prove necessary, would somehow be seen as legitimate when called by right authority (i.e., the pope) for just cause.[116] While today this proves to be a troubling aspect of Cusanus's life and teachings, we should, perhaps, nonetheless, be careful in our investigation of separating Cusanus the churchman from Cusanus the speculative dialogist.

Furthermore, we should also be cautious in classifying Cusanus's works. While *De concordantia catholica* and *De pace fidei* no doubt differ in context and content, both share a marked structural similarity in their beginning and ending with the whole and their emphasis on concordance, as well as holding together seeming opposites: pope and council, religious rites and religion. We seek to read Cusanus the cardinal and Cusanus the visionary in Cusanus's own words, and, as far as we are able, in his own context. And yet, as Cusanus's friend and fellow churchman Pius II surmised, the only earthly ruler and Platonic philosopher-king in the context of the fifteenth century with the potential to achieve temporal peace leading to lasting religious concord was the ruler of the city which bridged West and East and fused ancient thought and nascent empire, Constantinople and Istanbul: Mehmed the conqueror.

In the first four chapters of this study, we have tracked Cusanus's sojourn in search of religious concordance between Muslims and Christians in *De pace fidei* and "religio una in rituum varitate", as well as conciliar influences, philosophical and theological sources, and the idea of crusade and the paradox of peace.[117] Now we turn to Cusanus the visionary. With the next chapter we will approach Cusanus as visionary by first looking at Cusanus's visions of peace and his outline for dialogue as proposed to Juan of Segovia. We will also look at his move from Council to pope to prophet of religious peace.

---

116 On how the papal proponents of crusade transmitted and applied Augustine's views on just cause and legitimate authority, see Jonathan Riley-Smith, *What Were the Crusades?*, 3rd Edition (San Francisco: Ignatius Press, 2002).

117 *De pace fidei* I, 6.

While in this chapter we surmised an inferred and preliminary discussion on how Cusanus could preach crusade and propose dialogue, in those following we will also attempt to shed new light on another problematic in Cusanus studies: the vexing question of how Cusanus could shift from a conciliar to papal monarchist position. Citing Cusanus's own words, these chapters are but conjectures.[118] We now turn to address his visions of peace, followed by examining his move from council to pope to prophet of religious concordance. From there we proceed to a detailed analysis of Cusanus's conception of the Word of God in *De pace fidei* and how it relates to the metaphysics of his other major works.

---

118   *De coniecturis* I, 2.

CHAPTER 5

Visions of Peace

In the last days it will be, God declares,
that I will pour out my Spirit upon all flesh,
and your sons and your daughters shall prophesy,
and your young men shall see visions,
and your old men shall dream dreams.[1]

∴

Cusanus's library in Kues includes an exquisite early thirteenth-century copy of Hildegard of Bingen's *Scivias*.[2] The finely preserved and beautifully crafted medieval manuscript shows that Nicholas from Kues on the banks of the Mosel River was familiar with the visionary Hildegard from nearby Bingen on the Rhine. Hildegard, like Cusanus, was also both actively involved in the ecclesial and secular politics of her day and yet inclined to mystical contemplation. As with Cusanus, her stunning visions as recorded in the *Scivias* are truly cosmic in scope.[3] Cusanus's *De docta ignorantia* unfolds what Cusanus testified to be a concordant vision of the coincidence of opposites radiating from the very centre of the cosmos.[4] *De pace fidei* presents a cosmic and creative vision of one religion in the variety of rites as revealed by the Word of God through angelic ministration and hierarchy.[5] When seen together, the vision

---

1 Acts 2:17 NRSV.
2 Cod. Cus. 63. The date 1210 is found on f 140r "anno dominice incarnationis MCCX."
3 For English translation of *Scivias*, see Hildegard of Bingen, *Scivias*, translated by Mother Columba Hart and Jane Bishop (New York: Paulist Press, 1990). An example of Hildegard's cosmic visions is *Scivias*, vision two, a sweeping account of the creation and fall.
4 *De docta ignorantia, Epistola auctoris ad Dominum Iulianum Cardinalem*. On Cusanus and mystical theology, see Bernard McGinn, *The Presence of God, A History of Western Christian Mysticism: The Harvest of Mysticism in Medieval Germany* (New York: Herder and Herder, 2005), 432–483. McGinn focuses on Cusanus's contribution to mystical theology (as more than accounts of extatic experiences of God). Here we seek to integrate Cusanus's visions of illumination (mystical theology) with his dialogical and Christocentric approach to Islam in *De pace fidei*. See also: William J. Hoye, *Die Mystische Theologie des Nicolaus Cusanus* (Freiburg: Herder, 2004).
5 *De pace fidei* I.

of learned ignorance and *De pace fidei* further enlighten Cusanus's dialectic of religious concordance and peace on a truly cosmic scale. Thus far we have followed Cusanus's sojourn on the path to elusive religious peace. We traced his all embracing religious concordance of "una religio in rituum varietate", the context of late medieval Christian approaches to Islam, prominent philosophical and theological sources and the troubling interplay of religion and violence.[6] In this chapter, we observe Cusanus as visionary of religious peace by comparing his vision of learned ignorance with his vision of religious concordance. We will also peruse Cusanus's controversial move from conciliarist at the Council of Basel to papal apologist and how this relates to his visionary and prophetic call for peace between Christians and Muslims in *De pace fidei*.[7]

We now look briefly at two interrelated visions: *De docta ignorantia* and *De pace fidei*. How are these visions alike? What unites them? These visions have not yet been closely studied together.[8] A related and more vexing question also surfaces in our study, what unites Cusanus's hierarchical metaphysics of the Word of God in *De concordantia catholica* with *De pace fidei*? What correlates these writings points beyond to yet another still much debated interrelated query: why did Cusanus change from a councilarist to a papal monarchist? The dialectical and hierarchical answers to these analogous and interrelated questions of how to combine council and pope, rites and religion in the mind as well as the career of Cusanus, the master of learned ignorance and the coincidence of opposites, shed light on why he transitioned from adhering to the authority of the general council to loyally serving the pope. The visions of *De docta ignorantia* and *De pace fidei* present the viewer with a panorama of Cusanus's metaphysical thought on Christian-Muslim dialogue. While these visions are contemplative in design and metaphysical in scope, they also are grounded in the realm of temporal action. *De docta ignorantia* follows the attempt by Cusanus and the Roman Curia to reconcile Eastern and Western Churches. *De pace fidei* ensues after the bloodshed raging over confusion of religion and religious rites and the fall of Constantinople.[9] Furthermore, as Cusanus's Dionysian views on the papacy are developed within the context of fifteenth-century ecclesiological controversy, the contemplative vision of *De pace fidei* is located in the reality of Cusanus's plan for a general council between Muslims and Christians as expressed in his *Letter to John of Segovia*. The metaphysical

---

6 *De pace fidei* I, 6.
7 On Cusanus's religious dialogue as prophetic: *De pace fidei* unfolds the Word of God as preached by prophets. This same prophetic Word appears in the mind of Cusanus to once and for all lead the wise of the world to one religion in the diversity of rites (*De pace fidei* I, 4; II, 7).
8 I know of no major study or article that directly compares these two visions.
9 *De pace fidei* I, 1.

VISIONS OF PEACE 145

visions of *De docta ignorantia* and *De pace fidei* find their counterparts in the complex political life of Cusanus.

Envisioning Peace: *De docta ignorantia* and *De pace fidei*

While on a voyage from Constantinople to Venice in 1438 Cusanus received a vision of illumination. At the conclusion of *De docta ignorantia*, Cusanus describes the transcendental experience as "a celestial gift from the Father of Lights."[10] This divine benevolence was the revelation of learned ignorance, which knows that it does not know God. For Cusanus, echoing Anselm of Canterbury, "the maximum learning of ignorance" is connected to "the maximum, that beyond which there can be nothing greater."[11] In the prologue of *De docta*

---

10 *De docta ignorantia, Epistola auctoris ad Dominum Iulianum Cardinalem*, translation by Bond, 206. *De docta ignorantia* was completed by Nicholas of Cusa in his hometown of Kues in 1440. The revelation at sea occurred sometime between 27 November 1437 and 8 February 1438. The English translation of *De docta ignorantia* used in this work is by H. Lawrence Bond in: *Nicholas of Cusa: Selected Spiritual Writings*, trans. H. Lawrence Bond (New York: Paulist Press, 1997), pp. 85–206. See also the English translation by Jasper Hopkins, *Nicholas of Cusa On Learned Ignorance: A Translation and an Appraisal of De Docta Ignorantia*, (Minneapolis: The Arthur J. Banning Press, 1981). See also, "Nicholas of Cusa from Constantinople to 'Learned Ignorance': The Historical Matrix for the Formation of the *De docta ignorantia*", 135–164. Bond notes that while in Constantinople Cusanus probably procured a Greek edition of the works of Pseudo-Dionysius the Areopagite (141). Cusanus's return journey to Italy from Constantinople finds its metaphysical parallel in his fusion in *De docta ignorantia* of Eastern mystical thought, characterized by Pseudo-Dionysius, with the heightened focus on imitating Christ and the affective experience of salvation, as found in Western Europe in the fourteenth century. Cusanus combines the apophatic theology of the East as epitomized in Pseudo-Dionysius with the affective theology of the West as found in the *devotio moderna*, and further back still in the *Sermons on the Song of Songs* by Bernard of Clairvaux. This metaphysical and mystical melding of East and West is seen in book one (*De docta ignorantia* I, 26,) together with book three, which concludes with a cataphatic and concrete discussion of the Church and the affective call to virtue and imitating Christ (*De docta ignorantia* III, 12, 257). See also, Cranz, "Nicholas Cusanus and Dionysius Areopagita" in *Nicholas of Cusa and the Renaissance*, 109–136. Cranz observes that after his revelation on the return voyage from Constantinople, Nicholas of Cusa began to seriously study the works of Pseudo-Dionysius (118). See also, Casarella, "*His Name is Jesus:* Negative Theology and Christology in Two Writings of Nicholas of Cusa from 1440" in *Nichols of Cusa on Christ and the Church*, 281–307.

11 *De docta ignorantia* I, 2, 5, Bond, p. 89: "Maximum autem hoc dico, quo nihil maius esse potest." In Chapter 2 of the *Proslogion*, Anselm describes God as "something than which nothing greater can be thought" in: *Anselm of Canterbury, The Major Works*, eds. Brian Davies and Gillian Evans (Oxford: Oxford University Press, 1998), 87.

ignorantia, Cusanus speaks of his labour to formulate and express such an apophatic, yet concrete theological method of approaching the maximum where reason falters and ignorance prevails.[12] Yet for Cusanus, the toilsome endeavour which proves that the more one learns the more ignorant one becomes, originates in the innate muse of natural wonder, a thought provoking natural theology, which comes from the the delight we take in our senses.[13] Quoting the opening of Aristotle's *Metaphysics,* Cusanus writes, "So I think it consistent that wondering, the cause of philosophy, precedes the desire to know in order that the intellect, whose understanding is its being, will be perfected by the pursuit of truth."[14] This wonder driven "pursuit of truth" unfolds in three intricate books which correspond to the tripartite discussion of God, "the maximum," followed by the unitary universe, which is "the maximum from the absolute," and finally, Jesus Christ, the incarnate Word, who is the absolute maximum, the absolute minimum, the "universal goal" and the "most perfect end beyond all our capacity."[15] Only after diagrams of spheres, triangles and the dizzying mathematics of book one, the vast and vexing cosmology of book two, and the Chalcedonian Christology of book three, the reader of *De docta ignorantia* and the wise, but foolish student of that which cannot be known, realizes that the fullness of the coincidence of opposites and the subtle art of concordance, about which one wonders and seeks, must be revealed from

12   *De docta ignorantia,* prologus, Bond, p. 87.
13   Aristotle, *Metaphysics* I, 1, 980a.
14   *De docta ignorantia,* prologus, 87. Aristotle writes in *Metaphysics,* bk I, Chp 2, 982b: "For it is owing to their wonder that men both now begin and at first began to philosophize." Translated by W.D. Ross, in: Richard McKeon, ed., *The Basic Works of Aristotle* (New York: Random House, 1941), 692. On the act of knowing and God's being compare with Aquinas, who writes in *Summa Theologiæ* Ia., 16, 6, *De Deo,* "Nam esse suum non solum est conforme suo intellectui, sed etiam est ipsum suum intelligere; et suum intelligere est mensura et causa omnis alterius esse et omnis alterius intellectus; et ipse est suum intelligere et suum esse. Unde sequitur quod non solum in ipso sit veritas, sed quod ipse sit summa et prima veritas." "[God's] being is not only in conformity with his intellect, but is his very act of knowing; and his act of knowing is the measure and cause of all other being and all other intellect; and he himself is his own being and his own act of knowing. Hence it follows not only that truth is in God but also that he is the supreme and original truth." Thomas Aquinas, *Summa Theologiæ,* Volume 4 (1a, qq. 14–18), reprint of the Blackfriars edition (Cambridge: Cambridge University Press, 2006), 88–89.
15   *De docta ignorantia* I, 2, 5–8, Bond, pp. 89–90. Nicholas of Cusa's carefully worded statement about the universe being "the maximum from the absolute" appears to negate any notion of pantheism. In addition, in *De docta ignorantia,* book II, Chapter I, Section 97, Cusanus writes, "Indeed the universe is the creation, which necessarily derives from absolute and simply divine being" (Bond, p. 131).

God. It was through a contemplative vision of some kind from God, Cusanus writes, that he "was led to embrace incomprehensibles incomprehensibly."[16]

In 1453 Cusanus received another vision of illumination. At this point in his career Cusanus, the proposer of what he deemed the "barbarous ineptitudes" of *De docta ignorantia*, was now a cardinal, bishop of Brixen, and papal reformer for the German speaking lands.[17] News of the fall of Constantinople to the Ottoman Empire had just travelled by way of the Mediterranean to Venice and from there throughout Western Europe. The accounts of returning survivors concerning the fall of Constantinople caused much distress for political rulers, ecclesiastical leaders and the laity, yet led to little political or military response.[18] Cusanus heard the reports of the end of Byzantium and responded with a Platonic dialogue of universal religious peace based on what he intellectually saw. The dialogue is *De pace fidei*.[19] At the very beginning of the dialogue, Nicholas of Cusa writes of his vision,

> After the brutal deeds recently committed by the Turkish ruler at Constantinople were reported to a certain man, who had seen the sites of those regions, he was inflamed by a zeal for God; with many sighs he implored the Creator of all things that in his mercy he restrain the persecution, raging more than ever because of different religious rites. It happened that after several days—perhaps because of long continued meditation—a vision was revealed to this zealous man.[20]

Mehmed II is "the Turkish ruler" while the "certain man ... inflamed by a zeal for God" who remembered the sights of Constantinople is none other than Cusanus himself, who, as has been shown, visited Constantinople in 1437, sixteen years prior to the city's collapse and his consequent composition of *De*

---

16 *De docta ignorantia, Epistola auctoris ad Dominum Iulianum Cardinalem*, Bond, p. 206: "incomprehensibilia incomprehensibiliter".
17 *De docta ignorantia*, prologus, Bond, p. 87.
18 Steven Runciman, *The Fall of Constantinople 1453*, 160–181.
19 Other consulted English translations of *De pace fidei*: John Patrick Dolan, ed., *Unity and Reform: Selected Writings of Nicholas de Cusa*, (Notre Dame, IN: University of Notre Dame Press, 1962), 195–237, and Jasper Hopkins, *Nicholas of Cusa's De Pace Fidei and Cribratio Alkorani: Translation and Analysis* (Minneapolis, MN: The Arthur J. Banning Press, 1981).
20 *De pace fidei* I, 1, Biechler and Bond, p. 3: "Fuit ex hiis, quae apud Constantinopolim proxime saevissime acta per Turkorum regem divulgabantur, quidam vir zelo Dei accensus, qui loca illarum regionum aliquando viderat, ut pluribus gemitibus oraret omnium creatorem quod persecutionem, quae ob diversum ritum religionum plus solito saevit, sua pietate moderaretur."

pace fidei. It was on the return voyage from Constantinople that he received what he claimed to be divine enlightenment of learned ignorance. Constantinople plays a pivotal role in the visions of both learned ignorance and *De pace fidei*. The former vision occurred on the sojourn back from Constantinople and the latter resulted from the city's demise. The visions also relate to one another on a deeper metaphysical level. The vision of learned ignorance and the vision of *De pace fidei* are both visions of unity and perfection. In the vision of learned ignorance the method of apprehending God who is beyond knowing is perfected by the illumination of divine revelation. While in *De pace fidei* universal consent to religious concordance is made possible only through the mediation of the Word of God.

In the second vision of religious harmony, the dialogue reaches beyond the Church, of both West and East. It is a universal vision with a universal goal: concordance of the world's religions by way of the Word of God which leads to lasting peace. As in *De docta ignorantia*, God originates and initiates the vision. Cusanus prayed and prepared himself to receive a vision of contemplation. The vision on the return journey from Constantinople was preceded by serious meditative and scholarly attempts "to attain by different paths of learning" to finding harmony between maximum and minimum, religion and rites.[21] The argument and flow of *De pace fidei*, like *De docta ignorantia*, advance towards concordance. What is new about the vision of *De pace fidei* as compared to *De docta ignorantia* is that this revealed Word now travels beyond Christendom and encompasses the known religions of the world. Both visions struggle with the necessity of divine illumination to know the absolute maximum, the cosmos, and the incarnate Word, as well as religious harmony. The two visions show that knowledge of the divine and religious peace can only ultimately be realized through revelation, yet the revelation is not merely for the visionary.[22] Cusanus relates the visions to his context: namely Latin Christendom. And as with Aquinas, revelation is not just speculative and contemplative; it is also practical. It is precisely the combination of theory and practice, contemplation and action, vision and vocation that make sacred doctrine the noblest of sciences.[23]

---

21 *De docta ignorantia, Epistola auctoris ad Dominum Iulianum Cardinalem*, Bond, p. 205.

22 Cf., the return of the philosopher-king to the cave after beholding the sun, Plato, *Republic* VII, 516d–517b.

23 Aquinas, *Summa Theologiæ*, Ia. 1, 5. Aquinas writes, "Since the science of sacred doctrine is partly theoretical and partly practical, it ranks above any other science, whether theoretical or practical" (Davies, Leftow, 9). See also *Summa Theologiæ* Ia. 1, 4, responsio: "Unde licet in scientiis philosophicis alia sit speculativa et alia practica, sacra tamen

Envisioning Dialogue: Nicholas of Cusa's *Letter to John of Segovia*

Having glanced at the contemplative visions of unity and peace, we now glimpse what actually could be by comparing the proposed dialogical talking points in Cusanus's *Letter to John of Segovia* (1454) on plans for a Christian-Muslim dialogue or conference to the systematic theological structure of *De pace fidei*.[24] As we have seen, the dialogue of *De pace fidei* is Neoplatonic in genre, dialectical in argument, and conciliar is shape. Christology is the chief theological locus Cusanus explicates in *De pace fidei* and in his *Letter to John* on a proposed Christian-Muslim gathering to discuss religious concordance.[25] As with *De pace fidei*, Cusanus's *Letter to John* addressess the Christian concept of the Trinity before turning to Christology.[26] While *De pace fidei* was written as imaginative peacemaking for a Latin Christian audience, it was never altogether removed from reality. This may be seen in its immediate occasion, the fall of Constantinople, but also in the carefully selected sequence of theological talking points, which reveal sensitivity to genuine Muslim concerns, especially confusion and consternation over what Christians confess about Christ. Although Cusanus's letter to his old friend John of Segovia addresses the perceived need for a defence of the Christian faith as occasioned by the fall of Constantinople, it also contends for considerably more than apologetics.[27] The letter proposes late-medieval religious dialogue or dialectical conversation

---

doctrina comprehendit sub se utramque, sicut et Deus eadem scientia se cognoscit et ea quæ facit." According to Aquinas, sacred doctrina leads to beatitude beyond reason and insofar as it is a practical science, its aim is eternal happiness (*Summa Theologiæ* Ia, 5; Cf., *De pace fidei* XVI, 57). Moving in a similar direction, Cusanus's revealed visions of *De docta ignorantia* and *De pace fidei*, while employing reason, point beyond to reveal a complete theological method of unknowing (*De docta ignorantia*), and universal religious concordance (*De pace fidei*) through the enlightenment of peace from the hidden God.

24 The Latin text is found in vol. VII of the Heidelberg critical edition of Cusanus's writings, as well as *Nicolai de Cusa, De pace fidei*, Medieval and Renaissance Studies, Supplement III. The *Letter* is dated 29 December 1454 (*Epistula ad Ioannem de Segobia* III, p. 102, line 15). The pagination of the *Letter* is the same in both the Heidelberg edition and the Medieval and Renaissance Studies Supplement. For summary background information on the *Letter* and Cusanus's interactions with John, see Southern, *Western Views of Islam in the Middle Ages*, 86–94.

25 *De pace fidei* X–XV; *Epistula ad Ioannem de Segobia* II, p. 98, line 5–p. 100, line 15, which includes soteriology under Christology.

26 *Epistula ad Ioannem de Segobia* II, p. 97, line 20–p. 98, line 5; *De pace fidei* VII, 20-X.

27 *Epistula ad Ioannem de Segobia* I, p. 93, line 15 in the Heidelberg edition. Speaking of John, Cusanus writes, "Nam nunc fidei orthodoxae defensio exigebat talem zelosum atque apprime doctum."

from the context and starting point of shared philosophical tradition. Cusanus argues for the employment of reason and the illumination of revelation to promote a conference, or bringing together, of Christians and Muslims for the sake of religious concordance.[28]

Cusanus's *De pace fidei* was written as a sensible and imaginative 'letter' to his Christian readers in Western Europe on how to think about the complex correlations between Christianity and Islam following the fall of Constantinople.[29] While *De pace fidei* contends for religious concordance in general, the timing and context of the letter, as well as the imagined Muslim participants in the dialogue, disclose that he expressly had reconciliation with Islam in mind. Moreover, while *De pace fidei* reads as contemplative vision, when paired with his *Letter to John*—naïve as it may in hindsight be—it nonetheless uncovers what Cusanus thought possible in Christian-Muslim dialogue. In *De pace fidei* Cusanus assumes the aims of Platonic dialectic and classical theism as typified in the popular medieval summation of Western scholastic theology, Aquinas's *Summa Theologiæ*, and applies them to real Muslim theological concerns.[30] Throughout *De pace fidei* Cusanus unpacks in somewhat stilted but constructive conversational form how Muslims may employ reason to consent to the revealed 'sacred doctrine' of one religion in the variety of rites. He creatively reasons in ways that hopefully might prove congenial to Muslims. Echoing the opening of *De docta ignorantia*, Cusanus begins *De pace fidei* with the basic tenets of apophatic theology: God is hidden and cannot be known.[31] God reveals the concordance of religion hierarchically through angels and the Word of God. Like the foundational first question of the *prima pars* of Aquinas's *Summa Theologiæ*, the prologue of *De pace fidei* aims to reveal the big picture to the reader. Additionally, the whole becomes parsed and only fully realized through the respectful art of conversation, or in

---

28 *Epistula ad Ioannem de Segobia* II, p. 100, line 15 in the Heidelberg edition, "conferendum".
29 *De pace fidei* I, 1: "Unde, ut haec visio ad notitiam eorum qui hiis maximis praesunt aliquando deveniret, eam quantum memoria praesentabat, plane subter conscripsit."
30 Aquinas, *Summa Theologiæ* Ia. 1. Aquinas's dialectical method of the *Summa Theologiæ* developed out of classroom lecture and discussion. Similarly, the shape of *De pace fidei* originated from Cusanus's scholarly interest in Islam, his journey to Constantinople, his experience in learning scholastic thought in lectures at the University of Heidelberg and the many hours spent participating in various church councils.
31 *De docta ignorantia* I, 1; I, 26; *De pace fidei* I, 4–5. Cf., Aquinas, *Summa Theologiæ* Ia, 2. For a similar theological order, see book II of *Cribratio Alkorani*: God as ineffable mystery, apophatic, mystical theology, *Cribratio Alkorani* II, 1; *De Deo, Cribratio Alkorani* II, 2–3; *De Deo trino, Cribratio Alkorani* II, 5–11; Christology and soteriology, *Cribratio Alkorani* II, 12–19.

the case of the *Summa Theologiæ*, by way of dialectical argumentation. The religious leaders of the dialogue, especially the Muslim interlocutors, employ reason dialectically in order to achieve consent to one religion in the variety of rites.[32] Cusanus envisions the dialogue through the Word of God conversationally and sequentially: first, *De Deo*, specifically, one God as philosophical concept of Wisdom and Word, followed by *De Deo trino*, God as "unity" (Father), "equality" (Son), and "nexus" (Spirit).[33] The general order and common terms, according to Cusanus, are meant to appeal to collective philosophical concepts as assumed by both medieval Christians and Muslims.[34]

Having considered the similarities, Cusanus moves on to treat the differences. Cusanus was certainly aware that Muslims object to the belief that Jesus the Messiah is the Son of God.[35] Thus, he spends considerable time in *De pace fidei* dealing with Christology only after discussing Wisdom, Word, and plurality in unity in the context of *Logos* theology. He seeks common ground on the concentric concepts of Wisdom and Word as related to Deity, and unity, equality and nexus in Trinity, before dealing with the more divisive issue of who Jesus is. Cusanus unpacks Christology in much the same way he expounds the Trinity, viz. by appealing to universal expressions and aspirations: e.g. Jesus as source and supplier of happiness and immortality.[36]

The contemplative and felicitous conceptualization of religious concordance in *De pace fidei* becomes concrete in aspirations for a Christian-Muslim conference as proposed in Cusanus's Christocentric *Letter to John*. In the Letter, Cusanus explicitly mentions *De pace fidei* right before he discusses the outline

---

32   Cf., Aquinas, *Summa Theologiæ* Ia, 1, 1; I, 8.

33   *De Deo* on Wisdom and the Word, *De pace fidei* IV–VII; *De Deo trino* on unity, equality, nexus, *De pace fidei* VIII–XI; Biechler, Bond, p. 25. Cf., Aquinas, *Summa Theologiæ*, *De Deo*, Ia. 2–26; *De Deo trino*, Ia. 27–43.

34   Cf., *Epistula ad Ioannem de Segobia* II, p. 98, line 5: "Expertus sum tam apud Iudaeos quam ipsos Teucros non esse difficile persuadere trinitatem in unitate substantiae."

35   *Epistula ad Ioannem de Segobia* II, p. 98, line 5: "Sed circa unionem ypostaticam, in qua principaliter ultra unum Deum colentes nostra fides consistit, non minus difficile erit nunc quam semper ab initio." *De pace fidei* XI, 30; *Cribratio Alkorani*, alius prologus, 15; I, 9, 51.

36   *De pace fidei* XV; *Cribratio Alkorani* II, 18, 153; Cf., Aquinas, *Summa Theologiæ* Ia. 1, 1: *responsio*: "Dicendum quod necessarium fuit ad humanam salutem esse doctrinam quamdam secundum revelationem divinam præter philosophicas disciplinas quæ ratione humana investigantur. Primo quidem quia homo ordinatur a Deo ad quemdam finem qui comprehensionem rationis excedit."

of the proposed Christian-Muslim gathering.[37] More importantly, Cusanus follows a similar order of theological *loci* that accentuates the importance of Christ. By way of comparison, book one of the *Cribratio Alkorani* also deals almost exclusively with the Gospel of Jesus Christ and Christology as found in the Qur'an.[38] Cusanus's *Letter* is divided into three main sections: salutations and introduction, outline for a proposed Christian-Muslim conference, and a concluding discussion on the importance of accurately studying the Qur'an and John's now lost translation, which foreshadows Cusanus's *Cribratio Alkorani*.[39]

In the pivotal and explicitly theological second part of the *Letter*, Cusanus first discusses the reasonableness of the Trinity, albeit briefly.[40] The heart of the proposal pulsates Christ.[41] In discussing the hypostatic union of the divine and human natures in Christ, the chief and lasting point of disagreement between Christians and Muslims, Cusanus says that he had even inquired with others who had more knowledge of Islam, a theme underscored in *Cribratio Alkorani*.[42] His presentation and defence of the hypostatic union in terms of the absolute maximum and minimum of the infinite, bears some similarities to the terminology applied to Christ in *De docta ignoranta*.[43] According to Cusanus, since Christ is the highest one (and here Cusanus notes how the Qur'an refers to Christ as Word and Spirit), the grace he has cannot be greater. It also, then, cannot be lesser because it is infinite.[44] This infinite grace is

---

37 *Epistula ad Ioannem de Segobia* II, p. 96, line 20: "Visum est mihi omnino ita agendum cum infidelibus, uti placere conspicio reverendissimae paternitati vestrae, et de hoc scripsi libellum parvulum quem nominavi *De pace fidei*."

38 See especially, Chapters 9–20. Chapters 1–8 discuss the Gospel of Jesus Christ, and only when the Qur'an agrees with the Gospel may be it called the right way (I, 6, 39). Cusanus looks for agreement between the Gospel and the Qur'an.

39 On John's work on the Qur'an, *Epistula ad Ioannem de Segobia* I, p. 93, line 15, "transtulit Alchorani discussionem"; III, p. 101, lines 10–15: "Perficiat igitur reverendissima paternitas vestra; ita pro Dei reverential supplico et requiro [on this work of translation]."

40 *Epistula ad Ioannem de Segobia* II, p. 97, lines 20–25.

41 Throughout Part II of the *Letter to John*, Cusanus uses the title Christ to refer to the hypostatic Word of God.

42 *Epistula ad Ioannem de Segobia* II, p. 98, line 15: "Ista pars [hypostatic union] erit, uti semper fuit, difficilis valde"; *Epistula ad Ioannem de Segobia* II, p. 98, line 20: "Contuli aliquando cum certis, quibus dixi an ex Alchorano pateat aliquem Christo praeferri posse." *Cribratio Alkorani*, prologus, 2–4.

43 *Epistula ad Ioannem de Segobia* II, p. 98, line 20–p. 99, line 10; *De docta ignorantia* I, 2; III, 1. Cf., *De pace fidei* XII, 39.

44 *Epistula ad Ioannem de Segobia* II, p. Cf., *Cribratio Alkorani* bk. I, Chps. 17–18.

absolutely maximal and found in the person of Christ.[45] Thus, while Cusanus inquires of others and consults the Qur'an, he offers his own contribution to Christian-Muslim dialogue on the hypostatic union according to the principles of learned ignorance. In addition, in *De docta ignorantia* Cusanus cites the same passage from Avicenna's *Metaphysics* on paradise as he does in *De pace fidei* and discusses the importace of the crucifixion and the Eucharist, all of which revolve around the person and work of Christ.[46] *De pace fidei* presents the same theological order: hypostatic union, crucifixion of Christ, eternal happiness, paradise, and Eucharist.[47] The conference, had it happened, would have concentrated almost exclusively on Christ (Christology, soteriology, sacramentology) and imitated the imaginative heavenly gathering of *De pace fidei*.

Cusanus's *Letter to John* evidences that his ideas for Christian-Muslim dialogue and conversation were fixed not only in reality, but also in his understanding of Christ, the hypostatic Word of God. His *Letter to John* further reveals consistency in his thought on the importance of the Word of God and Christology in his conversation and engagement with Islam. The *Cribratio Alkorani* also reveals a real searching for concordance in and through Christ in order to end schism.[48] All of this suggests that we do well to nuance the categorization of *De pace fidei* as "literature of utopia" and mere "renaissance optimism".[49] While *De pace fidei* reads as creative and contemplative, we have argued that it is also rooted in conciliar realities and the aspirations of Cusanus's active ecclesial career. As Christology arises from the person of Christ, so the dialogue surfaces from the life and experience of Cusanus himself. Although *De pace fidei* presents a more idealized and sophisticated theological discussion, Cusanus's concise *Letter to John* tersely captures his hope for actual Christian-Muslim discussion as centered on the crux of the matter: Christ as *Logos*. Improbable as *De pace fidei* and the *Letter to John* would be, when examined in light of Cusanus's own career and context, they reveal the extent of what he thought possible. The threads of contemplation and action, visions and deeds, are woven into the very fabric of Christian theology and outline the Christocentric pattern of Cusanus's religious concordance in

---

45 *Epistula ad Ioannem de Segobia* II, p. 98, line 20–p. 99, line 5.
46 *Epistula ad Ioannem de Segobia* II, p. 99, lines 15–20; *De pace fidei* XV, 52. Avicenna, *Metaphysics*, Cod. Cus. 205. *Epistula ad Ioannem de Segobia* II, p. 99, line 25 (crucifixion); p. 99, line 25–p. 100, line 10 (Eucharist).
47 *De pace fidei* XI–XII (hypostatic union); XIV–XV (crufixion of Christ, eternal happiness, paradise); XVIII (Eucharist).
48 *Cribratio Alkorani*, preface.
49 *De pace fidei*, introduction by Biechler and Bond, xxvi–xxvii.

his encounter with Islam. After considering illumined peace and fixing our attention on Cusanus's intended plans to realize elusive religious unity, we now consider one final complicated aspect of Cusanus's visionary thought as connected to real life events: his controversial move from council to pope and how this relates to his prophetic call for conciliar dialogue in *De pace fidei*.

Envisioning Unity: From Council to Pope to Prophet of Religious Peace

In 1433 an aspiring young canon lawyer submitted a treatise to the Council of Basel on unity in the Church. The author of the conciliatory work was a humanist with a penchant for discovering ancient and forgotten sources in monastic libraries. German by birth and culture, he also studied in Italy where he imbibed the renaissance. As we have seen, he was a profound intellectual, prone to constructive concepts of unanimity and with a predilection for Neoplatonic hierarchical gradations. Pacific in philosophical temperament, he was also a conciliarist. The title of the composition is, of course, *De concordantia catholica* and it was presented to the council by its up-and-coming author Nicholas of Cusa.[50] The impressive gathering of theologians at Basel convened in 1431 and followed the general councils of Constance (1414–1418) and Siena (1423–1424). As the successor of these councils, the ecumenical gathering at Basel, which was called in order to continue the reform of the church, faced many of the same challenges as its predecessors. Pope Martin V convoked the council and it was presided over by his appointment as president, Cardinal Julian Cesarini.

The extent to which Martin V and Cesarini influenced the thought of Cusanus is a pertinent question which continues to perplex Cusa scholarship. Although Cusanus joined the Council of Basel in 1432 and thereafter submitted his treatise, *De concordantia catholica*, a pacific work which speaks of the natural concordance between hierarchy from above and consent from below, the

---

50 In 1417 at a time when the renaissance was thriving south of the Alps, Cusanus transferred his studies from the University of Heidelberg to the University of Padua, a center of humanism, medicine, and civil and canon law. Sigmund, *Nicholas of Cusa and Medieval Political Thought*, 23. Cusanus's knowledge of anatomy is evident in *De concordantia catholica* III, 41, where at the end of the entire treatise the concord of church and empire is compared to one healthy, fully functioning human body in all its many finely tuned intricacies.

pope and the membership of the general council, the one and the many, he nonetheless left the council in 1437 leaning in favour of the papacy.

Why this seemingly sudden change of loyalties? In only four years since the completion of *De concordantia catholica* the harmony of which he once wrote now resounded with dissidence and discord. Relations between Martin V's impulsive successor Eugenius IV and the council worsened, and by 1435 deputations at Basel forbade outright the payment of annates and taxes to Rome. Then in 1436 the majority of the council voted to pursue reunion with the Greek Church in Basel or Avignon, while the pope, Cesarini and Cusanus favoured a city in Italy. The dispute over where to hold the council of union resulted in Cusanus and Cesarini leaving Basel for Italy to join the pope. As he had done as a young man, Cusanus once again went south of the Alps. This time it was not to study canon law but to serve in the papal curia. This new career path would soon take Cusanus as far as Constantinople. Representing the older, more traditional view of the reasons why Cusanus changed allegiance from council to pope, Henry Bett writes, "What was the secret of his change of front? Probably the turbulent conduct and the extreme measures of the council itself."[51] Bett also argues that the matter of reunion of the Greek and Latin churches directly influenced Cusanus's decision.[52] Indeed, Cusanus himself affirms this same view.[53] Yet, this move was not without controversy. Donald Duclow contends that "Nicholas's conversion to the papal cause remains the most controversial move in his career."[54]

Which side of the reformation one affirmed was largely predetermined by the opinion of commentators from previous centuries. If one was against the pope, as was Johann Kymeus who wrote a tract against Cusanus in 1538 titled *The Popes Hercules Against the Germans*, Cusanus was a Judas-type figure who betrayed conciliar ideals for the wealth of Rome.[55] From the standpoint of the papal party, Cusanus's change of loyalties epitomized the stature and efficiency of the papacy over against the conciliar gridlock of Basel. Was this really a conversion, as Duclow suggests, or, given Cusanus's parallel political theories about hierarchy and consent, was it rather a natural next step? Paul Sigmund

---

51 Henry Bett, *Nicholas of Cusa* (London: Methuen & Co., 1932), 28.
52 Bett, *Nicholas of Cusa*, 29.
53 Cusanus writes in his *Oration at the Diet of Frankfurt* (1442), "Postremo dico, quod Grecis reductis qualitercumque non potuit Basilee concilium esse universalem militantem ecclesiam representans." Latin text in *Nicholas of Cusa: Writings on Church and Reform*, 201.
54 Bellitto, *Introducing Nicholas of Cusa*, 33.
55 Aeneas Silvius bestowed on Cusa the title "Hercules of the Eugenians" for his support of Pope Eugene IV.

argues that Cusanus understood church government to consist properly of a harmonious constitutional relationship between a representative council and a vibrant papacy. Sigmund writes,

> Yet when the division [in the council] took place, he reverted to an older integralist view also present in his thought which saw society and government as a harmonious organism of interrelated, functionally differentiated, and hierarchically graded parts. This harmonious cooperation was guaranteed by the operation of the Holy Spirit, and its structure reflected the hierarchical structure of the universe outlined by the Neo-Platonic writers. Consent was unanimous and representation was personal. The council was not a *universitas* of all the faithful but a gathering of the various orders of the church hierarchy under the pope and guided by the Holy Spirit.[56]

Sigmund rightfully highlights Cusanus's use of the concept of hierarchy as found in ancient and medieval Neoplatonic writers. Cusanus's Neoplatonic views on hierarchy are found in the first two chapters of book one of *De concordantia catholica*, and are articulated yet again in the council of the religions of the world presided over by the Word and his emissaries, Peter and Paul, in the dialogue of *De pace fidei* (1453). Sigmund further contends that in the writing of *De docta ignorantia* in 1440 conceptions of representation and consent "were fundamentally altered, so as to permit the development of a new theory of papal supremacy."[57] For Sigmund, hierarchical views were always present in Cusanus, yet they were redefined in *De docta ignorantia*. Similarly, Watanabe argues that the discord of the Council of Basel signalled for Cusanus the departure of the Holy Spirit, an end to universal harmonious consent and unity in diversity which in turn led him to embrace the papacy.[58]

There are also those who explain Cusanus's shift from council to pope in terms of practicalities, including Theodor Stumpf in the nineteenth century, who attributed personal ambition as the overarching motive of the decision.[59] Sigmund calls this "the 'opportunist' hypothesis."[60] In support of this view,

---

56 Sigmund, *Nicholas of Cusa and Medieval Political Thought*, 230–231.
57 Sigmund, *Nicholas of Cusa and Medieval Political Thought*, 243.
58 Watanabe, *The Political Ideas of Nicholas of Cusa*, 113.
59 Sigmund, *Nicholas of Cusa and Medieval Political Thought*, 226. Theodor Stumpf, *Die Politischen Ideen des N. Von Cues: ein Beitrag zur Geschichte der Deutschen Reformbestrebungen im Fünfzehnten Jahrhundert* (Köln, 1865), 101.
60 Sigmund, *Nicholas of Cusa and Medieval Political Thought*, 226.

there survives a letter written by Ambrogio Traversari, the papal representative at Basel, to an Italian bishop stating that Cusanus had requested his support for papal approval of his appointment as provost of Münster-Maifeld, a lucrative post.[61] More recently, Joachim Stieber posits the reason for the change as a mixture of Cusanus's commitment to a hierarchical conception of the church and personal gain.[62] In response to all of the reasons suggested over the years, Gerald Christianson thinks that the debate over why Cusanus left the council for Pope Eugenius IV in 1437 will probably never be resolved.[63]

Owing to the historical ambiguity and the enduring reputation of Cusanus in the history of the church, as well as in the history of ideas, the question concerning why he changed sides from the council to the pope remains an important, if not an unsolvable, quandry. It is important for what it reveals about his thought and, with regard to this present study, how it illumines his account of the concordance of the world's religions in the hierarchical Word of God. Beyond the pragmatic and political factors there appears, perhaps, hints of a metaphysical rationale revealing the deep coherence of Cusanus's thought about the relationship between the one acting from above and the many from below. Contra Sigmund, *De docta ignorantia* does not present a new paradigm of representation and consent so as to replace the ecclesial concord described in *De concordantia catholica* in order to allow for papal domination. A synthetic look at the tripartite structure and Neoplatonic movement of *De docta ignorantia*, reveal an underlying hierarchical and hypostatic principle which renders his move from council to pope thoroughly consistent with his thought both during his service at Basel and later as cardinal. This is especially true of the foundational first chapters of book one of his *De concordantia catholica* as well as the dialogue *De pace fidei*,

Before attempting to address this long-standing contentious question, a closer look at Martin V and cardinal Cesarini and their influence on Cusanus's move from council to pope is in order. Martin V's effect on Cusanus was indirect, but nonetheless, owing to the ancient and abiding stature of his office, considerable. His election to the papacy in 1417 effectively ended the Great Schism. The Council of Constance met in response to three rival claimants to

---

61   Sigmund, *Nicholas of Cusa and Medieval Political Thought*, 220.
62   Bellitto, *Introducing Nicholas of Cusa*, 34; Joachim Stieber, "The 'Hercules of the Eugenians' at the Crossroads: Nicholas of Cusa's Decision for the Pope and Against the Council in 1436–37—Theological, Political, and Social Aspects" in: Christianson, et al., *Nicholas of Cusa in Search of God and Wisdom*, 242.
63   Gerald Christianson, "Cusanus, Cesarini and the Crisis of Conciliarism" in: Bocken, *Conflict and Reconciliation: Perspectives on Nicholas of Cusa*, 92.

the one chair of St. Peter. Selecting Martin V as the sole pope of the Catholic Church was an integral component of what the Council decreed in *Haec Sancta*, namely, that the ecclesiastical representatives of Western Europe, with the full support of the Holy Roman Emperor, Sigismund, ambitiously proposed to reform the church in "its head and its members."[64] While the reform was intended to move beyond the papacy to encompass the Church as a whole, it began with the restoration of a single head over the many members. Just as the Latin Church confesses in *Quicunque vult* commonly known as the Athanasian Creed, there are not three gods, but one God, so the general council would in no way tolerate three popes. God is one and there is but one head of his body on earth. *Haec Sancta* also stated explicitly that the general council of the Catholic Church holds its power directly from Christ. Hence, even the pope, who by divine decree was essential to the governance and sacramental functioning of the church, was nonetheless subject to Christ, represented in and through the council as a whole. As pope, the strong-willed Martin dealt with restoring the Papal States after the chaos resulting from not only the Great Schism, but the Babylonian Captivity of the pope in Avignon as well. He was begrudgingly compelled by the proponents of Constance to accept the new conciliar reality of the Western church initiated at Constance and which met *en force* at Basel. Although Benedict XIII and Clement VIII lingered on as antipopes until 1429, by the time the Council of Basel was underway in 1431 Martin was sole pope. After years of ecclesial discord, there was now only one pope and a new beginning for the unified church which is reflected in the confident tone of *De concordantia catholica* (1433). The very title of the work reveals its constructive and optimistic aim: lasting harmony between the pope, the one head of the church, and its many members as represented in the general council.

Another important member of the church who had risen through the ranks of the many was Cardinal Julian Cesarini. Unlike Pope Martin V, who played a substantial but secondary role in the formation of Cusanus's thought, Cesarini was his mentor and friend. In 1440 Cusanus addressed his most famous writing, *De docta ignorantia*, to Cesarini. To look at Cesarini, we first overview *De docta ignorantia*, which presents the *via negativa* towards 'not knowing' the Absolute Maximum. The Absolute Maximum is beyond number, indivisible and infinite unity.[65]

Unfolding from the Absolute Maximum is the "Maximum from the Absolute," which is "universal unity" contracted in the plurality of all things.[66]

---

64   *Haec Sancta*, 6 April 1415, Tanner, *Decrees of the Ecumenical Councils*, Vol. 1, 409. Crowder, *Unity, Heresy and Reform*, 83.
65   *De docta ignorantia* I, 5, 14, Bond, p. 93.
66   *De docta ignorantia* I, 2, 6, Bond, p. 89.

The culmination of the search for learned ignorance is where the one, the Absolute Maximum, intersects the many: the Word made flesh. Jesus Christ is one with the Absolute Maximum through whom all things come into existence, and who, Cusanus writes, "is the most perfect end beyond all our capacity."[67]

The final chapter of the third and last book of *De docta ignorantia* on Christology concludes with a discussion of ecclesiology. In order fully to appreciate the significance of this discussion of the church and the movements of God to humanity and humanity to God, it is beneficial to look earlier in the same book, where Cusanus establishes the nexus of the one and the many in the person of Christ. He writes that "all things exist in Jesus as in the Word, and every creature exists in this highest and most perfect humanity, which universally enfolds all created things, so that all fullness dwells in him."[68] Cusanus's Christology determines not only his teachings on creation, but also his ecclesiology as centered on Jesus in *De docta ignorantia* and the Word of God in *De pace fidei*. For Cusanus, "God exists in unity with the maximum humanity of Jesus, for the maximum human can exist only maximally in God".[69] According to human capacity, and beyond that which finite minds can understand, God reveals the fullness of God's Wisdom and God's Word as Son "in a sensible form and in a form similar to ourselves," and, yet, "the fullness of all things".[70] The descent of the Word into union with the flesh and the human intellect is, as Aquinas says in the preface to question two of the *prima pars* of his *Summa Theologiæ*, "our road to God."[71] The structure of Aquinas's all-encompassing *Summa* is, as we have seen in Chapter 1 of this study, "*exitus et*

---

67 *De docta ignorantia* I, 2, 7, Bond, p. 90.
68 *De docta ignorantia* III, 4, 204, Bond, p. 179: "Et ita in Iesu, qui sic est aequalitas omnia essendi, tamquam in Filio in divinis, qui est media persona, Pater aeternus et sanctus Spiritus existunt, et omnia ut in Verbo, et omnis creatura in ipsa humanitate summa et perfectissima universaliter omnia creabilia complicanti, ut sit omnis plenitudo ipsum inhabitans." Cf., *De pace fidei* II, 7; XII, 38–39; XIII, 43.
69 *De docta ignorantia* III, 4, 204, Bond, p. 179.
70 *De docta ignorantia* III, 5, 211, Bond, p. 182: "Hac licet remotissima similitudine supra id, quod intelligi per nos potest, alleviamur parumper in nostra meditatione, quoniam Pater aeternus immensae bonitatis nobis volens divitias gloriae suae et omnem scientiae et sapientiae plenitudinem ostendere Verbum aeternum, Filium sum, qui ista et plenitudo omnium existit, nostris infirmitatibus compatiens, quoniam aliter quam in sensibili et nobis simili forma percipere non poteramus, ipsum secundum nostram capacitatem manifestans, humana natura induit per Spiritum sanctum sibi consubstantialem." Cf., *De docta ignorantia* III, 2, 192; *De pace fidei* II, 7–III, 8.
71 St. Thomas Aquinas, *Summa Theologiæ*, Volume 2 (1a., 2–11), reprint (Blackfriars edition) (Cambridge: Cambridge University Press, 2006), 3.

reditus," the Neoplatonic pattern of emanation and return.[72] As in the overall schema of Aquinas's *Summa*, there is also structurally in *De docta ignorantia* the many issuing forth from the one, the Absolute Maximum, and the bringing back of the the many to fullness in the one through the incarnate Word by means of his hierarchical Church which extends from earth to heaven and heaven to earth. The first book of *De docta ignorantia* presents the apophatic path to the Absolute Maximum. The final chapter of book one, concludes with the reader lost in darkness.

God is neither one nor more than one. According to the theology of negation nothing other than infinity is found in God. Consequently, negative theology holds that God is unknowable either in this world or in the world to come, for in this respect every creature is darkness, which cannot comprehend infinite light, but God is known to God alone.[73]

Book two ends in much the same way as book one. In discussing the wonders of the universe, Cusanus writes, "In these things that are so marvellous and so varied and diverse we discover through learned ignorance, in keeping with what we have already stated, that we are unable to know the reason of all the works of God."[74] The starry heavens above which declare the glory of God invoke and entice the intellect to continual contemplation.[75] Yet as book one and two of *De docta ignorantia* state, God and his creation are too wonderful to know. The seeker of God, the "wisely ignorant" pilgrim, desires to know "the

---

72 M.D. Chenu, O.P., *Toward Understanding Saint Thomas*, 304. On the Neoplatonic schema of the Summa, Chenu writes, "Such is the plan of the *Summa theologiae*, such the movement which it translates: *Ia Pars*—emanation from God-the principle; *IIa Pars*—return to God-the end; and because, *de facto*, by God's free and utterly gratuitous design (sacred history reveals this to us) this return is effected through Christ-the man-God, a *IIIa Pars* will study the Christian conditions of this return" (304–305).

73 *De docta ignorantia* I, 26, 88, Bond, pp. 126–127: "deus nec unum est nec plura. Et non reperitur in deo secundum theologiam negationis aliud quam infinitas. Quare secundum illam nec cognoscibilis est in hoc saeculo neque in futuro, quoniam omnis creatura tenebra est eo respectu, quae infinitum lumen comprehendere nequit, sed sibi solus notus est." Cf., *De pace fidei* V, 15; VI, 17: the dialogue proper of *De pace fidei* begins with the apophatic wisdom that God is not many, etc. Cf., Aquinas, *Summa Theologiæ*, prima pars, questions 3–11.

74 *De docta ignorantia* II, 13, 179, Bond, p. 168: "In hiis tam admirandis rebus, tam variis et diversis, per doctam ignorantiam experimur iuxta praemissa nos omnium operum Dei nullam scire posse rationem, sed tantum admirari, quoniam magnus Dominus, cuius magnitudinis non est finis." Cf. *De pace fidei* I, 3: "tu [God] tamen concreasti eidem ea omnia per quae, excitatus admiratione eorum quae sensu attingit".

75 *De docta ignorantia* II, 13, 179: "in admirationem ex munda machina"; Psalm 19:1.

works of God." What begins in wonder ends with the imparting of the wonderful, the supernatural wisdom from God which is mere foolishness to those untrained in learned ignorance, namely, the incarnation and ministry of Jesus Christ.[76] *De docta ignorantia* concludes not in "the cloud of unknowing," but in the hierarchy of the church which spans heaven and earth, an idea transmitted through Pseudo-Dionysius and Eriugena, with each of whom Cusanus was well acquainted.[77] God may be "unknowable in this world or in the world to come," yet, as Cusanus writes in *De concordantia catholica*, the celestial and ecclesiastical hierarchy is knowable through the bishops and priests, and through them to the laity and the Holy Roman Empire and even, to quote Christian Scripture, "to the ends of the earth."[78]

Like *De docta ignorantia*, the structure of *De concordantia catholica* unsurprisingly follows a three part division that finds its completion in the fullness of the incarnate Word. In the prologue to the treatise Cusanus outlines the

---

76 *De docta ignorantia* III, 4; 1 Corinthians 1:18–25.
77 *The Cloud of Unknowing* is the title of an anonymous, apophatic work, probably written in the second half of the fourteenth century. The expression originally comes from *The Mystical Theology* of Dionysius the Areopagite, where in the description of the ascent of Moses up the mountain, "he plunges into the truly mysterious darkness of unknowing" (3, 1001A, in: *Pseudo-Dionysius: The Complete Works*, Luibheid, 137). Cusanus cites this passage from Dionysius in his *Apologia doctae ignorantiae* (1449): "Nam id, quod improperat quaeritur in docta ignorantia, uti Dionysius noster, cuius hodie festa agimus, in Mystica theologia sic cum Moyse in caliginem ascendendum instruit. Tunc enim reperitur Deus, quando omnia linquuntur; et haec tenebra est lux in Domino" (*Apologia* 29). Cusanus refers directly to Dionysius throughout the *Apologia*. Sigmund points out that the discussion of the celestial and ecclesiastical hierarchy in *De concordantia catholica* I, 2 is mainly drawn from Eriugena (Sigmund, *Nicholas of Cusa and Medieval Political Thought*, 27). Cf. *On the Division of Nature (De divisione naturae)*, introduction, where Eriugena discusses the hierarchy of being, in: John F. Wippel and Allan B. Wolter, O.F.M., *Medieval Philosophy: From St. Augustine to Nicholas of Cusa* (New York: The Free Press, 1969), 120. Sigmund also notes that Cusanus had a copy of Eriugena's *De divisione naturae* with his own marginal notes now no longer at his library in Kues. On this matter Raymond Klibansky and Hildebrand Bascour add, "Nam contigit nobis ut e libris Cusani in diversas Europae partes dissipatis inter alios reperiremus hos codices manu eius adnotatos: *Timaeum* Platonis et Macrobium, Scotum Eriugenam *De divisione naturae*, Petri Abailardi *Theologiam*, Marcum Paulum *De consuetudinibus orientalium regionum*, Henrici Bate *Speculum divinorum et quorundam naturalium*" (*Nicolai de Cusa De Pace Fidei cum Epistula ad Ioannem de Segobia*, xxxv). Cusanus refers to Eriugena in his *Apologia doctae ignorantiae* as "John the Scot" in the context of a list of commentators on *The Mystical Theology* of St. Denis, and as "Iohannem Scotigenam" (*Apologia* 30).
78 Acts 1:8.

work.[79] First he discusses the Church as a whole in book one. He then studies the priesthood in book two and finally turns to the empire in book three. The priesthood is compared to the soul, the empire to the body. Hence, the church and empire are one soul and body. Cusanus's presentation of the church as a whole does not begin with the many. Rather, he begins with the one, the incarnate Word, and the Word's representative hierarch on earth, the pope. Although detailed discussion of the general council is nowhere to be found in book one, in Chapter 15, Cusanus mentions that "in decisions on matters of faith which is why he [the pope] possesses the primacy, he is subject to the council of the Catholic church."[80] And while this statement pays homage to the council, it also, more importantly, affirms the pope's primacy and appears in the context of a discussion of how the Bishop of Rome is the head of the church militant. In Cusanus's ecclesiology, the church as a whole is found most perfectly in Christ and, as will be shown below, by a certain divine likeness in his supreme representative on earth, the Bishop of Rome. First and foremost, Cusanus accentuates the dialectical and hierarchical nature of the Word of God: "Concordance is the principle by which the Catholic Church is in harmony as one and many—in one Lord and many subjects."[81] For Cusanus, "this concordance is highest truth itself,"[82] and the highest truth is none other than Christ, the Word of God.[83] At the end of the first chapter of book one of *De concordantia*, Cusanus states,

> In summary, therefore, we may say that Christ is the way, the truth and the life, and the head of all creatures, the husband or spouse of the church, which is constituted in a concordance of all rational creatures—with him as the One, and among themselves, the many—in various [hierarchical] gradations.[84]

---

79 *De concordantia catholica*, prologus, 3, Sigmund, p. 4: "In my treatise on the Catholic concordance, I believe that it is necessary to examine that union of faithful people that is called the Catholic Church, as well as the parts that together make up that church—i.e, its soul and body. Therefore we will consider first the church itself as a composite whole, then its soul, the holy priesthood, and thirdly its body, the holy empire."

80 *De concordantia catholica* I, XV, 61, Sigmund, p. 43.

81 *De concordantia catholica*, I, 1, 4, Sigmund, p. 5: "Concordantia enim est id, ratione cuius ecclesia catholica in uno et in pluribus concordat, in uno domino et pluribus subditis."

82 *De concordantia catholica* I, 1, 7, Sigmund, p. 7: "Quoniam haec concordantia est ipsamet veritas summa."

83 *De pace fidei* II, 7.

84 *De concordantia catholica* I, 1, 8, Sigmund, p. 7: "Unde haec est summa dicendorum, quod Christus est via, veritas et vita et omnium creaturarum caput, maritus sive sponsus

In summary, therefore, we may say that Christ is the way, the truth and the life, and the head of all creatures, the husband or spouse of the church, which is constituted in a concordance of all rational creatures—with him as the One, and among themselves, the many—in various [hierarchical] gradations.[85]

Jesus is the one soul and body of the hierarchy of the church and empire. As the God-man Christ spans heaven and earth, the infinite and the finite. This is also why book three of *De concordantia catholica* concludes with a comparison of the harmonious workings of church and empire to one soul and body, a reprise of the first three chapters of book one. Right before discussing the ecclesial and global metaphor of the human body, Cusanus posits that all spiritual power comes through Christ alone.[86] Cusanus also states in the context of the divinely appointed role of the priesthood to forgive and retain sins, that "there is a single power from God of binding and loosing and of giving life to all, although among the members there seem to be some who are greater and others of lesser importance."[87] The pope should always remember, the post-great schism Cusanus concludes, that his divinely graced superiority from Christ alone over this single power of absolution was intended by God for the proper ordering of the hierarchy and the peace of faith.[88]

De concordantia catholica shows that, according to Cusanus, the pope is the highest representative of the priesthood on earth and by the Holy Spirit mediates the Word to the lesser ecclesiastical orders. Through the indwelling of the Word by the nexus of the Holy Spirit and by virtue of the consent of natural law, the pope's *cathedra* embodies the divine principle of concordance most perfectly.[89] Cusanus further writes, "the Roman pontiff should be aware that the vital harmony of the church is preserved by the divine and canonical

---

ecclesiae, quae per concordantiam creaturarum omnium rationabilium ad eum unum et inter se plurium constituitur secundum varias graduationes." Cf., John 14:6; Colossians 1:18; Ephesians 5:25–32. Cf., *De pace fidei* II, 7.

85 *De concordantia catholica* I, 1, 8, Sigmund, p. 7: "Unde haec est summa dicendorum, quod Christus est via, veritas et vita et omnium creaturarum caput, maritus sive sponsus ecclesiae, quae per concordantiam creaturarum omnium rationabilium ad eum unum et inter se plurium constituitur secundum varias graduationes." Cf., John 14:6; Colossians 1:18; Ephesians 5:25–32. Cf., *De pace fidei* II, 7.
86 *De concordantia catholica* III, 41, 582, Sigmund, p. 318.
87 *De concordantia catholica* III, 41, 584, Sigmund, p. 318.
88 *De concordantia catholica* III, 41, 582.
89 On the Word dwelling in all ranks of being, see *De concordantia catholica* II, 2, 10; *De pace fidei* II, 7. Nexus (Holy Spirit) and consent are major themes in the imagined heavenly religious council of *De pace fidei*. Cf., *De concordantia catholica* I, 9, 44–45.

sanctions, which are all rooted in one source, the Holy Spirit and the natural law."[90] For Cusanus clearly affirms that in the church "there is one *cathedra* and one rule established in hierarchical grades."[91] Cusanus goes on to say, "that the true and certain chair [*cathedra*] of Peter in which all his successors sit, is one."[92] And he concludes, "that whoever says that he is a Christian must of necessity say that his chair is joined to the chair of the successors of St. Peter and is united in association with that chair."[93] For Cusanus, there is one chair of Peter in the one church, Christ's emissary and vicar on earth. In *De pace fidei*, Cusanus extends this idea of Petrine unity to include by analogy all religions as one religion in the variety of rites under the conciliar head of the Word of God. In this latter treatise, the Word of God leads the discussion, as the pope would chair the council "so that the erroneous notions of which there are a great many concerning your Word might be rooted out and truth might continuously shine forth."[94] According to *De pace fidei*, the Word is called on by God to correct error concerning the very same Word, and, thereby to achieve world religious concordance.

In the dialogue of *De pace fidei*, Cusanus harmonizes Peter and the Word of God through the convergence of the prophetic role of Christ and the apostolic ministry of the first pope for the advancement of peace and unity. For Cusanus Christ is the prophetic Word in whom the diversity of religions become one in the variety of rites. Cusanus introduces Peter into the dialogue of *De pace fidei* precisely on the topic of Christology. The Word first deals with the more abstract concepts of Wisdom, *Logos* and Trinity. Representing the magisterium of the Catholic Church, Peter addresses the theme of Christology proper or the incarnation of the Word of God, as well as soteriology: the data of revelation. In the Gospel of Mark, Jesus famously asked Peter, "But who do you say that I am?"[95] Peter's speech in *De pace fidei* answers this question.[96] Cusanus introduces Peter by observing that the apostle "has undertaken the explanation of this part [viz. Christology]."[97] The participants of the religions of the Word are implored to hear him for "he will sufficiently teach everything that is hidden"

---

90 *De concordantia catholica* III, 41, Sigmund, p. 318.
91 *De concordantia catholica* I, 6, 36, Sigmund, p. 24: "Unde sicut episcopatus unus, ita una cathedra et una praesidentia gradualiter et hierarchice constituta."
92 *De concordantia catholica* I, 14, 56, Sigmund, p. 38.
93 *De concordantia catholica* I, 14, Sigmund, p. 39.
94 *De pace fidei* III, 9: "ut fallaciae quae plurimum sunt circa Verbum tuum extirpentur et sic veritas continue elucescat." Translation by Biechler and Bond, p. 10.
95 Mark 8:29 NRSV.
96 *De pace fidei* XI–XV.
97 *De pace fidei* X, 28. Translation by Biechler and Bond, p. 30.

so that all may consent to one religion in the variety of rites.[98] Beyond the Christocentric catechetical and confessional role of Peter as unveiled in the ongoing ministry of the apostolic bishops, preeminently in the pope, there exists the hierarchical rank of the vicar of Christ in the gradation of being.

According to Catholic medieval cosmology and ecclesiology, Christians participate in the community through their divinely appointed ranks on the ecclesiastical hierarchy of pope, bishops, priests, laity and citizens.[99] "Hence", Cusanus writes, "just as there is one episcopate, so there is one *cathedra* [lit.—chair] and one rule established in hierarchical grades."[100] Furthermore, Cusanus understands the Bishop of Rome, as by virtue of his divine office and through the endowed graces of the Holy Spirit, to represent or sit in the chair (*cathedra*) of the ascended Christ, "the Eternal pontiff" for the well being of the commonwealth of church and empire.[101] After Jerusalem, where Christ "the Highest pontiff washed the church in His Blood", Rome is deemed primary see by divine rite and apostolic and conciliar tradition for the preservation of peace and unity.[102] Selection from above (divine grant) meets consent and corroboration from below (apostolic and conciliar tradition of the church catholic), much like *De pace fidei*, where God the Father selects the Word to reveal and lead the dialogue, which in turn is confirmed through reason and free consent by the philosophers from the ends of the earth for the sake of realizing religious peace and unity. The one and the many affirm the Roman *cathedra* as the center of the vital harmony of the church. In *De pace fidei*, as in *De concordantia catholica*, the force of canons of the councils, in the words of Cusanus, "is derived not from the pope nor from the head of the council but only from a single concordant consent."[103] The concluding image of the human

---

98   *De pace fidei* X, 28. Translation by Biechler and Bond, p. 30. Cf., *De pace fidei* I, 6; III, 9.
99   *De concordantia catholica* preface, 3.
100 *De concordanita catholica* I, 6, 36, Sigmund, p. 24. "Unde sicut episcopatus unus, ita una cathedra et una praesidentia gradualiter hierarchice constituta."
101 *De concordantia catholica* I, 3, 13, Sigmund, p. 11; *De concordantia catholica* preface, 3; I, 6, 36; I, 9, 44; I, 14, 56.
102 *De concordantia catholica* I, 16, 64, 66, Sigmund, pp. 46–47: "the Roman see rightly possesses the primacy by the statutes of the councils, because of its secular importance, [and] by divine grant, for the increase of the faith and the preservation of peace, and on account of having had so many holy popes, more than thirty of whom in succession were crowned as martyrs for their faith." Cf., the primacy and importance of Jerusalem in *De concordantia catholica* I, 16, 64; *De pace fidei* III, 9.
103 *De concordantia catholica* II, 8, 100, Sigmund, 79. Cf., De pace fidei III, 9: "et contentatur omnem religionum diversitatem communi omnium hominum consensu in unicam concorditer reduci amplius inviolabilem."

body in *De concordantia catholica* ultimately refers to the Body of Christ, the Word made corporeal and corporate, the beginning and end of hierarchy. The highest divinely mandated office on earth, the papacy, which, in the metaphor of the body Cusanus deems to be "the soul in the head", derives authority and effectiveness from Christ.[104] As the soul gives life to the body, so the papacy enlivens the church on earth and promotes the seeking of peace and unity through the Word of God.

The hierarchical ecclesiology of *De concordantia catholica* reflects the hierarchical theology of *De docta ignorantia*. In *De docta ignorantia*, God may be known to God alone (book I), only God makes himself known cryptically in the cosmos (book II), and more assuredly through the perspicuous revelation of his Word as unfolded through the person and work of Jesus and hierarchical gradations (book III). Through the illumination of the Word, the seeker after concordance then knows all created things are signs of the Word of God, and, since this Word was made flesh, "Jesus therefore is the end of all things."[105] The apophatic theology of Dionysius and his medieval transmitters is evident in the argument of books one and two of *De docta ignorantia*. The constructive fusion of the negative and the positive paths to God becomes clear in the transition from book two to book three. The enigmatic Dionysian darkness of the first book of *De docta ignorantia* leads to the insufficient wonder of the middle book and finally concludes with the cataphatic final book, where Cusanus recounts the incarnation, death, resurrection and ascension of Christ, the essential data of the Christ event.

Unsurprisingly, as Latin Trinitarian theology does not stop at the Father, but progresses in eternal generation to the Son and the Spirit from Father and Son, so also Cusanus's *De docta ignorantia* follows an advancing tripartite structure. As the Spirit is the bond between Father and Son, so in Cusanus's discussion of the incarnate Word, the Spirit connects the one human and divine Christ with the many members of the church through the mediating hierarchy.[106] There is one hypostatic hierarchy with all of the ecclesial distinctions in their proper place. Personality and distinction are affirmed in the one hierarchy of the Word with the many distinct but perfectly interconnected gradations.

---

104 *De concordantia catholica* I, 41, 583, Sigmund, p. 318.
105 *De docta ignorantia* III, 11, 247, Bond, p. 198: "omnia igitur creata signa sunt Verbi Dei. Omnis vox corporalis verbi mentalis signum. Omnis mentalis verbi corruptibilis causa est Verbum incorruptibile, quod est ratio. Christus est ipsa incarnata ratio omnium rationum, quia Verbum caro factum est. Iesus igitur finis est omnium."
106 *De pace fidei* X, 27.

As apex and rungs of the ladder itself of the ecclesiastical hierarchy sits the one whom Dionysius calls the hierarch. Dionysius conceives that "Jesus" is "the source and the perfection of every hierarchy."[107] Dionysius also says that a hierarch refers to "a holy and inspired man, someone who understands all sacred knowledge, someone in whom an entire hierarchy is completely perfected and known."[108] The hierarch hypostatically represents Christ and brings to those below him in the hierarchy the light of the Word. *De docta ignorantia* concludes not in darkness, but light. The attainment of learned ignorance leads not to the silence of unknowing, but to the divinely revealed and established hierarchy of the church in all its various gradations. At the conclusion of *De docta ignorantia*, the post-script and letter to Cesarini, Cusanus recounts how he received the illumination of learned ignorance from God.[109] What he had long since laboured naturally to acquire, he now receives by illumination from above. Grace does not abolish the many, but through the nexus of the Holy Spirit, the many are brought to perfection in and through the one hierarch.[110] Like *De docta ignorantia*, *De concordantia catholica* does not end in intellectual blindness. The final image of the treatise, the metaphor of the body, is more than a late-medieval lesson on human anatomy. There is one body (Christendom) with many parts. The parts are identified as ranks of church and empire, and each diverse function works in flawless synchronization with the whole, all of which metaphorically embodies the one revealed hierarchy of the incarnate and enlightening Word.

Given the hierarchical nature of the Word unfolding in the plurality of the hierarchy, it is not surprising that Cusanus dedicated *De docta ignorantia* to cardinal Cesarini, a hierarch himself of the Roman church or, to put in Cusanus's terms, a prelate who participates in the power of the papacy "in a contracted way."[111] Their collegial friendship and close working relationship make the acknowledgement a natural choice.[112] Yet, their friendship was one forged

---

107 *De ecclesiastica hierarchia* I, 2, 373B. Translation by Colm Luibheid. Cf., *De ecclesiastica hierarchia* II, 1, 393A; *De docta ignorantia* III, 12, 262.
108 *De ecclesiastica hierarchia* I, 3, 373C. Translation by Colm Luibheid.
109 *De docta ignorantia, Epistola auctoris ad Dominum Iulianum Cardinalem* Bond, p. 206; James 1:17.
110 Cf., Aquinas, *Summa Theologiæ* Ia., 1, 8.
111 *Letter to Rodrigo Sánchez de Arévalo* 10: "in sua particularitate Petri potestatem contracte participans, eandem (salva contractione) quam Petrus habet potestatem." Latin text and English translation in *Nicholas of Cusa: Writings on Church and Reform*, Izbicki, 443.
112 Gerald Christianson notes that Cusanus and Cesarini had much in common. They both were trained in canon law at the University of Padua and they both strived for concord in the Church and unity between the Latin and Greeks. Cesarini, who did not write a

by ideas and their adherence to the pope over the council adhered to their Neoplatonic views of the hierarchy of being extending from the one to the many. Even so, their hierarchical thoughts were not without consequence. Cesarini was killed at the Battle of Varna in 1444, which saw the Ottomans crush the crusaders. As a loyal devotee of the pope, he was an avid proponent of the crusade. His unflinching support for the papal side cost him his life. One may only wonder if Cusanus secretly dedicated *De pace fidei*, his response to the fall of Constantinople and religious violence, to the memory of Cesarini. *De pace fidei* makes explicit in metaphorical dialogical form what is implicit as metaphysical hierarchy in *De docta ignorantia* and *De concordantia catholica*. As the maximum contracted from the absolute finds perfect synthesis in Jesus Christ, so the many rites from the contracted maximum find universal synthesis through the same Wisdom and Word of God.[113] While a potential dedication of *De pace fidei* to Cesarini is merely conjecture, what can be stated more precisely is that in *De concordantia catholica* Cusanus, writing on behalf of the council and in consultation with Cesarini, offers a nuanced prominence to Rome.[114] It is true that Cusanus, who moved in humanist circles while a student of canon law in Padua, was among the first to detect that the so-called 'Donation of Constantine' was a forgery.[115] This may cause one to wonder even further why he joined the papal side in the debate against the conciliarists at Basel. It is worth noting, though, that in the same context in which Cusanus uncovers the forgery of the Donation of Constantine, he argues that the ruse was not necessary to prove the validity and salutation of the Roman see.[116]

---

treatise, was Cusanus's intellectual guide. Bocken, *Conflict and Reconciliation*, 95. Cusanus praises Cesarini's knowledge of Latin and Greek in the prologue to *De docta ignorantia*.

113   *De docta ignorantia* I, 2, 5–7.
114   See for example, *De concordantia catholica* II, 18, 158, 161.
115   *De concordantia catholica* III, 2, 295, 308.
116   Cusanus writes, "It should not be necessary to support the divine, praiseworthy, and most excellent first see of Rome with ambiguous arguments of this kind which were taken from these letters and inserted in the *Decretum* of Gratian" (*De concordantia catholica* III, 2, 311, Sigmund, pp. 221–222). On a similar note, Henry Bett observes that Cusanus also suspected the authenticity of Pseudo-Dionysius. In the margins of one of his manuscripts, Cusanus wrote, "Considera an loquatur (Athanasius) de Dionysio Areopagita sicut videtur; et tunc mirum quod Ambrosius, Augustinus et Hieronymous ipsum Dionysium non viderunt, qui fuerunt post Athanasium. Damascenus etiam Dionysium allegat, qui fuit post illos, tempore saeculi VIII. Gregorius Papa ante Joh. Damascenum etiam Dionysium allegat" (Bett, 19, note 2. Cod. Cus. 44, f. 1). Just as the discrediting of the Donation of Constantine and the Pseudo-Isidorian Decretals did not diminish the stature of the papacy for Cusanus, so also his suspicions of Pseudo-Dionysius did not seem to lessen his high regard for the Areopagite's apophatic and hierarchical ideas.

Cusanus affirms that by virtue of divine mandate and ancient tradition and enduring status, the Bishop of Rome is the head of the universal church. Indeed, for Cusanus, "Peter is the cornerstone of the Church, in whom is enfolded the whole edifice."[117] Furthermore, "Peter has all the power of Christ so that he can build up the Church not yet built up."[118] In Peter, according to Cusanus, the faithful and every principate of Christendom are enfolded. *De pace fidei* globally and mystically unfolds Peter's foundational role through the dynamic and dialectical Word of God to embrace all religious rites and build up the faithful of the world who consent to one religion.[119]

Finally, we consider the *Verbum*-metaphysic of Cusanus's pro-papal *Letter to Rodrigo Sánchez de Arévalo*, archdeacon of Treviño (1442). The letter, written after Cusanus's vision of learned ignorance and subsequent move to the papal side, begins with a profound discussion of the Word of God very similar in conceptual content to the opening of *De pace fidei*. The letter was written in the midst of lingering disturbances in the Latin Church over the fraught relationship between the Council of Basel and the pope, so that Rodrigo may "hunt down a final and truer conjecture according to the rules of learned ignorance."[120] Indeed, once these principles "become evident" and "open the intellect," Rodrigo and the reader will affirm the rightness of the pope's (Eugenius IV) prerogative of transferring the general council of Basel to Ferrara so that "the Council of Union with the Eastern Church should be held in the place most convenient for its business", as well as how he justly attempted through excommunication to dissolve the remaining fracas of those who refused to move south of the Alps.[121] Cusanus hopes that the readers' intellect will be illumined sufficiently to see the Word of God enfolded and unfolded

---

117 Sermon CLX, 3. Translation by Izbicki, *Nicholas of Cusa: Writings on Church and Reform*, p. 479. "Petrus est lapis aedificii ecclesiae, in quo totum complicatur aedificium sicut in lapide fundamenti, sine quo esse nequit aedificium, et in quo sistit aedificium."
118 Sermon CCLXXXVII, 7. Translation by Izbicki, *Nicholas of Cusa: Writings on Church and Reform*, p. 487. "Habet etiam Petrus omnem Christi potestatem, ut aedificare possit ecclesiam nondum aedificatam."
119 Sermon CCLXXXVII, 8: "In Petro est complicatio omnium fidelium et omnis principatus et omnis potestas ligandi et solvendi." *De pace fidei* I, 1; I, 6; II, 7.
120 *Letter to Rodrigo Sánchez de Arévalo* 1, Izbicki, pp. 430–431: "ultimam verioremque coniecturam secundum regulas doctae ignorantiae venari valeas."
121 *Letter to Rodrigo Sánchez de Arévalo* 15, Izbicki, pp. 446–447: "Haec, si ad liquidum extendantur, intellectum aperiunt…quando concilium pro reductione orientalis ecclesiae in eo loco, ubi magis rebus agendis congruebat, institueret atque ob hoc omnes alias congregationes dissolveret, et patres a Basilea absolveret, ut ad tam sanctam unionem libere concurrere possent." The goal is to concur together, to meet as one in concordance.

in the papacy as means of unity.[122] Analogously, Cusanus envisions the general religious dialogue of *De pace fidei* to be held in Jerusalem as the polis best suited for realizing that the diversity of the religions are but one through the enlightenment of the prophetic and dialectical Word of God.[123] And in his *Letter to John*, Cusanus seeks that the proposed council take place in the area of the Mediterranean for the convenience of the merchants who will escort the interested zealous Muslim faithful.[124] The principle of unity as revealed and guided by the enlightenment of the method of learned ignorance through the Word of God direct and outline Cusanus's attempts at seeking unity both between Eastern and Western Churches and between Muslims and Christians.

In his *Letter to Rodrigo* seeking ecclesial concordance, the first truth that Cusanus seeks and finds is the Word of God. Cusanus writes in a passage that would later be transmitted to the religions of the world in his vision of *De pace fidei*, "since all things are in the Word of God, through which all things came into existence, that Word then enfolds all things and through It all things are unfolded in a diversity of difference, participating the Word Itself."[125] The diversity of all things exists, according to Cusanus, through participation in the

---

122   *Letter to Rodrigo Sánchez de Arévalo* 6. According to Cusanus, the Word of God as enfolded and unfolded through Peter is enfolded and unfolded in his successor, the pope: "Hoc insuper modo Petri capitis ecclesiae huius complicativa virtus non nisi in explicata a se ecclesia potest appraehendi." *Letter to Rodrigo Sánchez de Arévalo* 14: "Sic et Petrus in ecclesia in ipsis sanctorum regulis vivere dicitur, quamdiu illa utilitati aedificandae ecclesiae praestat adiumentum." According to Cusanus, the continuation of the ancient general councils is also unfolded to the church through Peter and his successors. Yet, when unity is threatened, as was the case at Basel, the rump council abused its power to build up the Church, and, thereby, loses its legitimacy by frustrating plans of union with the Greek Church and instigating schism by electing an antipope (Felix v).

123   *De pace fidei* III, 9: "Et advocatis angelis qui omnibus nationibus et linguis praesunt, cuilibet praecepit, ut umum peritiorem ad Verbum caro factum adduceret...locum deputans Iherusalem ad hoc aptissimum."

124   *Epistula ad Ioannem de Segobia* 11, p. 97, line 15 in the Heidelberg edition. "Verum quia in terris Sarracenorum reperiuntur multi zelosi fideles, qui et mores atque fundamenta eorum optime sciunt et semper student ipsis obviare, illos colligere ex Kayro, Alexandria et Caffa expediret, et mercatores modum haberent eos adducendi."

125   *Letter to Rodrigo Sánchez de Arévalo* 1, Izbicki, p. 431: "quod quoniam omnia in verbo Dei sunt, per quod omnia in esse prodierunt, tunc verbum ipsum est omnia complicans, et omnia per ipsum explicata sunt in varietate alteritatis, ipsum verbum participantia." Cf., *De pace fidei* 11, 7.

Word of God.[126] Comparatively, in *De pace fidei*, all religious rites exist as praise of one God in so far as the Word of God enfolds and unfolds all things.[127] Indeed, as apophatic maxim of Cusanus, God ever remains "unknown and ineffable to all", and, yet, sought in existence itself through "different rites by different ways" and "named with different names."[128] Thus illumination by the Wisdom and Word of God is needed: whether through prophets or prelates. Furthermore, Cusanus writes to Rodrigo, "All rational creatures, therefore, can achieve the ultimate happiness in no other way than by participating the grace of Jesus."[129] Thus illumination by the Word of God through the method of learned ignorance in which believers touch the grace of Jesus is unfolded "through enigma and mirror image, or faith."[130] For Cusanus, the enigma of both finite existence and the diversity of religious rites unfold as the many from the infinite and unknown one. Cusanus writes, "Since, however, a multitude can participate unity only in a varied diversity, the Church cannot subsist, consequently, except in a varied participation of unity."[131] The remainder of the letter unfolds this through the agency of the pope whose power is to unite the ecclesiastical hierarchy that which is divided as the Word of God unites ontologically through the cosmic and transcendent unfolding and enfolding of all things. According to Cusanus, "There is no power under heaven which can diminish his authority to bring the erring back to the fold."[132] The pull of return (*redditus*) is the uniting power of the unfolding and enfolding Word of God as unfolding and enfolding through the mediation of Peter and his papal successors.

---

126 *Letter to Rodrigo Sánchez de Arévalo* 1: "sed in alteritate participantium exoritur alteritas creaturarum."
127 *De pace fidei* I, 4; II, 7.
128 *De pace fidei* I, 5, Biechler, Bond, p. 6: "Quid existens nisi esse? Tu ergo, qui es dator vitae et esse, es ille qui in diversis ritibus differenter quaeri videris et in diversis nominibus nominaris, quoniam uti es manes omnibus incognitus et ineffabilis." Cf., *De docta ingnorantia* I, 26.
129 *Letter to Rodrigo Sánchez de Arévalo* 2, Izbicki, pp. 431–433: "Omnes igitur rationales creaturae non aliter quam participatione gratiae Jesu foelicitatem ultimam consequuntur."
130 *Letter to Rodrigo Sánchez de Arévalo* 3, Izbicki, pp. 432–433: "saltem ipsam in aenigmate et speculo seu fide attingat." Cf., *De pace fidei* I, 5.
131 *Letter to Rodrigo Sánchez de Arévalo* 6, Izbicki, pp. 436–437: "Quomodo autem multitudo unitatem non nisi in varia alteritate potest participare, no potuit ecclesia nisi in varia participatione unitatis subsistere." Cf., *De pace fidei* I, 4: "Sed nosti, Domine, quod magna multitudo non potest esse sine multa diversitate."
132 *Letter to Rodrigo Sánchez de Arévalo* 15, Izbicki, p. 447: "ita non est potestas sub coelo, quae eius possit auctoritatem minuere, quominus errantes ad ovile reducat." Cf., *De pace fidei* III, 8–9.

Although Cusanus moved from the side of the council to that of the pope, what remained remarkably consistent in his theology from *De concordantia catholica* through *De pace fidei* and beyond was his dynamic understanding of the Word of God as embracing all things as their ultimate source of unity. The visions of *De docta ignoratia* and *De pace fidei* come into a shared focus through the lens of Cusanus's dialectical and hierarchical Word of God. The *Letter to Rodrigo*, penned subsequently to the vision of learned ignorance, provides more dialectical specificity than the presentation of the Word of God in the opening chapters of book one of *De concordantia catholica*. In the *Letter to Rodrigo*, we see the dialectic of the *Verbum explicatio-complicatio*, which would later be applied in *De pace fidei* to incorporate the religions of the world. Yet even in the opening of *De concordantia catholica* the idea appears, perhaps not as well elaborated as it later would be, concordantly running dispositively through the ranks of being. Put another way, the essential metaphysical framework for the Word of God in *De pace fidei* is already present in Cusanus's first major work. Cusanus extends the *Verbum* centered Christology from the *Letter to Rodrigo* to the religions of the world in *De pace fidei*. While *De concordantia catholica* offers a more balanced approach to the relationship between pope and council, from early on this focus on the *Verbum* remains in Cusanus's career right through *De pace fidei* and even in his final major writing, the *Cribratio Alkorani*, where he sifts the Qur'an to disclose the Word of God. *De pace fidei* also presents a balance of sorts between the Word of God as the analogue of the eternal pontiff and the council of world religious leaders. According to Cusanus's argument, the council is needed to consent to and to achieve lasting religious peace. While Cusanus's allegiances changed from council to pope, his predilection for real and imagined councils which promoted unity as chaired by the pope, whether it be between Eastern and Western Churches or between Islam and Christianity, remained a constant. Where the *Letter to Rodrigo* looks for peace between council and pope, *De pace fidei* seeks the same among the world religions. For Cusanus, the Word of God unites that which is divided and disparate. The pope, Christ's emissary on earth, in whom, according to Cusanus, the Word of God is unfolded and enfolded, amends division and avoids schism.

Cusanus was a cardinal and humanist, but also a theologian of the Word of God and proponent of the Dionysian celestial and ecclesiastical hierarchy. The common underlying hypostasis uniting the Christological arguments of both *De docta ignorantia* and *De concordantia catholica* is the Word of God. For Cusanus this preincarnate Wisdom (*Logos*) and incarnate Word assume an earthly representative in the hierarchy of infinite and finite things in the hierarch. The hierarchical working of the Word through the Spirit in the church is perhaps most clearly represented in Cusnaus's example of the magnetic stone found in the pivotal Christocentric beginning of *De concordantia cátholica*. Citing a passage from Ambrose, Cusanus writes in what is perhaps his most lucid passage on the hierarchical action of the Word of God,

> Thus I think of the Word from above as like a magnetic stone the power of which extends through everything down to the lowest being. Its infinite power is not lacking down through the ranks, but there is a marvellous order of interconnection among finite and limited creatures.[133]

The Word of God is how the hierarchy of being functions and how seekers of God realize the peace of faith. In the analogy, iron rings stand for human nature. The further away the chain of rings descends from the magnetic stone, the weaker the pull of unity. For as the magnetic power of the Word on human nature declines in subsequent generations and degenerates into ignorance of the Word and thence to religious and political confusion and, according to *De pace fidei*, the mistaking rites for religion, so the magnetic rock of the Word of God draws wise seekers of the peace of faith closer into concordance in rational human nature as "hypostatically united to divinity by grace in Jesus Christ."[134] According to Cusanus's transmission of Ambrose's analogy of the magnetic stone, the stone itself represents the human nature of Christ, while the inner, unseen force encompasses the infinite intellectual and divine nature of the *Logos*, and, as Divine Wisdom, the concordant principle of the cosmos. Furthermore, the Word of God in *De concordantia catholica* is represented by the holy priesthood, what Cusanus deems the soul of the church which extends to the body, the Holy Roman Empire, and beyond. Indeed, in *De concordantia catholica* Cusanus displays his knowledge of geography in describing the relationship of the nations of the world with the Holy Roman Empire, which would later be mapped out further in the characters of *De pace fidei*.[135] The Empire many be the body, but as the final metaphor of the treatise reveals, the priesthood is the soul. The highest capacity of this soul is of course the

---

133 Ambrose, *Ad Sabinum*. *De concordantia catholica* I, 2, 10, Sigmund, p. 9: "Sic verbum supernum lapidem imaginor, cuius virtus penetrat cuncta usque ad ultimum, non quod gradatim deficiat virtus infinita, sed ut finitis et terminatis creaturis insit mirabilis conexionis ordo."

134 *De concordantia catholica* I, 2, 10. *Letter to Rodrigo Sánchez de Arévalo* 2, Izbicki, pp. 430–431: "Nam omnis creatura rationalis, in natura rationali humana, per gratiam in Christo Jesu divinitati hypostatice unita gratiam elevationis ad unionem Dei." Cf., *De pace fidei* I, 4; II, 7–III, 8.

135 *De concordantia catholica* III, 6, 343.

papacy. Beyond sordid political and sundry practical concerns lies the deeper metaphysical and magnetic reason why Cusanus joined the papal contingent thereby revealing the full contours of his hierarchical world view. The cosmic hierarchy cascading from the coincidence of infinite and finite and the union of the heavenly church triumphant (Pseudo-Dionysius's *Celestial Hierarchy*) with the pilgrim church on earth (the *Ecclesitical Hierarchy*) through the hypostatic union of natures in the hierarch Christ concordantly concludes *De docta ignorantia* and indeed had appeared already seven years previously in the opening chapters of his first major work *De concordantia catholica*.[136]

Why did Cusanus leave the conciliar camp for the papal side following the Council of Basel? As the necessary earthly unfolding of the incarnate Word in the ecclesiastical hierarchy, the pope intermediates between the one absolute maximum (*De docta ignorantia*) and the consent of the many in the church catholic and the Holy Roman Empire (*De concordantia catholica*), and prophetically beyond the confines of Christendom to all the nations of the world and to every religious rite therein (*De pace fidei*). The pope as successor of Peter serves, for Cusanus, as the divinely appointed earthly means of restoring unity, both between the Eastern and Western Churches and among the many rites of the world's religions. Cusanus states, "the pope transferred the council [Basel] in order to preserve the unity of the Church and to reunite the Greeks."[137] The vision of *De pace fidei* presents the imagined universal council of religions. The Word chairs the session and then empowers Peter to continue the discussion so that Muslims, Hindus and Jews may consent to the concordance of the peace of faith. As the church "exists as a unity in a varied diversity", the pope's own ministry as a "coincidence of opposites" focuses, according to Cusanus, on attaining the virtue of unity and concordance of all things through the Word of God which unfolds and enfolds all things.[138]

Commenting on a passage centered on the Son of God as Wisdom from the Father at the outset of *De concordantia catholica*, Cusanus cites Augustine's description of Christ as one and the same idea expressed in different languages and various sacrificial rites. In a passage which sounds remarkably like the

---

136   *De docta ignorantia* III, 12, 262. Cf., *De concordantia catholica* I, 1, 8; I, 2, 12.
137   *Dialogus concludens Amedistarum errorem ex gestis et doctrina concilii Basiliensis*, 23, pp. 308–309. Translation by Izbicki. "Nunc autem, quando reductio Grecorum instabat, propter conservare unitatem ecclesie et reducere Grecos transtulit concilium."
138   *Letter to Rodrigo Sánchez de Arévalo*, 6, Izbicki, pp. 436–437: "Unitas igitur in varia alteritate ecclesia existit. Et sicut unitatis virtus non nisi in participata alteritate attingi potest, sic nec complicantis principii virtus aliter quam in explicatis principiatis potest apprehendi." Cf., *Letter to Rodrigo Sánchez de Arévalo* 1.

thesis concerning "one religion in the variety of rites" at the start of *De pace fidei*, he states: "for one and the same religion is observed at one time by some customs and signs, at other times by others, earlier in a more hidden fashion and later more openly, earlier by a few and later by a larger number."[139] In *De pace fidei*, the Wisdom and Word of God, and later through his earthly representative Peter, the wise hierarch, reveal the hidden truth that the various rites coincide in one religion through Cusanus's contemplative general council for the peace of the world.[140] Furthermore, Cusanus posits, "this is according to the intellectual rule of learned ignorance, that the Church is in the pontiff in an enfolded manner."[141] In *De docta ignorantia* the absolute maximum is one with the Word, Jesus Christ, who exists beyond the grasp of reason as the goal of the universe, and who is unfolded and enfolded in this world in the ecclesiastical hierarchy. In the argument of *De concordantia catholica* the pope receives his unfolded and enfolded place in the magnetic hierarchy and his power to attain unity as hierarch through the Spirit directly from the Word of God, the beginning and end of the chain of being. In this world, the one Word and many gradations of the ecclesiastical hierarchy come together most fully in the hierarch, the Bishop of Rome, the active and temporal unfolding of the unifying and concordant power of Christ.

Long since his move from council to pope and his illuminating vision of learned ignorance, Cusanus received a transcendent glimpse of concord where the hierarchy of the Word extended from Rome to the known world of the mid-fifteenth century. Years after Cusanus left the Council of Basel, he received what he testified to be a vision of a heavenly general council. Owing to the fall of Constantinople to the Ottomans, reunion with the Greek Church was no longer a matter of compelling urgency. By this time, the conciliar movement had also run its course. The one-time member of the Council of Basel recounts how a certain zealous man who had once seen the sites of Constantinople was distraught over the violence caused by differing religious beliefs and the collapse of Byzantium. Perhaps in remembrance of the death of his mentor Cesarini while on crusade against the Ottomans, Cusanus prays for an end to

---

139 Augustine, *Ad Deogratias* q. II, Sections 9–11. Augustine refers to the universal and global dispensation of divine knowledge and grace in and through Christ from the Old to New Testament and beyond. *De concordantia catholica* I, 3, 14, Sigmund, p. 11: "sicut in varietate linguarum idem [idea: Christ] pronuntiatur...Aliis enim tunc moribus et signis, aliis nunc, et prius occultius et postea manifestius, et prius a paucioribus, postea a pluribus una et eadem religio sanctificatur et observatur." Cf., *De pace fidei* I, 4–6; III, 8–9; XIX, 68.

140 *De pace fidei* XIX, 68.

141 *Epistola ad Rodericum de Trevino*, 14, Izbicki, pp. 446–447: "Et hoc est iuxta regulam intellectualem doctae ignorantiae, in pontifice esse ecclesiam complicative."

religious violence and receives a vision of religious peace. Cusanus responds to the fall of Constantinople not with military bombast, but by inventively envisioning a religious general council in Jerusalem, universal city of David, Jesus, and Mohammad, to the end that the participants of the many religions might unanimously consent to one religion in a variety of rites and fulfill what was serenely agreed upon in Cusanus's mind.[142] The recounting of in dialogue form of the vision of *De pace fidei* by Cusanus reveals a dynamic interplay of contemplation and action, council and pope, hierarchy from above and consent from below, played out on a truly global scale. In *De pace fidei*, as in *De docta ignorantia* and *De concordantia catholica*, the one meets the many through the incarnate Word, "the Eternal Pontiff."[143] Indeed, Cusanus deliberately designates Christ as pontifex: the bridge between the one and the many. He "who is and who was and who is to come" presides at the council of *De pace fidei* in person and through his emissaries, the first pope Peter and the great apologist Paul.[144] There is a characteristically Cusanian coinciding of opposites and bringing together of the one, the Absolute of *De docta ignorantia*, with the contracted many from the Absolute, the orders of church and empire of *De concordantia catholica*, and the diverse religions of *De pace fidei* into the unity of the *Logos* and the incarnate Word through his supreme earthly representative, the pope, the "unfolded from Peter".[145] For Cusanus, the successor of Peter in whom, by the power of the Holy Spirit, the one Absolute and the contracted many of the faith in all their differing religious rites most fully meet, necessarily exists for the well being of the universal church of God this side of heaven.

In this chapter we have seen Cusanus's visions of concordance and considered plans for action, as well as the centrality of the papacy and the prophetic voice of religious peace. In the next chapter we penultimately look synthetically at Cusanus's concentric concept of the Word of God in *De pace fidei* and how his metaphysic of concordance unfolds to embrace four of his major works. From there we will ultimately consider in the final chapter of this work the exclusive and inclusive nature of his Christocentric approach to Islam in *De pace fidei*.

---

142   *Epistula ad Ioannem de Segobia* 11, p. 100, line 15 in the Heidelberg edition. "Ego tamen, etsi omnino cum ipsis potius putem conferendum quam bellandum."
143   *De concordantia catholica* I, 3, 12, Sigmund, p. 11.
144   Revelation 1:8.
145   *Epistola ad Rodericum de Trevino* 11, Izbicki, pp. 442–443. "In hoc video murmurationes exoriri, quae facile tolluntur universali sacro principe [the pope] advertente se Petri successorem post ecclesiam a Petro explicatam."

CHAPTER 6

The Word of Peace

> He [Christ] is the image of the invisible God, the firstborn of all creation; for in him all things in heaven and on earth were created, things visible and invisible, whether thrones or dominions or rulers or powers—all things have been created through him and for him. He himself is before all things, and in him all things hold together.[1]

⁂

De pace fidei expounds Cusanus's Christocentric and Platonic-panoramic prayer for religious peace. In the dialogue diverse global religious rites and complex theological propositions are joined together as one religion through the dialectical and hierarchical Word of God. All things, including diverse religious practices, have been created by God, according to Cusanus, through Christ and for Christ.[2] This Word of God comprises, for Cusanus, the ancient and conciliar Christian conception of providential Wisdom and the incarnate *Logos*.[3] Echoing the New Testament of the Christian Scriptures, the dynamic Word of God in *De pace fidei* is before all things, and in him all things, notably both Islam and Christianity, connect. Cusanus bookends this Platonic dialogue in the turbulent realm of temporality, or in Augustinian terms, the flux of dissimilarity.[4] *De pace fidei* begins with a fervent petition for an end to violence caused by conflicting rites for religion and concludes with the nations of the world consenting to one religion in the variety of rites.[5] What remains constant amidst and above the fluctuations of religious confusion is the Word of God through which all things are unfolded and enfolded.[6] Here we see the expansive scope of Cusanus's vision of world religious peace. His imaginative and mystical prayer for peace ascends to the heavenly throne thereby moving

---

1 Colossians 1:15–17 NRSV.
2 *De pace fidei* I, 6–III, 9; Cf., Colossians 1:16.
3 *De pace fidei* IV; X, 27.
4 Augustine, *Confessions* II, 1 (1); VII, 10 (16); Cf., Plato, *Statesmen* 273d.
5 *De pace fidei* I, 1; XIX, 68.
6 *De pace fidei* II, 7.

inward to the soul and upward to the altitude of reason.[7] Here we not only observe the full scope of immanence and transcendence, self and God, but also the sweep of time: Cusanus recounts the conversation of *De pace fidei* from memory.[8] He recollects (*memoria*), in the Platonic and Augustinian sense (*anamnesis*), what the immortal soul should already know, yet what becomes confounded by ignorance (*ignorantia*) and clouded by conjecture (*coniecturis*).[9] In the centre of memory, Cusanus pneumatically unfolds the enfolding Word of God as inherent Wisdom, form of forms, presupposed by all that brings together heaven and earth, God and self, intellect and will, religion and rites.[10]

Cusanus recounts his Christocentric and all-encompassing dialogue of religious peace from memory. His recollection of the *Gloria in Excelsis* from the Gospel of Luke further illumines Cusanus's notion of peace in direct relation to the unifying Word of God.[11] *Sermon CLXVIII*, preached on Christmas, 1455, in his diocese of Brixen on the lectionary text of Luke 2:14 exegetes the metaphysics of peace and its perfection in the person of Christ, harking back to themes reminiscent of *De pace fidei*.[12] As in *De pace fidei*, Cusanus further develops his constructive concept of peace through the prompting of angelic visitation and annunciation.[13] And like *De pace fidei*, magnetic peace is mediated hierarchically (via angels from God to the Logos) and dialectically (the *terminus a quo* of natural philosophy to the *terminus ad quem* of the incarnate Christ).[14] In the Sermon, Cusanus reflects on the nature of peace as perfected in Christ. This peace may be recalled by the likes of Plato and Aristotle, yet owing to the fall of Adam and the subsequent wages of sin, the unruly soul disorients concordant discourse and divides what should be whole.[15] While philosophy

---

7   *De pace fidei* I, 2.

8   *De pace fidei* I, 1.

9   Augustine, *Confessions* X, 8 (12); Plato, *Meno* 81d, 82a–86c; *De pace fidei* I, 1: "memoria"; I, 3–4; II, 7; III, 8.

10 *De pace fidei* V, 13; XI, 29: "forma formarum"; XIII, 45: "hinc video hunc magistrum et mediatorem, naturae humanae supremitatem perfectionis et principatum tenentem, ab omnibus praesupponi."

11 Luke 2:14 and one of the chief parts of the western mass, which would regularly echo from altar in the Cardinal's mind.

12 *Sermon CLXVIII* in *Nicolai de Cusa Opera Omnia*, vol. 18, edited by Silvia Donati, Rudolf Haubst et al. (Hamburg: Felix Meiner, 2007), 219–223.

13 *De pace fidei* I, 1–2. Both *Sermon CLXVIII* and *De pace fidei* assume angels mediating the Wisdom and Word of God, Christ.

14 *Sermon CLXVIII*, 1; *Sermon CLXVIII*, 7: "De hac pace Christi considera quo modo sic praeordinatum est ab initio, ut esset mundus unus et omnia in eo, cuius finis esset Christus."; *De pace fidei* I, 3; III, 9.

15 *Sermon CLXVIII*, 4; *Sermon CLXVIII*, 10. Cf., *De pace fidei* III, 8. Cf., Romans 6:23.

may smooth the stony way to finding God, theology and sacred revelation remain requisite for beatitude in a manner redolent of Aquinas.[16] As in *De pace fidei*, the revelation of religious concord begins in the Brixen sermon with the Trinity followed by Christology.[17] Christ marks the end of the search for happiness and peace.[18] The union of God and man in Christ is the supreme peace.[19] This peace as found in the person and work of Christ—creator, mediator and end—enlightens and enables the soul to realize immortality and beatitude.[20] Here we fully appreciate the sublime doctrine of Cusanus's word of peace. Peace, like Christ, the source of peace, is one, and in this unity there exists a coincidence of opposites and the coming together of all things: cause and effect, infinite and finite, intellectual conceptions and active realizations, mystical contemplation and consensus of religious concord.[21]

From cathedra and pulpit to speculative religious discourse and dialogue we are reminded that the centre of this synthetic study on *De pace fidei* is Cusanus's multivalent and irenic concept of the Word of God. Our previous chapter covered how contemplation and action coincide through the Word of God in Cusanus's *De pace fidei*. We posited how his pacific and prophetic *Verbum* metaphysic of religious concordance illumines greater understanding of his contentious shift from council to pope. Having examined philosophical and theological influences and the context and contours of Cusanus's Christocentric search for religious concordance and peace, even the complicated connection of crusade and dialogue, we realized that Cusanus's conception of the divine *Logos* holds together one religion in the variety of rites. Since *De pace fidei* proposes a dialectical synthesis of the world's religions, notably of Christianity and Islam, through the Word of God, we now consider one concluding aspect of religious concordance: how this synthesis of peace relates to the Christology of four of Cusanus's other major writings: *De docta ignorantia*, *De concordantia catholica*, *Cribratio Alkorani*, and *De visione Dei*.

---

16 Aquinas, *Summa Theologiæ* Ia, 1, 1; *De pace fidei* XIII, 44; *Sermon* CLXVIII, 1, 4, 6, 10.
17 *Sermon* CLXVIII, 3: "Haec coincidentia in se considerate esset pax tricausalis unitatis." On Christology see *Sermon* CLXVIII, 7. *De pace fidei* on the Trinity, Chps. VII–X, on Christology, Chaps. XI–XV.
18 *Sermon* CLXVIII, 6, 10; *De pace fidei* XIII, 45: "Et quoniam omnium spes est aliquando consequi posse felicitatem, propter quam est omnis religio".
19 *Sermon* CLXVIII, 6: "Unio deitatis cum humanitate est suprema pax." Cf., *De pace fidei* XII, 39.
20 *Sermon* CLXVIII, 7, 9; *De pace fidei* XIV, 49.
21 *Sermon* CLXVIII, 2: "In illo Alpha et O, principium et finis coinciderent." Cf., Revelation 22:13; *Sermon* CLXVIII, 6: "Pax videtur unio circumferentis ad centrum, et locus pacis et quietis est centrum."

These important works are not normally viewed as correspondent, and are often classified as mismatched. *De docta ignorantia*, is categorized as speculative thought, *De concordantia catholica* as conciliar and political, *Cribratio Alkorani* as apologetical and polemical, and *De visione Dei* as a masterpiece of mystical theology.[22] Cusanus himself hints at these distinct designations.[23] Yet what underlies the arguments of these writings remains remarkably continuous. Cusanus's Chalecodonian and hierarchical, dialectical Christology from early in his theological career of *De concordantia catholica*, expands to embrace the diversity of the religions of the world in his mystical and imaginative dialogue of *De pace fidei*. In this chapter we present a case study on connecting four aspects of Cusanus's Christology from selections of four of his major works as compared with the account of the Word of God Christology in *De pace fidei*; in our final chapter we shall evaluate the tension between relative exclusivity and inclusivity in Cusanus's Christocentric approach to Islam. Having begun this study by examining how in *De pace fidei* all things dialectically and hierarchically cascade from and return to the Word of God, in this chapter we expand this *Verbum* metaphysic and Christology of *De pace fidei* to embrace the Christology of four of his major works.[24] While this case study is in no way meant to be exhaustive, here we aim to examine how the structure of the dialogue of *De pace fidei* progresses from the one Word and Wisdom of God to the many religions, and then back again from the many to the one by comparing specific aspects and sections of Cusanus's Christology in *De pace fidei* with particular characteristics and pericopes on the Christology of the four above mentioned works: the unfolding Word (*De pace fidei* and *De docta ignorantia*), the magnetic Word (*De pace fidei* and *De concordantia catholica*), the inherent Word (*De pace fidei* and *Cribratio Alkorani*), and the enfolding Word (*De pace fidei* and *De visione Dei*). By viewing the parts in relation to the whole, we are able to discern the encompassing arc of emanation and return, the full sweep of Cusanus's concept of religious concordance: how within Christ all things, including Christianity and Islam, hold together for peace.

---

22 For general overview on the standard classification of Cusanus's works, see Bellitto, et al., *Introducing Nicholas of Cusa*, and Watanabe, *Nicholas of Cusa: A Companion to his Life and his Times*.

23 *De docta ignorantia*, prologue and concluding epistle; *De concordantia catholica*, preface; *Cribratio Alkorani*, dedicatory preface; *De visione Dei*, dedication.

24 Chapter one.

The Unfolding Word: *De docta ignorantia* and *De pace fidei*

The Christian poet T.S. Eliot famously versified, "In my end is my beginning."[25] The same claim may be made of the conclusion of *De docta ignorantia*. As we have seen in the previous chapter, in the epilogue of *De docta ignorantia* Cusanus professed to have received a revelation from God. He would later reflect this in his vision of a single religion in a variety of rites in *De pace fidei*.[26] Cusanus states in the *Apologia doctae ignorantiae* that he received a method or 'via' of theological discourse in the form of the coincidence of opposites.[27] In the *Apologia* he even suggests the framework for *De pace fidei* on specific rites being confused with religion itself owing to confusion wrought by long standing custom.[28] According to Cusanus, God makes known a method and way of true theology and peace which originates in visions and contemplation and cannot ultimately be transcribed.[29] Moreover, the conclusion of *De docta ignorantia* proved to be a new dialectical beginning of sorts for Cusanus.[30] Over the next nearly twenty-five years he would reveal and apply the hidden and visionary principles of learned ignorance in various dialogues, treatises and sermons. Christ, the Word of God, as God and man, infinite and finite, reveals and perfects this method of knowing the unknown through the Holy Spirit.[31] Our present discussion concentrates on the new beginning found at the end of *De docta ignorantia*, in the final chapter to be precise.[32] Cusanus brings his method of learned ignorance to a close with a weighty discussion of the

---

25   T.S. Eliot, *Four Quartets*, East Coker (New York: Harcourt, Brace and Company, 1943), 17.

26   *De docta ignorantia*, *Epistola auctoris ad Dominum Iulianum Cardinalem*: "credo superno dono a patre luminum, a quo omne datum optimum"; *De pace fidei* I, 1: "visio quaedam eidem zeloso manifestaretur".

27   *Apologia doctae ignorantiae* 7: "oppositorum coincidentiam . . . via"; *De docta ignorantia*, prologus: "ratiocinandi modum".

28   *Apologia doctae ignorantiae* 7: "Nam tanta est vis longaevae observantiae, quod citius vita multorum evellitur quam consuetudo, – uti experimur in persecutione Iudaeorum, Sarracenorum et aliorum pertinacium haereticorum, qui opinionem usu temporis firmatam legem asserunt, quam vitae praeponunt." Cf., *De pace fidei* I, 1: "persecutionem, quae ob diversum ritum religionum"; *De pace fidei* I, 4: "Habet autem hoc humana terrena condicio quod longa consuetodo, quae in naturam transisse accipitur, pro veritate defenditur."

29   *Apologia doctae ignorantiae* 5: "theologiam veram non posse litteris commendari . . . Est enim theologia de regno Dei; et hoc magister noster Christus occultatum in abscondito thesauro declaravit." On peace as goal of this method, *Apologia doctae ignorantiae* 54.

30   *De coniecturis*, preface and prologue.

31   *De docta ignorantia*, *Epistola auctoris ad Dominum Iulianum Cardinalem* 264; *Apologia doctae ignorantiae* 54.

32   *De docta ignorantia* III, 12.

hierarchy of the church. Why should he conclude an apophatic discourse on abstract philosophical and theological reasoning with concrete ecclesiastical hierarchy? Astute readers would expect book three to conclude in much the same way as books one and two: with the mystery of unknowing God and self.[33] Why, then, compose a final chapter on the church?

The key to understanding book three of *De docta ignorantia*, namely Christ "the end of all things", unlocks why Cusanus concludes his method of unknowing God and self with the celestial and ecclesiastical hierarchy.[34] Cusanus begins his third and final book by investigating "the maximum that is both absolute and contracted, Jesus Christ, the ever blessed."[35] Furthermore, Cusanus adds, "we call on him to be the way to himself who is the truth, that by this truth, now through faith and later through obtaining, we may be alive in him and by him who is eternal life."[36] Straightaway, Cusanus recaps the argument of books one and two. The first book, he states, shows that the one absolute maximum is simple. The second book examines the universe contracted in plurality. Cusanus begins his third book on Christ, who is "both contracted and also absolute", by proceeding to note the contracted diversity of opinions on genus, species, and number according to the diversity of religions and regions.[37] This mystifying expression of plurality, Cusanus asserts, is God's own providential work so that each nationality would be content within its own region and customs for "unity and peace."[38] Similarly, in *De pace fidei*, Cusanus states that different regions worship God in various rites so as to increase devotion by the many of the one true God. Throughout the structure and content of *De docta ignorantia* and *De pace fidei* the hierarchical Word of God, the "maximum, which is both contracted and also absolute", brings differing opinions and religious rites together in one peace of faith and perfects the method of knowing the unknown (*De docta ignorantia*).[39] Echoing this cosmic goal of concordant harmony and perfection, Cusanus writes proleptically at the Christocentric conclusion of his *Apologia doctae ignorantiae*, "for by every

---

33   *De docta ignorantia* I, 26; II, 13, 180.
34   *De docta ignorantia* III, 11, 247, translation by Bond, p. 198.
35   *De docta ignorantia* III, prologue, 181, translation by Bond, p. 169.
36   *De docta ignorantia* III, prologue, 181, translation by Bond, p. 169.
37   *De docta ignorantia* I, 2, 7, translation by Bond, p. 90. *De docta ignorantia* III, 1, 182; III, 1, 189.
38   *De docta ignorantia* III, 1, 189, translation by Bond, p. 173.
39   *De docta ignorantia* I, 2, 7, translation by Bond, p. 90: "Et quoniam tale cum absoluto, quod est terminus universalis, unitur, quia finis perfectissimus *supra* omnem capacitatem nostram, de illo maximo, quod simul est contractum et absolutum, quod Iesum semper benedictum nominamus".

movement we seek only peace; and the Peace which surpasses all the senses is our peace".[40] In cosmic structure and prayer Cusanus demonstrates the effect of the circular and consubstantial nature of Christ upon human intellect and will, wherein, both as way and end, the knowledge of God and knowledge of self conjoin and transcend discursive reasoning and unfold in truth and life. Cusanus's method of learned ignorance as the way to unity and peace becomes hierarchically played out "by every movement" in and through Christ.[41] In *De pace fidei*, Cusanus applies this same logic and method of Christ as the unfolding Word who, through movements and ministrations of angels and the apostolic succession of Peter and Paul, hierarchically illumines each region and religion of the world by the timeless reality of one religion in the variety of rites.

Cusanus's presentation on the ascension of Jesus in book three of *De docta ignorantia* most clearly highlights the role of the unfolding Christ in his conception of the celestial and ecclesial hierarchy of unity and peace. Unsurprisingly, we find here also comparisons with *De pace fidei*. Because Christ has ascended, he "is the center and circumference of intellectual nature, and because the intellect embraces all things, he is above all things."[42] Indeed, Cusanus continues, drawing upon Christian Scripture, because Christ ascended above the heavens so that he would fill all things, "he is truth itself, he reigns in the intellectual heavens" and seated at the centre of the intellectual heavens and rational spirits, he is the life and end of human beings.[43] Cusanus envisions *De pace fidei* occurring in the heaven of reason.[44] Therefore Christ, as the center of all rational spirits, is not "situated along the circumference but is seated at the center" of the dialogue. From this centre, he interacts with the imagined

---

40   *Apologia doctae ignorantiae* 54, translation by Jasper Hopkins: "Nam cum omni motu non quaeratur nisi pax, et haec pax, quae exsuperat omnem sensum, sit pax nostra". Cf., Philippians 4:7; John 15:5; *De docta ignorantia* III, 12, 257. For Cusanus, Jesus Christ, the Word of God, is the source of peace, without whom nothing can be accomplished.
41   *Apologia doctae ignorantiae* 54, translation by Hopkins.
42   *De docta ignorantia* III, 8, 232, translation by Bond, p. 191: "Ipse centrum atque circumferentia intellectualis naturae est et, cum intellectus omnia ambiat, supra omnia est".
43   *De docta ignorantia* III, 8, 232, translation by Bond, p. 191: "Sic igitur supra omnem locum et omne tempus ad incorruptibilem mansionem, supra omne id, quod dici potest, intelligimus Christum ascendisse, in hoc quod supra omnes caelos ascendit, ut adimpleret omnia; qui cum sit Deus, est omnia in omnibus, et ipse regnat in caelis illis intellectualibus, cum sit ipsa veritas, et non secundum locum potius in circumferentia quam centro sedens, cum sit centrum omnium rationabilium spirituum, ut vita eorum. Et propter hoc intra homines hoc regnum caelorum etiam esse ipsa affirmat, qui est fons vitae animarum finisque earum." Cf., Ephesians 4:10.
44   *De pace fidei* XIX, 68: "caelo rationis".

participants and unfolds to the circumference the concordance of religious peace.[45] Moreover, in Cusanus's examination of the ascension in *De docta ignorantia*, he writes in what later would be applied to *De pace fidei*, "there is no perfect religion, leading to the final and most desired end of peace, that does not embrace Christ as mediator and savior, God and human, the way, the truth, and the life."[46] Here Cusanus wonders why, based on his interpretation of Islam, Muslims identify Christ as "the maximum, most perfect, and immortal human", but fail to perceive him to be divine.[47] In *De pace fidei*, Cusanus would propose his own unique way of unfolding the answer to this question through the conciliar agency of Christ, the Word of God. And for Cusanus "through Christ alone human nature can attain to incorruptibility."[48]

After discussing the ascension of Jesus and the soul's desire for union with the ineffable and infinite, Cusanus concludes book three of *De docta ignorantia* with the hierarchy of the church precisely because this is how the unfolding Word of God properly works to bridge the gap between unknowing and knowing, divine and human, angels and the blessed, church triumphant and church militant, religion and rites. Cusanus proposes a dialectical account whereby every rational nature which looks to Christ in faith, hope and love, is united, while the distinct personal truth of each nature is nonetheless retained with Christ in a graduated hierarchical order that spans heaven and earth, angels and the blessed.[49] "Consequently," Cusanus writes, "each of the blessed, while the truth of each's being is preserved, exists in Christ Jesus as Christ and through him in God as God, and God, remaining the absolute maximum, exists

---

45   *De docta ignorantia* III, 8, 232, translation by Bond, p. 191; *De pace fidei* III, 8.

46   *De docta ignorantia* III, 8, 229, translation by Bond, p. 190: "Vides, ni fallor, nullam perfectam religionem homines ad ultimum desideratissimum pacis finem ducentem esse, quae Christum non amplectitur mediatorem et salvatorem, Deum et hominem, viam, vitam et veritatem." Cf., *De pace fidei* XIII, 45; XIV, 49.

47   *De docta ignorantia* III, 8, 230, translation by Bond, p. 190: "perfectissimum et immortalem hominem". Cf., *De docta ignorantia* III, 8, 229.

48   *De docta ignorantia* III, 8, 230, translation by Bond, p. 190: "tamen adhuc super omnia necessarium est Christum Deum et hominem credi, per quem solum natura humana ad incorruptibilitatem potest pervenire." Cf., *De pace fidei* XIV, 48–49.

49   *De docta ignorantia* III, 12, 260: "Deinde omnis rationalis natura Christo Domino, remanente cuiuslibet personali veritate, si ad Christum in hac vita summa fide et spe atque caritate conversa fuerit, adeo unita existit, ut omnes, tam angeli quam homines, non nisi in Christo subsistant; per quem in Deo, veritate corporis cuiusque per spiritum absorpta et attracta, ut quilibet beatorum, servata veritate sui proprii esse, sit in Christo Iesu Christus, et per ipsum in Deo Deus, et quod Deus eo absoluto maximo remanente sit in Christo Iesu ipse Iesus, et in omnibus omnia per ipsum."

in Christ Jesus as Jesus and through him in all things as all things."[50] Similarly, in *De pace fidei*, each religious rite remains in its full nature and expression with the one religion through Christ, the Word of God just as the one person of Christ remains in two full natures: divine and human. As Cusanus writes at the conclusion of *De docta ignorantia*, "In no other way [than through the hypostatic Christ, the Word of God] can the church be more one. For the more the church is one, the greater it is."[51] *De pace fidei* expands the church, makes it greater, in order to embrace and unite all religious rites in a single universal religion hypostatically through the second person of the Trinity, thereby even coincidentally connecting diverse religious rites to the hidden and unknown God. According to Cusanus, the more united this church of one religion becomes, the greater the global and supernatural peace of faith.

Where is the church in *De pace fidei*? In a narrow sense, Cusanus notes the priesthood at the very end of *De pace fidei*.[52] In a broad sense for Cusanus the bishop and cardinal, the church is everywhere: late-medieval Christendom was an accepted and unquestioned reality and what is ubiquitous may be contextually assumed. Yet, in an overarching metaphysical sense, the church is present, in Cusanus's estimation, right at the beginning in the heavenly and angelic council, and expanded throughout as the Word unfolds the peace of faith hierarchically through Peter and Paul with the consent of the remaining and diverse many imagined participants to the ends of the earth. To echo *De docta ignorantia* and the *Apologia doctae ignorantiae*, the Church of *De pace fidei* in its hypostatic relation to Christ, the Word of God, is not "situated along the circumference but is seated at the center" and extends outward in the dynamic unfolding and enfolding of all things in concentric movements of peace, from center to circumference to reveal "the perfect religion" of "unity and peace".[53] The more the heavenly council remains one, the more the church is one with the variety of rites remaining just as in the ascended incarnate Word of God human nature remains enfolded within God and there reflects "the face of all peoples".[54] This universal and incarnate Word as centre unfolds

---

50 *De docta ignorantia* III, 12, 260, translation by Bond, p. 204.
51 *De docta ignorantia* III, 12, 261, translation by Bond, p. 204: "Nec potest ecclesia esse alio modo magis una. Nam ecclesia unitatem plurium, salva cuiusque personali veritate, dicit absque confusione naturarum et graduum. Quanto autem magis ecclesia est una, tanto maior."
52 *De pace fidei* XIX, 67.
53 *De docta ignorantia* III, 8, 232, translation by Bond, p. 191; *De pace fidei* II, 7; *Apologia doctae ignorantiae* 54; *De docta ignorantia* III, 8, 229, translation by Bond, p. 190; *De docta ignorantia* III, 1, 189, translation by Bond, p. 173.
54 *De pace fidei* XIII, 43, translation by Biechler, Bond: "facies omnium gentium".

in celestial and ecclesial hierarchy at the conclusion of *De docta ignorantia*. Indeed, as Eliot writes, "What we call the beginning is often the end / And to make an end is to make a beginning."[55] This beginning of the hierarchical unfolding of religious concordance continues at the imaginative end of *De pace fidei* with peace announced to the world and the enfolding of many rites into their source: the one Word and God of peace.[56]

The Magnetic Word: *De concordantia catholica* and *De pace fidei*

The incarnate Christ unfolds by attraction. Owing to human finitude and weakness and because humanity "could not grasp the Word except in a sensible form and in a form similar to ourselves, God revealed the Word according to our capacity."[57] One powerful analogy that Cusanus employs is that of magnetic stone. In the metaphysical preface to the argument of *De concordantia catholica* he compares the Word of God to a magnetic stone whose power from above extends below to the lowest rank on the chain of being in "a marvellous order of interconnection among finite and limited creatures."[58] This "marvellous order" embraces the intricate workings of church (church triumphant, church sleeping, i.e., purgatory, and church militant) as well as Holy Roman Empire, the commonwealth of Christendom.[59]

We have already explored this analogy in depth in the previous chapter. Here we seek to examine Cusanus's extension of the same Christocentric example to the unfolding of peace between Christians and Muslims. In *De concordantia catholica*, the infinite power hidden in the magnetic stone represents the divinity of Christ, while the outer shell refers to his finite human nature. The concentric rings attached to the stone are various orders of celestial and ecclesial hierarchy. In *De pace fidei*, Cusanus elaborates upon the analogy of the Word of God as magnetic stone in light of the complex and pivotal Chalcedonian theological locus of the two natures of the person of Christ—"that Christ alone is the loftiest man and the Word of God."[60] In the guise of the character Peter he addresses a Persian Muslim,

---

55   T.S. Eliot, *Four Quartets*, Little Gidding, 38.
56   *De pace fidei* XIX, 68.
57   *De docta ignorantia* III, 5, 211, translation by Bond, p. 182. Cf., *De pace fidei* II, 7.
58   *De concordantia catholica* I, 2, 10, translation by Sigmund, p. 9.
59   *De concordantia catholica*, preface, 3; I, 4, 19.
60   *De pace fidei* XII, 39, translation by Biechler and Bond: "Christum solum altissumum hominem et Verbum Dei."

Take this example, although it is a remote one: a magnet draws iron upward, and by adhering to the magnetic ore the nature of the iron does not subsist in its own weighty nature, otherwise it would not hang in the air, but in accordance with its nature it would fall towards the center of the earth. Yet in the power of the magnet's nature the iron, by adhering to the magnet, subsists in the air and not by the power of its own nature according to which it could not be there. Now the iron's nature is inclined in this way to the magnet's nature because the iron has in itself a likeness to the magnet's nature, from which it is said to have taken its origin. So if the intellectual human nature should adhere in the closest way to divine intellectual nature, from which it has received its being, it would adhere to it as inseparably as to the font of its life.[61]

This "remote example" illustrates how the Word of God attracts far to near from near to far. The magnetic ore is the intellectual and divine nature of the Word of God. The iron stands for the intellectual nature of human beings. Created in the image of the invisible God, and owing to its likeness to the magnet's power in its immateriality, human intellectual nature adheres magnetically to the Word of God.[62] As the Word is manifested in stone, it exists as universal and finite, and, hence, becomes potentially knowable by analogy and accommodation to all as beginning, way and end. This magnetic attraction becomes necessary, as Cusanus notes in dialogue between Peter and the Persian, "for between contracted wisdom, i.e., human wisdom, and wisdom per se, which is divine and maximum and infinite, there always remains an infinite distance."[63]

How, then, to mind the gap between contracted wisdom and infinite wisdom? The Word of God as "eternal Wisdom" and "omnipotent art" spans the metaphysical-material divide through the human intellectual nature in human beings, hence, the noetic metaphors of the magnet as incarnate Word and

---

61   *De pace fidei* XII, 40, translation by Biechler and Bond: "Cape exemplum, licet remotum. Lapis magnes attrahit sursum ferrum, et adhaerendo in aere magneti natura ferri non in sua ponderosa natura subsistit—alias enim non penderet in aere, sed caderet secundum naturam suam versus centrum terrae—, sed in virtute naturae magnetis ferrum magneti adhaerendo subsistit in aere, et non virtute propriae naturae secundum quam ibi esse non posset. Causa autem cur inclinetur sic ferri natura ad naturam magnetis est, quia ferrum gerit in se similitudinem naturae magnetis, a qua ortum recepisse dicitur. Sic, dum natura intellectualis humana adhaereret naturae intellectuali divinae propinquissime a qua recepit esse, illi adhaereret ut fonti vitae suae inseparabiliter."
62   Genesis 1:27; John 1:18. Cf., *De visione Dei* XXIV, 112–113.
63   *De pace fidei* XII, 36, translation by Biechler and Bond: "Nam inter sapientiam contractam, scilicet humanam, et sapientiam per se, quae est divina et maxima atque infinita, semper manet infinita distantia."

iron as intellectual nature.[64] While in *De concordantia catholica* the analogy of the magnetic stone applies to the complex hierarchy of church and empire within Christendom, in *De pace fidei* it extends by way of illumination (that is to say, through 'common grace' in creation) and dialectical consent to all those seekers of happiness and immortality, including Muslims, who may be so magnetically united in intellectual nature. Cusanus even envisions *De pace fidei* to be set in the altitude of reason, wherein the magnetic Word and Wisdom of God attracts the wise of the world to leave behind the "weighty nature" of mistaking rites for religion and to ascend to the peace of faith.[65] This ascension to the peace of one religion is made possible through the hierarchical-dialectical magnetism of the ascended Christ.[66] The magnetic Word accomplishes, at least imaginatively and metaphysically in Cusanus's mind, global peace through the unfolding Word of Wisdom of God. This same Word is also inherent in creation and in significant religious and philosophical writings as Wisdom and creator and end of all things.[67] As such, this magnetic and omnipresent art of the Word of God waits to be discovered by the magnetically attracted intellect. As we shall see, one such important text where the inherent Word of God heuristically appears is the Qur'an.

The Inherent Word: *Cribratio Alkorani* and *De pace fidei*

Cusanus's library in Kues, Germany includes a copy of Robert of Ketton's twelfth-century Latin translation of the Qur'an.[68] On the surface this would appear to be rather humdrum even by late-medieval standards. There were many copies of Ketton's Qur'an in circulation in late-medieval and early-modern Western Europe.[69] Indeed, as Thomas Burman points out, "when European Christians read the Qur'an any time between the mid-twelfth and late seventeenth century, they usually read Robert's version."[70] As the saying

---

64 *De pace fidei* XII, 37, translation by Biechler and Bond: "sapientiae aeternae, Verbo aut arti omnipotenti".
65 *De pace fidei* XII, 40; *De pace fidei* I, 1–2, translation by Biechler and Bond. Cf., *Cribratio Alkorani* I, 6, 42; *Cribratio Alkorani* II, 17, 148; *De visione Dei* XXV, 116.
66 *De pace fidei* XIII, 45; *De pace fidei* XIV, 49.
67 *De pace fidei* XIX, 68.
68 Cod. Cus. 108 f 30v–107.
69 Burman, *Reading the Qur'an in Latin Christendom, 1140–1560*. Burman notes that there are twenty-five medieval and early modern manuscripts of Robert's translation and it would be printed in editions of 1543 and 1550. One of these manuscripts is Cod. Cus. 108 (15).
70 Burman, *Reading the Qur'an*, 15.

THE WORD OF PEACE   189

goes though, you should never judge a book by its cover, especially old books. For Cusanus not only left his hospice his books, but also his annotations inside them. His copy of the Qur'an is full of his glosses and manicules. Cusanus's marginalia reveals much about how he read the Qur'an. Indeed these notes on the shared prophets and saints of Christianity and Islam serve as an interpretative key to unlocking his heuristic approach to the Wisdom of the Qur'an as found implicitly in *De pace fidei* and explicitly in *Cribratio Alkorani*.[71]

In Cod. Cus. 108, his copy of Robert of Ketton's translation of the Qur'an, we see Cusanus's heuristic approach to Islam: a searching for religious concordance through sifting for the inherent Word of God. Cusanus discovers many themes and characters from the Word of God, viz. Christian Scripture. He notes "paradise" in the margins eight different times on eight different folios.[72] He indicates the episode "Cain and Abel."[73] Cusanus glosses that the Qur'an rightly lauds Abraham, Isaac and Jacob.[74] Abraham is clearly noted in Cusanus's own hand, as is Isaac.[75] Abraham is further noted for his help for Lot and his valiant struggle against idolatry.[76] Indeed the father of the Abrahamic faiths is noted by Cusanus throughout his copy of the Qur'an. The great prophet Moses also appears prominently in Cusanus's marginalia, and his appearance before Pharaoh is especially noted.[77] Cusanus notes Saul and David, David and Nathan, and Solomon.[78] Job and Jonah are also noted, as well as Zachariah and John the Baptist.[79] Of all the names, three occur again and again: Abraham, Moses and the Virgin Mary. Cusanus writes how the Qur'an affirms Mary's perpetual virginity.[80] More importantly, Cusanus also notes in the margins how the Qur'an affirms Christ as both Son of Mary and Son of God, and the house of God as

---

71 For example. Cusanus cites the Qur'an (5:48) in *De pace fidei* I, 6; (3:40) in *De pace fidei* XII, 39, on Christ and the analogy of the magnetic stone.
72 "de paradiso": Cod. Cus. 108 f 31r, f 76r, f 88r, f 90r, f 94v, f 95r, f 96r, f 104v. Cf., *Cribratio Alkorani* II, 19, 154.
73 "de abel et chain" Cod. Cus. f 45r.
74 "laudat abha ysaac et iacob" Cod. Cus. 108 f 90r.
75 Cod. Cus. 108 f 33r, 50r; "ysaac" f 89v.
76 Cod. Cus. 108 "De Loth" f 80v; on Abraham and idolatry f 74v, f 79r, f 83v; "Nota de Abraham" f 80r.
77 Cod. Cus. 108 "de moysa" f 45r, f 81r, On Moses "de moysa" f 91v; "de moysa" before Pharaoh f 79v.
78 Cod. Cus. 108 Saul and David f 35v; "De David et Nathan" f 90r; "de salomone" f 81r.
79 Cod. Cus. 108 f 90r; f 75r; f 37r.
80 Cod. Cus. 108 f 72r: "beam aria virgo." Mary is also mentioned by Cusanus on f 102r: "Maria filia Joachim", and "De maria" f 37v.

the abode of peace, which are theological themes in both *De pace fidei* and *Cribratio Alkorani*.[81]

While this pastiche of references to peace fails to cover some of Cusanus's more polemical points on Islam in the *Cribratio Alkorani*, it nonetheless behooves careful readers to place condemnations of Islam in the context of the belligerent times, as well as the perspective of Cusanus's more irenic and constructive notes.[82] The majority of Cusanus's notes in the margins of Cod. Cus. 108 aim at religious understanding and concord in accordance with the Word of God. Indeed, Cusanus's notes in the margins of Cod. Cus. 108 reveal how he sifted and searched the Qur'an for evidence of concordance with Christ and Scripture. He notes the various prophets found in both the Bible and Qur'an. He even writes in the margin: "The true history of Moses and Pharaoh."[83] Most previous Christian studies of the text were written to contradict the Qur'an, not to affirm it. Cusanus's *Cribratio Alkorani* is intended to be a careful 'sifting' of the Qur'an: separating the wheat of Wisdom and enlightenment from the chaff of ignorance and malice. Rather than reject the Qur'an outright, Cusanus distinguishes between what Mohammad received from divine revelation and what he misconstrued on account of either ignorance or vain speculation.[84] Thus for Cusanus, the prophet Muhammed is indeed a prophet, in so far as he proclaims and upholds the Christian Gospel and Christ, the Word of God, in the line of the other prophets he noted in the margins of his Qur'an (Cod. Cus. 108).[85] For Cusanus, the Qur'an affirms Jesus as the Word of God.[86] And one studies the Qur'an to study Christ. Furthermore, it is the Qur'an, not Christian Scriptures that have been corrupted to obscure this truth, and this refutes the

---

81   Cod. Cus. 108 "de Ihu filio Marie" f 44v; "filii Marie" f 46r; "de Ihu Marie filio" f 47r; "de filio Dei" f 33r; "de domo Dei" f 33r. Cf., *De pace fidei* XI, 32: XII, 41; XIII, 45; *Cribratio Alkorani* I, 15; I, 17; I, 19. The abode of peace in *De pace fidei* is the visionary heavenly council of religious concordance and Jerusalem, city of David, Jesus and Mohammad (*De pace fidei* III, 9 and XIX, 68).

82   On Cusanus's sometime polemical refutation, see *Cribratio Alkorani* III, 3, 170: "Est igitur ultima resolutio probationis omnium, quae in Alkorano lenguntur, gladius."

83   "Vera historia de moyse and pharaone", Cod. Cus. 108 f 82r.

84   *Cribratio Alkorani*, prologus, 10: "Intentio autem nostra est praesupposito evangelio Christi librum Mahumeti cribrare est ostendere illa in ipso etiam libro haberi, per quae evangelium, si attestatione indigeret, valde confirmaretur, et quod, ubi dissentit, hoc ex ignorantia et consequenter ex perversitate intenti Mahumeti evenisse Christo non suam gloriam sed dei patris et hominum salutem, Mahumeto vero non dei gloriam et hominum salutem sed gloriam propriam quaerente."

85   *Cribratio Alkorani*, prologus 9.

86   *Cribratio Alkorani* alius prologus 1, 13, 16.

traditional Muslim assertion that Christians have corrupted their Scriptures and added plurality to divine unity. For Cusanus, Christ is inherent throughout the Qur'an as the divine Word, and may be discovered there heuristically.

The second prologue of the *Cribratio Alkorani* makes explicit Cusanus's implicit and inherent understanding of the Word and Wisdom of God, both as common grace and the revealed fullness of grace.[87] Cusanus states in the treatise's thesis that "there will be no difficulty in finding, in the Koran, the truth of the Gospel, although Muhammad himself was very far removed from a true understanding of the Gospel."[88] Throughout the *Cribratio Alkorani* Cusanus attempts to make near what appears to be far removed by uncovering Christ, the Word of God, within the centre of the Qur'an. In Cusanus's heuristic reading of the Qur'an, God sent his Word as the Word of God and son of Mary and supreme envoy of which no greater envoy can be conceived.[89] This same Cusanian project of carefully discerning the Word of God appears at the centre of *De pace fidei*. Cusanus devotes significant discussion, five chapters out of nineteen (eleven through fifteen), to discovering Christology and soteriology. Notably, Cusanus states, in what would later be considerably expanded in the *Cribratio Alkorani*, that since Muslims "say that Christ is the Word of God" they inherently acknowledge that he is God and truth, in whom all things unfold and enfold as illustrated in the all-seeing icon of Christ in *De visione Dei* as "the face of all peoples".[90]

The Enfolding Word: *De visione Dei* and *De pace fidei*

In 1453, the same year that he wrote *De pace fidei*, Cusanus composed his visionary treatise *De visione Dei* which endures as a masterpiece of Western mysticism made popular in the twentieth century and beyond through its

---

87 *Cribratio Alkorani* alius prologus 14.
88 *Cribratio Alkorani* alius prologus 16, translation by Jasper Hopkins: "Non igitur erit difficile in Alkorano reperiri evangelii veritatem, licet ipse Mahumetus remotissimus fuit a vero evangelii intellectu."
89 *Cribratio Alkorani*, alius prologus 15: "Misit autem secundum ipsum Christum, quem dicit verbum dei et filium Mariae. Quare cum verbum dei sit eiusdem naturae, cuius est deus, cuius est verbum—omnia enim dei deus sunt ob simplicissimam eius naturam –, quando voluit deus summum legatum mittere, misit verbum suum, quo non potest maior legatus concipi." Cf., *De pace fidei* XII, 39; Anselm of Canterbury, *Proslogion* 2.
90 *De pace fidei* XI, 30, translation by Biechler and Bond: "Sed cum vos omnes qui legem Arabum tenetis, dicatis Christum esse Verbum Dei—et bene dicitis—necesse est et quod fateamini ipsum Deum." *De pace fidei* II, 7; XIII, 43. See also, *De pace fidei* XI, 31–32.

promotion by two noted scholars of mysticism: Evelyn Underhill and Bernard McGinn.[91] *De visione Dei* explores seeing and unseeing God through an all-seeing icon of the face of Christ and the enfolding of all things within his omnipresent gaze.

By the time he wrote *De visione Dei*, Cusanus was a well-known author and philosopher. From 1451–1452 Cusanus, inclined to the contemplative, was now also serving as apostolic legate to the German people, especially entrusted with the practical and trying task of renewing spirituality in German speaking lands, travelling throughout what is now Belgium, the western portion of Germany and Austria.[92] While on his mission of spiritual reform and renewal, he visited various Benedictine monasteries, including the centuries old Benedictine abbey of Tegernsee (founded on lake Tegern in the mid-eighth century, perhaps, as medieval legend has it, by monks from the famed Benedictine house of St. Gall) in the idyllic Bavarian Alps, where he briefly stayed from 31 May to 2 June 1452.[93]

As his tranquil sojourn at the abbey and his correspondences show, Cusanus was close friend of the reform minded Caspar Ayndorffer (abbot of Tegernsee from 1426–1460). He was made abbot by papal authority and, for his restoration of monastic discipline in accordance with the Rule of Benedict, became known as the second founder of the abbey of Tegernsee. In a letter written in early 1454 to his friend, spiritual advisor, Cusanus, abbot Ayndorffer

---

91   Nicholas of Cusa, *The Vision of God*, translated by Emma Gurney Salter with introduction by Evelyn Underhill (New York: Cosimo, 2007). Bernard McGinn "Seeing and Not Seeing: Nicholas of Cusa's *De visione Dei* in the History of Western Mysticism" in Cusanus: *The Legacy of Learned Ignorance*, edited by Peter J. Casarella (Washington, D.C.: The Catholic University of America Press, 2006), 26–53. See also discussion of Cusanus's mystisim with special focus on *De visione Dei* in McGinn, *The Harvest of Mysticism in Medieval Germany*, vol. IV of the *Presence of God: A History of Western* Christian Mysticism (New York: Crossroad, 2005), 432–483.

92   On Cusanus's liturgical and ecclesial reforms, see: Robert R. Bond, *The Efforts of Nicholas of Cusa as a Liturgical Reformer* (Salzburg: Druckhaus Nonntal, 1962); Donald Sullivan, "Cusanus and Pastoral Renewal: the reform of popular religion in the Germanies", *Nicholas of Cusa on Christ and the Church*, 165–173; "Reform" by Brian A. Pavlac, *Introducing Nicholas of Cusa*, 59–112.

93   In her introduction, Underhill describes the details of Cusanus's spiritual direction of the monks of the Abbey of Tegernesee (Nicholas of Cusa, *The Vision of God*, translated by Emma Gurney Salter, introduction by Evelyn Underhill (London: J.M. Dent and Sons, 1928), xi). Hopkins also discusses Cusanus's interactions with the brothers (*Dialectical Mysticism*, 3).

of Tegernsee thanks the cardinal for two of his works which he had recently received: *De visione dei* and *De pace fidei*.[94]

De visione dei was expressly written by Cusanus for the monks of Tegernsee. Cusanus dedicates his promised treatise on mystical theology to his esteemed brothers of Tegernsee.[95] *De visione dei* was also written for them as a practical and 'Jesus' centered guide on mystical ascent to God. Along with the treatise, Cusanus tells us in his preface that he sent the monks an icon of the all-knowing God.,[96] The icon, presumably, was of the face of Christ, perhaps even, as Cusanus suggests in the preface to *De visione Dei*, the famous late-medieval image of the face of Christ upon the towel of Veronica.[97] Contextually and theologically, the reader may reasonably assume that the image was indeed an icon of Christ through also noting Christian Scripture where Christ is clearly identified as the "εικων" of the invisible God, as Cusanus was well aware. We may also mark that the all-knowing or all-seeing figure, as the work describes, ultimately centers

---

[94] In a letter to his friend and spiritual mentor Cusanus, composed sometime between 15 January and 12 February 1454, the abbot of Tegernsee, A. Gaspard Aindorrffer (Caspar Ayndorffer) writes, "Dirigo rescriptos et relectos per fraters libellos *De Visione Dei* et *De Pace fidei*, solita et humili confidencia petens alios nobis cum presentibus transmitti, scilicet: librorum Dyonisij novam translationem, similiter libros Eusebij noviter in latinum translatos, et specialiter mustum *berillum*, ut videamus in docta ignorancia et alibi que multis obscura videntur, precipue de coincidencia contradictoriarum, de spera infinita, etc." (E. Vansteenberghe, *Autour de la Docte Ignorance: une controverse sur la théologie mystique au XVe siècle*, in: *Beiträge zur Geschicte der Philosophie des Mittelalters: texte und untersuchungen*, band XIV, heft 2–4 (Münster: Aschendorffsche Verlagsbuchhandlung, 1915), 120. Vansteenberghe's study includes a number of letters between Cusanus and Ayndorffer. See also: Nicolai de Cusa, *De Visione Dei*, edidit Adelaida Dorothea Riemann, *Nicolai de Cusa Opera Omnia*, vol. 6 (Hamburg: Felix Meiner Verlag, 2000), ix–x. On the contents of the above letter, Vansteenberghe notes, "L'abbé s'en réjouit, mais ne peut croire que Dieu demande au cardinal de s'y retirer.—Il le remercie pour la dédicace du *De Visione Dei*, et lui renvoie ce livre ainsi ... *De Pace fidei*—Il désire maintenant les nouvelles traductions de Denys et d'Eusébe; le *De Beryllo*, qui permettra de mieux comprendre le *De Docta ignorantia*, en particulier pour ce qui regarde la coincidence des contraires et la spère infinie" (Vansteenberghe, 119). This letter shows how the Benedictine monks of Tegernesee were not only avid readers of Cusanus, but also eager students of the apophatic mysticism of Pseudo-Dionysius, which permeated Cusanus's writings, especially *De pace fidei* and *De visione Dei*.

[95] *De visione Dei*, dedication, 1: "Pandam nunc, quae vobis dilectissimis fratribus ante promiseram circa facilitatem mysticae theologiae."

[96] *De visione Dei*, preface, 2: "videntis tenentem, quam iconam Dei."

[97] *De visione Dei*, preface, 2. Cusanus writes of a similar image of "Veronicae" in his chapel at Koblenz.

upon Jesus, the discussion of whom concludes this treatise.[98] For Cusanus, Jesus, the Word made flesh, is the means by which mystical ascent to beatitude or knowing fully what here is ascertained enigmatically through learned ignorance, as well as final union with God, is disclosed, traversed and ultimately achieved. *De visione Dei* paints the vivid palette of Cusanus's Christology as the all-seeing Word of God from whom all things are unfolded and in whom are all things enfolded. This same universally unfolding and enfolding Word of God becomes globally focused in Cusanus's dialogue *De pace fidei*.[99]

De pace fidei and *De visione Dei* enfold Cusanus's metaphysics of the Word of peace and concordance. While orthodox Islam denounces images in worship or piety, *De visione dei* ultimately transcends image and icon to peer into the obscure cloud of God's ineffable essence, the famous 'cloud of unknowing', beyond what Cusanus calls "the wall of paradise", even beyond Cusanus's famous concept of the coincidence of opposites.[100] Having hit the wall, Cusanus writes from within this garden of rapturous paradise and draws to himself "the lover, the lovable and the bond between them."[101] Cusanus finds in himself, now beyond all images and analogues, past the ardent propelling of desire, that he is this love and that this bond of love is one with lover and beloved in essence.[102] Herein, the Word and words, icon and viewer enfold as one. Cusanus writes, "For in you, who are a lovable God, enfolding all that is lovable, you love all that which is lovable, so that thus they would see with me by what alliance or bond you are united to all things."[103] Cusanus continues that the "lovable God" and the begotten "lovable God", love from love, light from light, through whom everything which exists can exist "who are loving and willing God enfold all things in yourself, who are lovable God."[104] From this Word of God, for

---

98 Colossians 1:15; *De visione Dei* XXV.

99 *De pace fidei* II, 7.

100 *De visione Dei* XVII, 74, translation by Bond, p. 268.

101 *De visione Dei* XVII, 76, translation by Bond, p. 269: "Ego sum amans, ego sum amabilis, ego sum nexus." Cf., *De pace fidei* on the Trinity and the nexus or Spirit: VIII, 24.

102 *De visione Dei* XVI, 68–69; XVII, 77.

103 *De visione Dei* XVIII, 80, translated by Bond, p. 271: "In te enim, Deo amabili, omnia amabilia complicanti omne amabile amas, ut sic viderent mecum, quo foedere aut nexu sis omnibus unitus."

104 *De visione Dei* XIX, 83, translation by Bond, p. 272: "Tu enim Deus volens seu amans in te Deo amabili complicas omnia. Omne enim, quod tu Deus vis aut concipis est in te Deo amabili complicatum." According to Avicenna, "If this is established, then let us proceed to say this: that Being which is too exalted to be subject to the governance must be the highest object of love, because It must be the maximum in goodness. And the highest subject of love is identical with the highest *object* of love, namely, Its high and sublime

Cusanus, flows "life into all who believe" for the perfection of all who love God.[105] The path to perfection beyond all affirmations and negations of Deity is found in the concept and the reality, the sign and the thing signified, the Word of God who is eternal *Logos* and therefore unknown and incarnate Jesus and therefore knowable; and universally, in the vision of *De pace fidei*, beyond icon and image to the self, "the face of all peoples", everyone.[106]

Cusanus envisions that in and through Christ, finite and infinite, human and divine coincide. In *De pace fidei*, the religious rites of the various religions of the world coincide in the Word and Wisdom of God, namely Christ. For Cusanus Divine Wisdom is fully known in the face of Christ, which sees all and encompasses all faces. This all-seeing, omniscient face of Christ reflects the faces of all humanity and shows the way to religious concordance and one religion in the variety of religious rites. *De pace fidei* and *De visione Dei* convey Cusanus's unique mystical conceptualization of the Word of God as Face and Icon of understanding humanity and religious peace. In *De visione Dei*, Cusanus employs the late-medieval cultural artifact of the all-seeing icon of the face of Jesus. The same image is cited and abstracted in *De pace fidei*. Jesus, the Word-Icon of God, is the mode of seeing, object of understanding and the mediator of Cusanus's complex concept of the deep interrelatedness of Islam and Christianity. The Word of God as icon reflects the face of all humanity and enlightens seekers of the peace of faith, especially the prophets of God, which, for Cusanus, include the Prophet Mohammed, a profound reconfiguration of late-medieval religious beliefs. While *De pace fidei* and *De visione Dei* are often interpreted as unrelated in style and substance, we see concordance between Cusanus's understanding of the Word of God in *De pace fidei* and the icon of Jesus in *De visione Dei*.

De visione Dei ends with the eucharistic enfolding of the vision and its beholder in the Wisdom and Word of God. Cusanus writes that "every intellect

---

Essence. Because the good loves the good through that attainment and penetration whereby it is connected with it, and because the First Good penetrates Itself in eternal actuality, therefore Its love for Itself is the most perfect and complete. And because there is no distinction among the divine qualities of Its Essence, love is here the essence and the being purely and simply, i.e. in the case of the Pure Good." *Risalah fi'l-'ishq* (*A Treatise on Love*, c. 1030) transl. Emil Fackenheim.

105 *De visione* Dei XXIV, 114, translation by Bond, p. 286: "Tibi Iesu gratias ago, quoniam ad hoc tuo lumine perveni. In lumine enim tuo video lumen vitae meae, quo modo tu verbum influis omnibus credentibus vitam et perficis omnes te diligentes."
106 *De pace fidei* XIII, 43.

must submit itself through faith to the Word of God" and that the "intellect is nourished by the Word of Life," the delectable food of Wisdom and charity,[107] as nourishing intellectual food at the beginning of *De pace fidei*,[108] and again as nourishing eucharistic food at the conclusion.[109] As the Wisdom of God is both eternal *Logos* and incarnate Christ, so too, the food that is Wisdom is both intellectual and earthly nourishment. We behold the altarpiece at Cusanus's chapel in Kues with the central panel depicting the crucified Christ. Cusanus appears in his cardinal's hat kneeling before Jesus on the cross. For cardinal Cusanus, the peace of faith is more than a concept or philosophical maxim. The heart of the matter, the centre of concordance, is the eternal Word and Wisdom of God, the bread and wine from heaven given to eat and drink in the eucharistic feast. The same Word of God made flesh in the broken body of Christ imparted in the Mass on the altar for which the altarpiece was designed, in order that minds may be renewed through Wisdom to seek peace and concord. It is ultimately the crucified One who gathers together the divided religious rites into one religion as the scattered grains of wheat are gathered into one transcendent loaf of unity and life.

Cusanus's heart lies buried before this altar of charity and altarpiece of the crucified Word of peace. Above and adjacent to the altar reside Cusanus's books. This famous library includes the final and 'official' version of *De visione Dei*, Cod. Cus. 219, commissioned, edited and corrected by Cusanus himself and completed sometime after April 1464. Cusanus marked the text in what would have been his final reading of *De visione Dei* before his death in August 1464 exactly on his discussion of the Trinitarian union of Father and Son in the nexus of the Spirit, where, in addressing God, he wrote some ten years prior, "Your union and your concept is act and arising work, in which are the act and unfolding of all things."[110] *De pace fidei* ends with the opening of ancient books and the recollection of what is long forgotten in order to retrieve the concordance of one religion in the variety of rites through the eternal Wisdom and incarnate Word of God from whom all things are unfolded and in whom all things are enfolded and from whom arise acts of charity for the bond of amity.[111] At the end of his lifelong search for concordance, Cusanus remembers

---

107 *De visione Dei* XXIV, 112, 113, translation by Bond.
108 *De pace fidei* IV, 12.
109 *De pace fidei* XVIII.
110 *De visione Dei* XIX, 83, translation by Bond: "Et unio tui et tui conceptus est actus et operatio exsurgens, in qua est omnium actus et explicatio." Cod. Cus. 219 f 17r with mark made in Cusanus's hand.
111 *De pace fidei* I, 6; II, 7; XIX, 68.

the axiom of his theology, that in the Word of God "all things hold together" for peace.[112]

Cusanus's sublime conception of the Word of peace, in whom all things hold together for the concordance of the one and the many, demonstrates the unity of the corpus of his writing. The four Christological angles of our case study: the unfolding Word (*De pace fidei* and *De docta ignorantia*), the magnetic Word (*De pace fidei* and *De concordantia catholica*), the inherent Word (*De pace fidei* and *Cribratio Alkorani*), and the enfolding Word (*De pace fidei* and *De visione Dei*), fit together to form a unified whole which provides greater insight into the unanimity of Cusanus's theology. The central Word of God extends to the four corners of these seemingly unrelated works and pervades them with the cosmic arc of concordance as unfolding hierarchically from the Word, magnetically coursing through the Word, and enfolding to the Word for the harmony of religion and the consummation of peace.

---

112   Colossians 1:17 NRSV.

CHAPTER 7

For the Peace of Jerusalem

Pray for the peace of Jerusalem.[1]

∵

In 1446 Cusanus wrote a brief and bizarre treatise on the end of the world: *Coniectura de ultimis diebus*.[2] In the work, Cusanus surmises that the world will end sometime between 1700 and 1734.[3] While today this seems eccentric, in the context of the fifteenth century, conjectures on the ensuing apocalypse were far from strange. Cusnus's predictions are patterned on Augustine's eight epochs found in the conclusion of the *City of God* and the pervasive apocalyptic speculation of Joachim of Fiore.[4] Fears of the impending end of the world would continue well after Cusanus with the likes of the Dominican Savonarola and the magisterial reformer Martin Luther, who was often depicted in his time as the prophetic second Elijah sent to proclaim the return of Christ.[5] Cusanus also believed he lived in the latter days. In a Letter to Jacob von Sirck from October 1453 after the fall of Constantinople, Cusanus writes, "I fear greatly that this violence may defeat us, for I see no possible uniting in resistance. I believe that we must address ourselves to God alone, though He will not hear us sinners."[6] In *De pace fidei*, Cusanus claims that his prayer, at least mystically and metaphysically, has been answered.[7]

---

1   Psalm 122:6 NRSV.
2   *Opuscula I: De Deo abscondito, De quaerendo Deum, De filiatione Dei, De dato patris luminum, Coniectura de ultimis diebus, De genesi*, edited by P. Wilpert (Hamburg: Felix Meiner, 1959).
3   *Coniectura de ultimis diebus* 127.
4   Augustine, *De civitate Dei*, bk. XXII, Chp. 30. On Joachim and Savanarola, see: *Apocalyptic Spirituality: Treatises and Letters of Lactantius, Adso of Montier-en-Der, Joachim of Fiore, the Franciscan Spirituals, Savonarola*, trans. Bernard McGinn (New York: Paulist Press, 1979). On Luther as Elijah of the last times, see, *The Four Horsemen of the Apocalypse*, 23–25.
5   For more on Cusanus and the end of the world, see Donald D. Sullivan, "Apocalypse Tamed: Cusanus and the Traditions of Late Medieval Prophecy," *Journal of Medieval History* 9 (1983) 227–236.
6   Quoted in Karl Jaspers, *Anselm and Nicholas of Cusa*, edited by Hannah Arendt and translated by Ralph Manheim (New York: Harvest, 1966), 170.
7   *De pace fidei* I, 1.

At the conclusion of this study, what is worth noting is not the conjectured end of the world, but why Cusanus even forges ahead with his speculation. After all, Jesus of Nazareth had warned that no one knows the hour of his coming, which implied the condemnation of those vain seers who attempted to wrest knowledge of the future away from God.[8] According to Cusanus, one may only endeavor to know in this lifetime the incomprehensible truth, even though in this world of conjectures, and echoing Augustine, we only know incomprehensible truth through symbolism that is infinitely distant from the truth itself.[9] Or, as he says in his *Apologia doctae ingnorantiae*, that true theology remains hidden in sacred Scripture, the very Word of God.[10] Cusanus, speculates, he says, because he claims to know only this Word of God, namely, the pre-incarnate *Logos* and the person of Christ.[11] In Christ, according to the dialogical structure of Cusanus's *De pace fidei*, the metaphysical and the physical coincide. As we have seen, *De pace fidei* identifies the Word of God as *Logos* and incarnate dialogist.[12] Indeed, for Cusanus, Christ is the very Wisdom of God.[13] Therefore, this Divine Word-Wisdom is the ground for speculating about time and eternity, and, indeed, as has been argued in this study, the basis and starting point for his conciliar and complicated approach to Islam in *De pace fidei* and *Cribratio Alkorani*.[14] Furthermore, according to Cusanus every human assertion on what is true is conjecture, yet when connected to Christ, the hypostatic union, the very way and truth, these conjectures become closer to hidden wisdom.[15] This truth, as we have seen in *De pace fidei* and in the prologue to the *Cribratio Alkorani*, is none other than the Word and Wisdom of God in whom all things are unfolded and from whom are enfolded.[16]

Throughout this study we have focused on Cusanus's Christocentric and sapiential philosophical and theological approach to Islam as expounded in *De pace fidei*. This study has synthetically examined the metaphysics of Cusanus's dialectical *Verbum-Logos* dialogue with Islam. As Cranz has noted, for Cusanus, the cosmic and incarnate Christ forms the basis of an entire Christian philosophy to such a degree that the more he studies the cosmos the more he sees Christ as the center of the coincidence of opposites wherein the many rites

---

8   Mark 13:32; Matthew 24:36.
9   *Coniectura de ultimis diebus* 123. Cf., *De pace fidei* XVI, 55; Augustine, *De doctrina Christiana*, I, 4–5.
10 *Apologia doctae ignorantiae* 4.
11 *Coniectura de ultimis diebus* 124.
12 *De pace fidei* III, 8; IV, 10; X, 27.
13 *Coniectura de ultimis diebus* 124; 1 Corinthians 2:2; Colossians 2:3.
14 *De pace fidei* III, 9; *Cribratio Alkorani* prologus, 8–10.
15 *De Coniecturis* I, prologus; *De pace fidei* II, 7; John 14:6.
16 *De pace fidei* II, 7; *Cribratio Alkorani* prologus, 8–10; *Idiota de sapientia* I, 21–23.

coincide within one religion.[17] Following the methodological lead of Augustine, Gadamer and Cranz we identified Cusanus's hermeneutic of one religion in the variety of rites through signs and things signified as flowing from and returning to the *Verbum* of God as metaphysics of Muslim-Christian dialogue.[18] This Word speaks words in the dialogue form of *De pace fidei* and enlightens Cusanus to write words of religious concordance. As his *Idiota de sapientia et de mente* and *De venatione sapientiae* reveal, the master of learned ignorance spent his scholarly and spiritual life searching for the Wisdom and peace of God which surpasses all understanding.[19] In *De pace fidei*, Cusanus searches and claims to find the Divine Wisdom of religious concordance. For the mysterious and cosmically generating Wisdom cries out in the streets to be readily welcomed by laymen (*idiota*) and even the proponent of "the barbarous ineptitudes" of learned ignorance, Cusanus himself.[20] And yet, this Wisdom leads to greater insight: the final vision of God, whereupon, "God grants that He be made visible to us without enigma."[21] While Cusanus spent his life hunting for this known yet unknown Wisdom, he did so largely alone. As Karl Jaspers notes, Cusanus is the only major thinker of his century who did not belong to any school or found a school.[22] He was in some ways a metaphysical loner, much like that of the great scholars of the ninth century, e.g. John Scotus Eriugena. And yet, his ideas remain and he sometimes seems strangely at home in our multi-religious age. His solitary quest for the plenitude of Wisdom uncovers a new Christocentric and communal understanding of religious peace.

While Cusanus may have been a metaphysical loner in his own time, his Christocentric ideas on religious peace in *De pace fidei* are deeply rooted in ancient Hellenic thought and the Bible, Wisdom as consubstantial of reason and revelation. As we have shown, the Christology of *De pace fidei* is Johannine. Indeed for Cusanus and the author of the Gospel according to John, there is nothing beyond the horizon of the Word.[23] Cusanus's cosmic Christology of *De pace fidei* also transmits the ancient Hebraic wisdom tradition of the Book of Proverbs and the Hellenic Lady Wisdom of Boethius's *Consolation*.[24] As in the

---

17 Cranz, "Saint Augustine and Nicholas of Cusa in the Tradition of Western Christian Thought," 298.
18 Augustine, *De doctrina Christiana*, I, 4–10; Gadamer, *Truth and Method*, 435–436.
19 Philippians 4:7.
20 Proverbs 8–9; *De docta ignorantia*, prologus, Bond, p. 87.
21 *Idiota de sapientia*, Führer, 49. Latin: "sine quo in hoc mundo Dei visio esse nequit, quousque concesserit Deus, ut absque aenigmate nobis visibilis reddatur."
22 Jaspers, *Anselm and Nicholas of Cusa*, 164.
23 John 1:1–18; *De pace fidei* II, 7.
24 Proverbs 8–9.

Gospel of John, there are two dialectical aspects to Cusanus's Christological approach to Islam: universalist and exclusivist.[25] As late-medieval churchman, Cusanus inherited the universalist and exclusivist Christology of the ecumenical councils of Nicaea (325) and Chalcedon (451). The former council included the fundamental tenet of catholic faith that the *Logos* is the same substance as God (*homoousios, unius substantiae cum patre*) and through whom all things came to be, while the latter incorporated Pope Leo's famous Tome, which stated that the incarnate *Logos*, the Son of God, is one person in two natures (divine and human, "unitatem personae in utraque natura").[26] Leo's Tome, which, we have seen, serves as prolegomena to the *Cribratio Alkorani*, weaves together the two threads of universality and exclusivity into the one tapestry of Christ. Leo quotes Proverbs and the Gospel of John, "As Wisdom built a house for herself, the Word was made flesh and dwelt among us", and this Word becomes flesh so that the proper character of both natures is maintained and come together in a single person.[27] Here we discover anew again how Cusanus's Christology in *De pace fidei* is simultaneously orthodox and conciliar.

While Cusanus's sapiential ideas of religious concordance are rooted in reason and revelation, in conciliar and constructive thought, they are also formulated within the catholic historical theological tradition. Another angle for viewing Cusanus's dialectic of reason and revelation, the exclusivity and universality of his Christology as evidenced in *De pace fidei*, sees Cusanus inheriting the catholic exclusivity of the third century bishop Cyprian of Carthage and the philosophical openness of Clement of Alexandria (c150–c.215). We first consider Cyprian and Cusanus's exclusivity as concentrated in unity. It was Cyprian who famously quipped, "outside the church, there is no salvation" (*extra ecclesiam nulla salus*).[28] Cusanus, much like Cyprian, was

---

25 John 1:1–18; 14:6. On universalist *Verbum* Christology see, *De pace fidei* VI. On exclusivist Christology, see *De pace fidei* XI.
26 Council of Nicea, *Expositio fidei CCCXVIII partum* in Tanner, *Decrees of the Ecumenical Councils*, vol. 1, 5. Leo's Tome, *Epistula Papae Leonis*, Tanner, *Decrees of the Ecumenical Councils*, vol. 1, 80.
27 *Cribratio Alkorani*, preface, *Pio Secundo Universalis Christianorum Ecclesiae Summo Sactissimoque Pontifici*. Leo's Tome, Tanner, *Decrees of the Ecumenical Councils 1*, 78: "Feciditatem virginis spiritus sanctus dedit, veritas autem corporis sumpta de corpore est, est aedificante sibi sapientia domum *verbum caro factum est habitavit in nobis*, noc est in ea carne quam sumpsit ex homine et quam spiritu vitae rationalis antimavit. Salva igitur proprietate utriusque naturae et in unam coeunte personam."
28 Cyprian of Carthage, Epistle LXXII, *Ad Jubajanum de haereticis baptizandis*, Section 21: "Salus extra ecclesiam non est." See also how Cyprian is quoted by Pope Boniface VIII in the high water mark of the medieval papacy, *Unam sanctam* (1302).

adamant in maintaining the unity of the Catholic Church, especially in the face of heresies and schisms threatening to rend concordance asunder. For Cyprian and Cusanus, the source of this unity is Christ as represented on earth by the bishops, and preeminently, the Bishop of Rome.[29] In *De concordantia catholica*, Cusanus notes from ancient tradition there is one cathedra and one rule established in hierarchical gradations.[30] Cusanus's ecclesial career may be aptly described as that of seeking unity and avoiding schism, and, as we have argued, this meant seeking out the primacy of the earthly hierarch, namely, the pope, as medium of universal concordance, be it between Eastern and Western Churches or Christianity and Islam.[31] Cyprian asks rhetorically, "If a man does not hold fast to this oneness of the Church, does he imagine that he still holds the faith?"[32] We have seen in the preface to the *Cribratio Alkorani*, turning us back again to Leo's Tome, that Cusanus considers Islam to be the ancient Nestorian heresy now continued as sect. We have also considered throughout this study how in *De pace fidei* Cusanus conceives that schisms exist because through longstanding custom many confuse rites for religion and become lost in the diffuse manifestations of the one unity of religion.[33] The goal of *De pace fidei* is the eradication of global religious schism through conciliar and Christocentric dialogue. In *De ecclesiae catholicae unitate*, Cyprian allegorizes the seamless garment of the crucified Christ, which, according to the Gospel of John, was not divided into many but remained one as symbolizing the church as one people knit together in harmony.[34] Furthermore, for

---

29 Cyprian, *De Ecclesiae catholicae unitate*, 4–6. On the primacy of the Roman chair, see 4 (first edition, note the two versions of the treatise on this pivotal section): "Super illum aedificat ecclesiam et illi pascendas oves mandat et, quamvis apostolis omnibus parem tribuat potestatemm unam tamen cathedram constituit et unitatis originem adque rationem sua auctoritate disposuit. Hoc erant utique et ceteri quod fuit Petrus, sed primatus Petro datur et una ecclesia et cathedra una monstratur". Latin text found in: Cyprian, *De Lapsis and De Ecclesiae Catholicae Unitate*, text and translation by Maurice Bévenot (London: Oxford University Press, 1971), 62.

30 *De concordantia catholica* I, 6, 36: "Unde sicut episcopatus unus, ita una cathedra et una praesidentia gradualiter et hierarchiæ constituta."

31 Cusanus naturally addresses his *Cribratio Alkorani* to Pope Pius II because Pius as Pope, like Pope Leo the Great, sits in the one cathedra of concordance as instrument of unity and the ending of schism.

32 Cyprian, *De Ecclesiae catholicae unitate*, 4 (second edition, note the two versions of the treatise on this pivotal section): "Hanc ecclesiae unitatem qui non tenet, tenere se fidem credit?" For English translation and above and Latin text, see: Cyprian, *De Ecclesiae Catholicae Unitate*, Bévenot, 64–65.

33 *De pace fidei* I, 4.

34 Cyprian, *De Ecclesiae Catholicae Unitate* 7, Bévenot, 69. Cf., *Unam sanctam*.

Cyprian and Cusanus, "the Church forms a unity, however far she spreads and multiplies by the progeny of her fecundity."[35] And, for Cyprian, "You cannot have God for your Father if you no longer have the Church for your mother."[36] Towards the pivotal and foundational beginning of *De concordantia catholica*, which as has been proposed in this study serves as theological foundation as centered on the magnetic Word of God for *De pace fidei*, Cusanus cites this very same passage of Cyprian.[37] There he writes that "concordance is highest truth itself" and after citing Cyprian, describes how those in the church are united to Christ.[38] Cusanus writes,

> Christ is the way, the truth, and the life, and the head of all creatures, the husband or spouse of the church, which is constituted in a concordance of all rational creatures—with him as the One, and among themselves, the many—in various [hierarchical] gradations.[39]

Cusanus, like Cyprian before him, clearly connects the unity of the church to the person of Christ. Yet, in a distinctly innovative turn, moves beyond the confines of the Catholic Church in *De pace fidei* to include Judaism, Islam, and Hinduism by hierarchical gradation of one religion in the variety of rites. Pope Boniface VIII had affirmed the universal primacy of Peter more than a century prior to *De pace fidei* and a millennium after Cyprian. As Boniface expanded Cyprian's primacy of Rome to encompass the world in *Unam sanctam*, so Cusanus expands his notion of the church to be that of one religion in the variety of rites. Cusanus's Catholic Church of *De pace fidei* embraces manifold religious

---

35 Cyprian, *De Ecclesiae Catholicae Unitate* 5, Bévenot, 65: "Ecclesia una est quae in multitudinem latius incremento fecunditatis extenditur." Cf., *De concordantia catholica* I, 1, 7; I, 6, 35; I, 8, 43; I, 14, 58; XV, 60; II, 17, 141; II, 26, 209; II, 34, 256. Consider also the global scope of the church or one religion in the variety of rites in *De pace fidei*.
36 Cyprian, *De Ecclesiae Catholicae Unitate* 6, Bévenot, 65: "Habere iam non potest Deum patrem qui ecclesiam non habet matrem." Cf., *De concordantia catholica* I, 1, 7. Cited by Cusanus in context of arguing for the primacy of Peter and Rome: *De concordantia catholica* I, 6, 35.
37 *De concordantia catholica* I, 1, 7.
38 *De concordantia catholica* I, 1, 7.
39 *De concordantia catholica* I, 1, 8, translation by Sigmund. Cf., John 14:6. "Unde haec est summa dicendorum, quod Christus est via, veritas et vita et omnium creaturarum caput, maritus sive sponsus ecclesiae, llquaell per concordantiam creaturarum omnium rationabilium ad eum unum et inter se plurium constituitur secundum varias graduationes."

rites.[40] These religious rites are coincidently and consubstantially joined as one concordance of peace through the dialogical *Verbum* and by way of his hierarchical emissaries, most notably, the apostle and first pope, Peter.[41] Both Cyprian and Cusanus stress the importance of ecclesiastical hierarchy. Each seeks unity as emanating from Christ and through the Vicar of Christ, for it is the *Verbum* of God that reveals the religious concordance of one religion in the variety of rites dialectically, one theological proposition by one. The conversation continues with Peter, who sits in the earthly chair of Christ, "the Eternal Pontiff," which, as we have seen, has major implications for Cusanus's move from council to pope.[42]

While Cyprian and Cusanus both stress the exclusivity of the church and primacy of Peter, Clement of Alexandria represents the universality of Christology and the favoured role of Greek thought as echoed in *De pace fidei*. By comparing Cyprian and Clement with *De pace fidei* we see the scope of the dialectical tension of inclusivity and exclusivity as centered in the Word and Wisdom of God. Clement lived during the Alexandrian revival of Platonic studies, which we know now as Middle Platonism. As Justin Martyr found Christianity through first finding Greek philosophy and by an encounter with an old man by the sea, Clement also was well versed in Hellenic thought and was one of the first theologians to harmonize Christianity and philosophy.[43] In a representative passage on Greek thought, Clement writes, "The ideas, then, which they have stolen, and which are partially true, they know by conjecture and necessary logical deduction: on becoming disciples, therefore, they will know them with intelligent apprehension."[44] Christian theologians may plunder from the Egyptians and appropriate the Platonists.[45] As we have noted in this study, we find concepts pilfered from Greek thought throughout *De pace fidei*. Like Augustine before him, Cusanus brings Neoplatonic philosophy into the service of catholic truth. Yet, as Cranz notes, Cusanus goes further than Augustine in transmitting Neoplatonic thought and ancient Christology in that through the incarnation of the Word of God he discovers "the basis of a

---

40 *De pace fidei* XIX, 67: "Ubi non potest conformitas in modo reperiri, permittantur nationes—salva fide et pace—in suis devotionibus et cerimonialibus."
41 Peter leads the conversation of *De pace fidei* from Chapters XI to XVI.
42 *De concordantia catholica* I, 3, 13.
43 Justin Martyr, *Dialogue with Trypho*, Chapters 3–8.
44 Excerpt from Clement of Alexandria's *Miscellanies*, quoted in: *Readings in Philosophy of Religion: Ancient to Contemporary*, edited by Linda Zagzebski and Timothy D. Miller (Oxford: Wiley-Blackwell, 2009), 491.
45 Augustine, *De doctrina Christiana* II, 11, 60.

complete metaphysic."[46] For Cusanus, the hypostatic Word of God has its own exclusive substantial reality (*contra* modalism), and the Word universally flows through all things. Yet, as we have seen, Cusanus aims to hold the universal and the exclusive together in his approach to Islam in *De pace fidei*. He sees all this, according to the prologue to the dialogue, through the art of contemplation as the complete metaphysic of religious peace. God reveals the truth of one religion in the variety of rites. To echo Anselm of Canterbury, Cusanus sees and believes in order to understand the religious concordance of the Word of God. For Cusanus, the Athens so praised by Clement coincides with Jerusalem, the City of God as reason coincides with revelation to form one universal metaphysic of unity. For Cusanus, unlike Tertullian, Athens has everything to do with Jerusalem.[47] Thus the dialogue begins in a metaphorical Athens as signified by the Greek dialogist and concludes in the heavenly and earthly Jerusalem where the unity of the peace of faith is pronounced as concurrent with ancient philosophy and Christian theology as one complete religious metaphysic.[48]

In *De pace fidei*, Cusanus dialectically and hierarchically holds together Athens and Jerusalem, reason and revelation, universalist and exclusivist outlooks, conciliar-catholic tradition and the pragmatic concerns of the present as all centered in the cosmic and incarnate Christ.[49] As this marks the conclusion of this study, one final summary way of reviewing the two aspects of the universalist and exclusivist polarities of Cusanus's Christology focuses on the master of learned ignorance's love of cataphatic and apophatic theology, which, as we have seen, extends hierarchically throughout *De pace fidei*. He begins the theological talking points of the dialogue with the Word as Truth and Wisdom, which embraces all things and is embraced by the philosophers.[50] What humanity can say about God arises, then, to allude to Denys, from the sum total of creation, but also, more precisely for Cusanus, from the sum total of religious rites. Cusanus believed that Wisdom made the world. Therefore, this cosmos is rationally knowable by all seekers after truth. Yet, for Cusanus, all human assertions are but conjectures. Thus, the revelation of Wisdom made flesh is

---

46 Cranz, "Saint Augustine and Nicholas of Cusa", 313.
47 Tertullian, *Prescriptions Against the Heretics*, quoted in: *Readings in Philosophy of Religion: Ancient to Contemporary*, 488.
48 *De pace fidei* IV; XIX, 68. On the primacy of Jerusalem as city of ecclesiastical and hierarchical synthesis, see *De concordantia catholica* XVI, 64.
49 For a succinct overview of the universalist and exclusivist impulses of Christology, see *World Religions: A Sourcebook for Students of Christian Theology*, edited by Richard Viladesau and Mark Massa (New York: Paulist Press, 1994), 9–16.
50 *De pace fidei* II, 7; IV–VI.

required in order to clarify the confusion of rites with religion, or of creation with creator.

Cataphatic verbosity may lend itself to catastrophic confusion of words for the Word. The names for God "are fittingly derived from the sum total of creation".[51] Indeed, according to Denys, theologians praise God "by every name—and as the Nameless One."[52] And, indeed, since God created all things, everything shares in beauty and is good.[53] Denys's hierarch, the Word of God, appears as the central character of Cusanus's religious dialogue and as the foundation of his conception of one religion in the variety of rites.[54] We see a Dionysian, cataphatic (universalist) side to Christology: the Word embraces all things. Even so, this Word speaks for the hidden God who remains ever unknown and unknowable.[55] Within this cataphatic sum total of creation, some rites are better than others, and some theological, dialogical points are higher than others. According to Denys and Aquinas, hierarchy operates as from the lower to the higher by way of the middle—according to the so-called '*lex divinitatis*'.[56] As Dionysius says, theologians discuss hierarchies in order to make known the ranks of heaven, but also to reveal the mystery of God.[57] "The most evident idea in theology, namely, the sacred incarnation of Jesus for our sakes, is something which cannot be enclosed in words nor grasped by any mind."[58]

What can be grasped with more certainty is that Christology and the sacred incarnation of the preexistent *Logos* comes to the fore in Cusanus's conversation with Islam. Moreover, as this study has shown, it is unsurprising that this Christological approach to Islam in *De pace fidei* is not only conciliar, but also hierarchical and dialectical, echoing, as it does, the impact of church polity, ecclesiology and Neoplatonic and Dionysian gradations and genre. Christ mediates between lower and higher, between discursive rites and speculative religious concordance. The angels receive the truth of one religion in the variety of rites in intellectual purity, while humanity receives it by means of sensible

---

51 *De divinis nominibus* I, 7, 597A. Translation by Colm Luibheid. Cf., *De pace fidei* VII, 21: "Nam nomina quae Deo attribuuntur, sumuntur a creaturis, cum ipse sit in se ineffabilis et super omne quod nominari aut dici posset."

52 *De divinis nominibus* I, 6, 596A. Translation by Colm Luibheid.

53 *De coelesti hierarchia* II, 3, 141C.

54 *De ecclesiatica hierarchia* II, 1, 393A.

55 *De pace fidei* I, 4; I, 5; II, 7.

56 Ephesians 1:20–21; *De coelesti hierarchia* III, 1, 164D; *Unam sanctam*; Aquinas, *Summa Theologiæ* Ia., 108, 1; *Summa Theologiæ* Ia., 108, 6.

57 *De coelesti hierarchia* II, 5, 144C.

58 *De divinis nominibus* II, 9, 648A. Translation by Colm Luibheid.

signs.[59] The Word mediates this concordance from the angels (higher) to humanity (lower). The dialogue proper of *De pace fidei* begins more generally (concepts of Divine Wisdom and Word) and then emanates, by the end of the imagined conversation, to touch upon all forms of diverse rites and practices. Yet, the dialogue concludes with the stillness of peace, which surpasses all human power of utterance. Final realization of religious peace remains mystical and speculative, beyond this world, the *theoria* of vision, the end as envisioned in the dialogue to be the New Jerusalem. The dialogue is bookended as Cusanus's own recollection of an intellectual vision and as culmination of the contemplation of religious concordance.[60] Cusanus attempts to unfold the enigmatic aspect of Wisdom and the Word from memory in the flux of conjecture as peering through a mirror darkly.[61] What does shine forth in *De pace fidei* is Christ as both creative cataphatic revealer of the concordance of every conceivable religious rite and as narrow apophatic, mystical way to unity beyond the dialogical finite conundrum "where a sentence has both a beginning and an ending."[62]

As we have arrived at the end of this study, we conclude that Cusanus's Christocentric exclusivist-inclusivist synthesis of religious concordance is formulated through the concepts and categories of Greek philosophy. This examination of *De pace fidei* has sought to present a particular case study of how the intellectual worlds of the three Abrahamic religious traditions interacted and created similar patterns of thought through Greek philosophy.

In order to summarize the comprehensive conceptual framework of Hellenism as background to *De pace fidei*, we look to the eminent former McGill professor and founder of McGill University's Institute of Islamic Studies, Wilfred Cantwell Smith. In the beginning of his now classic study, *The Meaning and End of Religion*, Cantwell Smith traces the use of the concept of *religio* in the West and uncovers its shifting meaning.[63] The origins of the word *religio* are found in Greco-Roman usage and centered on the performance of religious rites. This universal aspect of the pantheon resonates with Cusanus's famous thesis, "religio una in rituum varietate."[64] From there, Smith notes, "The one

---

59 *De coelesti hierarchia* I, 1–3, 120B-124A; Aquinas, *Summa Theologiæ* Ia, 108, 1; *De pace fidei* I, 2; XVI, 55.
60 *De pace fidei* I, 1; XIX, 68.
61 *De pace fidei* I, 1.
62 Augustine, *Confessions* IX, x (24). English translation by Henry Chadwick (Oxford: Oxford University Press, 1998), 171.
63 Wilfred Cantwell Smith, *The Meaning and End of Religion: A New Approach to the Religious Traditions of Mankind* (New York: Mentor Books, 1964), Chapter 2.
64 *De pace fidei* I, 6.

sense of the term *religio* that is found fairly steadily through the Middle Ages is a development from meaning 'rite', namely the specialized designation of the monastic life as *'religio'*."[65] That Cusanus was familiar with this connotation of *religio* may be found in his correspondence with the Benedictine monks of Tegernsee on his treatise *De visione Dei*, which we noted in the last chapter of this study. From religious orders Smith then moves onto the great renaissance Platonist, Marsilio Ficino's contribution to the meaning of *religio* in his *De christiana religione*.[66] While briefly considering Aquinas's use of the word *religio* he passes over Cusanus's *De pace fidei*.

Cusanus's frequent use of the word *religio* in *De pace fidei* echoes ancient Hellenic ideas, and also that great harmonizer of Neoplatonism and Christianity, Augustine.[67] In *De vera religione*, Augustine explores the universal nature of *religio*, but also moves to the contemplative in regards to the Christian faith. Cusanus read *De vera religione* and cites the work in *De pace fidei*.[68] Augustine argues that the good and blessed life "is to be found entirely in the true religion wherein one God is worshipped and acknowledged with purest piety".[69] Vestiges of this true religion are to be found everywhere through the agency and providence of Divine Wisdom.[70] Even so, Augustine summons lovers of wisdom to "turn to God so that we may deserve to be illumined by his Word, the true light."[71] This path is open to everyone. There is one God alone to be worshipped, according to Augustine, "and his Wisdom who makes every wise soul wise."[72] And Augustine concludes *De vera religione* by urging "Let our religion bind us to the one omnipotent God, because no creature comes between our minds and him whom we know to be the Father and the Truth, i.e., the inward light whereby we know him."[73] As Smith detects, Augustine barely mentions Christianity in *De vera religione*. "The culmination is mystic,"[74] much like the

---

65   Smith, *Meaning and End of Religion*, 33.
66   *Libro di Marsilio Ficino Fiorentino della Cristiana religione* (Published both in Latin and Italian in 1474 or early 1475).
67   Cusanus employs *religio* or declensions of the same 27 times throughout *De pace fidei*.
68   *De pace fidei* II, 7; *De vera religione* 39. See critical apparatus of the Heidelberg Edition, vol. VII, p. 8.
69   Augustine, *De vera religione* I, 1, *Augustine: Earlier Writings, The Library of Christian Classics*, vol. VI, translated by John H.S. Burleigh (Philadelphia: Westminster Press, 1953), 225. Cf., *De pace fidei* I, 5–6.
70   *De vera religione* XXXIX, 72, p. 262. Cf., *De pace fidei* IV, 10–12.
71   *De vera religione* XLII, 79, p. 266.
72   *De vera religione* LV, 112, p. 282.
73   *De vera religione* LV, 113, p. 282.
74   Smith, *Meaning and End of Religion*, 31.

ideal religious dialogue as envisioned by Cusanus in the framework of contemplation.[75] For *religio* is the bond that unites creatures to the Creator, the Truth and inner light of revelation. Smith reminds us that the non-Augustinian introduction into eighteenth-century Europe of the post enlightenment notion of revealed religion has led to confusion.[76] Cusanus, as inheritor of ancient and Augustinian contemplative and universal concepts of religion, reminds readers who venture into his conceptual context that God does not reveal religions, but rather God reveals God's self as way and means to beatitude and religious concordance: the Word in relation to words, the finite in hierarchical dialectical gradations to the infinite. Cusanus's religion is not one of the religions, but the religion: the peace of faith for the peace of the cosmos.

In Cusanus's all-encompassing conception of one religion in the variety of rites we detect not even a hint of Pascal's matter of the heart or Schleiermacher's intuition of the numinous universe[77] As Biechler and Bond note, there are indeed pointers to Luther in *De pace fidei* on religion and justification by faith.[78] For Cusanus, this peace of faith is bonded to its object: the Word, the dialogical-incarnational and cosmic-hierarchical Word of God through whom all things are enfolded and unfolded.[79] Cusanus even peers subtly ahead to a central tenet of confessional Lutheran theology: the ubiquity of Christ.[80]

At the conclusion of this work, we observe that Cusanus's ideas on one religion in the variety of rites are not without criticism. Here, for brevity's sake, we propose but a few. First and foremost, Cusanus had no real exposure to Muslims. While given that for a churchman of his time and place he was remarkably well versed on Islam, nonetheless, he sounds today naïve in his belief that

---

75   *De pace fidei* I, 1.
76   Smith, *Meaning and End of Religion*, 116.
77   "Le coeur a ses raisons que la raison ne connaît point; on le sait en mille choses. Je dis que le coeur aime l'être universel naturellement, et soimême naturellement selon qu'il s'y adonne; et il se durcit contre l'un ou l'autre à son choix" (Blaise Pascal, *Pensées* (277), edited by Léon Brunschvicg (Paris: 1897), 66). In his second speech, Schleiermacher writes, "I entreat you to become familiar with this concept: intuition of the universe. It is the hinge of my whole speech; it is the highest and most universal formula of religion on the basis of which you should be able to find every place in religion, from which you determine its essence and its limits" (Friedrich Schleiermacher, *On Religion: Speeches to its Cultured Despisers*, translated and edited by Richard Crouter (Cambridge: Cambridge University Press, 1996), 24).
78   On faith in *De pace fidei*, see introduction to the English translation of *De pace fidei* by Biechler and Bond, xxxvi–xlviii.
79   *De pace fidei* II, 7.
80   *Formula of Concord*, Article VIII.

rational discourse could indeed achieve lasting religious peace between these two great Abrahamic faiths. Secondly, Cusanus may indeed be guilty of the fallacy of equivocation: while the theological subjects may be same for Christians and Muslims—for example God, Word, prophets—the predicates are different. Thirdly, in our fragmented contemporary world, we have, no doubt, lost faith in the power of logical, dialectical thought as envisioned in *De pace fidei*. Perhaps, it never really worked in reality but only in the imaginations of thinkers like Plato and Cusanus. Finally, what would Cusanus say about Christ being the way, the truth, and the life?[81] In other words, what about the uniqueness of Christ as mediator between the infinite and finite, God and humanity? For Augustine, this was not to be found in the books of the Platonists.[82] Cusanus seems to suggest in *De venatione sapientiae* the Wisdom-Word is found everywhere, or at least in all of the great thinkers, pagan and Christian alike. And, the *Cribratio* shows that he found Wisdom as incarnate in Christ in the Qur'an too. Perhaps, in the end, Cusanus conceives of an all-encompassing religion unrecognizable to both Christians and Muslims. While Cusanus's conception of religious concordance may appear today as delusional or disturbing, we would do well to approach him through his own words. This study has argued that in order fully to appreciate Cusanus's thesis of one religion in the variety of rites, readers must note how he understands the peace of faith through the Word of God metaphysically, as rooted in Hellenic thought and the plentitude of ancient conciliar Christology.

On this last objection, as formulated with the Christian tradition over the emptying of the uniqueness of Christ, the prolific twentieth century theologian Hans Urs von Balthasar provides a more penetrating critique of the metaphysics of Cusanus's Logo-centric *De pace fidei*. Balthasar zeroes in on the universality and apparent lack of exclusivity in the cardinal's Christology. In volume five of his massive *The Glory of the Lord: A Theological Aesthetics*, Balthasar concludes that for Cusanus, "the philosophical systematic passes over directly into the theological."[83] Perhaps, instead of a passing over, there is a merging of opposites or coincidence of rites in one religion—the former are "taken up" into the latter. As Karl Jaspers comments, "For Cusanus, speculative philosophical thinking and the Christian faith merge into one."[84] How they merge into

---

[81] John 14:6.
[82] Augustine, *Confessions* VII, ix, 13–14.
[83] Hans Urs von Balthasar. *The Glory of the Lord: A Theological Aesthetics, Vol. V: The Realm of Metaphysics in the Modern Age*. Translated by Oliver Davies, et al. (San Francisco: Ignatius Press, 1991), 245.
[84] Jaspers, *Anselm and Nicholas of Cusa*, 55.

one is through the dialectical and hierarchical Word of God within the mise en scène of contemplative vision. For Balthasar, Cusanus represents one of the great attempts "to see Biblical revelation once again within the total form of a theology that organically includes philosophy."[85] Balthasar traces the passing over into the theological beginning with *De concordantia catholica* through *De pace fidei*. "It suffices to say about that, that the speculative background for both (as least as strongly as for Augustine's *City of God*) is Platonic."[86] In *De concordantia catholica* and *De pace fidei*, the earthly church must imitate as best as it can the heavenly Jerusalem.[87] Balthasar further observes, that, for Cusanus, "There is one thing above all to be avoided: schism."[88] How Cusanus avoids schism, according to Balthasar, is through engaging and encompassing the whole cosmic spectrum. Balthasar writes,

> Cusa endeavours as a Catholic to think universally and broadly within the Church; he wants to understand the Church, like the incarnate God in Christ, only against the cosmic background; even the ecclesiastically positive must be utterly transparent to the whole truth between God and man.[89]

For Balthasar Cusanus appears to have tied the knot of philosophy and theology too tightly, in that "he projects the world-religions on to the background of the (Platonic-)philosophical and thus, as has been shown, sees in Christ above all the Logos, the perfect teacher of Wisdom who has appeared."[90] And yet, it appears that the expression of the Wisdom-Word as imagined but nonetheless incarnate dialogist itself is the way to showing the fullness of the concordance of infinite and finite, and that in this Word all rites, indeed, the sum total of all acts of adoration in creation, find their fulfillment.[91] Perhaps, the knot has slackened owing to a failure to adhere to Cusanus's Christocentric metaphysics of *De pace fidei*. It is in Cusanus's tying together of philosophy and theology, the universal and exclusive, that the full cosmic and concordant glory of the Word of God shines forth.

---

85   Hans Urs von Balthasar, *The Glory of the Lord: A Theological Aesthetics, Vol. 1: Seeing the Form*, translated by Erasmo Leiva-Merikakis (San Francisco: Ignatius Press, 1982), 79.
86   von Balthasar, *The Glory of the Lord*, vol. 5, 245.
87   von Balthasar, *The Glory of the Lord*, vol. 5, 245.
88   von Balthasar, *The Glory of the Lord*, vol. 5, 245.
89   von Balthasar, *The Glory of the Lord*, vol. 5, 245.
90   von Balthasar, *The Glory of the Lord*, vol. 5, 246.
91   *De pace fidei* II, 7-III, 9.

Balthasar's criticism bears consideration, and, indeed, Cusanus was not without detractors of his cosmic theological method in his own day. This study has suggested that the connection between heavenly and earthly, church and world, is tied together in Christ, who is both divine wisdom (universalist) and the incarnate Word (exclusivist). As Leo's Tome shows, and as cited by Cusanus at the outset of *Cribratio*, what he sought to avoid was schism. For Cusanus this meant the schism of Christianity and Islam, or any schism between reason and revelation, or between the exclusivity and inclusivity of ancient and conciliar Christology. The *concordantia* is in and through Christ the Wisdom of God. With this in mind we may formulate three general approaches to religion and religious diversity: all religions are the same, all religions are different, or religions exist as unity in plurality. Cusanus comes closest to the third option. For Cusanus, religion is one and cosmic in range and effect, yet rites are many and diffuse in practice. The rites remain distinct and yet wholly part of one religion. Cusanus seems to hold universal and exclusive together dialectically and discovers through imagined contemplative and conciliar dialogue a religious synthesis. There are striking similarities here to the fourth-and fifth-century conciliar Christological debates and formulations over holding to one *hypostasis/persona* in two distinct but inseparable natures. *De pace fidei* sometimes accentuates the exclusive character of the Christian faith, while at other times highlights the universal scope of Wisdom through the plethora of religious rites. Ultimately, though, for Cusanus truth is found in the Word of God, who "is all and in all."[92] While, no doubt, this may prove troubling to Christians and Muslims today, it seems to be truer to Cusanus's thought and intentions. By letting Cusanus speak we might hear something new for our age. This study began with a close reading of the text and the assumption that *De pace fidei* has something to say to the complexities of our multi-religious world.

De pace fidei concludes with the peace of Jerusalem, the political and allegorical city holy to Jews, Christians and Muslims, a place of shared sacred importance.[93] This study of the fifteenth century has looked at relations between two of the religions of Abraham: Christianity and Islam. In our age, Jerusalem still represents a city of religious hope and division. As sign of hope and prayer for the peace of Jerusalem, the Second Vatican Council issued *Nostra Aetate* (28 October 1965). In one succinct paragraph, the Council declared:[94]

---

92 *De pace fidei* 11, 7; Colossians 3:11 NRSV.
93 *De pace fidei* XIX, 68.
94 *Nostra Aetate* or *Declaration on the Relation of the Church to Non-Christian Religions* (28 October 1965), *Vatican Council II, vol. 1, The Conciliar and Post Conciliar Documents*, new

> The Church has also a high regard for the Muslims. They worship God, who is one, living and subsistent, merciful and almighty, the Creator of heaven and earth, who has also spoken to men. They strive to submit themselves without reserve to the hidden decrees of God, just as Abraham submitted himself to God's plan, to whose faith Muslims eagerly link their own. Although not acknowledging him as God, they venerate Jesus as a prophet, his virgin Mother they also honor, and even at times devoutly invoke. Further they await the day of judgment and the reward of God following the resurrection of the dead. For this reason they highly esteem an upright life and worship of God, especially by way of prayer, almsgiving and fasting.[95]

The Council goes on in the next paragraph to lament that many quarrels have developed over the centuries between Muslims and Christian, and that "a sincere effort be made to achieve mutual understanding; for the benefit of all men, let them together preserve and promote peace, liberty, social justice and moral values."[96] *Nostra Aetate* does not address more controversial theological quandaries, such as whether or not the Qur'an is a revelation of God, nor does it comment on the place of the Prophet Mohammed within the Catholic faith. Instead of attempting to provide detailed summaries of the common points of interest or disagreement, *Nostra Aetate* only constructively hints at common teachings. Elaboration is left to continued dialogue and mutual understanding. The ongoing work of finding common ground and conversation instead of conflict continues in such landmark efforts like the textually focused *A Common Word*. This open letter of peace explores Scripture and the Qur'an on the love of one God and love of neighbour.[97] While noting *Nostra Aetate*, we also mention the more recent *Dominus Iesus* (6 August 2000), which points back to Cyprian and Boniface VIII ("Extra ecclesiam nulla salus est"). It appears again that in the teachings of the Roman Catholic Church concerning other religious traditions we have both tendencies at play: inclusion and exclusion, universalist and exclusivist. At times, Cusanus's approach bears similarities with the Roman Catholic theologian Karl Rahner's understanding of an anonymous

---

revised edition, edited by Austin Flannery (Northport, NY: Costello Publishing, 1996), 738–742.

95 *Nostra Aetate, Vatican Council II*, vol. 1, 739–740.
96 *Nostra Aetate, Vatican Council II*, vol. 1, 740.
97 See the summary and abridgment to *A Common Word* in: *A Common Word: Muslims and Christians On Loving God and Neighbor*, 28–29.

Christian.[98] Yet, in *De pace fidei*, the anonymous Christian is led to the exclusive truth of one religion in the variety of rites by the very Word of God. According to Cusanus, the anonymous Christian becomes synonymous through Christ.

While Cusanus lived in what he conjectured were the last days, he creatively constructed the contemplative dialogue of *De pace fidei* as religious synthesis in a world drastically demarcated by belief. Of course, *contra* Cusanus, the world did not end in the eighteenth-century. Against his archetypal meditations on the peace of faith, violence perpetuated by religion persists. Throughout the vicissitudes of past and present, Cusanus's prayer for religious peace resonates. The fifteenth century, while no stranger to end-time fervor, was in Southern's terms, "a moment of vision" for Christians perceiving Islam.[99] These visions of peace were soon eclipsed by realities of war. Today, through religious dialogue like *A Common Word*, we perchance glimpse the moment of vision anew. Contemplation on what Louis Massignon called the potential for the *point vierge* between Christians and Muslims.[100] Amidst proponents of apocalyptical clashes of civilizations and religious conflagration, Cusanus's *De pace fidei* reminds Christians and Muslims of shared philosophical concepts and the recurrent need for respectful and honest conversation. From a Christian perspective, Cusanus maintains the tension between universality and exclusivity inherent in ancient and conciliar Christology. In so doing, he ultimately points to the dialectical and hierarchical cosmic fullness of the hypostases of the *Logos*. While Christians and Muslims will continue to differ on fundamental points of belief and practice, adherents of both great Abrahamic faiths pray along with Cusanus for peace. Cusanus's heart lies buried before the altar in the chapel of his cherished hospice and library whereupon prayers ascend for the peace of Jerusalem, the city holy to Jews, Christians and Muslims. For the fifteenth-century theologian Nicholas of Cusa, the common word of peace

---

98   Karl Rahner, "Christianity and the Non-Christian Religions" in *Readings in Philosophy of Religion: Ancient to Contemporary*, 459–464. See also Rahner's response to criticism by Balthasar and others, "Observations on the Problem of the 'Anonymous Christian'", Karl Rahner, *Theological Investigations*, vol. XIV, translated by David Bourke (New York: Seabury Press, 1976), 280–294. Rahner writes that concerning the reality of the anonymous Christian "neither can nor should be contested by a Catholic Christian or theologian" (282).

99   The title of Chapter 3 of Southern, *Western Views of Islam in the Middle Ages*.

100   "*Point vierge*" Massignon (Foucauld au desert: devant le Dieu d'Abraham, Agar et Ismael) via Merton, *Conjectures*, 148. Merton writes, "the 'point vierge' of the spirit, the center of our nothingness where, in apparent despair, one meets God—and is found completely in His mercy." Perhaps, this study best concludes with the suggestion that the mystery of God's mercy may be a nexus of dialogue between Christians and Muslims.

between Christians and Muslims is none other than the prophet of Jerusalem, Jesus the Christ.

As we have seen, Cusanus wrote *De pace fidei* the same year (1453) as he penned his mystical masterpiece *De visione Dei*. We now conclude this chapter on the theolical horizons openend by Cusanus's Christocentirc influence on Christian-Muslim dialogue and prayer for the peace of Jerusalem by surveying a great Christian mystical theologian of the twentieth century, Thomas Merton, who, like Cusanus, wrote on the mystery of contemplation and religious diversity. Like Cusanus, Merton was also very interested in the relationship between Christianity and Islam.[101] Merton's autobiographical *The Seven Storey Mountain* has been hailed as a twentieth century *Confessions*.[102]

In a letter to the Pakistani Sufi Abdul Aziz, dated 26 December 1962, Merton notes with sadness the death of a shared friend, the famous Christian scholar of Islam, Louis Massignon.[103] Merton had first become acquainted with Massignon in 1958, maintaining a friendship with him until his death in 1962. Massignon had in turn introduced Merton to Azis, who corresponded from 1960 until Merton's death in 1968.[104] Merton and Aziz were each mystics, though from different religious traditions; Merton of the catholic mystical way and Aziz of the path of Sufism. While both Merton and Massignon were priests,

---

101 Merton's interest in Islam is explored in *Merton & Sufism, The Untold Story: A Complete Compendium*, edited by Rob Baker and Gray Henry (Louisville, KY: Fons Vitae, 1999).

102 William H. Shannon, the Founding President of the Thomas Merton Society, observes how Merton's *The Seven Storey Mountain* has been described as a twentieth century "version" of the *Confessions* of St. Augustine. Thomas Merton, *The Seven Storey Mountain: An Autobiography of Faith*, with "Note to the Reader" by William H. Shannon (New York, Harcourt, 1999), xix.

103 Thomas Merton, *Thomas Merton: A Life in Letters, the Essential Collection*, edited by William H. Shannon and Christine M. Bochen (New York: HarperOne, 2008), 345. For an overview and study of Merton's correspondence with Abdul Aziz, see William Apel, *Signs of Peace: the Interfaith Letters of Thomas Merton* (Maryknoll, NY: Orbis, 2006), 9–27. See also Sidney H. Griffith, "'As One Spiritual Man to Another': The Merton-Abdul Aziz Correspondence" in *Merton & Sufism, The Untold Story: A Complete Compendium*, 101–129.

104 On Merton and Massignon, see Herbert Mason, "Massignon and Merton" in *Louis Massignon au cœur de notre temps*, edited by Jacques Keryell (Paris: Éditions Karhala: 1999), 247–258; Sidney H. Griffith, "«Un entretien sur toutes choses, humaines et divines» La correspondance entre Louis Massignon et Thomas Merton," Keryell, 259–278; Sidney H. Griffith, "Merton, Massignon and the Challenge of Islam" in *Merton & Sufism*, 51–78. See also Apel, *Signs of Peace*, 12. See also: Mary Louise Gude, *Louis Massignon: The Crucible of Compassion* (Notre Dame, IN: University of Notre Dame Press, 1996).

Merton of the Latin Rite and Massignon of the Greek Catholic Melkite rite,[105] Merton, Massignon and Aziz were also bound by a deeper, more innate desire; they were all three avid seekers of Wisdom, Sophia, in all of its multivalent and mysterious manifestations. Massignon was famous for his work on the great Sufi al-Hallâj, *La Passion d'al Husayn ibn Mansour al-Hallâj: martyr mystique de l'Islam*, first published in 1922, and for his landmark *Essai sur les Origines du Lexique Technique de la Mystique Musulmane* also first published in 1922 with a second, revised edition in 1954.[106] What Merton has to say about Massignon's death is also memorable, even prophetic. "It seems to me," Merton writes, "that mutual comprehension between Christians and Moslems is something of very vital importance today, and unfortunately it is rare and uncertain, or else subjected to the vagaries of politics." Given the recent history of Christian-Muslim relations, it's clear that "the vagaries of politics" have often obscured mutual comprehension. Massignon, Aziz and Merton remind seekers after peace that there exists, however hidden in the enigma of signs and things signified, the *point vierge* of the human spirit where God and self are known in the merciful, compassionate One (*Bismillah al-rahman al-rahim*).[107]

Upon hearing the news of the fall of Constantinople to the Ottomans in 1453, the philosopher and prelate Nicholas of Cusa composed *De pace fidei*, in the form of an irenical dialogue between Christians and Muslims. The Ottoman conquest of Constantinople, the ancient capital of the Eastern Roman Empire and home of the famous ancient church Hagia Sophia, sent shock waves throughout Western Europe and provoked calls for a crusade from Pope Nicholas V and the Roman curia. Indeed these calls for crusade would continue throughout the fifteenth and well into the sixteenth century. Unlike many of his fellow churchmen, however, Cusanus responded to the fall of Constantinople not with a call to arms, but with an invitation to conversation. For

---

105   Merton was ordained as Father M. Louis, O.C.S.O., 26 May 1949, the Feast of the Ascension. Massignon was ordained in 1950.

106   Louis Massignon, *Essai sur les Origines du Lexique Technique de la Mystique Musulmane*, 2nd Edition (Paris: J. Vrin, 1954). An example of Massignon's comparison of Christianity and Islam is found in Chapter four of his essay where he writes, "Si la Chrétienté est, fondamentalement (1), l'acceptation et l'imitation de Christ, *avant* l'acceptation de la Bible—en revanche, l'Islam est l'acceptation du Qor'ân *avant* l'imitation de Mohammed" (139). For English translation of the *Essai*, see Louis Massignon, *Essay on the Origins of the Technical Language of Islamic Mysticism*, translated by Benjamin Clark (Notre Dame, IN: University of Notre Dame Press, 1997).

107   "Point vierge", Massignon (Foucauld au desert: devant le Dieu d'Abraham, Agar et Ismael) via Merton, *Conjectures of a Guilty Bystander* (London: Sheldon Press, 1977), 148; see also Apel, *Signs of Peace*, 16; Griffith, "Merton, Massignon and the Challenge of Islam," 64.

a church leader of his age and place, he was remarkably well versed in the thought and traditions of Islam. His personal library in Bernkastel-Kues, Germany contains various Western theological writings on Islam, as well as works by the great early-medieval Muslim philosopher Avicenna. In Cusanus's library well-marked works by Arab philosophers, such as Averroës and Al-Ghazali, stand side by side with Aquinas' *Summa Theologiæ*, Plato's *Republic* and the sermons of Meister Eckhart.[108] Cusanus points to a shared font of Sophia as channelled through Abraham and Plato, revelation and reason, monotheism and mysticism.

On the common ground of Greek philosophy, the intellectual worlds of the three Abrahamic religious traditions interacted, creating similar patterns of thought in dealing with crucial religious concepts. Furthermore, the impact of Greek philosophy on Christian and Muslim theologians and philosophers provided them a shared synthetic and hermeneutical paradigm. There are many Platonic or Neoplatonic influences on Cusanus's method of learned ignorance and the coincidence of opposites in the Wisdom and Word of God: Plato, Aristotle, Proclus, Denys, Avicenna, Aquinas, and Eckhart. From Antiquity to the Middle Ages, during which philosophy and religious thought were closely aligned and intertwined, the dynamic encounter between Greek philosophical tradition and the three Abrahamic religions shaped the contours of Western intellectual history. And this is especially true for Cusanus. As his library shows, on the common ground of Greek philosophy, he interacted with the intellectual traditions of Islam through such thinkers as Al-Ghazali and Averroës, and employed similar modes of thought in dealing with the doctrine of God and Wisdom, the Word and words, unity and plurality, Being and beyond Being.[109] For Cusanus, the three Abrahamic faiths—Judaism, Christianity, and

---

108 Cod. Cus. 177, Plato's *Phaedrus* with numerous notes and markings by Cusanus (Cod. Cus. fs. 108–111). Cod. Cus. 178, Latin translation of Plato's *Republic* also with notes and markings by Cusanus. See especially, Cod. Cus. 178f. 132r, book six of Plato's *Republic*. On Thomas Aquinas, see Cod. Cus. 68, *prima pars*, *Summa Theologiæ*, with notes by Cusanus on f. 124v, question 93 of the *prima pars* of the *Summa Theologiæ*. Cod. Cus. 21, fs. 137r–172v, sermons by Meister Eckhart in Latin, with notes or markings by Cusanus on almost every page.

109 Cod. Cus. 205 with writings by Arab philosphers; Cod. Cus. 298 (Avicenna) with note by Cusanus on f. 79v. See also Cod. Cus. 299 with Avicenna's *Liber de anima* with markings by Cusanus on f. 21v. Cod. Cus. 107 and 108 on Islam both contain numerous notes by Cusanus. Cod. Cus. 195 contains the *Liber de causis* and Proclus's *Elements* both of which are written in the same script by the same scribe with notes and markings by Cusanus throughout. The two works were meant to be read together. Cusanus has many notes on Prop. 20 of Proclus's *Elements* (Cod. Cus. 195f. 38r). Cusanus also references Plato thrice

Islam—are Western monotheistic religions shaped by the contours and categories of Greek thought. Thus, Greek philosophy, and, with regard to Cusanus, Neoplatonic dialectical and hierarchical thought in particular, provided medieval Christians, Muslims and Jews with collective insights into the mystery of the essence of God and the wonders of the cosmos. And for Cusanus, the coincidence of opposites is hypostatically found and surpassed in Christ, Holy Wisdom, Hagia Sophia, enlightenment and enlightener, who is both God and man and the way to God, and God the unknowable, the very reconciliation and transcender of the many rites of the one religion. The *point vierge* of Cusanus's sapient dialogical approach to the interrelation between Christianity and Islam is centered in the unfolding and enfolding, the hidden-revealed Wisdom and Word of God as evocatively and dialectically explicated in Cusanus's *De pace fidei*.

Merton carefully studied Cusanus. He translated into English Cusanus's apophatic dialogue *De Deo abscondito* (*Dialogue on the Hidden God*) where God is ultimately unknown and yet, paradoxically, attainable.[110] The dialogue describes searching for God beyond mere names and words and leads the 'pagan' in the dialogue to a deeper understanding of what God is by saying what God is not.[111] And ultimately, God is not known, and this nonetheless is a *learned* ignorance. Cusanus was deeply influenced by apophatic thought, especially as found in the writings of Pseudo-Dionysius.[112] It is a learned ignorance, apophaticism turned outward, globally expanded in *De pace fidei*. In a letter from New Year's Day, 1964 to R.J. Zwi Werblowsky, a prominent scholar of comparative religion, Merton also notes how the 'pagan' character in the dialogue *De Deo abscondito* is a superficial Christian.[113] Merton writes how he found comfort

in his notes in the margins of *Liber de causis* (Cod. Cus. 195f. 4r, f. 7r, f. 8r), and Pseudo-Dionysius twice (Cod. Cus. 195f. 5v, f. 8r). See also, notes and markings by Cusanus in Cod. Cus. 185, Proclus's *Platonic Theology*, fs. 89r, 91r, 93r, 93, 103r. We draw special attention to the interplay of Plato and Proclus and Denys (Pseudo-Dionysius the Areopagite) in Cusanus's notes.

110   *De Deo abscondito, Dialogue About the Hidden God, a Translation by Thomas Merton* (New York: Dim Gray Bar Press, 1989). First published in the summer 1966 issue of the *Lugano Review*.
111   *De Deo Abscondito* 1, 10–11, 15. Cf., *De pace fidei* 1, 4.
112   Cods. Cus. 43–45, 96 are the works of St. Denys. For notes by Cusanus, see Cod. Cus. 45f. 89r; Cod. Cus. 96f. 257r.
113   Thomas Merton, *The Hidden Ground of Love: The Letters of Thomas Merton on Religious Experience and Social Concerns*, edited by William H. Shannon (New York: Farrar, Straus, Giroux, 1985), 587. Merton writes, "I send you a mimeo of a translation of a very short piece of Nicholas of Cusa. Here again the intention is in no sense apologetic, where he

in turning to Cusanus after reading Hannah Arendt on the Eichmann case and the moral disorientation of the West indeed, as Merton writes, "a sordid examination of the conscience of *the entire West*".[114] For Merton, though, reason and conscience must not give way to what he calls "the insane cruelties of our bureaucratic age."[115] The 'West' may be burdened by bureaucracy, but for Merton and Cusanus, it also represented, at least at its best, a living repository and transformer of ancient Greek thought and Christian and Muslim revelation, an intellectual setting for mystical ascent, and modality of belief in one God. For Cusanus (and indirectly, for Merton) the superficial Christian is one who does not see that God is both hidden (unknowable, apophatic) and knowable in revelation (cataphatic) both *without*, i.e. in Jewish and Christian Scripture, and, also, albeit conditionally or as it pertains to Christ, in the Qur'an, and *within*, that is in the conscience and the poetic muse of Wisdom. By way of Cusanus and other great thinkers and writers, Merton creatively borrowed the elastically recurring neologism of *coincidentia oppositorum*.

Christopher Pramuk's masterful study of Cusanus's Christology in *Sophia: the Hidden Christ of Thomas Merton*, succeeds in showing how Sophia, the unknown and unseen Christ, "centered and in many respects catalyzed Merton's theological imagination in a period of tremendous social, political, and religious fragmentation."[116] The same may be said of Cusanus concerning his Christocentric and sapiential understanding of Islam in *De pace fidei*: Sophia, the unknown and unseen Christ, the *Verbum Dei*, Jesus, centers, unifies and catalyzes the seeming *coincidentia oppositorum* of Christianity and Islam as one religion in a variety of rites in his own uncertain time rent by tremendous social changes such as in the discovery of the so-called 'New World', the Renaissance, the advent of heliocentrism, and the nascent Scientific Revolution. Cusanus's age was also rife with political challenges: the Hundred Years' War, the rise of Islam through the rapidly expanding Ottoman Empire. Most pressingly, Cusanus's troubled century witnessed religious fragmentation on a near apocalyptic scale: the papal schism, the subsequent conciliar movement of the fifteenth century, and the oncoming Reformation. According to orthodox and catholic Christian doctrine, as confessed by both Merton and Cusanus, the incarnation of the *Verbum* is indeed the ultimate *coincidentia oppositorum*

---

pits a 'pagan' against a 'Christian.' In point of fact, one of the things that strikes the alert reason is that the 'pagan' is really a 'Christian' of the superficial type" (587).

114 Merton, *Conjectures*, 278.
115 Merton, *Conjectures*, 278.
116 Christopher Pramuk, *Sophia: The Hidden Christ of Thomas Merton* (Collegeville, MN: Liturgical Press, 2009), xxiii.

of God and man; and yet, as God, Christ Jesus is also beyond every *coincidentia oppositorum* as the one infinitely and utterly unutterable and unknowable God. Chapter 3 of Pramuk's study, "In the Belly of a Paradox: the Archaeology of Merton's Sacramental Imagination", aptly demonstrates how Merton's conviction that there exists an inherent relationship among all expressions of wisdom in and through the Wisdom of God extends to non-Christians, including pre-Christian Hellenic philosophers and Muslims.[117] For Merton and Cusanus, the *Logos*, *Verbum*, Sophia, pulsates from the centre which is both a centre and not a centre, and magnetically emanates inherent sublime power throughout existence.

Cusanus's *De pace fidei* begins and ends in Jerusalem, the place Pope Urban II, in his sermon in 1095 announcing the first crusade at the Council of Clermont, called the navel or centre of the earth, the city holy to Jews, Christians and Muslims,[118] a city of violence and peace, discord and concordance. Toward the conclusion of *De pace fidei*, the representatives of the world's religions are sent back to instruct their peoples in the one religion in a variety of rites. They are then compelled to meet again in Jerusalem, the old and the new, literal and figurative city straddling heaven and earth. Beginning in Jerusalem, religious peace will then emanate to the ends of the earth. The dialogue of *De pace fidei* closes in Jerusalem with the opening of books. At the end of the dialogue, the representatives of the world's religions search the ancient Greek and Latin sources where they discover that from the very beginning of Western philosophy, all religious diversity consists in multiple rites rather than in the worship of the one God. One of the central conceptual theologocal concepts used by Cusanus in *De pace fidei* is the city as nexus, as the political, temporal and eternal setting for the synthesis of religious concord: the topography of realizing religious peace and the geography of dialectical discourse.

Cusanus begins his mystical vision of *De pace fidei* in the flux of becoming, the dissimilarity of religious strife. The visionary, Cusanus himself, prays ardently for peace. He then ascends intellectually by divine grace into the heaven of reason, the angelic, metaphysical realm of abstraction where peace is realized hierarchically and dialectically given by God almighty (the Father) through the Word and Wisdom of God (the Son), and then through Peter (the papacy) and Paul (the rational and missionary impulse of the church catholic).

---

117   See especially, Pramuk, *Sophia*, 121–129.
118   For the description of Jerusalem as 'the navel of the earth' see Robert the Monk's chronicles of the events of the First Crusade and his rendition of the sermon by Pope Urban II at the Council of Clermont. (*Robert the Monk's History of the First Crusade, Historia Iherosolimitana*, translated by Carol Sweetenham (Aldershot, UK: Ashgate, 2006), 81).

For Cusanus, the one religion presupposes the Word of God from whom, in whom, and by whom the peace of faith is achieved (both *fides qua creditur* and *fides quae creditur*). Cusanus's originality here lies in how he applied this Neoplatonic understanding of learned ignorance to Islam: knowing that one does not know God, knowing that one does not know the one, instead of knowing only the many rites, knowing and unknowing Christian-Muslim dialogue through the *Logos* and Wisdom of God.

Cusanus transmits the Greek archetypal idea of the *polis* as nexus of religious concordance. The two cities: Constantinople, which for Cusanus was the primary repository of Neoplatonic thought, and Jerusalem, which in the Western medieval mind was the centre of the Earth, spatially and symbolically mark the Greek-patterned geography for the social imaginary of Christian-Muslim dialogue in *De pace fidei*. For Cusanus the *Logos* of concordance extends by gradation to all being; so also religious peace, as realized dialectically and hierarchically through the *Logos*, extends from the city of Jerusalem to Constantinople and throughout the world—a hierarchical geography of the chain of being and the chain of cities. At one point in history, after the unsettling events of the fall of Constantinople and the troubles that religious persecution bring, Cusanus wrote how he saw a vision of what intellectually already is and pragmatically could be.[119]

There are broad conjectural and even urban similarities between Merton and Cusanus's search for shared wisdom between Christians and Muslims. While different in tone and time, both mystics sought Sophia as the way of finding common ground and concordant peace. Merton wrote on the life of faith, "The tendency of our modern society and of all its thought and culture is to deny and to deride this simple, natural awareness, and to make man from the very beginning both afraid of faith and ashamed of it."[120] Indeed, by looking back to Hagia Sophia as found in the Abrahamic faiths and ancient Greek thought (revelation and reason), Merton retrieves the importance of faith found within. He presses on, "The first step to living faith is then, as it has always been one way or another, a denial and a rejection of the standards of thought complacently accepted by rationalistic doubt."[121] For Merton, seekers of Sophia must press on beyond the vagaries of politics and the smog of

---

119 *De pace fidei* I, 1; XIX, 68.
120 Thomas Merton, *Life and Holiness*, New York: Herder and Herder, 1963, 96. Merton dedicated this work in memoriam to Louis Massignon (d. 1962).
121 Merton, *Life and Holiness*, 96.

modern doubt to discover the *point vierge*.[122] Cusanus waited in hope on the way to perpetual peace, the way to Jerusalem. Merton too waited in hope for peace. And the providential God of peace was with him as he traveled to a great chain of cities "from Prades to Bermuda to St. Antonin to Oakham to London to Cambridge to Rome to New York to Columbia to Corpus Christi to St. Bonaventure to the Cistercian Abbey of the poor men who labor in Gethsemani" even to as far as Bangkok.[123] Indeed, Merton died while seeking religious concordance while attending a conference of Eastern and Western monks in Thailand. Cusanus's vision of *De pace fidei* and Merton's own search for Sophia ultimately coalesce with the *telos* of Scripture and the end of things, the sight of the new Jerusalem coming down from above, the eternal abode of peace, the time beyond time when the many will be one, and the journey to religious concord consummated.

---

122   *Conjectures*, 148. Merton writes, "the 'point vierge' of the spirit, the center of our nothingness where, in apparent despair, one meets God—and is found completely in His mercy."
123   *The Seven Storey Mountain*, 462.

CONCLUSION

Nicholas of Cusa's Christocentric Approach to Islam

Nicholas of Cusa's religious dialogue *De pace fidei* (1453) presents his unique Christological approach to Islam. The fall of Constantinople in 1453 compelled Cusanus to unfold and elaborate his theological synthesis of religious concordance. Throughout his life Cusanus sought to square the circle, i.e. to reconcile humanity with divinity, the Eastern and Western Churches, council and pope, Christianity and Islam. This study has examined Cusanus's multivalent search for unity by looking closely at his conversation with Islam in the light of his constructive Christology and his concomitant conception of the 'concordant' Word of God.

We began this study of Cusanus's universalist and exclusivist Wisdom-Word metaphysic of Christian-Muslim dialogue by marking the philosophical and theological sources of *De pace fidei*, which includes the foremost Platonic and Neoplatonic influences of hierarchy and dialectic, as well as the Greek and Christian idea of the polis as nexus of religious concordance, which culminates in a gathering together of the world's religions in Jerusalem. This included examining in detail Cusanus's unique Christocentric approach to Islam through his crucial conception of the coincidence of many and diverse rites within one religion. We situated *De pace fidei* within Cusanus's life-long pursuit of ecclesial reform and compared it with other Christian approaches to Islam in the late Middle Ages. Furthermore, we observed similarities that Cusanus's path to religious peace in *De pace fidei* shares with Bonaventura's famous *Itinerarium mentis in Deum,* and considered the influence of Plato's *Republic* upon Cusanus's search for religious peace in connection with his correlative and life-altering theological method of 'learned ignorance' (*docta ignorantia*). We even wondered the reality of how Cusanus could simultaneously preach crusade and dream of religious concord within the context of late-medieval Christendom's conflicts with the Ottoman Empire. Through close consideration and comparison of Cusanus's two related visions of *De pace fidei* and *De docta ignorantia* we surveyed his main metaphysical ideas as they relate to his conception of Christian-Muslim dialogue. We also investigated the ordering of the theological loci of *De pace fidei* as indicative of an actual blueprint for dialogue with Muslims, and his plans for a Christian–Muslim council found in his correspondence with his fellow student of Islam, John of Segovia. Moreover, we saw how Cusanus's unique metaphysic of Christian–Muslim dialogue assists in comprehending his controversial Dionysian move at the Council of Basel from the conciliar side to that of the pope, and finally to a prophetic and visionary voice for Christian-Muslim conciliar conversation. We then explored in detail how the structure of the dialogue of *De pace fidei* proceeds from the one Word and Wisdom of God by bringing together Cusanus's Christology in *De pace fidei* with the Christology of his other major works: namely, *De docta ignorantia, De concordantia catholica, Cribratio Alkorani,* and *De visione Dei*. Finally, we evaluated the inherent conciliar tension and taut dialectic of exclusivity and inclusivity within Cusanus's Christological approach to Islam.

Cusanus's sapiental dialogue of *De pace fidei* presents a profoundly dialectical account of the cosmos as actively flowing from, centered in, and returning to the Word and Wisdom of God. The dialogue moves within the broad metaphysical framework of Neoplatonic tradition, from confusion and disunity towards understanding and thence to affirmation of the inherent relatedness of all religions or, more exactly for Cusanus, religious rites, through their common participation in the Word of God as emanating into all things and present in all things. In Cusanus's vision of *De pace fidei* Christianity and Islam both derive from the Word, move through the Word, and return to the Word. Cusanus's better known treatise *De docta ignorantia* begins by maintaining an apophatic 'knowing' which does not properly 'know' God (i.e. 'learned ignorance), and concludes with a detailed discourse on the hierarchy of the Christian church, which is precisely where the argument of *De concordantia catholica* takes its own point of departure. For Cusanus, a full account of creation's participation in the Wisdom of God necessarily expands beyond the confines of fifteenth-century Christendom as presented in the argument of *De concordantia catholica* to embrace the particlulars of the major religions of the world which, as set out by him in the mystical synthesis of *De pace fidei*, he shows to be linked together through the magnetic power of the all-embracing Word of God. Here the Word of God extends by gradation into all being, and to all religions, and, like a magnetic stone, draws the representatives of the world's religions—most notably Islam—into the lasting unity of "the Peace of Faith" by means of a universal participation in the Word and Wisdom of God: *religio una in rituum varietate.*

Throughout *De pace fidei,* Cusanus consistently affirms both the diversity of rites and the universality of religious expression found in the shared *Logos* theology of Islam and Christianity. While substantive unity of the religions is realized at the level of a common participation in the cosmic Word of God, hierarchical distinctions are nonetheless maintained between the various differing religious cults and ethical practices of Christians and Muslims. While critical scholarship tends largely to view the Christological arguments of *De concordantia catholica* and *De docta ignorantia* as disparate and unrelated in substance, this research has demonstrated their underlying connection through a careful exposition of their deep hierarchical and dialectical Christocentric concordance in the argument of *De pace fidei*. Two other major writings of Cusanus, which are categorized by Nicholas of Cusa scholars as dissimilar in style and content to *De pace fidei* —namely, *Cribratio Alkorani* and the mystical treatise *De visione Dei*—are also closely related in substance to the dialogue of religious peace through their shared emphasis on the primary principle of the concordant 'Word of God'. Even in the opening discussion of the early treatise *De concordantia catholica* the idea appears, perhaps not as well elaborated as it would later come to be; the magnetic power of the divine Word extends dispositively throughout the diverse ranks of being. The essential metaphysical framework for the concordant Word of God in *De pace fidei* is already present in *De concordantia catholica* as theological prolegomena for his *De concordantia religionum*. Far from being comprised of recycled materials from his other writings, *De pace fidei* constitutes a creative synthesis of Cusanus's cosmology, Christology, political theory, mystical theology, and Christocentric approach to Islam. At the conclusion of this study, we propose that Cusanus, the master of learned ignorance and ardent seeker after metaphysical unity and coinceiential polarity, continues to have something profoundly constructive to say in the crucial contemporary conversation between Christians and Muslims.

Bibliography

Select Manuscripts in Nicholas of Cusa's Library, Kues, Germany

Cod. Cus. 107 consists of medieval Christian apologetical writings on Islam.
Cod. Cus. 108 includes Robert of Ketton's Latin translation of the Qur'an.
Cod. Cus. 177, 178 consist of works by Plato.
Cod. Cus. 205, 298, 299, 300 are various works of Avicenna.
Cod. Cus. 300, 301, 310 comprise writings of Averroës.

Select Manuscripts in the Vatican Library

Ott. lat. 347.
Urb. lat. 401.
Vat. lat. 1787.
Vat. lat. 5994.

Primary Sources—Latin Editions of Cusanus

Baur, Ludwig. *Cusanus-Texte III. Marginalien 1. Nicolaus Cusanus und Ps. Dionysius im Lichte der Zitate und Randbemerkungen des Cusanus.* Heidelberg: Carl Winter, 1941.
Bormann, Karl. *Cusanus-Texte III. Marginalien 2. Proclus Latinus: Die Exzerpte und Randnoten des Nikolaus von Kues zu den Lateinischen Übersetzungen der Proclus-Schriften 2.2 Expositio in Parmenidem Platonis.* Heidelberg: Carl Winter, 1986.
Nicholas of Cusa. *Nicolai de Cusa Opera Omnia iussu et auctoritate academiae litterarum heildelbergensis ad codicum fidem edita.* 22 Volumes. Leipzig-Hamburg: Felix Meiner, 1932–2012.
Nicholas of Cusa. *De docta ignorantia.* Edited by E. Hoffmann, and R. Klibansky. Leipzig: Felix Meiner, 1932.
Nicholas of Cusa. *Idiota de sapientia, Idiota de mente, Idiota de staticis experimentis.* Edited by L. Baur. Leipzig: Felix Meiner, 1937.
Nicholas of Cusa. *Directio speculantis seu de non aliud.* Edited by L. Baur and P. Wilpert. Leipzig: Felix Meiner, 1944.
Nicholas of Cusa. *De pace fidei cum epistula ad Ioannem de Segobia.* Edited by R. Klibansky and R. Bascour. Hamburg: Felix Meiner, 1959.
Nicholas of Cusa. *Opuscula I: De Deo abscondito, De quaerendo Deum, De filiatione Dei, De dato patris luminum, Coniectura de ultimis diebus, De genesi.* Edited by P. Wilpert. Hamburg: Felix Meiner, 1959.

Nicholas of Cusa. *De concordantia catholica*. Edited by G. Kallen. Hamburg: Felix Meiner, 1964.
Nicholas of Cusa. *De coniecturis*. Edited by J. Koch and C. Bormann. Hamburg: Felix Meiner, 1972.
Nicholas of Cusa. *De Venatione Sapientiae, De apice theoriae*. Edited by R. Klibansky and G. Senger. Hamburg: Felix Meiner, 1982.
Nicholas of Cusa. *Cribratio Alkorani*. Edited by L. Hagemann. Hamburg: Felix Meiner, 1986.
Nicholas of Cusa. *De visione Dei*. Edited by A.D. Riemann. Hamburg: Felix Meiner, 2000.
Nicholas of Cusa. *Apologia doctae ignorantiae ad codicum fidem edita*. Edited by R. Klibansky. Hamburg: Felix Meiner, 2007.
Nicholas of Cusa. *Sermones III (1452–1455)*. Edited by Silvia Donati, Rudolf Haubst, et al Hamburg: Felix Meiner, 2007.
Nicholas of Cusa. *Nicolai de Cusa De Pace Fidei cum Epistula ad Ioannem de Segobia*. Ediderunt Commentariisque Illustraverunt Raymundus Klibansky et Hilderbrandus Bascour, O.S.B. Medieval and Renaissance Studies Supplement III. London: Warburg Institute: 1956.
Nicholas of Cusa. *Acta Cusana: Quellen zur Lebensgeschichte des Nikolaus von Kues*. Edited by Erich Meuthen and Hermann Hallauer Hamburg: Felix Meiner, 1976–.
Nicholas of Cusa. *Die Philosophisch-Theologischen Schriften, Lateinisch—Deutsch*. 3 Vols. Edited by Leo Gabriel and Wilhem Dupré. Wien: Herder, 1989.
Senger, Hans Gerhard. *Cusanus-Texte III. Marginalien 2. Proclus Latinus: Die Exzerpte und Randnoten des Nikolaus von Kues zu den lateinischen Übersetzungen der Proclus- Schriften 2.1 Theologia Platonis, Elementatio theological*. Heidelberg: Carl Winter, 1986.

Select English Translations of Cusanus

Biechler, James E., and H. Lawrence Bond, eds. *Nicholas of Cusa on Interreligious Harmony: Text, Concordance and Translation of De Pace Fidei*. Lewiston, NY: The Edwin Mellen Press, 1990.
Dolan, John Patrick, ed. *Unity and Reform: Selected Writings of Nicholas de Cusa*. Notre Dame, IN: University of Notre Dame Press, 1962.
Nicholas of Cusa. *Writings on Church and Reform*. Translated by Thomas M. Izbicki. The I Tatti Renaissance Library. Cambridge, MA: Harvard University Press, 2008.
Nicholas of Cusa. *The Vision of God*. Translated by Gurney Salter and Introduction by Evelyn Underhill. New York: Cosimo Classics, 2007.
Nicholas of Cusa. *Nicholas of Cusa: Selected Spiritual Writings*. Trans. H. Lawrence Bond. New York: Paulist Press, 1997.

Nicholas of Cusa. *The Catholic Concordance*. Trans. Paul E. Sigmund. Cambridge: Cambridge University Press, 1995.
Nicholas of Cusa. *Nicholas of Cusa's De Pace Fidei and Cribratio Alkorani: Translation and Analysis (Second Edition)*. Trans. Jasper Hopkins. Minneapolis: The Arthur J. Banning Press, 1994. http://cla.umn.edu/sites/jhopkins/.
Nicholas of Cusa. *Toward a New Council of Florence: 'On the Peace of Faith' and Other Works by Nicolaus of Cusa*. Translated by William F. Wertz Jr. Washington D.C.: Schiller Institute, 1993.
Nicholas of Cusa. *The Layman on Wisdom and the Mind*. Trans. M.L. Führer. Ottawa: Dovehouse, 1989.
Nicholas of Cusa. *Nicholas of Cusa On Learned Ignorance: A Translation and an Appraisal of De Docta Ignorantia*. Trans. Jasper Hopkins. Minneapolis: The Arthur J. Banning Press, 1981.
Nicholas of Cusa. *Nicholas of Cusa's Debate with John Wenck: A Translation and an Appraisal of De Ignota Litteratura and Apologia Doctae Ignorantiae*. Trans. Jasper Hopkins. First Edition 1981. Minneapolis: The Arthur J. Banning Press, 1988. http://cla.umn.edu/sites/jhopkins/.
Nicholas of Cusa. *Of Learned Ignorance*. Trans. Germain Heron. London: Routledge & Kegan Paul, 1954.

Primary Sources

Abbot Suger. *On the Abbey Church of St.-Denis and its Art Treasures*. 2nd Edition. Edited and translated by Erwin Panofsky. Princeton: Princeton University Press, 1979.
Alighieri, Dante. *The Divine Comedy: Paradiso, Italian Text and Translation*. Trans. Charles S. Singleton. Princeton: Princeton University Press, 1975.
Alighieri, Dante. *The Divine Comedy 1: Hell*. Trans. Dorothy L. Sayers. London: Penguin, 1949.
Anselm of Canterbury. *The Major Works*. Edited by Brian Davies and G.R. Evans. Oxford: Oxford University Press, 1998.
Apel, William. *Signs of Peace: The Interfaith Letters of Thomas Merton*. Maryknoll, NY: Orbis, 2006.
Apocalyptic Spirituality: Treatises and Letters of Lactantius, Adso of Montier-en-Der, Joachim of Fiore, the Franciscan Spirituals, Savonarola. Trans. Bernard McGinn. New York: Paulist Press, 1979.
Aquinas, Thomas. *Commentary on the Book of Causes*. Trans. Charles R. Hess and Richard C. T Taylor. Washington, D.C.: Catholic University Press, 1996.
Aquinas, Thomas. *Summa Contra Gentiles, Book One: God*. Trans. Anton C. Pegis. Notre Dame: University of Notre Dame Press, 1975.

Aquinas, Thomas. *Summa Theologiae, Questions on God*. Edited by Brian Davies and Brian Leftow. Cambridge: Cambridge University Press, 2006.

Aquinas, Thomas. *Summa Theologiæ*, Volume 1 (1a., 1). Reprint (Blackfriars Edition). Cambridge: Cambridge University Press, 2006.

Aquinas, Thomas. *Summa Theologiæ*, Volume 2 (1a., 2–11). Reprint (Blackfriars Edition). Cambridge: Cambridge University Press, 2006.

Aquinas, Thomas. *Summa Theologiæ*, Volume 3 (1a, 12–13). Reprint (Blackfriars Edition). Cambridge: Cambridge University Press, 2006.

Aquinas, Thomas. *Summa Theologiæ*, Volume 4 (1a., 14–18). Reprint (Blackfriars Edition). Cambridge: Cambridge University Press, 2006.

Aquinas, Thomas. *Summa Theologiæ*, Volume 5 (1a., 19–26). Reprint (Blackfriars Edition). Cambridge: Cambridge University Press, 2006.

Aquinas, Thomas. *Summa Theologiæ*, Volume 6 (1a., 27–32). Reprint (Blackfriars Edition). Cambridge: Cambridge University Press, 2006.

Aquinas, Thomas. *Summa Theologiæ*, Volume 7 (1a., 33–43). Reprint (Blackfriars Edition). Cambridge: Cambridge University Press, 2006.

Aquinas, Thomas. *Summa Theologiæ*, Volume 8 (1a., 44–49). Reprint (Blackfriars Edition). Cambridge: Cambridge University Press, 2006.

Aristotle. *The Basic Works of Aristotle*. Edited and translated by Richard McKeon. New York: Random House, 1941.

Augustine, Saint. *City of God*. Trans. Henry Bettenson. London: Penguin Books, 2003.

Augustine, Saint. *City of God*. 7 Volumes. Loeb Classical Library. Cambridge, MA: Harvard University Press, 1957.

Augustine, Saint. *Confessions*. Trans. Henry Chadwick. Oxford: Oxford University Press, 1991.

Augustine, Saint. *Confessions*. Loeb Classical Library. Cambridge, MA: Harvard University Press, 1912.

Augustine, Saint. *De vera religione. Augustine: Earlier Writings*. The Library of Christian Classics. Vol. VI. Trans. John H.S. Burleigh. Philadelphia: Westminster, 1953.

Augustine, Saint. *On Christian Teaching (De Doctrina Christiana)*. Trans. R.P.H. Green. Oxford: Oxford University Press, 1997.

Augustine, Saint. *Sermons*. Trans. Edmund Hill, In *The Complete Works of St. Augustine: A Translation for the 21st Century*. Edited by J.E. Rotelle. Vol. 3.9. New York: New City Press, 1994.

Augustine, Saint. *The Trinity*. Trans. Edmund Hill, O.P. In *The Complete Works of St. Augustine: A Translation for the 21st Century*. Edited by J.E. Rotelle. Vol. 1.5. New York: New City Press, 1991.

Balthasar, Hans Urls von. *The Glory of the Lord: A Theological Aesthetics. Volume I: Seeing the Form*. Translated by Erasmo Leiva-Merikakis. Edited by Joseph Fessio and John Riches. San Francisco: Ignatius Press, 1982.

BIBLIOGRAPHY

Balthasar, Hans Urls von. *The Glory of the Lord: A Theological Aesthetics. Volume V: The Realm of Metaphysics in the Modern Age*. Translated by Oliver Davies, Andrew Louth, Brian McNeil, and John Riches. Edited by Brian McNeil and John Riches. San Francisco: Ignatius Press, 1991.

Bernard of Clairvaux. *In Praise of the New Knighthood*. Trans. M Conrad Greenia. Cistercian Fathers Series: 19B. Kalamazoo: Cistercian Publications, 2000.

Bernard of Clairvaux. *Five Books on Consideration: Advice to a Pope*. Trans. John D. Anderson and Elizabeth T Kennan. Cistercian Fathers Series: 37. Kalamazoo: Cistercian Publications, 1976.

Bhagavad Gita. Trans. Juan Macaró. London: Penguin Books, 1962.

Biblia Sacra Vulgata. Edited by Robert Weber and Roger Gryson. Stuttgart: Deutsche Bibelgesellschaft, 2007.

Boethius. *The Theological Tractates, The Consolation of Philosophy*. Trans. S.J. Tester. Cambridge, MA: Harvard University Press, 1973.

Bonaventure. *Works of St. Bonaventure: Itinerarium Mentis in Deum*. Volume II. Revised. Edited by Philotheus Boehner and Zachary Hayes. Saint Bonaventure, NY: Franciscan Institute, 2002.

Bonaventure. *The Souls Journey Into God, The Tree of Life, The Life of St. Francis*. Trans. Ewert Cousins. New York: Paulist Press, 1978.

Bonaventure. *The Mind's Road to God*. Trans. George Boas. Indianapolis/New York/Kansas City: Bobbs-Merrill, 1953.

Catherine of Siena. *The Letters of Catherine of Siena*. Volume IV. Trans. Suzanne Noffke O.P. Tempe, AZ: Arizona Center for Medieval and Renaissance Studies, 2008.

Catherine of Siena. *I, Catherine: Selected Writings of St Catherine of Siena*. Edited and translated by Kenelm Foster. OP and Mary John Ronayne. OP. London: Collins, 1980.

The Cloud of Unknowing. Trans. A.C. Spearing. London: Penguin, 2001.

Coogan, Robert. *Babylon on the Rhone: A Translation of Letters by Dante, Petrarch, and Catherine of Siena on the Avignon Papacy*. Potomac, MD: Studia Humanitatis, 1983.

Crowder, C. M.D. *Unity, Heresy and Reform, 1378–1460: The Conciliar Response to the Great Schism*. London: Edward Arnold, 1977.

Cyprian of Carthage. *De Lapsis and De Ecclesiae Catholicae Unitate*. Text and translation by Maurice Bévenot. London: Oxford University Press, 1971.

Dawson, Christopher, ed. *The Mongol Mission: Narratives and Letters of the Franciscan Missionaries in Mongolia and China in the Thirteenth and Fourteenth Centuries*. Translated by a nun of Stanbrook Abbey. London: Sheed and Ward, 1955.

Devotio Moderna: Basic Writings. Trans. John Van Engen. New York: Paulist Press, 1988.

Ferdowsi, Abolqasem. *Shahnameh: the Persian Book of Kings*. Translated by Dick Davis. New York: Penguin Books, 2006.

Flannery, Austin, ed. *Vatican Council II, Vol. 1, The Conciliar and Post Conciliar Documents*. New Revised Edition. Northport, NY: Costello Publishing, 1996.

Francis of Assisi. *Early Documents: Volume 1, The Saint*. Eds. Armstrong, Regis J., J.A. Hellmann, and William J. Short. New York: New City Press, 1999.

Gibb, H.A.R, ed. *The Travels of Ibn Battuta, A.D. 1325–1354*. 5 Vols. Translated with revisions and notes from Arabic text edited by C Defrémery and B.R. Sanguinetti, with annotations by C.F. Beckingham. London: The Hakluyt Society, 2000.

Hildegard of Bingen. *Scivias*. Trans. Mother Columba Hart and Jane Bishop. New York: Paulist Press, 1990.

Ibn Taymiyya. *A Muslim Theologian's Response to Christianity: Ibn Taymiyya's Al-Jawab al-Sahih*. Edited and translated by Thomas F. Michel. Delmar, NY: Caravan Books, 1985.

Jackson, Peter, ed. *The Mission of Friar William of Rubruck: His Journey to the Court of the Great Khan Möngke 1253–1255*. London: The Hakluyt Society, 1990.

Jones, J.R. Melville. *The Siege of Constantinople 1453: Seven Contemporary Accounts*. Amsterdam: Adolf M. Hakkert Publisher, 1972.

Kolb, Robert, and Timothy J. Wengert, eds. *The Book of Concord: The Confessions of the Evangelical Lutheran Church*. Minneapolis: Fortress Press, 2000.

Kohanski, Tamarah, ed. *The Book of John Mandeville: An Edition of the Pynson Text with Commentary on the Defective Version*. Medieval and Renaissance Texts and Studies. Vol. 231. Tempe: Arizona Center for Medieval and Renaissance Studies, 2001.

The Koran Interpreted: A Translation by A.J. Arberry. New York: Touchstone, 1996.

Llull, Ramon. *Selected Works of Ramon Llull*. Vol. 1. Edited and translated by Anthony Bonner. Princeton: Princeton University Press, 1985.

Luther, Martin. *Luther's Works. The Christian in Society III*. Vol. 46. Edited by Robert C. Schultz, and Helmut T. Lehmann. Philadelphia: Fortress Press, 1967.

Luther, Martin. *Luther's Werke*. Vol. 53. 1920. Weimar: Herman Böhlaus Nachfolger, 1968.

Meister Eckhart. *The Essential Sermons, Commentaries, Treatises and Defense*, Edited and trans. by Edmund Colledge. New York: Paulist Press, 2002.

Merton, Thomas. *Thomas Merton: A Life in Letters, the Essential Collection*. Edited by William H. Shannon and Christine M. Bochen. New York: HarperOne, 2008.

Merton, Thomas. *The Seven-Storey Mountain: An Autobiography of Faith*. New York: Harcourt, 1999.

Merton, Thomas. *Conjectures of a Guilty Bystander*. London: Sheldon Press, 1977.

Merton, Thomas. *Life and Holiness*. New York: Herder and Herder, 1963.

Pascal, Blaise. *Pensées*. Edited by Léon Brunschvicg. Paris: 1897.

Philippides, Marios, Editor and Translator. *Mehmed II The Conqueror and the Fall of the Franco-Byzantine Levant to the Ottoman Turks: Some Western Views and Testimonies*. Tempe: Arizona Center for Medieval and Renaissance Studies, 2007.

Philippides, Marios. Editor and Translator. *Emperors, Patriarchs and Sultans of Constantinople, 1373–1513: An Anonymous Greek Chronicle of the Sixteenth Century*. Brookline, MA: Hellenic College Press, 1990.

Philippides, Marios. Translator. *Byzantium, Europe, and the Early Ottoman Sultans, 1373–1513: An Anonymous Greek Chronicle of the Seventeenth Century (Codex Barberinus Graecus 111)*. New Rochelle, NY: Aristide D Caratzas, Publisher, 1990.

Philippides, Marios. Translator. *The Fall of the Byzantine Empire: A Chronicle by George Sphrantzes, 1401–1477*. Amherst, MA: The University of Massachusetts Press, 1980.

Piccolomini, Enea Silvio (Pope Pius II). *Euryalus und Lucretia, Lateinisch/Deutsch*. Edited by Herbert Rädle. Stuttgart: Reclam: 2009.

Piccolomini, Enea Silvio (Pope Pius II). *Reject Aeneas, Accept Pius: Selected Letters of Aeneas Sylvius Piccolomini (Pope Pius II)*. Edited and Translated by Thomas M. Izbicki, Gerald Christianson, and Philip Krey. Washington D.C.: The Catholic University of America Press, 2006.

Piccolomini, Enea Silvio (Pope Pius II). *Enea Silvio Piccolomini (Pius II) Euryalus und Lucretia (De Duobus Amantibus), Epistolae Selectae, Chrysis Comedia*. Edited by Anton F.W. Sommer. Vienna: Editiones Neolatinae Tom. 43, 2004.

Piccolomini, Enea Silvio (Pope Pius II). *Commentaries*. 2 Vols. Edited by Margaret Meserve and Marcello Simonetta. Cambridge, MA: Harvard University Press, 2003.

Piccolomini, Enea Silvio (Pope Pius II). *Selected Letters of Aeneas Silvius Piccolomini*. Translated and Edited by Albert R. Baca. Northridge, CA: San Fernando Valley State College, 1969.

Piccolomini, Enea Silvio (Pope Pius II). *Opera quae extant omnia*. Basiliae. Henrici Petri. Circa Mid-Sixteenth-Century. Reprint. Folio. Frankfurt: Minerva G. M. B. H., 1967.

Piccolomini, Enea Silvio (Pope Pius II). *Aeneae Sylvii Piccolominei Senensis Orationes Politicae, et Ecclesiasticae*. Edited by Joannes Dominicus Mansi. 2 Volumes. 1755.

Plato. *Complete Works*. Edited by John W. Cooper. Indianapolis: Hackett Publishing, 1997.

Plato. *The Symposium*. Trans. Christopher Gill. London: Penguin Books, 1999.

Plotinus. *Enneads*. 7 Vols. Trans. A.H. Armstrong. Cambridge, MA: Harvard University Press: 1989.

Plotinus. *The Essential Plotinus: Representative Treatises from the Enneads*. Trans. Elmer O'Brien. Indianapolis: Hackett Publishing: 1964.

Polo, Marco. *The Travels of Marco Polo*. Trans. by W. Marsden and T. Wright. Edited by Peter Harris. New York: Everyman's Library, 2008.

Polo, Marco. *The Travels of Marco Polo: The Complete Yule-Cordier Edition*. 2 Vols. 1920. New York: Dover, 1993.

Proclus. *Théologie Platonicienne*. 6 Livres. Edited and Translated by H.D. Saffrey and L.G. Westerink. Paris: Les Belles Lettres, 1978.

Proclus. *The Elements of Theology*. Second Edition. Trans. E.R. Dodds. Oxford: Clarendon Press, 1963.

Pseudo-Dionysius Areopagita. *Corpus Dionysiacum II, De coelesti hierarchia, De ecclesiastica hierarchia, De mystica theologia, Epistulae*. Edited by Günther Heil and Adolf Martin Ritter. Berlin: Walter de Gruyter, 1991.

Pseudo-Dionysius Areopagita. *Pseudo-Dionysius: The Complete Works*. Trans. Colm Luibheid. New York: Paulist Press, 1987.

Rahner, Karl. *Theological Investigations*. Vol. XIV. Translated by David Bourke. New York: Seabury Press, 1976.

Schleiermacher, Friedrich. *On Religion: Speeches to its Cultured Despisers*. Translated and edited by Richard Crouter. Cambridge: Cambridge University Press, 1996.

Tanner, Norman P., ed. *Decrees of the Ecumenical Councils*. 2 Vols. London: Sheed & Ward, 1990.

Tierney, Brian. *The Crisis of Church and State 1050–1300*. Toronto: University of Toronto Press, 1988.

Viladesau, Richard, and Mark Massa, eds. *World Religions: A Sourcebook for Students of Christian Theology*. New York: Paulist Press, 1994.

Virgil. *Aeneid*. 2 Vols. Loeb Classical Library. Trans. H. Rushton Fairclough. Cambridge, MA: Harvard University Press, 1999.

Wippel, John F., and Allan B. Wolter, eds. *Medieval Philosophy: From St. Augustine to Nicholas of Cusa*. New York: The Free Press, 1969.

Zagzebski, Linda and Timothy D. Miller, eds. *Readings in Philosophy of Religion: Ancient to Contemporary*. Oxford: Wiley-Blackwell, 2009.

Secondary Sources

Apostolov, Mario. *The Christian-Muslim Frontier: A Zone of Contact, Conflict or Cooperation*. London: RoutledgeCurzon: 2004.

Arbel, Benjamin, ed. *Intercultural Contacts in the Medieval Mediterranean*. London: Frank Cass, 1996.

Armour, Rollin, Sr. *Islam, Christianity, and the West: A Troubled History*. Faith Meets Faith Series. Maryknoll, NY: Orbis Books, 2002.

Avis, Paul. *Beyond the Reformation? Authority, Primacy and Unity in the Conciliar Tradition*. London: T&T Clark, 2006.

Babinger, Franz. *Mehmed the Conqueror and his Time*. Ed. William C. Hickman. Trans. Ralph Manheim. Princeton: Bollingen Series XCVI. Princeton University Press, 1978.

Baker, Rob and Gray Henry, eds. *Merton & Sufism, The Untold Story: A Complete Compendium*. Louisville, KY: Fons Vitae, 1999.

Bakos, Gergely Tibor. *On Faith, Rationality, and the Other in the Late Middle Ages: A Study of Nicholas of Cusa's Manuductive Approach to Islam*. Princeton Theological Monograph Series. Eugene, OR: Pickwick Publications, 2011.

Baş, Bilal. *Ecclesiastical Politics During the Iconoclastic Controversy (726–843): The Impact of Eusebian 'Imperial Theology' on the Justification of Imperial Policies*. Montreal: McGill University PhD Thesis, 2008.
Bellitto, Christopher M., Thomas M. Izbicki and Gerald Christianson, eds. *Introducing Nicholas of Cusa: A Guide to a Renaissance Man*. New York: Paulist Press, 2004.
Bett, Henry. *Nicholas of Cusa*. London: Methuen & Co., 1932.
Biechler, James, E. *The Religious Language of Nicholas of Cusa*. Missoula, MT: Scholars Press, 1975.
Bisaha, Nancy. *Creating East and West: Renaissance Humanists and the Ottoman Turks*. Philadelphia: University of Pennsylvania Press, 2004.
Black, Antony. *Council and Commune: The Conciliar Movement and the Fifteenth Century Heritage*. London: Burnes & Oates, 1979.
Black, Antony. *Monarchy and Community: Political Ideas in the Later Conciliar Controversy 1430–1450*. Cambridge: Cambridge University Press, 1970.
Bocken, Inigo, ed. *Conflict and Reconciliation: Perspectives on Nicholas of Cusa*. Leiden: Brill, 2004.
Bond, Reverend Robert R. *The Efforts of Nicholas of Cusa as a Liturgical Reformer: Pars Dissertationis Ad Lauream In Facultate S. Theologiae Apud Pontificium Athenaeum*. "Angelicum" De Urbe. Salzburg: Pontificium Athenaeum Internationale "Angelicum", 1962.
Boulting, William. *Æneas Silvius (Enea Silvio De' Piccolomini—Pius II): Orator, Man of Letters, Statesman, and Pope*. London: Archibald Constable and Company, 1908.
Brecht, Martin. *Martin Luther: The Preservation of the Church, 1532–1546*. Trans. James L. Schaaf. Minneapolis: Fortress Press, 1993.
Brockopp, Jonathan E., ed. *The Cambridge Companion to Muhammad*. Cambridge: University Press, 2010.
Burgevin, Frederick H. *Cribratio Alchorani: Nicholas Cusanus's Criticism of the Koran in Light of His Philosophy of Religion*. New York: Vantage Press, 1969.
Burman, Thomas E. *Reading the Qur'ān in Latin Christendom, 1140–1560*. Philadelphia: University of Pennsylvania Press, 2007.
Calvino, Italo. *Invisible Cities*. Trans. William Weaver. Orlando: Harcourt, 1974.
Campbell, Tony. *The Earliest Printed Maps 1472–1500*. London: The British Library, 1987.
Casarella, Peter J., ed. *Cusanus: The Legacy of Learned Ignorance*. Washington D.C.: The Catholic University of America Press, 2006.
Castelli, Enrico. *Cusano e Galileo*. Padova: CEDAM, 1964.
Chenu, M.D. *Toward Understanding Saint Thomas*. Trans. A.M. Landry O.P., and D. Hughes O.P. Chicago: Henry Regnery Company, 1964.
Christianson, Gerald, and Thomas M. Izbicki, eds. *Nicholas of Cusa On Christ and the Church: Essays in Memory of Chandler McCuskey Brooks for the American Cusanus Society*. Leiden: E.J. Brill, 1996.

Christianson, Gerald, and Thomas M. Izbicki, eds. *Nicholas of Cusa in Search of God and Wisdom.* Leiden: E.J. Brill, 1991.

Christianson, Gerald, Thomas M. Izbicki, and Christopher M. Bellitto, eds. *The Church, the Councils & Reform: The Legacy of the Fifteenth Century.* Washington, D.C.: The Catholic University of America Press, 2008.

Costigliolo, Marcia. "Qur'anic Sources of Nicholas of Cusa." *Mediaevistik* 24 (2011): 219–238.

Cranz, F. Edward. *Nicholas of Cusa and the Renaissance.* Edited by Thomas M. Izbicki, and G Gerald Christianson. Aldershot: Ashgate: 2000.

Cranz, F. Edward. "Saint Augustine and Nicholas of Cusa in the Tradition of Western Christian Thought." *Speculum* 28 (1953): 297–316.

Cunningham, Andrew and Ole Peter Grell, eds. *The Four Horsemen of the Apocalypse: Religion, War, Famine and Death in Reformation Europe.* Cambridge, UK: Cambridge University Press, 2000.

Daniel, Norman. *Islam and the West: The Making of an Image.* Oxford, UK: Oneworld, 1993.

Duclow, Donald F. *Masters of Learned Ignorance: Eriugena, Eckhart, Cusanus.* Burlington, VT: Ashgate, 2006.

Düx, Johann M. *Der Deutsche Cardinal Nicolaus von Cusa und die Kirche Seiner Zeit.* 2 Volumes. Regensburg: Joseph Manz, 1847.

Eimeren, Wilhelm van. *Cusanus: Historischer Roman.* Münster: Aschendorff, 2008.

Enea Silvio Piccolomini Papa Pio II: Atti del Convegno per il Quinto Centenario Della Morte e altri Scritti Raccolti da Domenico Maffei. Siena: Società Tipografica «Multa Paucis» Varese, 1968.

Euler, Walter Andreas. *Unitas et Pax: Religionsvergleich bei Raimundus Lullus und Nikolaus von Kues.* Würzburg: Echter Verlag, 1995.

Euler, Walter Andreas and Tom Kerger, ed. *Cusanus und der Islam.* Trier: Paulinus Verlag, 2010.

Farrow, Douglas. *Ascension and Ecclesia: On the Significance of the Doctrine of the Ascension for Ecclesiology and Christian Cosmology.* Grand Rapids: Eerdmans, 1999.

Flasch, Kurt. "Docta ignorantia und negative Theologie." *Nicolai de Cusa Opera Omnia: Symposium zum Abschluß der Heidelberger Akademie-Ausgabe, Heidelberger, 11. Und 12. Februar 2005.* Edited by Werner Beierwaltes und Hans Gerhard Senger. Heidelberg: Universitätsverlag Winter, 2006.

Flasch, Kurt. *Nikolaus von Kues. Geschichte einer Entwicklung: Vorlesungen zur Enführung in seine Philosophie.* Frankfurt am Main: Klostermann, 1998.

Fleury, Cynthia. *Dialoguer avec L'Orient: Retour á la Renaissance.* Paris, France: Presses Universitaires de France, 2003.

Ford, David F. *The Future of Christian Theology.* Chichester, UK: Wiley-Blackwell, 2011.

Foucault, Michel. *History of Madness*. Edited by Jean Khalfa. Translated by Jonathan Murphy and Jean Khalfa. London: Routledge, 2006.

Francisco, Adam S. *Martin Luther and Islam: A Study in Sixteenth-Century Polemics and Apologetics*. Leiden: Brill, 2007.

Freely, John. *The Grand Turk: Sultan Mehmet II—Conqueror of Constantinople and Master of an Empire*. New York: Overlook Press, 2009.

Gadamer, Hans-Georg. *Truth and Method*. 2nd Edition. Translated by Joel Weinsheimer and Donald G. Marshall. London: Contiuum, 2004.

Gandillac, Maurice de. "Neoplatonism and Christian Thought in the Fifteenth Century: Nicholas of Cusa and Marsilio Ficino." In *Neoplatonism and Christian Thought, Studies in Neoplatonism: Ancient and Modern*. Vol. III. Edited by Dominic J O'Meara. Norfolk, VA: International Society for Neoplatonic Studies, 1981.

Gandillac, Maurice de. *Nikolaus von Cues: Studien zu Seiner Philosophie un Philosophischen Weltanschauung*. Düsseldorf: Verlag L. Schwann, 1953.

Gandillac, Maurice de. *La politique de Nicolas de Cues*. Rome: Atti Congresso Internazionale di Studi Umanistici, 1952.

George-Tvrtkovic, Rita. "After the Fall: Riccoldo de Montecroce and Nicholas of Cusa on Religious Diversity." *Theological Studies* 73 (2012): 641–662.

Gestrich, Helmut. *Nikolaus von Kues 1401–1464: Leben und Werk im Bild*. Mainz: Verlag Hermann Schmidt, 2006.

Gilson, Étienne. *Les Métamorphoses de la Cité de Dieu*. Louvain: Publications Universitaires de Louvain, 1952.

Gude, Mary Louise. *Louis Massignon: The Crucible of Compassion*. Notre Dame, Indiana: Unviersity of Notre Dame Press, 1996.

Hadot, Pierre. *Éloge de la Philosophie Antique*. Paris: Éditions Allia, 2009.

Harries, Karsten. *Infinity and Perspective*. Cambridge, MA: The MIT Press, 2001.

Hartzheim, Casparo. *Vita Nicolai de Cusa*. Trier 1730. Frankfurt: Minerva GMBH, 1968.

Haubst, Rudolf. *Über Nikolaus von Kues als Seelsorger: Drei Predigten vor Cusanus-Festakademien*. Trier: Paulinus-Verlag, 1977.

Haubst, Rudolf. *Die Christologie des Nikolaus von Kues*. Freiburg: Verlag Herder, 1956.

Hesse, Hermann. *Siddhartha*. Translated by Hilda Rosner. New York: Bantam Books, 1971.

Hoffmann, Hans Werner. *Nikolaus von Kues und Proklos. Eine Interpretatio Christiana*. Dissertation. Philosophischen Fakultät de Universität. Düsseldorf, 1998.

Housley, Norman, editor. *Crusading in the Fifteenth Century: Message and Impact*. New York: Palgrave Macmillan: 2004.

Hoye, William J. *Die Mystische Theologie des Nicolaus Cusanus*. Freiburg: Herder, 2004.

Hudson, Nancy J. *Becoming God: The Doctrine of Theosis in Nicholas of Cusa*. Washington D.C.: The Catholic University of America Press, 2007.

Huizinga, Johan. *The Autumn of the Middle Ages*. Trans. Rodney J Payton and Ulrich Mammitzsch. Chicago: University of Chicago Press, 1996.

Izbicki, Thomas M. and Christopher M. Bellitto, eds. *Nicholas of Cusa and his Age: Intellect and Spirituality: Essays Dedicated to the Memory of F. Edward Cranz, Thomas P. McTighe, and Charles Trinkaus*. Leiden: Brill, 2002.

Izbicki, Thomas M. *Reform, Ecclesiology, and the Christian Life in the Late Middle Ages*. Aldershot, UK: Ashgate Variorum, 2008.

Jacobi, Klaus. *Die Methode der Cusanischen Philosophie*. Freiburg: Verlag Karl Alber, 1969.

Jaspers, Karl. *Anselm and Nicholas of Cusa*. Edited by Hannah Arendt. Trans. Ralph Manheim. New York: Harvest Book, 1974.

Johnston, Mark. *The Evangelical Rhetoric of Ramon Llull: Lay Learning and Piety in the Christian West around 1300*. Oxford: Oxford University Press, 1996.

Kelly, J.N.D. *The Oxford Dictionary of Popes*. Oxford: Oxford University Press, 1986.

Keryell, Jacques, ed. *Louis Massignon au cœur de notre temps*. Paris: Éditions Karhala: 1999.

Klibansky, Raymond. *The Continuity of the Platonic Tradition During the Middle Ages with a New Preface and Four Supplementary Chapters Together with Plato's Parmenides in the Middle Ages and the Renaissance with a New Introductory Preface*. Reprint 1943. München: Kraus International Publications, 1981.

Koetsier, T., and L. Bergmans, eds. *Mathematics and the Divine*. Amsterdam: Elsevier, 2005.

Kritzeck, James. *Peter the Venerable and Islam*. Princeton: Princeton University Press, 1964.

Küng, Hans, et al. *Christianity and World Religions: Paths to Dialogue*. Trans. Peter Heinegg. New York: Orbis Books, 1993.

Ladner, Gerhart B. *The Idea of Reform: Its Impact on Christian Thought and Action in the Age of the Fathers*. Eugene, OR: Wipf & Stock, 2004.

Larner, John. *Marco Polo and the Discovery of the World*. New Haven: Yale University Press, 1999.

Laursen, John Christian, ed. *Religious Toleration: "The Variety of Rites" from Cyrus to Defoe*. New York: St. Martin's Press, 1999.

Levy, Ian Christopher, Rita George-Tvrtkovic and Donald F. Duclow. *Nicholas of Cusa and Islam: Polemic and Dialogue in the Late Middle Ages*. Leiden: Brill, 2014.

Marx, J. *Verzeichnis der Handschriften-Sammlung des Hospitals zu Cues bei Bernkastel a./Mosel*. Trier: Druck der Kunst-und Verlagsanstalt Schaar & Dathe, Komm.-Ges. a. Akt., 1905.

Marx, J. *Verzeichnis Handschriften-Sammlung des Hospitals zu Cues bei Bernkastel a./Mosel*. Trier: 1905. Frankfurt: Minerva G.M.B.H, 1966.

Massignon, Louis. *Essay on the Origins of the Technical Language of Islamic Mysticism*. Trans. Benjamin Clark. Notre Dame, IN: University of Notre Dame Press, 1997.

Massignon, Louis. *Essai sur les Origines du Lexique Technique de la Mystique Musulmane*. 2nd Edition. Paris: J. Vrin, 1954.

McGinn, Bernard. *The Harvest of Mysticism in Medieval Germany (1300–1500). Vol. IV of The Presence of God: A History of Western Mysticism*. New York: Herder and Herder, The Crossroad Publishing Company, 2005.

Meserve, Margaret. *Empires of Islam in Renaissance Historical Thought*. Cambridge, MA: Harvard University Press, 2008.

Meuthen, Erich. *Nicholas of Cusa: A Sketch for a Biography*. Trans. by David Crowner and Gerald Christianson. Washington, D.C.: Catholic University of America Press, 2010.

Meuthen, Erich. *Nikolaus von Kues 1401–1464, Skizze einer Biographie*. Münster: Aschendorff, 1985.

Miller, Clyde Lee. *Reading Cusanus: Metaphor and Dialectic in a Conjectural Universe. Studies in Philosophy and the History of Philosophy*. Volume 37. Edited by Jude P. Dougherty. Washington D.C.: The Catholic University of America Press, 2003.

Miroy, Jovino de Guzman. *Tracing Nicholas of Cusa's Early Development: The Relationship Between De concordantia catholica and De docta ignorantia*. Louvain: Éditions Peeters, 2009.

Mitchell, R.J. *The Laurels and the Tiara: The Life and Time of Pius II, Scholar, Poet, Statesman, Renaissance Pope*. New York: Doubleday, 1962.

Mitteilungen und Forschungsbeiträge der Cusanus-Gesellschaft 12 (MFCG). Mainz: Matthias-Grünewald-Verlag, 1977.

Moorman, John. *History of the Franciscan Order: From Its Origins to the Year 1517*. 1968. Chicago: Franciscan Herald Press, 1988.

Necipoglu, Nevra. *Byzantium Between the Ottomans and the Latins: Politics and Society in the Late Empire*. Cambridge: Cambridge University Press, 2009.

Nederman, Cary J. *Worlds of Difference: European Discourses of Toleration, c. 1100—c. 1550*. University Park, PA: The Pennsylvania State University Press, 2000.

Nicol, Donald M. *The Last Centuries of Byzantium, 1261–1453*, 2nd Edition. Cambridge: Cambridge University Press, 1993.

Nicol, Donald M. *The End of the Byzantine Empire*. New York: Holmes and Meier, 1979.

Nicolle, Jean-Marie. *Mathématiques et métaphysique dans l'œvre de Nicolas de Cues*. Paris: Presses Universitaires du Septentrion, 2001.

Oberman, Heiko A. *The Harvest of Medieval Theology: Gabriel Biel and Late Medieval Nominalism*. Grand Rapids: Baker Academic, 2000.

O'Conner, Flannery. *A Good Man is Hard to Find and Other Stories*. New York: Harvest, 1955.

O'Malley, John, Thomas M. Izbicki, and Gerald Christianson. *Humanity and Divinity in Renaissance and Reformation: Essays in Honor of Charles Trinkaus.* Leiden, E.J. Brill, 1993.

Ortayli, Ilber. *Discovering the Ottomans.* Trans. by Jonathan Ross. Markfield, UK: Kube Publishing, 2009.

Pamuk, Orhan. *Istanbul: Memories and the City.* Trans. Maureen Freely. New York: Vintage Books, 2004.

Pieper, Josef. *The Silence of St. Thomas.* Trans. John Murray and Daniel O'Connor. South Bend, IN: St. Augustine's Press, 1999.

Pramuk, Christopher. *Sophia: The Hidden Christ of Thomas Merton.* Collegeville, MN: Liturgical Press, 2009.

Renard, John. *Islam and Christianity: Theological Themes in Comparative Perspective.* Berkley, CA: University of California Press, 2011.

Riccati, Carlo. *"Processio" et "Explicatio", La doctrine de la creation chez Jean Scot et Nicolas de Cues.* Naples: Bibliopolis, 1983.

Riley-Smith, Jonathon. *What Were the Crusades?* Third Edition. San Francisco, CA: Ignatius Press, 2002.

Riley-Smith, Jonathon. *The Crusades: A Short History.* New Haven: Yale University Press, 1987.

Roggema, Barbara, Marcel Poorthuis, and Pim Valkenberg, eds. *The Three Rings: Textual Studies in the Historical Trialogue of Judaism, Christianity and Islam.* Peeters Leuven: Thomas Instituut Utrecht, 2005.

Runciman, Steven. *The Fall of Constantinople 1453.* Cambridge: Cambridge University Press, 1965.

Sabatier, Paul. *Vie de S. François d'Assise.* Paris: Librairie Fischbacher, 1894.

Sahas, Daniel J. *John of Damascus on Islam: the "Heresy of the Ishmaelites".* Leiden: Brill, 1972.

Sasse, Hermann. *We Confess Anthology.* Trans. Norman Nagel. St. Louis: Concordia, 1999.

Shriver, George H., ed. *Contemporary Reflections on the Medieval Christian Tradition: Essays in Honor of Ray C. Petry.* Durham, NC: Duke University Press, 1974.

Sigmund, Paul E. *Nicholas of Cusa And Medieval Political Thought.* Cambridge, MA: Harvard University Press, 1963.

Smith, Wilfred Cantwell. *The Meaning and End of Religion: A New Approach to the Religious Traditions of Mankind.* New York: New American Library, 1964.

Southern, R.W. *Western Views of Islam in the Middle Ages.* Cambridge, MA: Harvard University Press, 1962.

Stieber, Joachim W. *Pope Eugenius IV, the Council of Basel and The Secular and Ecclesiastical Authorities in the Empire: The Conflict over Supreme Authority and Power in the Church.* Leiden: E.J. Brill, 1978.

Sullivan, Donald D. "Apocalypse Tamed: Cusanus and the Traditions of Late Medieval Prophecy." *Journal of Medieval History* 9 (1983): 227–236.

Szarmach, Paul E., ed. *An Introduction to The Medieval Mystics of Europe*. Albany, NY: State University of New York Press, 1984.

Tamburello, Dennis. *Ordinary Mysticism*. New York: Paulist Press, 1996.

Taylor, Charles. *Modern Social Imaginaries*. Durham, NC: Duke University Press, 2004.

Thorndike, Lynn. "John of Seville." *Speculum* 34 (1959): 20–38.

Tierney, Brian. *The Foundations of the Conciliar Theory*. Cambridge: Cambridge University Press, 1955.

Turner, Denys. *The Darkness of God: Negativity in Christian Mysticism*. Cambridge, UK: Cambridge University Press, 1995.

Underhill, Evelyn. *Mysticism*. Stilwell, KS: Digireads.com Book, 2005.

Vansteenberghe, Edmond. *Le cardinal Nicolas de Cues (1401–1464): l'action—la pensée*. 1920. Frankfurt: Minerva, 1963.

Volf, Miroslav, Ghazi bin Muhammad, and Melissa Yarrington, eds. *A Common Word: Muslims and Christians on Loving God and Neighbor*. Grand Rapids: Eerdmans, 2010.

Volkmann-Schluck, K.H. *Nicolaus Cusanus: Die Philosophie im Übergang vom Mittelalter zur Neuzeit*. Frankfurt: Vittorio Klostermann, 1968.

Wallis, R.T. *Neoplatonism*. Second Edition. London: Bristol Classical Press, 1995.

Watanabe, Morimichi. *Nicholas of Cusa: A Companion to His Life and His Times*. Edited by Gerald Christianson and Thomas M. Izbicki. Burlington, VT: Ashgate, 2011.

Watanabe, Morimichi, ed. *American Cusanus Society Newsletter*. Vols. XXIII, 2 (2006)—XXVIII, 2 (2011). Brookville, NY: Long Island University C. W. Post Campus, 2006–2011.

Watanabe, Morimichi. *Concord and Reform: Nicholas of Cusa and Legal and Political Thought in the Fifteenth Century*. Edited by Thomas M. Izbicki and Gerald Christianson. Aldershot, Great Britain: Ashgate Variorum, 2001.

Watanabe, Morimichi. *The Political Ideas of Nicholas of Cusa With Special Reference to His De Concordantia Catholica*. Geneva: Librairie Droz, 1963.

Watts, Pauline Moffitt. *Nicolaus Cusanus: A Fifteenth-Century Vision of Man*. Leiden: Brill, 1982.

Wolf, Anne Marie. *Juan de Segovia and the Fight for Peace: Christians and Muslims in the Fifteenth Century*. Notre Dame, Indiana: University of Notre Dame Press, 2014.

Wood, Frances. *Did Marco Polo go to China?* London: Secker & Warburg, 1995.

Yamaki, Kazuhiko, ed. *Nicholas of Cusa: A Medieval Thinker for the Modern Age*. Richmond, UK: Curzon Press, 2002.

Index

A Common Word   17, 213 n. 97, 214
Al-Ghazali   3, 44, 217
angels   22 n. 15, 34, 35, 36, 37, 38, 46 n. 127, 88, 97, 98, 137, 139 n. 106, 150, 178, 183, 184, 206, 207
apocalypse   120 n. 22, 198
Apologia doctae ignorantiae   69, 70 n. 79, 90, 100, 101, 102, 103, 106, 107, 109, 110, 113 n. 112, 161 n. 77, 181, 182, 183 n. 40, 185, 199
apophatic theology   39, 40, 53, 60, 68, 70 n. 77, 93, 109, 145 n. 10, 146, 150, 160, 161 n. 77, 166, 168 n. 116, 171, 182, 193 n. 94, 205, 207, 218, 219, 224
Aquinas, Thomas   8, 24, 27 ns. 38–39, 35, 60, 85, 89, 110, 146 n. 14, 159 n. 71, 217
Aristotle   29, 42 n. 109, 63 n. 44, 70, 99, 108, 146, 178, 217
Athens   45, 50 n. 5, 76, 112, 113, 119, 122, 124, 205
Augustine   4, 7, 8, 9, 22 n. 15, 28 n. 43, 29, 30, 33, 34, 35, 36, 45, 46, 56, 64 n. 46, 65 n. 54, 68, 70, 72, 74, 93, 109, 110, 113 n. 112, 122, 128, 136, 141 n. 116, 161 n. 77, 174, 175 n. 139, 177 n. 4, 178 n. 9, 198, 199, 200, 204, 205 n. 46, 207 n. 62, 208, 210, 211, 215 n. 102
Averroës (Ibn Rushd)   29, 217
Avicenna (Ibn Sina)   3, 44, 70, 108, 153, 194 n. 104, 217
Ayndorffer, Caspar   192, 193 n. 94

Bakos, Gergely Tibor   11, 12
Balthasar, Hans Urs von   210, 211, 212, 214 n. 98
Bernard of Clairvaux   78, 128, 129, 132, 133, 134, 145 n. 10
Bernardino of Siena   98, 133, 134
Biechler, James E.   3 n. 13, 9, 10, 12, 13, 79 n. 115, 83 n. 128, 96, 209
Boethius   42, 43 n. 111, 45, 200
Bonaventura   16, 86, 87, 88, 89, 90, 91, 92, 93, 94, 96, 97, 98, 99, 100, 103, 113, 114, 223
Bond, H. Lawrence   3 n. 11, 3 n. 13, 12, 13, 61, 98, 145 n. 10, 209
Book of Acts (*Acts of the Apostles*)   37, 69, 112, 113, 120

Brigit of Sweden   20
Buddhism, Buddhists   82
Byzantium   49, 60, 122, 147, 175

Capistrano, John of   132
cataphatic theology   40, 93, 106, 109, 145 n. 10, 166, 205, 206, 207, 219
Catherine of Siena   20, 132, 133, 134
Cesarini, Julian   77, 129, 131, 132 n. 67, 154, 155, 157, 158, 167, 168, 175
Christian-Muslim dialogue   9, 12, 13, 17, 28 n. 42, 56, 84, 85, 121, 122, 137, 144, 149, 150, 153, 215, 221, 223, 224
Christology   8, 9, 12, 13, 14, 15, 16, 17, 24 n. 28, 34, 39, 43 n. 118, 44, 61 n. 36, 62 n. 39, 64 n. 47, 65, 66, 69, 73, 84, 88, 91, 93, 94, 97, 99, 103, 107, 108, 114, 137, 146, 149, 150 n. 31, 151, 152, 153, 159, 164, 172, 179, 180, 191, 194, 200, 201, 204, 205, 206, 210, 212, 214, 219, 223, 224, 225
Clement of Alexandria   201, 204
coincidence of opposites   7, 14, 15, 27, 30, 43, 44, 50 n. 5, 100, 101, 102, 103, 106, 107, 108, 139, 140, 141, 143, 144, 146, 174, 179, 181, 194, 199, 217, 218
Coniectura de ultimis diebus   198, 199
Council of Basel   3 n. 10, 16, 51, 52, 57 n. 27, 58, 59, 77 n. 109, 83, 84, 121, 135, 144, 154, 156, 158, 169, 174, 175, 224
Council of Basel-Ferrara-Rome   57 n. 27, 49 n. 5
Council of Constance   48 n. 2, 50, 57, 65 n. 53, 66, 94, 157
conciliarism   47, 57 n. 27, 61, 77
Constantinople   3, 18, 19, 20, 23, 26, 33, 38, 44, 45, 47, 49, 50, 52, 53, 54, 56, 58 n. 30, 59, 60, 61, 68 n. 65, 71, 73, 77, 80, 81, 88, 91, 97, 99, 115, 116, 118, 119, 120, 122, 123, 126, 127, 129, 130, 131, 133, 134, 135, 140, 141, 144, 145, 147, 148, 149, 150, 155, 168, 175, 176, 198, 216, 221, 223
Cranz, F. Edward   7, 8, 9, 15, 145 n. 10, 199, 200, 204
Cribratio Alkorani   3 n. 11, 6, 7 n. 32, 8, 13, 14, 15, 17, 23 n. 20, 34, 46 n. 127, 55, 62 n. 41, 69, 78, 80, 81, 84, 85 ns. 131–132, 99, 104,

106, 126, 150 n. 31, 151 ns. 35–36, 152, 153, 172, 179, 180, 188, 189, 190, 191, 197, 199, 201, 202, 224, 225
crusade   16, 49 n. 5, 58 n. 30, 60, 71, 77, 78, 80, 81, 82, 83, 85, 89, 96, 114, 118, 119, 121, 124, 125, 126, 127, 128, 129, 130, 131, 132, 133, 134, 135, 137, 140, 141, 142, 168, 175, 179, 216, 220, 223
Cyprian of Carthage   126, 201

Dante   91 n. 11, 129 n. 56, 136, 137
De apice theoriae   31 n. 52, 52, 62 n. 40, 63, 68 n. 67, 69, 70, 71, 72, 74 n. 92, 86 n. 134
De concordantia catholica   4 n. 15, 11, 12, 13, 14, 15, 17, 49 n. 4, 50 n. 5, 51, 52, 53, 65 n. 53, 66 n. 60, 67, 68 n. 66, 69, 75 n. 96, 84, 90 n. 9, 103, 107, 116 n. 6, 119, 120 n. 19, 135, 137 n. 99, 138, 139, 140, 141, 144, 154, 155, 156, 157, 158, 161, 162 n. 79, 163, 164, 165, 166, 167, 168, 172, 173, 174, 175, 176, 179, 180, 186, 188, 197, 202, 203, 204 n. 42, 205 n. 48, 211, 224, 225
De coniecturis   5 n. 19, 43 n. 112, 63 n. 43, 90, 140 n. 114, 142 n. 118, 181 n. 30, 199 n. 15
De docta ignorantia   3 n. 11, 13, 14, 15, 16, 17, 19 n. 2, 23, 27, 30, 31, 33 n. 58, 42 n. 109, 43 n. 111, 44 n. 119, 60 n. 33, 62 n. 40, 69, 70 n. 79, 74 n. 92, 76, 77, 90, 91, 94, 100, 101, 103, 104, 106, 107, 108, 143, 144, 145, 146, 147, 148, 149 n. 23, 150, 152 n. 43, 153, 156, 157, 158, 159, 160, 161, 166, 167, 168, 172, 174, 175, 176, 180, 181, 182, 183, 184, 185, 186, 193 n. 94, 197, 200 n. 20, 223, 224, 225
De doctrina Christiana (Augustine)   4, 28 n. 43, 64 n. 46, 65 n. 54, 109, 136 n. 93, 199 n. 9, 200 n. 18, 204 n. 45
De pace fidei   3, 4, 5, 6, 7, 8, 9, 10, 12, 13, 14, 15, 16. 17, 18, 19 ns. 2–3, 20, 21, 22, 23, 24, 25, 26, 27, 28, 29, 30, 31, 32, 33, 34, 35, 36, 37, 38, 39, 40, 41, 42, 43, 44, 45, 46, 47, 48, 50, 52, 53, 54, 55, 56, 57 n. 27, 61, 62, 63, 64 ns. 46, 48, 49, 65, 66, 67, 68, 69, 70, 71, 72, 73, 74, 75, 76, 77 n. 110, 80, 81 n. 122, 82, 83, 84, 85, 86, 87, 88, 89, 90, 91, 92, 93, 94, 95, 96, 97, 98, 99, 100, 102, 103, 104, 105, 107 n. 82, 108, 109, 110, 111, 112, 113, 114, 116, 118, 120, 121, 122, 124, 127 n. 49, 135, 136, 137, 138, 139, 140, 141, 142, 143, 144, 145, 147, 148, 149, 150, 151, 152 n. 37, 152 n. 43, 153, 154, 156, 157, 159, 160 ns. 73–74, 162 n. 83, 163, 164, 165, 166 n. 106, 168, 169, 170, 171, 172, 173, 174, 175, 176, 177, 178, 179, 180, 181, 182, 183, 184, 185, 186, 187, 188, 189, 190, 191, 193, 194, 195, 196, 197, 198, 199, 200, 201, 202, 203, 204, 205, 206, 207, 208, 209, 210, 211, 212, 214, 215, 216, 218, 219, 220, 221, 222, 223, 224, 225
De vera religione (Augustine)   208
De visione Dei   13, 14, 15, 17, 39, 44, 45 n. 124, 69, 95, 106, 107, 109, 179, 180, 187 n. 62, 188 n. 65, 191, 192, 193, 194, 195, 196, 197, 208, 215, 224, 225
Dionysius the Areopagite (Denys, Pseudo-Dionysius)   20, 29, 35, 36 n. 75, 46 n. 127, 70 n. 77, 93, 99, 103, 107, 108, 193 n. 94, 205, 206, 217, 218 n. 109, 218 n. 112
Duclow, Donald F.   1 n. 2, 46 n. 127, 155
Dürer, Albrecht   52, 53, 54, 120 n. 22

Eckhart, Meister   100, 108, 109, 217
Eriugena John Scotus   32 n. 55, 161, 200
Euler, Walter Andreas   9, 10, 82 n. 124
Eusebius   46 n. 127, 104, 105, 106

fall of Constantinople   18, 19, 20, 23, 26, 33, 38, 44, 47, 49 n. 5, 53, 56, 58 n. 30, 60, 77, 88, 126, 129, 141, 144, 147, 149, 150, 168, 175, 176, 198, 216, 221, 223
Farrow, Douglas   107
Foucault, Michel   5
Francis of Assisi   81, 87, 93

Gadamer, Hans-Georg   5, 6, 9, 42, 200

Haubst, Rudolf   13
hierarchy   8, 15, 16, 27, 34, 35, 36, 38, 43, 46 n. 127, 61, 68 n. 65, 73, 74, 76, 88, 89, 90, 92, 93, 94, 96, 109, 129 n. 56, 136, 139, 140 n. 112, 143, 154, 155, 156, 161, 163, 165, 166, 167, 168, 171, 172, 173, 174, 175, 176, 182, 183, 184, 186, 188, 204, 206, 223, 224
Hildegard of Bingen   143
Hinduism, Hindus   20, 27, 39, 71, 88, 98, 108, 174, 203
Holy Roman Empire   49 n. 4, 120, 126, 161, 173, 174, 186
Hudson, Nancy J.   11, 14
Hussites   57 n. 27, 61

incarnation   1, 7, 22, 23, 30, 43, 44 n. 119, 64, 65, 66, 70 n. 81, 72, 73, 80, 91, 94, 103, 107, 122, 136, 161, 164, 166, 204, 206, 209, 219
Islam   3, 8, 9, 11, 12, 13, 14, 15, 16, 17, 18, 20, 21, 26, 27, 28, 34, 42, 43, 44, 45, 46, 47, 49, 51, 52, 53, 57, 59, 60, 62, 64, 73, 75, 77, 78, 79, 80, 81, 82, 83, 84, 85, 89, 91, 93, 97, 99, 115, 117, 118, 121, 122, 124, 127, 135, 136, 137, 143 n. 4, 144, 150, 152, 153, 154, 172, 176, 177, 179, 180, 184, 189, 190, 194, 195, 199, 201, 202, 203, 205, 206, 207, 209, 212, 214, 215, 216, 217, 218, 219, 221, 223, 224, 225
Izbicki, Thomas M.   13, 76, 124, 132 n. 67

Jerusalem   16, 17, 21 n. 11, 35, 36, 37, 50 n. 5, 56, 59, 61, 64 n. 47, 68 n. 65, 73, 74, 77, 80, 82 n. 126, 87, 88, 89, 90, 91, 93, 97, 99, 111, 112, 113, 114, 119, 120, 122, 124, 129, 165, 170, 176, 190 n. 81, 198, 205, 207, 211, 212, 214, 215, 220, 221, 222, 223
Jesus   23, 27, 31, 32, 36, 37, 41, 44 n. 119, 62, 63 n. 42, 68 n. 65, 69, 70, 72, 76, 87, 90, 91, 92, 94, 97, 100, 104, 106, 107, 109, 110, 111, 120, 134, 146, 151, 152, 159, 161, 163, 164, 166, 167, 168, 171, 173, 175, 176, 182, 183, 184, 185, 190, 193, 194, 195, 196, 199, 206, 213, 215, 219, 220
Jews, Judaism   6, 35, 39, 45, 71, 88, 98, 108, 174, 212, 214, 218, 220
John of Segovia   16, 28 n. 42, 62, 78 n. 113, 83, 84, 85, 121, 135, 140, 144, 149, 223

Klibansky, Raymond   15, 161 n. 77
Kues   1, 2 ns. 3–6, 14, 17, 51, 52, 82, 92, 95, 103, 143, 145 n. 10, 161 n. 77, 188, 196, 217

Lepanto, Battle of   130
Llull, Raymond   82, 83
Louis Massignon   214, 215, 216 n. 106, 221 n. 120
Luther, Martin   56, 67, 75, 77, 78, 79 n. 114, 198, 209

Marco Polo   54, 55, 56
Mecca   59, 61
Mehmed II   16, 39, 60, 84, 114, 115, 116, 117, 118, 119, 120, 121, 123, 124, 126, 127, 128, 147

Merton, Thomas   215, 216, 218, 219, 220, 221, 222
Mohammad (Prophet)   34, 54 n. 15, 71, 80, 176, 190
Miroy, Jovino de Guzman   11, 12, 14 n. 58

neoplatonism   45, 137, 208
Nestorianism   34, 55, 81, 84, 85, 134, 202

Ottoman Empire   49, 53, 119, 147, 219, 223

Paul (Apostle)   2, 20, 23 n. 18, 25, 42, 46 n. 127, 67, 69, 70 n. 79, 76, 91, 97, 111, 156, 176, 183, 185, 220
Pentecost   7, 89, 110, 112, 114
Peter (Saint)   25, 46 n. 127, 50, 67, 91, 97, 111, 125 n. 41, 127, 130, 156, 158, 164, 165, 169, 170 n. 122, 171, 174, 175, 176, 183, 185, 186, 187, 203, 204, 220
Peter the Venerable   78
Plato   16, 20, 31, 32, 42, 44, 55, 62 n. 40, 70, 71, 72, 74, 89, 95, 99, 101, 102, 104, 105, 106, 108, 109, 110, 113, 122, 148 n. 22, 161 n. 77, 177 n. 4, 178, 210, 217, 218 n. 109, 223
Plotinus   105, 106, 107 n. 81, 109 n. 90
Pope Boniface VIII   129, 201 n. 28, 203
Pope Eugene IV   58, 59, 77, 155, 157, 169
Pope Leo the Great   70 n. 79, 84, 126, 127 n. 50, 134, 201, 202, 212
Pope Martin V   50 n. 6, 58, 154, 155, 157, 158
Pope Pius II   2 n. 6, 16, 39, 58 n. 30, 71, 77, 84, 115, 116, 117, 118, 119, 122, 123, 124, 125, 126, 127, 128, 129, 131, 132, 133, 134, 135, 137, 141, 202 n. 31
Pope Urban II   77, 127 n. 50, 128, 130, 220
Pramuk, Christopher   219, 220
Proclus   20, 29, 44, 103, 104, 108, 137, 217

Qur'an   3, 6, 8, 23, 34, 40, 44 n. 120, 152, 153, 172, 188, 189, 190, 191, 210, 213, 219

religio una in rituum varietate (*De pace fidei*)   6, 9, 10, 12, 18, 19, 21, 22, 24, 25 n. 31, 26, 27, 28, 29, 30, 31, 32, 33, 34, 35, 36, 38, 40, 50 n. 5, 56, 61, 67, 68, 69, 73, 74, 75, 86, 88, 89, 91, 92, 96, 97, 207, 224
renaissance   52, 53, 56, 59, 72, 119, 124, 130, 133, 153, 154, 208, 219

INDEX

Republic (Plato)   16, 31, 40 n. 101, 55, 64 n. 46, 70, 72, 89, 101, 109, 110, 148 n. 22, 217, 223
Ricoldo da Monte Croce   79 n. 114, 83
Robert of Ketton   3, 40, 78, 79, 84, 188, 189

Smith, Wilfred Cantwell   207, 208, 209
Southern, R.W.   77, 81 n. 122, 83 n. 127, 85, 115 n. 3, 149 n. 24, 214
Sufism   45 n. 125, 215
Suger, Abbot of St. Denis   95
Summa contra gentiles (Aquinas)   8, 85
Summa Theologiæ (Aquinas)   23 n. 19, 24, 25, 26, 27, 28, 29, 35, 37, 43, 60 n. 32, 64 n. 46, 74, 75, 146 n. 14, 148 n. 23, 150, 151, 159, 160 n. 72, 167 n. 110, 179 n. 16, 206 n. 56, 207 n. 59, 217

Taylor, Charles   56 n. 25
Tertullian   124, 205
Trinity   1, 4 n. 15, 22, 24 n. 28, 33, 36, 38, 39, 46 n. 127, 70, 72, 73, 92, 109, 122, 137, 139, 149, 151, 152, 164, 179, 185, 194 n. 101
Troy   115, 119, 123, 124, 130

ubiquity (Christology)   209

Varna, Battle of   77, 129, 132 n. 67, 168
Vatican II (council)   62 n. 41, 212, 213
Verbum Dei (Christ)   3, 4 n. 19, 5, 6, 21, 22, 25, 26, 27, 28, 29, 31, 32, 34, 38, 41, 42, 44, 45, 46, 61 n. 36, 62, 63 n. 42, 64, 65, 66, 67, 73, 76, 86, 88, 89, 90 n. 8, 91, 96, 105, 138, 169, 172, 179, 180, 199, 200, 201 n. 25, 204, 219, 220
Virgil   115, 132

Watanabe, Morimichi   1 n. 1, 13, 76, 156
Wenck, Johann   100, 101, 102, 103, 106, 107, 108, 110, 114
Wisdom of God   2, 7, 9, 13, 15, 16, 17, 18, 21, 22, 23, 29, 34, 35, 36, 38, 39, 40, 44, 69, 72, 76, 95, 105, 113, 135, 137, 180, 188, 191, 195, 196, 199, 204, 212, 220, 221, 224

zeal   19, 81, 147, 170, 175